THE WIRRAL RAILWAY
AND ITS PREDECESSORS

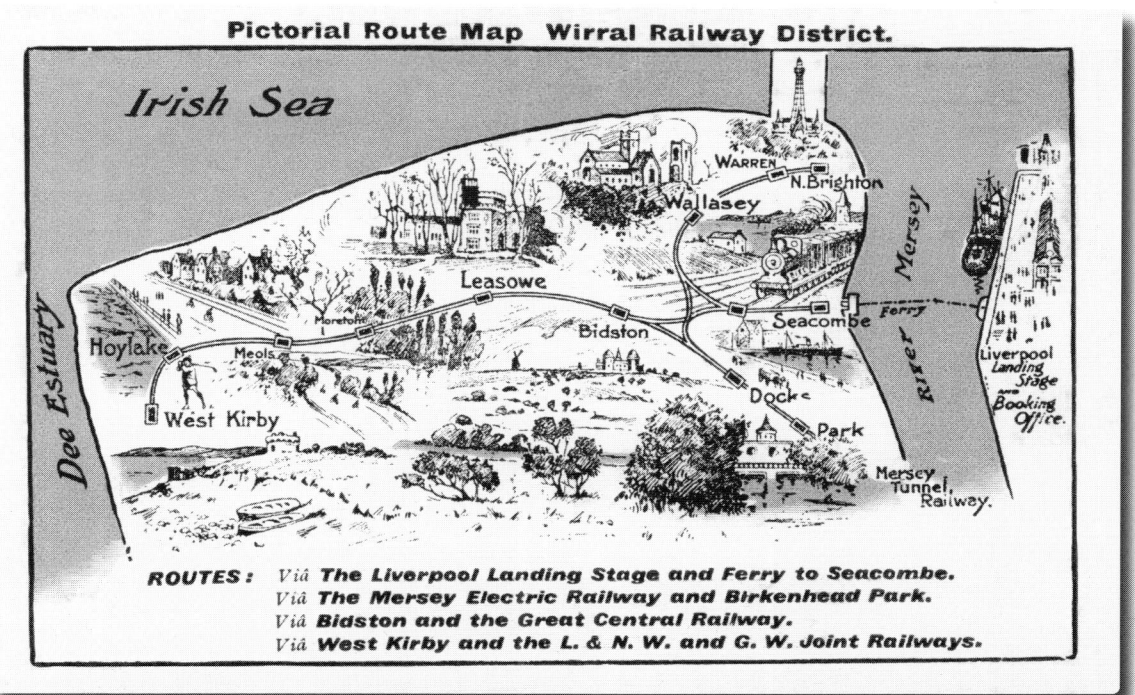

This pictorial route map of the Wirral Railway, shown in isolation from all connecting railways, was issued by the Company as a correspondence postcard in 1907. The reverse of the card can be found illustrated on page 129. JOHN ALSOP COLLECTION

Staff and passengers pose for the photographer at New Brighton station circa 1906. No. 15, one of the unusual 4-4-4 tanks delivered new to the Wirral in 1903, has just brought in a train from Birkenhead. Note the engine is seen in original condition, without the bunker rails with which it was later fitted to increase coal capacity. JOHN ALSOP COLLECTION

THE WIRRAL RAILWAY
AND ITS PREDECESSORS

T.B. Maund FCILT

Lightmoor Press

© Lightmoor Press & T.B. Maund 2009. Designed by Neil Parkhouse.
British Library Cataloguing-in-Publication Data. A catalogue record for this book is available from the British Library.

ISBN 13: 9781899889 38 9

All rights reserved. No part of this publication may be reproduced, stored in a retrieval system or transmitted in any form or by any means, electronic, mechanical, photocopying, recording or otherwise, without the written permission of the publisher.

LIGHTMOOR PRESS
Unit 144B, Lydney Trading Estate,
Harbour Road, Lydney,
Gloucestershire GL15 5EJ
www.lightmoor.co.uk

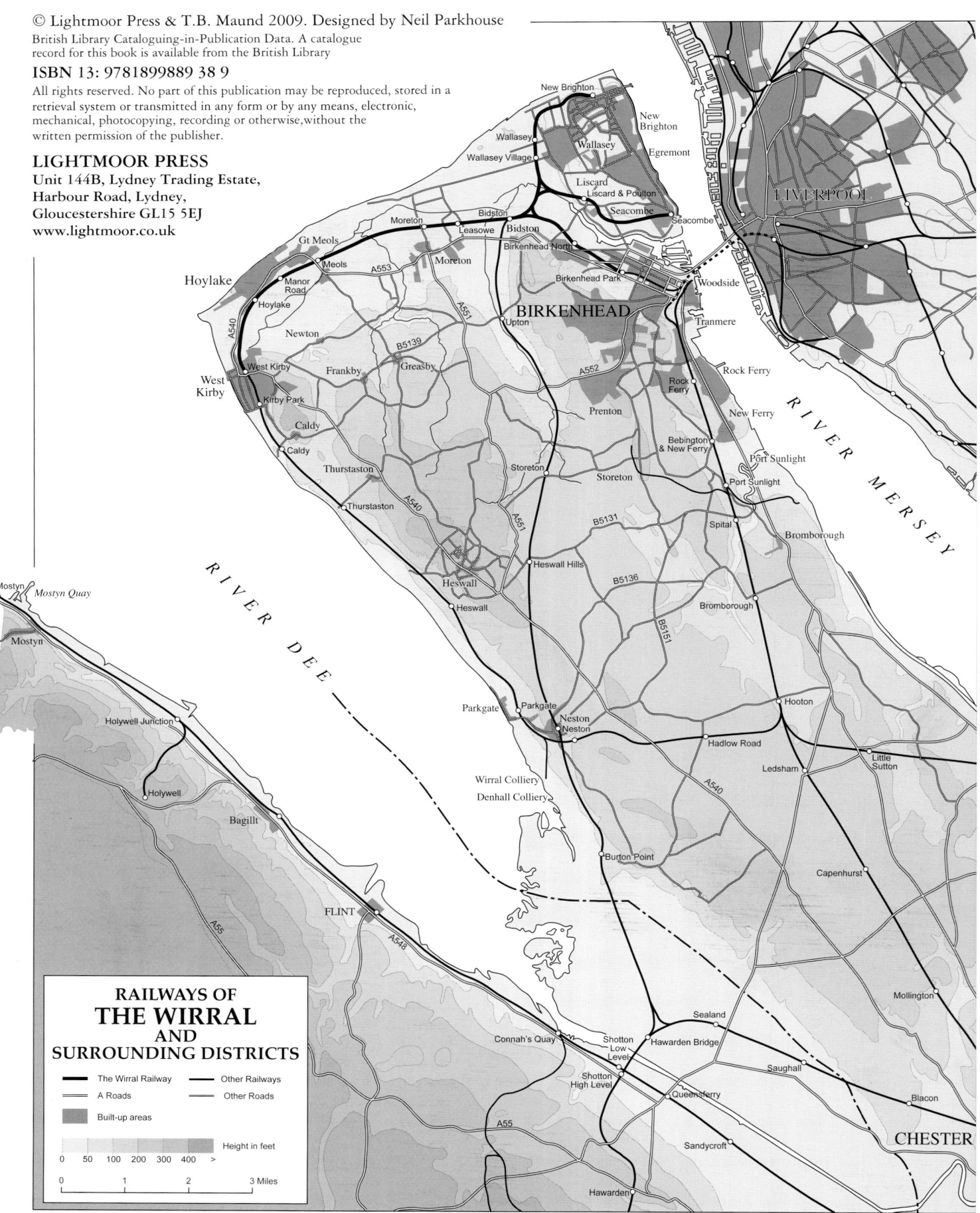

LIGHTMOOR PRESS is an imprint of BLACK DWARF LIGHTMOOR PUBLICATIONS LTD. Printed by TJ INTERNATIONAL, Padstow

CONTENTS

Introduction, Acknowledgements, Bibliography

Chapter One ... Page 7
THE HOYLAKE RAILWAY

* PROPOSED DEE CROSSINGS * MODIFIED PLANS * LEGAL ACTION * THE FIRST LOCOMOTIVES *
* THE HOYLAKE & BIRKENHEAD RAIL & TRAMWAY COMPANY * HOYLAKE & BIRKENHEAD LOCOMOTIVES *
* THE STREET TRAMWAY * THE WEST KIRBY AND DOCKS EXTENSIONS * SALE OF THE TRAMWAY *
* THE SEACOMBE, HOYLAKE & DEESIDE RAILWAY COMPANY * THE FIRST WIRRAL RAILWAY COMPANY *
* THE MERSEY RAILWAY * THE LIMITED COMPANY * PARK AND NEW BRIGHTON BRANCHES OPENED *
* THE SEACOMBE, HOYLAKE & DEESIDE LOCOMOTIVES * SIGNALLING *
* PROPOSED PURCHASE OF SEACOMBE, HOYLAKE & DEESIDE AND WIRRAL RAILWAYS *
* THE WELSH RAILWAYS UNION ACT *

Chapter Two ... Page 33
THE WIRRAL RAILWAY

* THE SEACOMBE BRANCH * IMPROVEMENTS TO THE WEST KIRBY LINE * THE SEACOMBE BRANCH OPENED *
* THROUGH FARES * THE FERRY CROSSING * WAY AND WORKS * GOODS TRAFFIC *
* PRIVATE SIDINGS, THEIR TRAFFIC AND LOCOMOTIVES * PRIVATE OWNER WAGONS ON THE WIRRAL SYSTEM *
* PASSENGER SERVICES: THE 1906 WORKING TIME TABLE * SIGNAL CABINS * * PROPOSED ELECTRIFICATION *
* THE SEACOMBE DODGER * INCREASED TRAFFIC * MANAGEMENT * LOCOMOTIVES * SECOND-HAND LOCOMOTIVES *
* WREXHAM, MOLD & CONNAH'S QUAY AND GREAT CENTRAL LOCOMOTIVES ON THE WIRRAL RAILWAY *
* LIVERY * PASSENGER STOCK * THE FINAL YEARS * SUGGESTED NEW BRIGHTON EXTENSION * HOYLAKE'S COMPLAINTS *
* THE END * THE ROUTE DESCRIBED: BIRKENHEAD PARK TO NEW BRIGHTON * SEACOMBE TO WEST KIRBY *

Chapter Three ... Page 131
THE WIRRAL IN LM&SR DAYS

* INTEGRATION OF THE WIRRAL LINES WITH THE LM&SR * CHANGES TO MOTIVE POWER * SERVICE LEVELS *
* BIRKENHEAD NORTH ENGINE AND CARRIAGE SHEDS * THE ELECTRIFICATION * PREPARATION OF THE LINE *
* CURRENT SUPPLY * MODERNISATION OF THE STATIONS * THE CHANGEOVER * ELECTRIC ROLLING STOCK *
* GOODS TRAFFIC * INDUSTRIAL SIDINGS AND LOCOMOTIVES * PRIVATE OWNER WAGON OPERATORS IN THE LM&S ERA *
* THE SECOND WORLD WAR * THE IMMEDIATE POST-WAR YEARS *

Chapter Four ... Page 182
FROM BRITISH RAILWAYS TO MERSEYRAIL

* CLOSURE OF THE SEACOMBE BRANCH * GOODS TRAFFIC – NEW BEGINNINGS, DECLINE AND CLOSURE *
* MERSEYRAIL * THE WIRRAL LINES TODAY *

Appendix 1 ... Page 217
The Wirral Railway's Accident Record

Appendix 2 ... Page 218
The Final Years of Mechanical Signalling on the Wirral

Appendix 3 ... Page 231
Wirral Railway Miscellany

Appendix 4 ... Page 232
The Locomotives of the Wirral Railway and its Predecessors

Appendix 5 ... Page 234
The Electric Rolling Stock

Appendix 6 ... Page 236
The Wirral Railway in 1914 (From *The Railway Magazine*)

Index ... Page 239

INTRODUCTION

The Wirral Peninsula, sandwiched between two major rivers, the Mersey and the Dee, is an attractive and diverse part of north Cheshire, encompassing sea and river, countryside and town, and both traditional and modern industry. To the west there is a background of Welsh hills, whilst to the east the Liverpool waterfront dominates the scene. Until the mid-19th century, the area was sparsely populated, with agriculture and fishing being the main occupations and the major settlements being Tranmere and Neston. A major tidal creek, the Wallasey Pool, stretched for over a mile inland and, as the land adjoining the Irish Sea was low-lying, there were areas of marshy ground which, until the building of an embankment in relatively modern times, was subject to flooding. Indeed, the name Wallasey is derived from the Celtic *'waleas eye'*, meaning Isle of Strangers, this north-eastern part of the peninsula having been cut off by the flood waters of the Irish Sea, the Mersey and the Pool in past centuries.

The growth of Liverpool as a major port from the 18th century onward was the catalyst for the development of Wirral as a dormitory for Liverpool workers; at first the upper classes sought refuge from the crowded and disease-ridden port area but, as steam ferries and safe landing facilities became established, the use of a ferry as part of the journey to work became commonplace for all classes of the population. Liverpool's industry and port facilities overflowed on to the Cheshire shore, the Wallasey Pool being developed as docks in the 19th century. Shipbuilding became important in Birkenhead as the traditional yards on the Liverpool shore were swept away by dock extensions. The roads leading north from Chester had been turnpiked and stage coach services were started connecting the ancient city with Neston and Parkgate (once an important port for Ireland), and with Liverpool by way of several ferries. The first railway on the peninsula, between Chester and Birkenhead, opened on 22nd September 1840, only ten years after the first inter-city line between Liverpool and Manchester; branches were added in due course and the Great Western and London & North Western railways, who leased these lines in perpetuity, established a monopoly which, in the view of many traders, was not advantageous to them.

The coastal strip across the north of the peninsula was much favoured by the well-to-do as a residential area and leisure resorts also developed, the firm, sandy beaches and the vistas of mountain and sea becoming a magnet for pleasure seekers. Until the later years of the 19th century, this was not good railway country as the population, although growing, was insufficient to support profitable facilities, whilst the marshy and sandy tracts of land made construction expensive. The aims of the original Hoylake Railway company, to build railways across the northern part of Wirral, may at first appear ill-conceived but the interests of the directors in other railway schemes in North Wales suggest that there was some grand plan, which nevertheless fell apart at an early stage. The aims of the first Wirral Railway company, which was formed later, were clearly concerned with linking up with other railways in North Wales and breaking the GW/L&NW monopoly. Unfortunately, this company was never able to raise sufficient money to complete its original scheme and disposed of its powers to others.

The amalgamation of these two local railways in 1891 under the Wirral title established one of the smallest British railway companies, with a track mileage of only twenty-four but with a highly intensive passenger service, most of which survives to this day. As Birkenhead and Wallasey grew into large towns and Hoylake and West Kirby expanded residentially, the Wirral Railway enjoyed its heyday but it was always run on a shoestring and absorption into the London, Midland & Scottish Railway in 1923 prevented the line falling into dereliction through the lack of funds for essential improvements. Until railway Grouping in 1923, the diversity of the Wirral peninsula was reflected in the existence of no fewer than five separate railway companies – the Great Western, London & North Western, Great Central, Wirral and Mersey. In addition, the Cheshire Lines Committee, a consortium of the Great Central, Great Northern and Midland railways, provided goods services. Even after Grouping there were still four, the Mersey remaining independent until Nationalisation.

This book endeavours to provide a comprehensive account of the origins of the constituent companies and their successors, including events on the freight side up to 1980. The Wirral lines were used for quite short distances by other railways and these are included. Modern development of the passenger services under the *Merseyrail* name is a complex story which has been fully dealt with in the present author's *Merseyrail Electrics – The Inside Story* (NBC Books 2001).

ACKNOWLEDGEMENTS

The author wishes to express his gratitude and thanks to many friends for their generous assistance in building up the story of the Wirral Railway. Particular thanks are due to John Ryan, who made available his private archives and valuable photograph collection to the author, and to John Horne for giving access to his photographic collection and for providing much additional information on goods services and private sidings, whilst Ian Pope has supplied information regarding private owner wagons on the Wirral system. Neil Parkhouse has sourced numerous further illustrations, provided much additional caption information and also corrected the long held misapprehension regarding the early photograph of Hoylake (page 12), in connection with which Harry Jack has also provided valuable assistance in regard to early locomotive details. Special thanks are due also to Messrs. John Alsop, J.N. Barlow, Grahame Boyes, Martin Jenkins, Ted Lloyd, Glynn Parry, E. Richards, T.G. Turner, the late John Ward and the late Bryan Wilson, who have made available documents and illustrations for publication, and also to the members of the Merseyside Railway History Group. The staff at the following institutions have also been most helpful in making available official plans, documents and illustrations: National Archives, Kew; Cheshire County Record Office; the National Railway Museum Library; the Record Office for Leicestershire, Leicester & Rutland; Wirral Metropolitan Borough Library.

BIBLIOGRAPHY

The Wirral Railway, Campbell Highet, Oakwood Press 1960
The Mersey Railway, G.W. Parkin, Oakwood Press 1965
Steel Wheels to Deeside, John W. Gahan, Countyvise/Avon Anglia 1983
Various issues of the *Railway Gazette, Railway Magazine, The Railway Observer, Railway News, Transport World*, and *Bradshaw's Guide*.
Biographical Dictionary of Railway Engineers, John Marshall, 2nd Edition, RCHS 2003
The Wrexham, Mold & Connahs Quay Railway, James I.C. Boyd, Oakwood Press 1991
The Last Merseyrail Signal Boxes, Merseyside Railway History Group 2004

CHAPTER 1
THE HOYLAKE RAILWAY

In 1860, the north-west corner of the Wirral peninsula, comprising the parishes of Great Meols, Hoose, Little Meols and West Kirby, had a population of less than 2,000 but its bracing climate, magnificent views of North Wales across the broad Dee estuary and spectacular sunsets were already attracting the attention of prosperous Liverpool and Birkenhead businessmen who found that they could build houses on cheap land and escape the smoke, grime and disease of the towns. Omnibus services were running between Little Meols (which stood between present day West Kirby and Hoylake, near Graham Road) and Woodside ferry by 1849. They ran what would nowadays be called a commuter service, with a journey in from Little Meols in the morning and a return trip around 4.30-5.00pm in the afternoon. On Sundays, the direction of the service was reversed, to cater for the needs of day visitors.

The first proposed railway scheme in the district was the abortive Birkenhead Docks & West Cheshire Junction Railway of 1862, which was planned to break the monopoly of the L&NW and GW Joint Railway between Chester and Birkenhead. From a junction with other railways in Delamere Forest, the line was planned to come up the centre of the peninsula to Bidston where it would have divided into three, one line to Seacombe ferry, one to Woodside ferry and the third to Hoylake. Despite influential support, however, the line was rejected by Parliament on 19th May 1862.

What was apparently a purely local scheme by a new company, the Hoylake Railway Company, was announced later in the same year. The intention was to construct a line from a point on the south side of Seacombe ferry, through Poulton, Bidston, Moreton, Saughall Massie, Great Meols and Hoose to Hoylake, *'adjoining the racecourse'*, with a branch line from Bidston to Birkenhead (Wallasey Bridge Road, near the Dock Cottages). Powers were sought to purchase, compulsorily or otherwise, the Wallasey Pool Bridge and Wallasey Bridge Road from the Wallasey Pool Bridge Company, which levied tolls. Robert Vyner, Squire of Bidston, owned part of the Pool and much of the land between Bidston and Leasowe. He had plans to build a dock, for which preparatory work had already been completed on the south bank where Bidston Dock was constructed much later. The former Birkenhead, Lancashire & Cheshire Junction Railway had already come up against this situation when seeking powers for an extension from Bridge End (Cathcart Street), Birkenhead to Seacombe and New Brighton in their failed 1853 Bill.

In the interests of clarity, modern names of roads are used in the following sections, although it will be appreciated that many did not exist at that time or were known by earlier names. The Hoylake Railway Co. planned to cross the Wallasey Pool obliquely, by means of a bridge of one 60 foot span and five 30 foot spans, each 9 feet 6 inches high. From Seacombe, the line would have followed fairly closely the north bank of the Wallasey Pool, which had already been enclosed to form the nucleus of the extended Birkenhead dock system, the Great Float. Poulton Bridge Road, on the north side of the Pool, was to be straightened in line with Wallasey Bridge Road on the south side. The junction between the Seacombe line and the Docks branch was to be at School Lane, Bidston, the line continuing to run along the south side of the 'Great Drain', which channelled the waters of the tiny River Birket into the Pool and drained the surrounding area. The terminal station was to be located on the south side of the junction of the present-day Birkenhead Road and Church Road. It should be borne in mind that, until the land reclamation work of the late 1870s, Seacombe ferry lay in a shallow bay and the proposed station would have been very close to the shore.

The Hoylake Railway Act received the Royal Assent on 28th July 1863; it authorised the construction of the line more or less as applied for and the creation of capital of £100,000 in £10 shares, with borrowing powers for a further £33,000. £99,000 was raised by debentures. The chairman, J. Everitt, a London banker, was also chairman of the Wrexham, Mold & Connah's Quay (WM&CQ), the Bishop's Castle, and Carmarthen & Cardigan railways and four more directors (Barnes, Edgeworth, Fynney and Penson) were also on the WM&CQ board. The company had as Engineer Benjamin Piercy, who held the same position with the WM&CQ and was regarded by some as a 'promoting engineer'. There is some suggestion that Piercy and his brother, Robert, in effect, acted as contractors for building the line, engaging sub-contractors for specific functions. No reference has been found to another contractor. The Piercys were extensively involved with railway construction in north and mid-Wales and later, in India, France and Sardinia. The Secretary (and later manager) was Braithwaite Poole, whose most recent appointment had been as manager, from 1861 to 1863, of the newly municipalised Wallasey Ferries. Poole had been Liverpool Goods Manager for the London & North Western Railway (L&NW), having been one of the first four such managers appointed after the formation of the company in 1846. He acted as senior manager and attended to the company's goods interests at the Railway Clearing House. However, he had been dismissed in 1856 for failing to deal with frauds by his staff. He was a flamboyant, controversial figure, who laboured tirelessly to promote the cause of the little company. In 1865, he helped to draft the Rules for the WM&CQ, further proof of the close relationship between the two companies.

It was very difficult to raise large sums of money to build isolated lines of this kind, particularly as the American Civil War had a devastating effect on the cotton trade and traffic handled at the port. The promoters can hardly have expected the line to thrive on the sparse residential and leisure traffic between Liverpool, Birkenhead and Hoylake. The Birkenhead docks scheme had been revitalised in 1858 following the creation of the Mersey Docks & Harbour Board, with responsibility for port facilities on both sides of the River Mersey and, doubtless, this played some part in the directors' plans. The close links with the WM&CQ suggests that the prime objective was to secure territory in the Wirral peninsula free of L&NW and Great Western (GW) influence and from where a Dee crossing could be established. There was grave dissatisfaction with the monopolistic behaviour of the GW in the Wrexham and Ruabon coal mining area and, consequently, there was strong support from the industrialists for an alternative route to Birkenhead, thus avoiding both the GW and the Chester bottleneck.

Proposed Dee Crossings

In November 1863, a Bill was submitted seeking to change the name of the company to the Birkenhead & Flintshire Railway Company and proposing to build a railway crossing the River Dee almost at its widest point, between Little Meols (present day West Kirby) and the Chester & Holyhead Railway (C&H) at Mostyn. The line, 6.44 miles long, would be carried on an embankment interspersed with three viaducts, the first of which, commencing about one mile from the Wirral shore, was to be 660 yards long with 64 openings of 30 foot span, 32 feet above low water. A further length of embankment, approximately half a mile long, was to be followed by another mile long viaduct with 170 30 foot openings. Another length of embankment would then lead onto a curved viaduct, 1,540 yards long, with 148 30 foot openings and one of 40 feet which could be raised to allow shipping to pass. This then led, by way of a two-furlong radius curve passing over the Mostyn Colliery railway, to a junction with the Chester & Holyhead line, a short distance south of Mostyn station. The plans show a curve from east to north only, whereas if the real objective were to establish a connection with the WM&CQ further down the line at Connah's Quay, which seems likely, a curve in the other direction would have been desirable.

Lord Stanley of Alderley owned all the land on the English side and the Trustees of Lord Mostyn owned the land on the Welsh side. Both objected to the Bill as did the clumsily named 'Company of Proprietors of the Undertaking for Recovering and Preserving the Navigation of the River Dee'. The Board of Trade supported the latter on the grounds of interference with shipping and the Bill failed. The scheme would have been enormously expensive and it is hard to envisage investors putting up sufficient money. It is though a fine example of the optimism of Victorian railway entrepreneurs, to whom a little matter of five or six miles of river was an obstacle to be tackled and, if possible, overcome. However, in the following year, an attempt was made to link the English and Welsh schemes of the promoters further upstream. A company styled the Dee & Mersey Junction Railway proposed a line from Connah's Quay across the Dee to join both the Hoylake Railway at Hoylake and the authorised but not yet constructed Hooton-Parkgate branch line of the L&NW & GW Joint Railway at Neston. The route was to pass under the C&H and there was to be a 352 yard tunnel under the river, the line falling at 1 in 55 on the Welsh bank and rising on the Wirral side near Burton Point at 1 in 80. Construction would have involved building a 50 foot coffer dam adjacent to the navigable channel. The whole scheme, which included dredging a deep channel to keep shipping clear of the coffer dam, was planned by John Frederick Bateman and Benjamin Piercy. The eminent railway engineer James Brunlees said the job was straightforward and could be finished in eighteen months. There was strong opposition from Chester city, the navigation interests and, of course, the L&NW and GW companies but the *coup de grace* came from the Board of Trade's opposition on the grounds of '*interference with tidal waters*' and the Bill was thrown out on 5th May 1865.

Meanwhile, in November 1864, the company deposited the Hoylake Railway (New Works) Bill, the main feature of which was a loop line running north west from Seacombe and following a route approximating to the present day Brighton Street, King Street and Seabank Road to New Brighton. From here, the line kept to the high ground, curving westwards from the end of Seabank Road (yet unmade) to a station near Portland Street. It then continued westward and south-eastward, crossing Grove Road approximately at the Warren Drive junction and Wallasey Road east of St. Hilary Brow, joining the Seacombe line near Wallasey Bridge Road. Two short chords would have enabled trains to run between New Brighton and Seacombe by the western side of the loop and to reach the eastern side avoiding Seacombe terminus. The company wished to establish a goods station adjacent to Seacombe ferry and sought powers to acquire approximately 2.5 acres of land across the road from the proposed passenger station and adjacent to Bowdler & Chaffer's shipbuilding yard.

There was much opposition from landowners, particularly Harold Littledale, Lord of the Manor of Liscard and the executors of Richard Smith, one time owner of Seacombe ferry and Lord of the Manor of Poulton-cum-Seacombe. A much bigger land acquisition was proposed east of the proposed Docks station, where powers to acquire were sought for about 28 acres, bounded by the West Float, Wallasey Bridge Road, Beaufort Road and the graving dock. However, Parliament approved only the western side of the loop terminating near Portland Street, New Brighton, a distance of 2.1 miles and this passed into law as the Hoylake Railway (New Works) Act 1865. Undeterred, the directors, who still had no railway in operation, came forward at the end of the same year with a further Extension Bill, this time from Hoylake to West Kirby and along the banks of the Dee to a point a little way inland from Parkgate, on Leighton road, a distance of 8.24 miles. The location of the terminus is, at first sight, puzzling, as it was not in line with the L&NW & GW Joint Railway's authorised Hooton-Parkgate line, which was already under construction at the time. The Hoylake-Parkgate branch was authorised by the Hoylake Railway (Extension) Act, 1866, which also approved the raising of a further £200,000 of capital. Power was also granted for the company and the WM&CQ to enter into agreements for the management and working of the line and the supply of rolling stock and '*officers and servants*'.

The following year, the board's strategy in keeping the Parkgate extension well away from the Joint line was revealed when the Hoylake Railway (Chester Extension) Bill, 1866 was deposited in Parliament. An 11-mile line was proposed between Parkgate and Chester, which closely resembled that proposed by the Birkenhead Docks & West Cheshire Junction Railway of 1862 and, in fact, would have closely followed the lines which were eventually built in the 1890s under the auspices of the Manchester, Sheffield & Lincolnshire Railway. Once more, the opposition of the L&NW & GW Joint Railway was a major factor in the rejection of these plans.

Modified Plans

Meanwhile, the directors, led by the chairman, J. Everitt, had decided to build the line from Hoylake to Bidston and the branch to Wallasey Bridge Road, as the company could not afford to build the Seacombe line with its expensive bridge across the Pool. Construction started in late 1864 or early 1865 and much levelling, filling and drainage was necessary near Bidston where the ground was marshy. The interests of Vyner had to be constantly given priority and the company agreed to build the line on the north side of the 'Great Drain' (the culverted River Birket), instead of the south side as authorised; this protected Vyner's dock scheme and facilitated the later connection with the dock lines.

Harold Littledale of New Brighton who was interested in several railway schemes, had joined the board by 1865 and became active in the affairs of the company. His firm, Littledale, Ridley & Bardswell, solicitors, handled much of the company's legal work. When sufficient work had been completed, the first locomotive was driven by Poole for 1¼ miles on 11th August 1865 and a temporary carriage shed was erected at Hoylake. The half-yearly meeting reported good progress and the contractor anticipated completion by 1st November. It was essential to have some connection with a ferry, either at Seacombe or Woodside, though the former would have involved crossing the toll

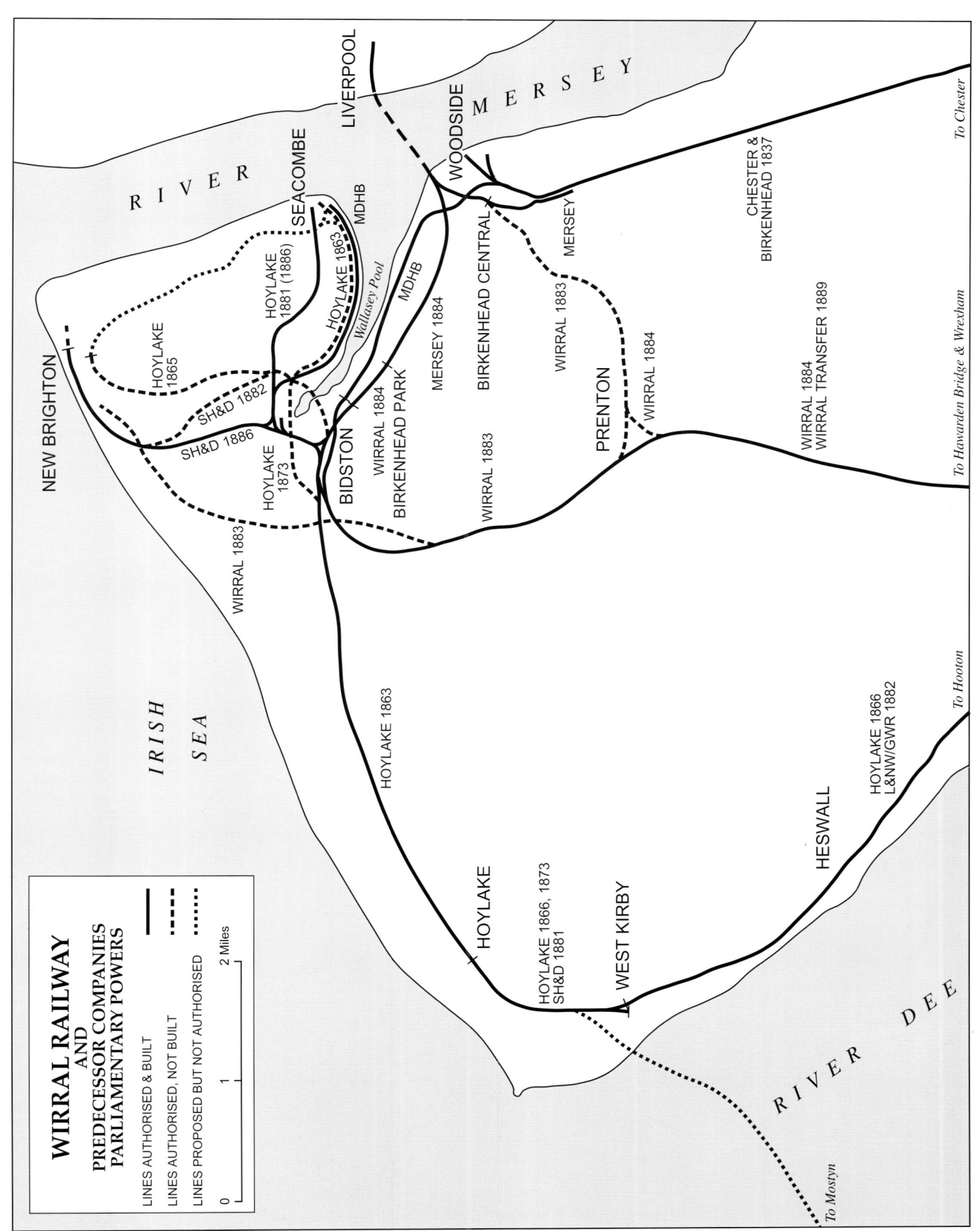

bridge at Poulton. There were negotiations with James McHenry of the Birkenhead Street Railway Co, operator of the first ever purpose-built tramway in the land, with a view to his line being extended from Birkenhead Park Entrance to Wallasey Bridge Road via what later became Laird Street. McHenry was ready and willing to do this but the Birkenhead Town Commissioners, whilst agreeing to the line's extension, would permit no passing loops, thus rendering it unworkable.

The railway had trouble with a sub-contractor and hopes of opening in January 1866 were dashed. There is some confusion about the date of opening. A Board of Trade inspection was carried out on 16th June by Captain Ritchie and there are reports of the line opening without ceremony on Monday 18th, on which date the company announced in the *Liverpool Mercury* that it was open for business. However, the Board of Trade was not entirely satisfied with the condition of the line as there was a further inspection on 2nd July 1866, on which date the regular service commenced between Docks station, Birkenhead and Hoylake, a distance of just under 5.4 miles. The original Docks station was situated on the west side of Wallasey Bridge Road, just north of Beaufort Road, some distance to the north of the present day Birkenhead North station. The line was primitive, with cinder platforms at the intermediate stations of Bidston, Moreton and Meols and the spartan wooden buildings were kept to the absolute minimum. There were refreshment rooms at Docks and Hoylake stations. Particulars of the original motive power remain sketchy but it seems the case that the company owned only one locomotive when the line first opened. Various reports say that it was a 2-2-2WT named *Ashton*, of which more later.

Originally there were six trains in each direction on weekdays and four on Sundays. The through journey occupied twenty minutes and, as it was single line, the times were arranged so that only one train was on the track at any one time. Initially, the passenger traffic exceeded expectations and no doubt there was considerable curiosity riding at first. Braithwaite Poole told a shareholders' meeting on the 31st August 1866 that no fewer than 30,000 passengers had been carried since opening, producing receipts of £1,000; this was not maintained and the winter traffic was very sparse indeed, one train being withdrawn in October 1866, whilst in January 1867, the service was further reduced to three trains Mondays to Fridays, four on Saturdays and two on Sundays. Summer services were increased to seven on weekdays and six on Sundays. The timetable was strongly criticised, particularly as the last train in summer left Hoylake as early as 7.00pm. The link with Liverpool was provided by horse drawn omnibuses, operated under contract by Thomas Evans, an established Birkenhead operator and one of the Birkenhead Improvement Commissioners, between Docks station and Seacombe ferry, over the toll bridge. However, there were other contenders as it is on record that Adam Fox of Church Road, Seacombe wrote to the Wallasey Local Board in 1868, complaining that he was being prevented from running between Docks station and Seacombe ferry by the Wallasey Pool Bridge Company.

The railway was the subject of regular comment in a Liverpool periodical, *The Porcupine*, which was highly critical of Poole's management. The issue of 14th July 1866 made several disparaging remarks about the manager, comparing him to the Admirable Crichton and then went on:

'... *The line was to be the cheapest, the carriages the finest and the management the most perfect in the world and the Sands of Hoylake were to be brought within half an hour of the Exchange Flags. At least, so said in chorus the weekly and daily press of Liverpool and Chester, not forgetting sly little 'puffs' insiduous in London and the provincial papers. At last after several delays and one false start, the Hoylake Railway is opened and so far, for any good it is to the hard-worked, dust-choked dweller in Liverpool, the line might just as well remained original soil. The few trains run at long and inconvenient intervals and the last train from Hoylake – in July, mind you – leaves at 7 p.m. about the hour when the ordinary business man might expect to join his family at dinner or tea – according to his tastes or social standing. So, after all the columns of puffing this 'Model Railway' – managed by the great Braithwaite Poole – comes to this. Already the public discontent is loud and general and unless something like a rational time-table is arranged and kept to, Mr Poole and his directors will find that something more than erratic genius is required to make a railway paying and popular*'

The cudgels were again taken up in the issue of 17th November 1866:

'*A meeting of the Hoylake Railway company was held ... when a report was read in which it was stated that 'the traffic has been regularly and efficiently conducted' and further 'that the result is*

Part of the original Birkenhead Docks station built by the Hoylake Railway, with the platform still extant on 26th October 1937. From September 1873, the station had a cross-platform interchange with the horse-drawn street trams of the Hoylake & Birkenhead Rail & Tramway Co. The tramway arrived along the road behind the fence, executing a ninety degree turn into the station to terminate along the far side of the platform. After closure in 1888, the old station was renamed Birkenhead Docks Goods but much of it was actually occupied by Birkenhead North engine shed and sidings. JOHN RYAN COLLECTION

encouraging.' Now is not this a trifle congratulatory? If these remarks are true, what about the indignation meetings at Moreton and elsewhere? What about the constant complaints of paucity of trains, especially at night? Furthermore, what about the gross muddle at the last Hoylake races? The results may be very encouraging to directors and secretaries but we fancy shareholders and the travelling public will not endorse this 'flattering tale'

During the second half of 1867, only 68,949 passengers were carried – 6,885 first class, 28,512 second class and 33,552 third class. Additional trains had been run, incurring more locomotive hours without attracting any more traffic. The adjourned meeting of shareholders in July 1868 heard a very dismal report. Shareholders complained that the directors failed to apply themselves to their duties and remarked that the chairman, Everitt, had attended only one meeting since November 1867. The company was seriously affected by the failure of the bankers, Overend & Gurney, who were deeply involved with several railway companies.

Legal Action

As he was owed £9,000 for his land, Mr Vyner obtained a Chancery Court decree in 1868; a further decree was obtained by Alexander Young, John Ball and The Imperial Mercantile Credit Association. Alexander Young was a well known City chartered accountant, a partner in the firm of Turquand & Young, and was probably acting on behalf of the shareholders. Young was deeply involved in railway affairs and claimed to know the chairmen and general managers of most of the principal railway companies. He held many railway directorships, including sitting on the board of the Neath & Brecon Railway Co. There were no funds available to pay any of them and other liabilities amounted to £20,000. An accountant was appointed to investigate. Braithwaite Poole resigned to become a railway consultant. In retirement, he lived at 14 Catherine Street, Birkenhead, an address which, years later, became familiar to thousands of Wirral residents as the head office of the Birkenhead & District Co-operative Society and appeared on every milk float, bread van *et al*. He died there on 3rd August 1888.

A Receivership Order was made on 13th February 1869, the Receiver being George Chandler. It was decided to continue operating the railway in the hope of selling it as a going concern and James Goulding, the traffic manager, looked after day-to-day operations. A new board of directors, elected on 7th September 1869, included Robert Vyner who seems to have exercised exemplary patience and restraint. The registered office was now in London. By that time it was known that receipts for the second half of 1868 and the first half of 1869 were £1,608 and £1,634 respectively and clearly the company had no money to meet its obligations. *Herapath's Railway Journal* of 25th September 1869 carried the following report:

'In pursuance of a Chancery Decree obtained by Mr Robert Vyner who had never been paid for his land, that portion of the Birkenhead and Hoylake Railway which runs through his property, was offered for sale by auction at the Queen Hotel, Chester on Saturday 18 September. One of the conditions of the sale was that the purchaser was to pay beyond his bid for the land for everything found upon it at a valuation made by the Auctioneers, Messrs. Churton and Elphick. The solicitor representing the Railway Company protested against anything but the land being sold but the auctioneer said he was acting under the authority of the Court of Chancery and proceeded to put up four 'lots'. The first was knocked down to Messrs. Roberts and Potts, Chester for £4,000, the only bid, the lot including the Dock Cottages Station, North Birkenhead (where the line commences), adjoining land, and the railway as far as lot 2, which included Bidston station and a length beyond this lot also being knocked down to Mr Roberts for £1,500. No offers were made for the other two lots. It was stated that Mr Roberts was acting for Mr Vyner'.

Vyner had temporarily rescued the company by buying back his own land but took no further immediate action. However, on 30th June 1870, a writ of ejectment was obtained from the High Sheriff of Cheshire and, on 4th July, bailiffs required the manager, James Goulding, to remove all rolling stock and plant from the Birkenhead end of the line. From the 8th July, trains from Hoylake terminated at Leasowe, where there was no proper platform, with an omnibus connection to and from Seacombe provided under contract to the railway company by Adam Fox. Other privately owned omnibuses restarted running between Hoylake and Woodside in July 1870, twice daily on Mondays to Fridays, three times on Saturdays and once on Sundays. Bradshaw records the resumption of a connection with Woodside in November 1870 but *Bradshaw's Railway Manual*, 1872 states '*This undertaking has fallen into bankruptcy, part of it is sold and the traffic suspended.*' This was incorrect as the railway never ceased working.

It is fortunate that the Receiver's account books have survived and these give a fairly complete picture of the company's activities in receivership. This was previously a period about which absolutely nothing was known. As one might expect with such a small line, much of the maintenance work was out-sourced. Several well-known names appear in the accounts; Thomas Brassey & Co, whose Canada Works were less than a mile from Docks station, supplied '*Mud Plugs for Engine*' in June 1869 for 12s 0d and carried out repairs for £1 1s 9d the following month. There were several similar items, including '*labour and material for repairing locomotive – £2 3s 7d*' on 22nd December. On 30th April 1869, Sharp, Stewart & Co. carried out repairs to an engine for 6s 0d. This strenghtens the belief that the company's first engine was of Sharp, Stewart manufacture. Robert Main, a Birkenhead coachbuilder who had assembled the first tramcars to run in England from American-built sections in 1860, was paid the not inconsiderable sum of £7 13s 6d in June 1869 for '*Sundry repairs to carriages*'; other carriage repairs were done by the Ashbury company of Manchester (for only 6s 0d), which might suggest the origin of the company's coaching stock. L. Sterne supplied '*patent buffers for carriages*' for £4 4s 0d. Many sundries such as oil, paint, grease, tallow, etc were supplied by Irving, Little & Co., a Birkenhead business which is still thriving today. On another occasion, they supplied '*sleepers to repair permanent way*' for the sum of £133 6s 8d. One unusual item noted in July 1871 was '*Repairing Guard's Watch 7s 6d.*'

The difficult cash flow position is reflected by the practice of ordering small quantities of tickets from the Edmondson company and timetable bills from a local printer. James Brandreth supplied break [*sic*] blocks. Coal was originally bought from Richard Evans & Co., owners of Haydock Colliery, but later orders were spread over several merchants. Each summer, the Receiver authorised modest expenditure on press advertising in eight or nine newspapers, both national and local.

The First Locomotives

It is rare nowadays for details of a railway company's locomotives to remain a mystery but that is what has happened in the case of the original Hoylake Railway, the minute books of which have not survived. It is likely that in the very early days the company owned only one locomotive, almost certainly second-hand, and there is a report of an occasion when this engine ran into a sand drift and became derailed, causing the last train from Hoylake to be drawn

A very early photograph of Hoylake terminus, which is now believed to show the opening in 1866. Previously, in numerous earlier publications, the picture has been consistently misidentified as being later than this, whilst the locomotive has been stated to be the ex-London & South Western Railway 2-2-2WT No. 36 *Comet*, bought by the HR in 1875. *Comet*, however, had large splashers and outside cylinders, which the engine seen here patently does not. The station staff, footplate crew and platelayers posing for the photographer, along with the large crowd of onlookers, would all suggest an 'occasion', probably the official commencement of regular services on 2nd July 1866. The locomotive is thus almost certainly the inside-cylindered 2-2-2WT *Ashton*, about which otherwise little is known, although it is thought to have been a Sharp, Stewart product. The builder's plate visible on the buffer beam is too indistinct to read but 'Sharp, Stewart' fits with the letter spacing. The condition of the engine's paintwork indicates the inability of early paints to stand up to the heat of locomotive boilers. When built the line had cinder ballast and the stations low cinder filled platforms, as depicted here, whilst on the right, part of the primitive wooden carriage shed can be seen. Also of note is the tall station signal, with lattice post, supplied by Stevens & Co. of Southwark. No semaphore arm is visible, suggesting that the signal consisted simply of a lamp which was hoisted up the post to give an indication to footplate crews. Most of the railway's coaching stock would also appear to be on view. Little is known about these early coaches, which may well have been bought second-hand; they were 4-wheelers and apparently the partitions only went partway to the roof. The seats were also bare wood and quite narrow, forcing passengers to sit upright. T.B. MAUND COLLECTION

by horses. There is also the question of how the early engines got to the completely isolated line, though it seems likely that they were brought by rail to a suitable point on the Mersey Docks & Harbour Board line and dragged by horses over the intervening distance to Birkenhead Docks station.

From the available information, it seems that the original engine was a 2-2-2 outside framed well tank with inside cylinders and allegedly named *Ashton*. It is believed to have had a tall chimney with the Ramsbottom ornamental cap, was left-handed and had a Sharp pattern regulator handle. The early photograph of Hoylake station (*opposite*), which has now been re-evaluated, almost certainly shows this engine and thus confirms these sparse details. It is suggested that it was of Sharp, Stewart origin and it is known that this company carried out several repairs to the locomotive during its time in the Wirral. The photograph also confirms nameplates were carried on the boiler sides although the name cannot be read. As an aside, the location of the renowned locomotive dealer I.W. Boulton's works was at Ashton but no reference to such an engine can be found in Bennett's *Chronicles of Boulton's Siding. Ashton* is said to have been sold to Haydock Colliery in the early 1870s but another report gives it as being offered for sale in 1878, which would seem more likely.

It is obvious that the line could not be worked successfully with only one locomotive. The notes of the late S.H. Pearce Higgins suggest that the second engine was a Sharp, Stewart 2-4-0 well tank built in 1858 and acquired from the North London Railway. However, other sources state that it was an 0-6-0T, which seems unlikely but possibly it acquired this wheel arrangement later in life. It has also been attributed to Fox, Walker and built in 1867, which again seems unlikely as that would make it new, whilst Highet asserts that the Hoylake Railway had two locomotives in 1866. Various reports give the name of the locomotive as *Magnet*. This engine is also reported to have later been sold into colliery use but much of this is speculative.

The Receiver's accounts include five quarterly payments of £124 7s 7d to a Charles Langley in respect of '*Hire of Engine*' but when the last payment was made on 13th April 1870, it is clear that it was the final hire purchase instalment. These five payments amounted to £621 but it is not known how long they had been going on before the receivership, nor indeed to what locomotive they refer. With the company having been experiencing financial difficulties for a number of years, they may even have equated to the clearance of the debt incurred with the purchase of *Magnet*. Alternatively, the only other logical albeit highly unlikely explanation is the existence of a third locomotive of which nothing is known. However, this remote prospect is further negated by what happened next.

Although no details are known, it seems likely that the company was experiencing motive power difficulties in 1870 and one can speculate that the original engines were giving trouble. Whatever the problem, in May 1870 the Receiver authorised expenditure of £100 on a locomotive named *Diamed* from 'A. Young'. It will be recalled that Alexander Young who was one of the plaintiffs in 1868 and would, in due course, become a director of the successor company and it would suggest that there were links with the men who were to rescue the line much earlier than was previously thought. In the accounts for 20th June 1870 there is an item for '*Hire of Locomotive from R. Young £55.00*'. This could, of course, have been a clerical error for A. Young.

The engine's name is also likely to be a clerical error and should almost certainly read *Diomed* (or *Diomede* as it was sometimes spelt), which comes from Greek mythology. Further, no *Diamed* appears in Pike's *Dictionary of Locomotive Names* but there are several named *Diomed, Diomede* and *Diomedes*. If the Hoylake did indeed buy a locomotive outright for £100, it is likely to have been very old and decrepit and, from the locomotives known to have carried the name *Diomed* or a variation thereof, there are five possible candidates:
a) *Diomed* – No. 52. 2-2-2. 1838. Grand Junction Rly*
b) *Diomed* – No. 131. 2-2-2. 4/1849. L&YR
c) *Diomed* – No. 52. 2-2-2. 11/1849. L&NWR
d) *Diomedes* – No. 69. 2-2-2. 10/1848. MS&LR
e) *Diomed* – No. 10. 2-2-2. 1846/7. East Lancashire Rly

The similarities in name, numbers and wheel arrangement serve only to muddy things further. However, of this list, the strongest candidates would seem to be a) and b). Grand Junction Railway No. 52 *Diomed* was built in 1838 by Walker Bros. of Bury as a 2-2-2 with 13ins by 18ins inside cylinders and 5 foot 6 inch driving wheels. Although costing £1,200 for the engine plus £160 for the tender when new, it would surely have been worth little more than £100 by 1870. However, it was sold in November 1849 and its whereabouts in the intervening years is unknown, the likelihood being that it was in industrial use. Lancashire & Yorkshire Railway No. 131 *Diomed* was also a tender engine, built by Bury, Curtis & Kennedy of Liverpool in 1849 and numbered 131. It had outside cylinders 15ins by 20ins and driving wheels of 5 feet 10 inches diameter. Renumbered 90 in 1850, it was transferred to the East Lancashire Division of the L&YR in 1862, following that company's takeover of the East Lancashire Railway. On transfer, it swapped both name and number with ELR 2-2-0 No. 610 *Diomed*. In 1866, *Diomed*, the erstwhile L&YR No. 90, was rebuilt as a 2-4-0 and it was eventually withdrawn in 1869. The engine's subsequent fate is unknown, scrapping obviously being a strong possibility but its arrival on the Wirral for the sum of £100 is also quite likely.

The fate of e), the ELR's No. 10 *Diomed*, following its name and number swap with L&YR No. 90, is also uncertain. An inside cylindered 2-2-2 built by Walker Bros. in 1846/7, the company carried out a repair on the engine for the ELR in February/March 1849. No. 10 was rebuilt as a 2-4-0 tank in 1854, in which condition it transferred to the L&YR in 1862. It is thought to have been replaced in April 1869 and it is conceivable it could have gone to the Wirral, where the Hoylake revived its old name

Lastly, c) and d) would seem to be the least likely candidates. L&NWR No. 52 *Diomed* was built at Crewe in November 1849, as a 2-2-2 with outside cylinders of 15ins x 20ins and 6ft driving wheels. Replaced by a new engine in September 1860, No. 52 was probably

---

* Pike's *Dictionary* gives the name of this engine as *Diomedes*. However, Harry Jack, who kindly provided much assistance regarding the possible identity of this engine, notes that Ted Craven, a very careful researcher into early locomotives, recorded it as *Diomed*.

L&YR No. 131 *Diomed*, one of the likely candidates for the engine which appeared on the Wirral. It is seen here at Manchester Road station in Burnley, still in pretty much original condition, sometime between 1862 and 1866, when it was rebuilt as a 2-4-0. JOHN ALSOP COLLECTION

renumbered to the duplicate list as No. 52A and was either sold or scrapped sometime between then and April 1862. Whilst it could have survived to turn up on the Wirral eight years later, L&NWR experts consider this unlikely. Finally, the Manchester, Sheffield & Lincolnshire Railway 2-2-2 of 1848, No. 69 *Diomedes*, was rebuilt as a Class '2' 2-4-0 in the early 1860s and seems to have survived in MS&L use until around 1880, which effectively rules this engine out altogether.

Whichever *Diomed* it actually was, following its arrival on the Hoylake Railway nothing more is known of the locomotive. Its subsequent fate is unrecorded, as there are no further references to it in any documents which have so far come to light. Indeed, Highet in his history makes no mention of it at all, such was its obscurity. However, coupled with the reference in the accounts of 20th June 1870 to '*Hire of Locomotive ... £55.00*', what this may indicate is that *Diomed* was indeed merely on hire, probably for just a few weeks because of problems with *Ashton* or *Magnet*, and the engine was never actually purchased at all. Whilst Young was authorised to spend £100, that does not mean he actually did so.

Traffic receipts show clearly that August Bank Holiday (then the first Monday in August) was the time of highest traffic, followed by Easter and a poor third by Whitsuntide. The weather could make or break these holidays and a wet summer could have serious consequences for the company. The year 1869 was the best during the receivership, whilst 1870 had a fairly good Easter, not so good Whit and with the curtailment at Leasowe affecting the rest of the year. The winter of 1871-72 was far better than 1869-70, when the takings fell to £9-£10 per week during December to April. From February 1871, revenue recovered suddenly from £9 to £23, the reason for this not being apparent. However, the change occurred at the beginning of the third financial year of the receivership, suggesting some change in accounting practice such as, for example, the spreading of contract (season ticket) receipts. From time to time in the summer, revenue was augmented by the sale of hay which grew beside the line. Substantial quantities were harvested raising £15-£20 on each occasion.

The wages were paid fortnightly and were steady at between £50 and £60 with very little seasonal variation. There were obviously some redundancies in July 1870, with a fall to £38 which rose quite soon to an average of £45. The wages account included '*petty expenses*' which are not identified and an unusual item could account for one or two sudden fluctuations.

Whilst it is certain that connecting omnibuses originally ran to and from Seacombe ferry, there is no doubt that a change to Woodside ferry was made at some time and this may have been done from the time of the curtailment of trains at Leasowe, though the address of Adam Fox, the contractor for the railway, was adjacent to Seacombe ferry. However, the accounts reveal a payment on 25th November 1870 of £2 1s 8d to '*the Woodside Ferry Co.*' (this would actually have been the Birkenhead Improvement Commissioners) in respect of an office. The use of Woodside would have avoided the use of the Poulton toll bridge and given the existence of the line a higher profile; its added visibility may well have contributed to the improvement in revenue in the later period of receivership.

Payments to Adam Fox for omnibus hire naturally correlate strongly with traffic receipts but his resources seem to have been sufficiently flexible to meet any sudden variations in traffic. The railway's weekly payments in the early stage were between £10 and £20 but in the rock-bottom period between November 1870 and mid-February 1871 he received only three payments, none exceeding £5. Thereafter, matters improved, reaching almost £60 in the August Bank Holiday week. In the winter of 1871-72 payments never fell below £16 and in July achieved £65.

The Hoylake & Birkenhead Rail & Tramway Company

Meanwhile, there were other forces at work, intent on putting the railway on a firm footing. On 5th May 1870, the Birkenhead Improvement Commissioners considered an application from '*landowners, and others interested in the Birkenhead, Hoylake and West Kirby neighbourhood*' who wanted to lay down a tramway connecting Woodside ferry and Docks station, and a deputation with detailed plans was received two weeks later. The matter was referred to the Surveyor and, in due course, approved, though settlement of the railway's financial affairs delayed progress. On 19th November 1870, a new company, the Hoylake & Birkenhead Tramway Co, was formed with a capital of £70,000 and it is possible that the conversion of the railway to a tramway was contemplated, as its principal objects were '*to construct, maintain and work tramways in Birkenhead, Bidston-cum-Ford and elsewhere in the County Palatine of Chester and to acquire, maintain and work the undertaking of the Hoylake Railway Co.*' The promoters were all London men and included A.C.S. Padeswell Hall, MP, James Walker and F.G.W. Fearon, Secretary of the Trust and Loan Co. of Upper Canada.

The new company immediately deposited a Bill in Parliament seeking powers to build a tramway between Woodside and Docks station. However, there were legal difficulties about the status of the company and the Bill was abandoned. Under an Act of 1st July 1872, the 1870 company was dissolved and a new company, the Hoylake & Birkenhead Rail & Tramway, was formed to take over the powers of the Hoylake Railway Company and build 3.02 miles of street tramway between Docks station and Woodside. There was an obligation to run two workmen's cars each way, not later than 7.00am and not before 6.00pm at not more than one halfpenny per mile with a minimum fare of 1d. The new company paid the Receiver £22,000 for the assets and goodwill of the old company and settled with Mr Vyner for his land. The Official Liquidator was Ashurst, Morris, Crisp & Co. of 6 Old Jewry, London E.C. but it was not until 1875 that the Hoylake Railway Company was wound up.

Officially trains resumed running through to the Docks station on 1st August 1872 but the last payment to the omnibus contractor was on 18th July and the *Liverpool Mercury* reported the reopening on 23rd July. There was an hourly service commencing at 9.40am from Docks and ending at 8.20pm from Hoylake. Single fares were 1st class 1s, 2nd class 8d and 3rd class 6d. The new company provided a service of twelve trains, which by the summer of 1877 had increased to fourteen. The *Liverpool Mercury* of 23rd July 1872, when announcing the reopening commented:

> '... giving an opportunity of spending a day at this delightful watering place and paying a visit to West Kirby than which a more beautiful place for the salubrity of its climate and beauty of the scenery does not exist within 50 miles of Liverpool.'

Hoylake & Birkenhead Locomotives

In accordance with the known facts, the H&B company took over two locomotives from the HR – *Ashton* and *Magnet*, with the fate of the mysterious *Diomed* unknown. In mid-1875, the company acquired another 2-2-2 well tank, built by the London & South Western Railway at Nine Elms in 1852, using a boiler, cylinders and wheels acquired from the Vulcan Foundry. It was one of eight locomotives dubbed the 'Sussex' Class and was named *Comet*, carrying the number 36, (which it retained); it had 5 foot 6 inch driving wheels, the others being 3 feet 6 inches in diameter, outside frames and 14½ins by 20ins stroke outside cylinders. It had been withdrawn by the L&SW in June 1872 and hired to the Isle of Wight (Newport Junction) Railway at £2

An outline drawing of the ex-L&SWR 2-2-2 *Comet* (not reproduced to scale), which arrived on the H&B in 1875 and remained there until 1881 at least. A quick glance at the way the smokebox casing typically flares into the outside cylinders and the large splasher for the driving wheel indicates that it cannot possibly be the locomotive in the early photograph of Hoylake. The 'Sussex' Class had 5ft 6ins driving wheels and 3ft 6ins leading and trailing wheels, and the water tanks a capacity for 560 gallons.

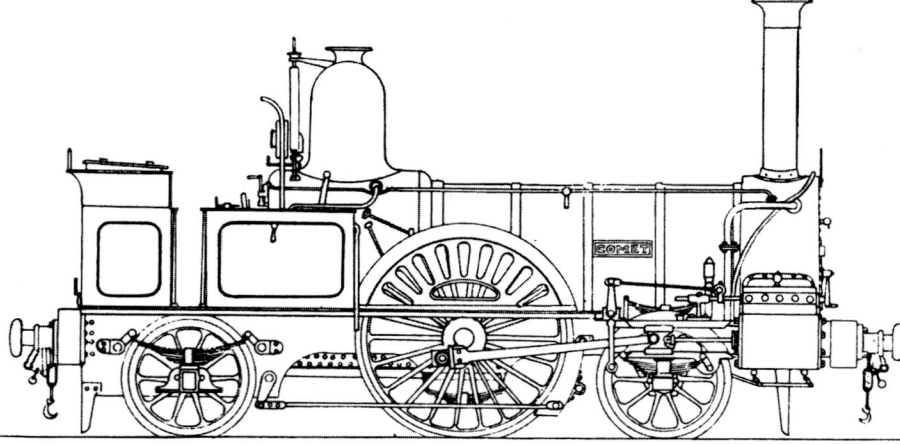

per day, where it remained until 1875 when it was sold to the Hoylake company for £325. It retained its L&SWR green livery throughout its service on the Wirral and, according to *An Illustrated History of LSWR Locomotives* by D.L. Bradley (Wild Swan Publications), was offered for sale on 11th November 1878 along with *Ashton* and sold in February 1879 to J. Lever & Co., Port Sunlight for £142. This, however, seems unlikely as it is a matter of record that the first sod of Port Sunlight soap works was not turned until 3rd March 1888. Lever had an earlier works at Warrington but only from 1885. However, Bradley records in his *Locomotives of the LSWR* (RCTS) that both *Comet* and *Ashton* were omitted from the company's Board of Trade returns on 30th June 1879, so they had at least been removed from the books. This suggests withdrawal perhaps with the intention of scrapping, although the latter may not have taken place until several years later.

Bradley also recorded a number of incidents from *Comet*'s career, as documented in the Hoylake & Birkenhead Company's minute books. Apparently it was involved in a minor accident when it left the rails on 13th August 1875, broke a crank axle in September 1877 and suffered a collapsed tube plate in May 1878.

The returns for 1874, 1875 and 1876 indicate that the company actually owned only one engine, probably *Comet*, with *Ashton* being out of service and written off in the accounts and *Magnet* by this date apparently disposed of. It also suggests that at least one other locomotive was being hired and the Liquidator's accounts for 30th January 1874 record the payment of £112 to the Great Western Railway for the hire of an engine.

By 1877, however, the company were declaring ownership of four engines. In 1876, things must have been getting difficult, with probably only one serviceable locomotive (*Comet*) available for traffic, so an order was placed with the Yorkshire Engine Co. of Sheffield for two 2-4-0 side tank engines, which, when delivered early in 1877, were given the numbers 1 and 2 and the names *West Kirby* and *Birkenhead* respectively (builders No's 356 and 357). They immediately took over the brunt of services with, as previously indicated, *Comet* and *Ashton* being offered for sale eighteen months later.

It was apparent, however, that a back up engine was still required. The Locomotive Superintendent of the Hoylake & Birkenhead Rail & Tramway Co., J.E. Medley, also held the same position for the Neath & Brecon Railway. In 1850, two 0-4-0 well tanks had been delivered by Stothert, Slaughter & Co. to the Monmouthshire Railway & Canal Co., being numbered 14 and 15 respectively. Of

ABOVE: Yorkshire Engine Co. official photograph of HR No. 2 *Birkenhead*, one of two 2-4-0 engines supplied new in 1877, the other being No. 1 *West Kirby*. The engine is seen here fully lined out but in the usual works grey for photography purposes. T.B. MAUND COLLECTION

RIGHT: *Birkenhead* poses in the Wirral, shortly after delivery. The gentleman holding the boiler handrail may well be J.E. Medley, the H&B's Locomotive Superintendent. The engine by now wears the H&B's black livery, whilst the lining appears to have been much simplified from the works photo. As traffic increased, these engines proved too light for the work and both were withdrawn in June 1891. *Birkenhead* was sold in 1892, hauling colliers trains in North Staffordshire and survived until 1922 following conversion to a stationary engine. JOHN ALSOP COLLECTION

In the late 19th century, Woodside ferry approach at Birkenhead was unique in being served by three horse tramway companies, the separate metals of which were not connected in any way. This reproduction from a painting by the late G.S. Cooper shows the situation in 1877, soon after the opening of the Hoylake Railway's line from Docks station. The railway company's tramcar is in the background and was a typical Starbuck car of the period. Car No. 7 of the Birkenhead Tramway Co., in the foreground, is today preserved and stands in the ferry terminal (right), now a listed building. T.B. MAUND COLLECTION

light construction, both appear to have been quickly converted to three axles by the addition of what was referred to as a pair of '*straining wheels*'. In 1870, No. 14 gained an 'A' suffix to its number on being replaced by a newer locomotive in the MR&CC fleet, with the same happening to No. 15 in 1872. Effectively now surplus to requirements, No's 14A and 15A were sold to the locomotive dealers Budd & Holt in October 1873. A month later, No. 14A was resold to the Neath & Brecon Railway for £1,500. No doubt when casting around for a back up engine in 1878, the company approached Medley and asked if the N&B had anything suitable. No. 14A, which may have been out of traffic at this time in any case, was evidently suggested and, following various repairs when it may also have been rebuilt as a 2-4-0, was purchased by the Hoylake Railway for £500 and was eventually despatched north on 24th March 1879.

In 1881, when the Seacombe, Hoylake & Deeside Railway took over the Hoylake Railway, the company's locomotive stock was recorded as four engines: No. 1 *West Kirby*; No. 2 *Birkenhead*; No. 3 (ex- N&B No. 14A); No. 36 *Comet*. The presence of the latter on the list, whilst it may have been of scrap value only, further scotches the theory that it was sold to J. Lever & Co. in 1879.

THE STREET TRAMWAY

By late 1871, the through Hoylake-Woodside omnibus service had been reduced to one journey each way on weekdays only, suggesting that the 'official' railway connection had secured most of the traffic. On resumption of the rail service, a temporary omnibus service was provided between Docks station and Woodside. An agreement with the Birkenhead Commissioners had been signed on 16th April 1872 and the new company lost no time in arranging for the construction of their tramway. As authorised, it consisted of mainly single line with eleven loops. It was to commence in two spurs on the north side of Woodside ferry approach, the double tracks to pass either side of a lamp in the centre of Hamilton Street, before turning right into Canning Street, which was also to be double track. It then ran by Sandford Street (returning via Taylor Street), Bridge Street, Marcus Street, Corporation Road, Beaufort Road (and its extension which belonged to Vyner) and Wallasey Bridge Road. In fact, although authorised to use Corporation Road throughout, the line was constructed along the parallel Cleveland Street, which was much wider and not so congested with carts going to and from the

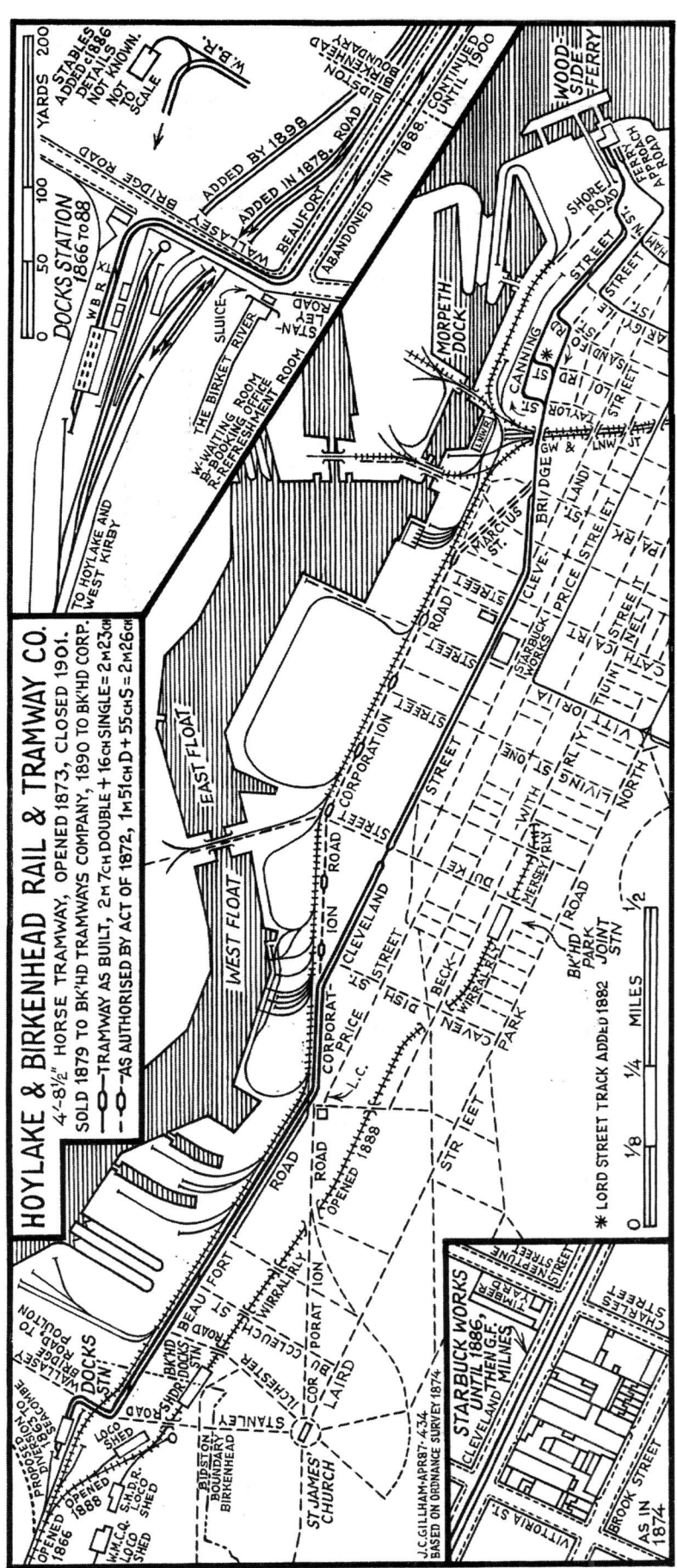

dock quays; this was done with the Commissioners' consent though without further powers. It was also built as double track for most of its length though, at the insistence of the Commissioners, the authorised double track in Hamilton Street was built as single alongside the kerb thus easing the gradient. This length of track is still in position beneath the tarmac in 2007. An annual rent of £200 was paid for the two sidings at Woodside, which were the property of the Commissioners who owned the Ferry Approach.

Construction commenced on 22nd April 1873, using a new form of rail recently patented by a tramway engineer, C.H. Beloe, who was well known locally. It consisted of steel rails weighing 30lbs per yard, bolted to cast iron sleepers; the cost was £3,368 per single track mile and it is interesting to note that the labour element of this amount was only £220. Curves were of 35 foot radius and the maximum gradient, on the climb from Woodside to Canning Street, was 1 in 19. Despite shortages of labour and materials, the Board of Trade inspection took place on 5th September, the inspecting officer, Maj-Gen Hutchinson, walking the full length of the line and riding back to Woodside. Public service commenced the following day, after an opening ceremony when four cars carried 100 invited guests to Docks station where they boarded a train for Hoylake, lunch being served in the new carriage shed. The establishment of a rail link with Woodside was celebrated by various special events in Hoylake, a regatta on 13th September, field sports on 15th and a pony meeting at the racecourse on 16th.

The tramway track ran into Docks station, where there was cross-platform interchange with the trains and this may well have been the first example of a facility of this kind. Stables were later erected nearby and the provision of horses was contracted out to Thomas Lloyd, a well-known figure in local transport circles. There seems to have been some dissatisfaction with his performance as the contract was terminated from 30th June 1876, after which he was replaced by W.W. Townson, a Liverpool veterinary surgeon who also ran omnibuses in Birkenhead. The tramcar manufacturer George Starbuck, whose factory was on the route, supplied, painted and repaired the cars. Starbuck, an American who had been closely associated with George Francis Train, the tramway pioneer, seems to have had a good relationship with the railway company as he was permitted to test his products on the tramway. On 11th May 1876, he tested a steam car built for Vienna, three round trips being made at an average speed of 10mph with 45 passengers aboard. The car handled the 1 in 19 gradient in Hamilton Street successfully but would not have been able to restart if it had needed to stop.

According to contemporary reports, the tramway rolling stock originally consisted of six single-deck cars seating 18 passengers; the saloons were 14 feet long and 6 feet 7 inches wide and weighed 1 ton 11 cwt. The overall length including platforms was 20 feet and they were 9 feet 3 inches high. However, all seem to have been rebuilt as double-deckers, by Starbuck no doubt, and two more similar cars were added in 1878. They were described as knifeboard double-deckers with eight windows a side and sliding shutters. 'Knifeboard' cars had a long back-to-back seat on the upper deck mounted on a clerestory which provided ventilation for the saloon. In 1876, an agreement was made with the Birkenhead Commissioners to keep the track in repair for £100 per annum.

LEFT: The only known photograph of one of the Hoylake & Birkenhead Railway tramcars – presumably, the railway's full title was not used for space reasons. Car No. 2 would have been one of the six single-deckers originally provided, which were rebuilt as double-deckers probably in the mid 1870s. It is likely that No. 2 was photographed outside Starbuck's works following this rebuild. The livery was red and cream, with 'The Hoylake Railway' lettering in red shaded with black. The lettering on the route board looks to be in cream shaded with black whilst the number and monogram were in gold. JOHN HORNE COLLECTION

BELOW: It was not unusual for early railway companies to offer inducements to encourage patronage of their trains and this handbill was issued in August 1876, offering free travel for up to five years to people building new houses in Hoylake and West Kirby. The extension to the latter was not opened until April 1878. T.B. MAUND COLLECTION

The London syndicate which had promoted the new company was also concerned with the Neath & Brecon, Belfast Central, Felixstowe Railway & Dock Co. and the Devon & Cornwall Railway. The general manager, F. Kirtley, and engineer and locomotive superintendent, J. E. Medley, also held these offices with the Neath & Brecon. James Goulding continued to act as local manager, the head office being in the Ferry Buildings at Woodside.

The Hoylake's line was completely isolated from other railways and it was hoped to remedy this situation by agreeing running powers with another projected concern, the Birkenhead, Chester & North Wales Railway Co. (BC&NW). This company, by an Act of 1873, had revived the 1862 scheme for a mid-Wirral line between Chester and Bidston with connections to both sides of the Great Float. The proposed junction with the Hoylake line was to be 350 yards west of Bidston station, *i.e.* much further west than the line which was ultimately built and a Bill was submitted moving the authorised line between Bidston and Poulton so that its junction would line up with the BC&NW. The latter intended to handle its passenger traffic by routing it into the projected Birkenhead Central station of the Mersey Railway over another authorised line leaving the main line at Prenton. However, no progress was made and on 25th November 1874, the Hoylake directors resolved to write to the BC&NW Co. '*regarding carrying out its Agreement with this company dated 23rd July 1873*'. As construction of the Mersey Railway had not then commenced, there was no progress and a Notice of Abandonment was issued in December 1877.

With a secure connection to Woodside, traffic on the line gradually increased. Express trams were run at peak hours, though just how this was arranged is not clear. Eventually, an additional short length of track was laid in Lord Street, the purpose of which was apparently to enable the fast cars to overtake the slow ones.

THE WEST KIRBY AND DOCKS EXTENSIONS

The H&B directors now felt confident enough to consider extensions to their railway line. The Hoylake & Birkenhead Railway & Tramway Act, 1873, authorised two extensions; the first was from Hoylake to West Kirby (1.225 miles) and the second was a short length to connect Docks station with the Mersey Docks & Harbour Board line in Beaufort Road, thus ending the isolation of the Hoylake line. The raising of additional capital of £24,000 and borrowing of £8,000 was also sanctioned. Negotiations for the acquisition of land started in 1875 and, in the August of the following year, a handbill was issued offering free tickets for up to five years to people building new houses in Hoylake and West Kirby.

Later on, tickets were sold in bulk to the Royal Liverpool Golf Club enabling its members to travel at single fare for the return journey. They were valid for a year after issue and available in reverse for members resident in Hoylake.

Tenders were let for the West Kirby extension in 1877 but progress was slow. The extension was single line as was the whole route at that time. However, pressure from the local council resulted in a road overbridge having to be built at Bridge Road, West Kirby, to double line standards, in place of the proposed level crossing. The directors fixed 1st January 1878 as the opening date but the line was not ready. Maj-Gen. Hutchinson carried out the Board of Trade inspection on 25th January and postponed the opening for a month, pending receipt of a Certificate to the effect that the extension would be worked by train staff as to mode No. 2 of Board of Trade regulations for working single lines. There was a further postponement on 4th March 1878 as the signals were not ready and the extension was at last opened on 1st April 1878. The original West Kirby station lay just to the south of the present day terminus on land later occupied by sidings and nowadays by the Concourse. Like everything else, it was a primitive affair.

In a further attempt to obtain some physical connection with other railways, the Hoylake directors and manager met the Works Committee of the Mersey Docks & Harbour Board on 25th May 1877, with a view to making the connection authorised as Railway No. 2 in their 1873 Act. The railway deputation asked that the Board's lines between Ilchester Road and the township boundary be put in repair but the Board, being concerned with dock traffic, did not really want this connection. However, they agreed to make

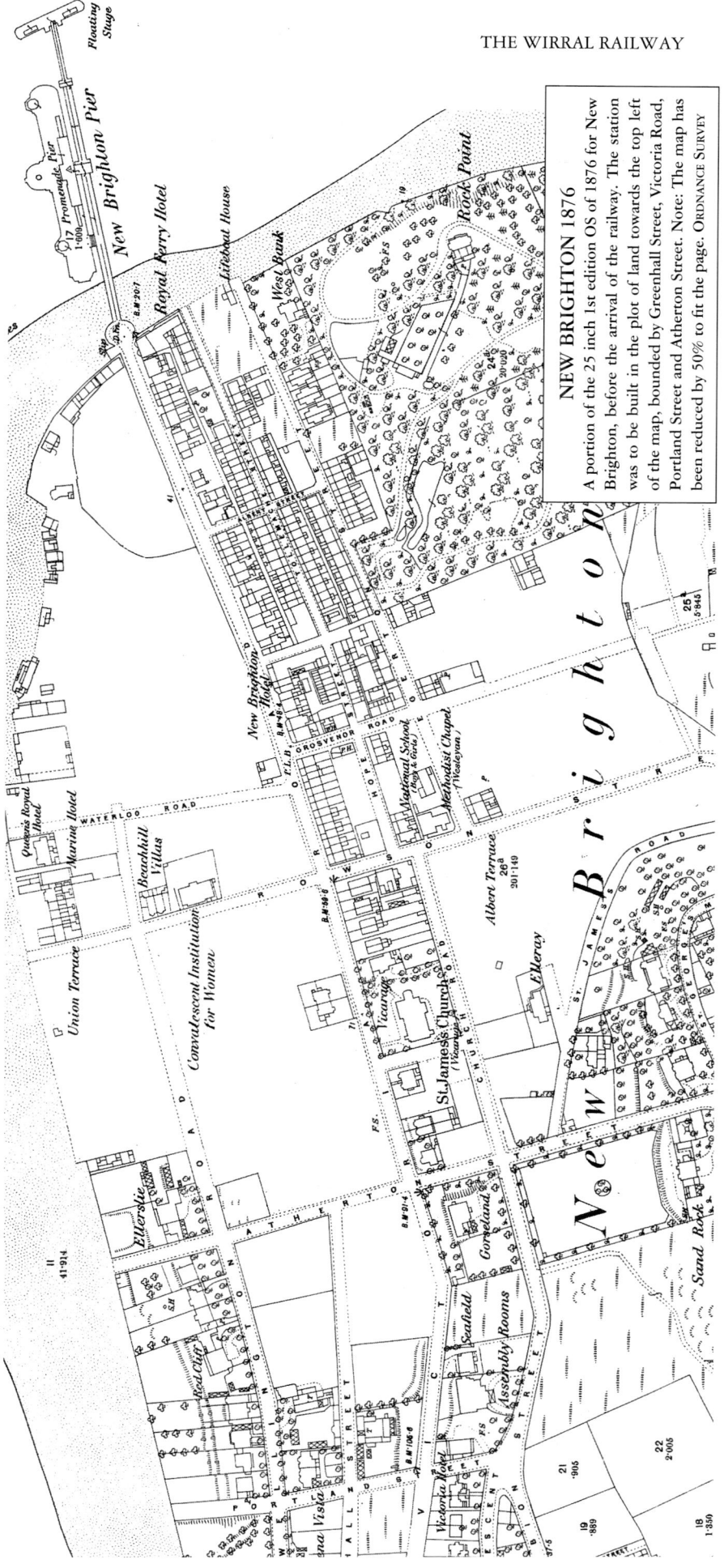

NEW BRIGHTON 1876

A portion of the 25 inch 1st edition OS of 1876 for New Brighton, before the arrival of the railway. The station was to be built in the plot of land towards the top left of the map, bounded by Greenhall Street, Victoria Road, Portland Street and Atherton Street. Note: The map has been reduced by 50% to fit the page. ORDNANCE SURVEY

the connection but did nothing and the Hoylake company made a further request on 25th January 1878, to the effect that the tracks be repaired *'for the benefit of those parties who are entitled to use them.'* This was tactless and the Works Committee stiffly resolved that *'the company be informed that it does not appear that the Company has any rights to use the line except with the permission of the Board.'* The company had to concede that this was so; possibly they had in mind the rights of the factory owners whose premises were built on Dock Board land.

Having laid the short connecting line (330 yards), the railway company sought permission to pass wagons over the Board's lines. This was granted on 19th July 1878, subject to certain charges being paid (see page 49). The Hoylake company would have gained very little traffic but for the intervention of the industrialists whose premises were now connected to the new line. These firms were the Board's tenants and, in December 1878, it was agreed that this entitled them to pay only sixpence per loaded wagon. In later years, the Board accepted the Wirral connection as legitimate but only when it became a source of traffic for the docks, perhaps with the creation of the Parkgate-West Kirby link in 1886 but certainly when the joint Manchester, Sheffield & Lincolnshire and Wrexham, Mold & Connah's Quay line reached Bidston in 1896.

SALE OF THE TRAMWAY

The tramway between Docks station and Woodside had long ceased to be just a railway feeder and it is possible that, by the late 1870s, local town traffic exceeded railway passengers. In 1879, the directors decided to dispose of it if they could and, after a period of negotiation, the Birkenhead Tramways Company, a body formed in 1877 to take over and extend the non-statutory 1860 company formed by G.F. Train, agreed to pay £27,500 for the line, eight cars and the sheds and stables at Wallasey Bridge Road, which were accessed by a triangular junction. The tramways company was obliged under the Agreement to provide an improved service, meet all trains and run a 10-minute service between 8.00am and 8.00pm at fares not exceeding 3d inside and 2d outside. They also had a duty to run *'two express through cars at the least, from or in connection with the morning trains without stopping for intermediate traffic.'* There was also a provision forbidding any tramway extensions beyond Bidston in the direction of Hoylake. The transfer took place on 12th October 1879.

THE SEACOMBE, HOYLAKE & DEESIDE RAILWAY COMPANY

The railway now came under more local control, Mr Henry Robertson (senior), the Wrexham ironmaster and founder member of the locomotive building firm, Beyer, Peacock & Co., becoming

HOYLAKE AND BIRKENHEAD RAILWAY.
TRAIN BOOK.

Thursday May 18th May/82

STATIONS.	Train	Commencing Numbers	Closing Numbers	No. of Passengers	Class	Rate	Amount	Amount by each Train
		8/38pm	8/53pm					
Moreton	3R	01	02	1		6	-6	
Hoylake	3	98	00	2		8	1.4	
	3R	48	49	1		1/-	1-	2.10
		8/27am		4				
Moreton	P	44	45	1		2	2	
	3R	02	03	1		6	6	
Hoylake	P	48	49	1		5	5	
	3R	49	52	3		1/-	3.0	
West Kirby	P	54	55	1		6½	6½	
	2R	87	88	1		1/6	1.6	6.1½
		9/38am		8				
Moreton	3R	03	04	1		6	6	
Meols	3R	28	30	2		9	1.6	
Hoylake	3	00	01	1		8	8	
	3R	52	53	1		1/-	1.0	
West Kirby	3	59	61	2		10	1.8	
"	3R	98	00	2		1/3	2.6	7.10
		10/38am		9				
Hoylake	2R	22	24	2		1/3	2.6	
	3R	53	55	2		1/-	2.0	
West Kirby	3	61	62	1		10	10	
"	1R	19	20	1		2/3	2.3	
"	2R	88	89	1		1/6	1.6	
"	3R	00	09	9		1/3	11.3	1.0.4
		11/38am		16				
Moreton	3	42	46	4		4	1.4	
Meols	3R	30	31	1		9	9	
Hoylake	1R	27	31	4		1/9	7.0	
	3R	55	60	5		1/-	5.0	
W Kirby	2	75	76	1		1/-	1.0	
	3	62	63	1		10	10	
	1R	10	12	2		2/3	4.6	
	2R	89	93	4		1/6	6.0	
	3R	09	21	12		1/3	15.0	2.1.5
				34				

A page from the Hoylake & Birkenhead Railway Train Book, dated 18th May 1882. The company had changed its name to the Seacombe, Hoylake & Deeside Railway a year earlier but were no doubt using up old stationery.

chairman. Mr R.C. de G. Vyner (son of the former squire, now deceased), Harold Littledale (previously on the board of the old company) and Frederic North of Stonebark, New Brighton (whose family name is remembered in North Drive near his residence) joined the board over the next few years, the latter as a nominee of Major John Cavendish Orred, a landowner. Henry Robertson (1816-88) was experienced in both railway and industrial affairs. He had been engineer to the Shrewsbury & Chester, Shrewsbury & Birmingham and Shrewsbury & Hereford railways, and had served the GW until the amalgamation of 1854; his interests included the Ruabon Coal Co., Westminster Colliery, Brymbo Colliery and Broughton Works. He had come to the Wrexham district during a slump in 1842 and spent £100,000 in revitalising collieries and works in the area. Upon his death in 1888, his place on the SH&D board was taken by his son, Henry Beyer Robertson. The new board considered the present title of the company to be too localised and proposed to change it to the Seacombe, Hoylake & Deeside Railway Company (SH&D), a title that indicated their future intentions. The registered office was at 84 Foregate Street, Chester, the office of Mr W.D. Haswell, who was destined to be the Secretary of the company and its successor until the Grouping in 1923. Under SH&D auspices, the shed at Birkenhead Docks was designated a workshop and excellent engineering work was done there under unsophisticated conditions.

The name change was authorised by the Seacombe, Hoylake & Deeside Railway Act, 1881, which reactivated the long-lapsed powers for the line between Bidston and Seacombe. Although the opening of the Mersey Railway was five years in the future, a public meeting at the Stanley Hotel, Hoylake in March 1881, was told that the prospects for the line were good, as the 'Mersey Subway', by then in the early stages of construction, had no competition. The route of the new line was similar to that authorised by the 1863 Act and Vyner, who still had hopes of his late father's dock scheme being completed, succeeded in having a number of onerous conditions inserted in the Act. Most of the land between Bidston and Poulton belonged to Vyner, who realised that a railway would be a useful adjunct to the dock. The railway company's land acquisitions were restricted to the purchase of sufficient land for building a double track railway, station works (including the necessary facilities for the Tramways Company) and a station at Poulton. In carrying the line over Wallasey Pool, the company was obliged to provide a swing or bascule bridge with an opening span not less than that of the existing bridge on Wallasey Bridge Road. However, if Vyner were to build his dock, the bridge had to be a double swing bridge with two 60 foot spans either side of the pivot. To facilitate his plans, the line had to leave the existing railway about 1,000 feet west of the point originally intended, and a much higher and more expensive embankment would have been required.

The Birkenhead Tramways Company petitioned against the Bill, complaining that they had paid £27,500 for the tramway and asserted that *'the railway company has greatly benefited since the tramway was managed by a skilled staff of directors and managers.'* As a new Docks passenger station was envisaged on the curve leading to the bridge, provision was made for altering the tramway layout. The Tramways Company was to be compensated to the extent of £500 per year if the railway was diverted to Seacombe.

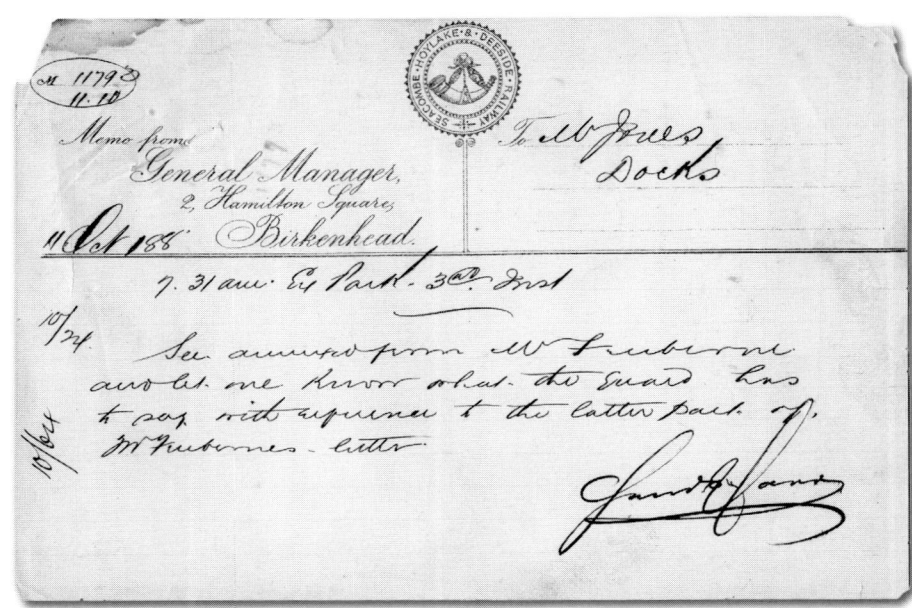

SH&D memo from the General Manager to Mr Jones, Docks station, 11th October 1888.

A further Act in 1882 authorised another line 2.235 miles long, commencing in the township of Poulton-cum-Seacombe and terminating west of Portland Street, New Brighton. The raising of additional capital of £60,000 was also sanctioned. The route was closer to Breck Road and Wallasey Village than the line which was eventually built and was clearly designed for running trains between Seacombe and New Brighton. Seacombe was an all-weather, all the year round ferry whereas New Brighton was unreliable in the winter. The company believed that New Brighton and Wallasey could develop in the same way as Hoylake and West Kirby, and that a substantial business and residential traffic could be built up to and from Seacombe. The cost of the works necessary to satisfy Vyner was prohibitive and the company felt that it would be impossible to obtain a return on the capital invested, so nothing was done for the time being.

THE FIRST WIRRAL RAILWAY COMPANY

In the meantime, on 13th June 1883, another concern, the Wirral Railway Company, was incorporated by Board of Trade Certificate, a rarely-used procedure authorised by the Railway Construction Facilities Act, 1864. Its objects were to provide a link between the Mersey Railway, then under construction, and the proposed Manchester, Sheffield & Lincolnshire Railway's (MS&L) line from Chester to Connah's Quay, near Shotwick. From that point, there would be a connection with the Wrexham, Mold & Connah's Quay line to Wrexham. However, the railways authorised by the Certificate linked New Brighton to the Mersey Railway's Birkenhead Central station by a roundabout route. Starting from a point in Warren Drive west of Victoria Road, the line would have crossed Wallasey Village and then turned south to follow the proposed 1873 diversion and BC&NW abandoned line. The Prenton Branch had been authorised in 1873 to follow a line south of Borough Road, at the time a new road, which followed a now culverted watercourse through the 'Happy Valley'. By 1883, this road had been developed and the proposed site of the Mersey Railway's Birkenhead Central station had been slightly changed, so the line was realigned to tunnel under Argyle Street South and Tranmere Hill, and cross Borough Road near Kingsland Road, where there was to be a station. The gradient from Central to Kingsland Road was to be 1 in 39.71, the tunnel section measuring 573 yards. The line then followed a route north of Woodchurch

ABOVE: SH&D consignment note, 6th March 1895.

LEFT: Requisition for contract tickets, 12th March 1892

Road with a station at Holm Lane. The land was purchased and lay fallow for many years and much of it is now a public recreation ground known as the Holm Field. Birkenhead Central station was designed to receive this line and the connections were slightly modified to make the junction further east by a drawing dated 9th December 1882; tunnel easements were negotiated with property owners in Holt Hill and the nearby Convent. Agreement was reached with the Earl of Shrewsbury & Talbot for land purchases and plots in Borough Road were bought from the liquidators of the Birkenhead Land & Investment Co. Ltd. There is a record of the purchase of No's 3, 5 and 7 Kingsland Road in 1885 and an agreement to extend the time available for purchase of the tramway stables in Borough Road.

In 1884, the Wirral applied to Parliament for lines (a) from Bidston to Birkenhead Park and (b) extending their authorised railway at Prenton to Neston, a distance of 6.22 miles. A rather tight curve was also proposed to enable trains to run from Birkenhead Central in the direction of Neston, where the station was to be slightly to the east of the town centre. This was authorised and, following agreement about junctions with the Manchester, Sheffield & Lincolnshire Railway, a further Bill was deposited in Parliament the same year, extending the line from Neston to join the MS&L near Shotwick, with another curve in the direction of Chester. This Bill also modified the earlier Act slightly, the junction at Bidston being moved nearer to the station. These proposals were authorised by the Wirral (Dee Extension) Railway Certificate 1884, which also permitted the Mersey, SH&D, MS&L and WM&CQ to *'pursue joint ventures'*. It stipulated that the Woodchurch-Birkenhead Central line should be in a cutting 18ft below road level.

The Mersey Railway

In 1883, the Mersey Railway between Birkenhead and Liverpool was under construction and plans were being made for the two railways to be linked. At that time, the Mersey was authorised between James Street, Liverpool and Green Lane, Birkenhead but no move was made to construct a link with the North Wirral lines. Meanwhile, the Wirral Railway had proposed to build a line from a point west of the Birkenhead Docks station of the SH&D to join the Mersey Railway at Hamilton Square. This line would have been in tunnel from a point near Aspinall Street. In November 1883, plans for linking the two lines were confirmed between the two companies but the meeting point was to be at Duke Street, not Hamilton Square, thus confining the tunnel section to the Mersey Railway. The Wirral agreed to delete the line between Duke Street and Hamilton Square (Railway No. 2 in their 1883 Bill) provided the Mersey obtained powers to make a connection. This was authorised by the Mersey Railway Act 1884.

The Mersey was in dire financial straits and would probably have done nothing if the Wirral had not threatened to extend to Hamilton Square. The first sod of the Wirral line was cut near the Birkenhead Showground (near the present day

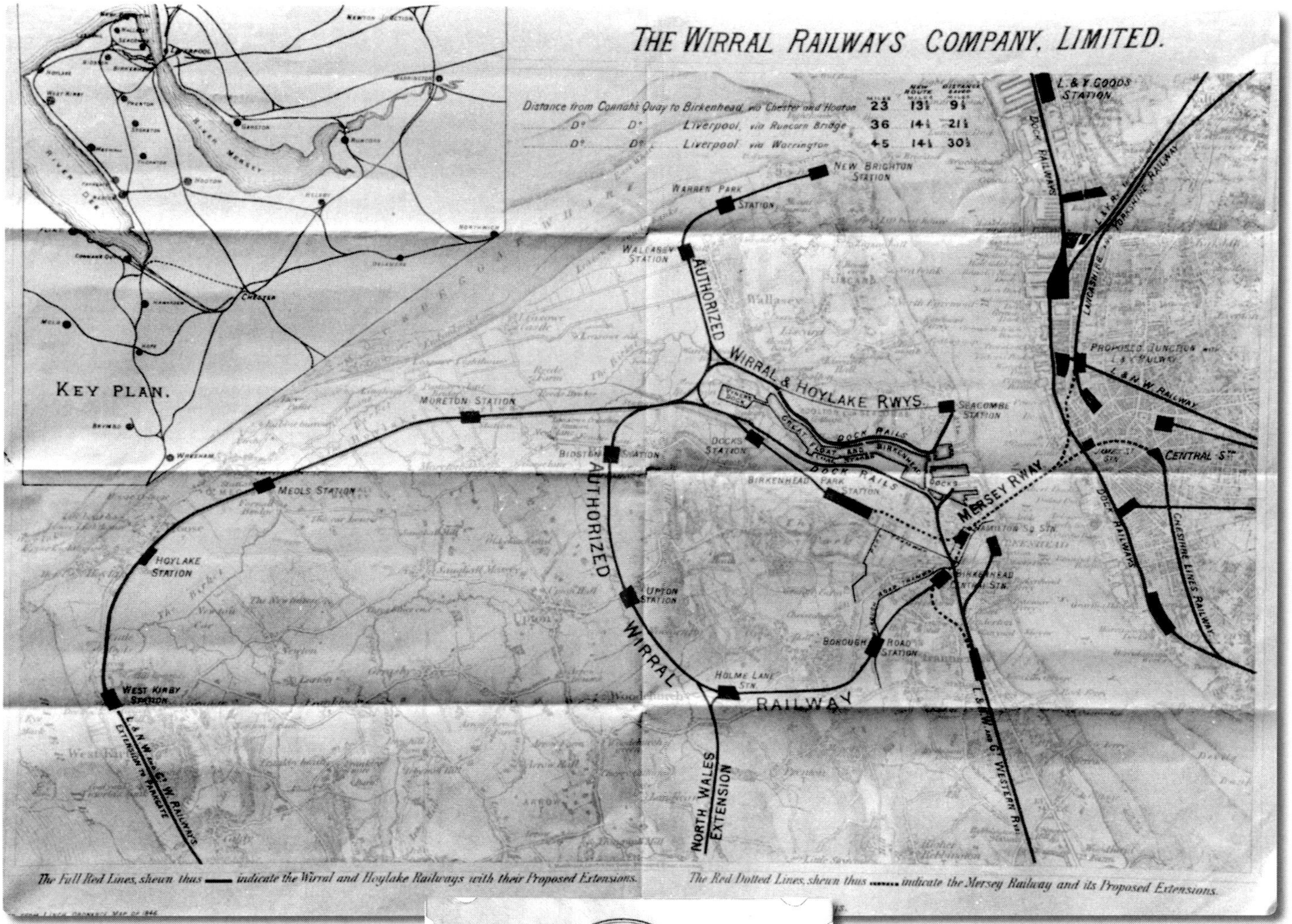

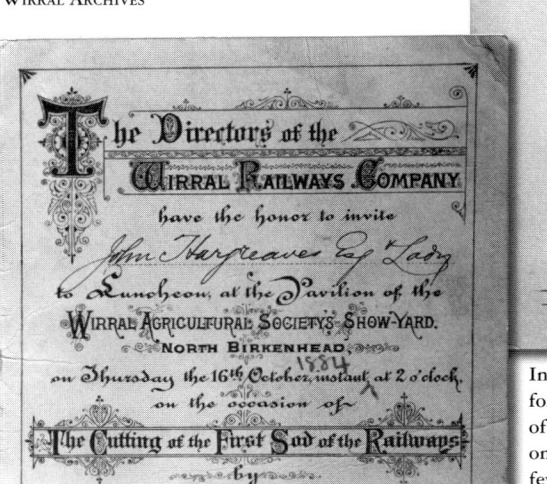

Above: This map accompanied the Prospectus for the Wirral Railways Company Ltd in 1884. Note the authorised line between Birkenhead Central and Holm Lane (Prenton), as well as Vyner's Dock at Poulton, neither of which were built. Courtesy Wirral Archives

The Directors of the Wirral Railways Company have the honor to invite John Hargreaves Esq & Lady to Luncheon, at the Pavilion of the Wirral Agricultural Society's Show-Yard. North Birkenhead, on Thursday the 16th October, instant, 1884 at 2 o'clock on the occasion of The Cutting of the First Sod of the Railways by The Right Honble W. E. Gladstone, M.P.

The favour of an early reply to 14, Cook St. Lpool is particularly requested

THE WIRRAL RAILWAYS

Thursday Oct: 16th 1884.

MENU

SOUP
Hare.

FISH
Salmon Trout en Aspic.
Fried Eels à la Tartar.

JOINT
Roast Beef.
Roast Chicken.
Westphalian Ham.
Boiled Round of Beef.
Veal & Ham Pie.

Vanilla Cream. Wine Jelly.
Cheese.

The Wirral Railways Company Limited.

SPECIAL TICKET.

Admit Mr Jno Hargreaves to the Show Yard of the Wirral Agricultural Society, North Birkenhead, at 2 o'clock on Thursday, 16th October, on the occasion of the Cutting of the First Sod of the Railways by the Right Honble. W. E. Gladstone, M.P.

DOORS OPEN AT 1 O'CLOCK; CEREMONY AT 2 O'CLOCK.

Offices: 14, Cook Street, Liverpool. Gill & Archer

Invitation card, admittance pass and menu for the ceremonial cutting of the first sod of the Wirral Railways by Mr Gladstone on 16th October 1884. In the event, only a few yards of this railway, the projected line to Hawarden, were laid. However, after the powers had been transferred jointly to the MS&L and WM&CQ companies, there was yet another 'First Sod' ceremony in 1892, this time at Hawarden Bridge but again carried out by Mr Gladstone. Courtesy Glynn Parry

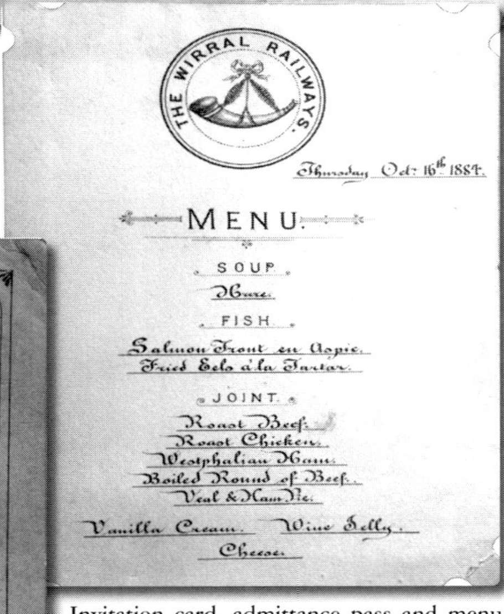

Gautby Road) on 16th October 1884 by the Rt Hon. W.E. Gladstone, MP, whose family home was at Hawarden. The Gladstones had business interests in Liverpool and a substantial investment in North Wales coal. Unfortunately, there was insufficient capital available to proceed and very little was done, the work being confined to the Bidston area.

The Limited Company

Yet a third company, the Wirral Railways Company Ltd, was formed in 1884, with a powerful board of directors overlapping those of the Seacombe, Hoylake & Deeside. They were Henry Robertson, MP, W.E. Gladstone,

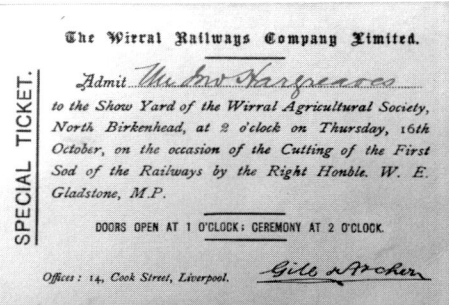

MP, R.C. de Grey Vyner, J.H. Darby of Brymbo, T.H. Jackson of the Manor House, Birkenhead, Harold Littledale, Frederic North and James Tomkinson of Willington Hall, Tarporley. The engineers were again, Brunlees, Fox & Bell. The limited company's objects were to buy the shares of the Wirral statutory company and the SH&D to form one statutory company. Agreements dated 1st July 1884 transferred the powers of the Wirral statutory company to the limited company and agreed the sale of the SH&D to the limited company. From this time on, the affairs of the three companies are inextricably interwoven and it is sensible to consider them as one.

In 1885, the SH&D company had alternative routes to Seacombe and New Brighton surveyed by their engineers. A route west of the Wallasey Pool was chosen and although the terrain was marshy and substantial embankments were needed, the cost was very much less than the 1881 route with its expensive swing bridge. A triangular junction east of Bidston ('Bidston Junction') would give access to a line leading northwards to Wallasey and New Brighton at a lower level than the 1882 line; the authorised terminus was to be in Rowson Street, much nearer the centre of things, near the Convalescent Institution for Women (which later became the Maris Stella Convent school). A second triangular junction ('Seacombe Junction') gave access to Seacombe, leaving the New Brighton line west of Poulton. The powers for the line across the Pool and the higher level New Brighton line were abandoned but an extension of time was granted for the other 1881 lines. A short connecting line was to leave the existing line almost at the throat of Docks station, crossing the 'Great Drain' to join up with the authorised Wirral line between Bidston and Birkenhead Park. All this was authorised by the SH&D Act, 1886.

On 1st August 1885, the Wirral limited company made an agreement with the Wirral statutory company for the latter to build the Birkenhead Park line and, on the same date, another agreement was made with the SH&D to build the New Brighton line; in each case the limited company was to be paid with the share capital of the other party to the value of the work completed. The latter agreement was amended on 13th June 1887 to take account of the contents of the SH&D Act 1886. As the mile long length between Park and a point near Docks was the only part of the original Wirral company's line to be built, an agreement was made in 1887 for it to be worked by the SH&D. Paid up shares were then issued in exchange for the acquired capital. The contract for the building of the Park and New Brighton lines was awarded to George Meakin and John William Dean of Birkenhead on 1st October 1885. In 1886, land for Birkenhead Park station was bought from William Laird, the shipbuilder, for £12,000, to be paid in equal shares by the Wirral and the Mersey companies. A Mersey & Wirral Joint Committee was formed to manage the station, three directors, Robertson, Egerton and Jackson being provisionally appointed.

The section of the New Brighton branch over the marshy land between Bidston Junction and the approaches to Wallasey was built as double track on an embankment. Beyond Wallasey, it ran through exposed sandhills close to the coastline and then hugged the hillside into New Brighton, some rock blasting being necessary. The question of the siting of New Brighton station occupied the attention of the directors during 1886-87. There had been a suggestion that, to save money, the line should terminate, at least for the time being, at Warren Point (sometimes referred to as 'Stonebark' which was Frederic North's residence) but it was too far out of the resort and there was no room for sidings. The authorised terminus at Rowson Street would involve either a steep gradient or building the station on an embankment and, in January 1887, it was decided to compromise and curtail the current works at Atherton Street, where temporary station buildings would be erected. There was adequate land on the north side to handle goods traffic. Plans for Birkenhead Park, Wallasey and the new Docks station were approved the following month, all to be built in brick not stone. Docks station, although on

The remains of the Hoylake Railway's Birkenhead Docks station on 26th October 1937, nearly fifty years after closure. The station had a short but chequered life. Following commencement of regular services on 2nd July 1866, the Hoylake's financial difficulties saw the station and this end of the line closed from 4th July 1870 to 1st August 1872, whilst from 6th September 1873, it was also served by the trams of the Hoylake & Birkenhead Rail & Tramway Company, until closure as a passenger station in 1888. Seen here on the platform is the old station building, which comprised the booking office at this end, with Spiers & Ponds' refreshment rooms beyond. The building had survived in use as part of the locomotive depot, latterly as an office for the chargeman fitter until more suitable accommodation was found for the unfortunate man. This view was taken near the end of the building's life as it was demolished along with the engine shed, which was in a similarly parlous state, after closure of the depot in 1938. JOHN RYAN COLLECTION

SEACOMBE HOYLAKE AND DEESIDE RAILWAY.

FEBRUARY, 1888.

DOWN TRAINS—WEEK DAYS.

Distance from Docks.	STATIONS.	1 a.m. pass.	2 a.m. pass.	3 a.m. pass.	4 a.m. pass.	5 a.m. pass.	6 a.m. pass.	7 a.m. pass.	8 a.m. pass.	9 a.m. pass.	10 a.m. pass.	11 a.m. pass.	12 a.m. pass.	13 a.m. pass.	14 a.m. pass.	15 a.m. pass.	16 a.m. pass.	17 a.m. pass.	18 a.m. pass.	19 a.m. pass.	20 p.m. pass.	21 p.m. pass.	22 p.m. pass.	23 a.m. goods.	24 p.m. pass.	25 p.m. pass.	26 p.m. pass.
m. ch.																					S	S		NS		S	S
... ...	B'head Park...dep.	7 1	7 31	7 45	8 1	8 15	8 31	8 45	9 1	9 15	9 31	9 45	10 1	1015	1045	11 1	1145	12 1	1245	1 1	1 15	1 31	1 45	...	2 1	2 15	2 31
0 73	Docks...„	7 4	7 34	...	8 4	8 18	8 34	...	9 4	9 18	9 34	...	10 4	1018	1048	11 4	1148	12 4	1248	1 4	1 18	1 34	1 48	1 53	2 4	2 18	2 34
... ...	Docks Goods...„																							1 53			
2 71	Wallasey......arr.	7 10	7 40	...	8 10	...	8 40	...	9 10	...	9 40	...	1010	...	...	1110	...	1210	...	1 10	...	1 40	...	...	2 10	...	2 40
... ...	Bidston Jnct. pass.	...	...	7 50	...	8 21	...	8 50	...	9 21	...	9 50	...	1021	1051	...	1151	...	1251	...	1 21	...	1 51	1 56	...	2 21	...
3 30	Moreton......dep.	...	...	...	...	8 25	...	...	...	9 25	...	...	...	1025	1055	...	1155	...	1255	...	...	...	1 55	2 0	...	...	...
5 11	Meols......„	...	...	...	...	8 30	...	...	...	9 30	...	...	...	1030	11 0	...	12 0	...	1 0	...	...	...	2 0	...	...	...	...
6 27	Hoylake { arr.	...	...	7 59	...	8 33	...	8 59	...	9 33	...	9 59	...	1033	11 3	...	12 3	...	1 3	...	1 29	...	2 3	2 8	...	2 29	...
	{ dep.	...	...	8 1	...	8 36	...	9 1	...	9 36	...	10 1	...	1036	11 4	...	12 4	...	1 4	...	1 31	...	2 4	2 31	...	2 31	...
7 43	West Kirby....arr.	...	...	8 4	...	8 39	...	9 4	...	9 39	...	10 4	...	1039	11 7	...	12 7	...	1 7	*	1 34	*	2 7	2 35	*	2 34	*

Distance from Docks.	STATIONS.	27 p.m. pass.	28 p.m. pass.	29 p.m. pass.	30 p.m. pass.	31 p.m. pass.	32 p.m. pass.	33 p.m. pass.	34 p.m. pass.	35 p.m. pass.	36 p.m. pass.	37 p.m. pass.	38 p.m. pass.	39 p.m. pass.	40 p.m. pass.	41 p.m. pass.	42 p.m. pass.	43 p.m. pass.	44 p.m. light eng.	45 p.m. pass.	46 p.m. pass.	47 p.m. pass.	48 p.m. pass.	49 p.m. light eng.	50 p.m. pass.	51	52
m. ch.				S	S						NS	NS			NS	NS											
... ...	B'head Park...dep.	2 45	3 1	3 15	3 31	3 45	4 1	4 31	4 45	5 1	5 15	5 31	5 45	6 1	6 15	6 31	6 45	7 1	7 25	7 45	8 1	8 45	9 45	1035	1115		
0 73	Docks...„	2 48	3 4	3 18	3 34	3 48	4 4	4 34	...	5 4	5 18	5 34	...	6 4	6 18	6 34	6 48	7 4	7 28	7 48	8 19	8 48	9 48	1038	1118		
... ...	Docks Goods...„																										
2 71	Wallasey......arr.	...	3 10	...	3 40	...	4 10	4 40	...	5 10	...	5 40	...	6 10	...	6 40	...	7 10	...	...	8 25	8 57	9 57	...	11 S 27		
... ...	Bidston Jnct. pass.	2 51	...	3 21	...	3 51	...	4 50	...	5 21	...	5 50	...	6 21	...	6 51	...	7 51	...	8 51	9 51	...	...	...	1121		
3 30	Moreton......dep.	2 55	...	...	...	3 55	...	S	...	5 25	...	S	...	6 25	...	6 55	...	7 55	...	8 55	9 55	...	...	...	...		
5 11	Meols......„	3 0	...	...	...	4 0	...	S	...	5 30	...	S	...	6 30	...	7 0	...	8 0	...	9 0	10 0	...	...	...	...		
6 27	Hoylake { arr.	3 3	...	3 29	...	4 3	...	4 59	...	5 33	...	5 59	...	6 33	...	7 3	...	8 3	...	9 3	10 3	...	...	...	1129		
	{ dep.	3 4	...	3 31	...	4 4	...	5 0	...	5 34	...	6 0	...	6 34	...	7 4	...	8 4	...	9 4	10 4	...	...	...	1130		
7 43	West Kirby....arr.	3 7	*	3 34	*	4 7	...	5 3	...	5 37	...	6 3	...	6 37	...	7 7	...	8 7	...	9 7	10 7	...	...	...	1133		

UP TRAINS—WEEK DAYS.

Distance from West Kirby.	STATIONS.	1 a.m. cars.	2 a.m. cars.	3 a.m. pass.	4 a.m. light eng.	5 a.m. pass.	6 a.m. light eng.	7 a.m. pass.	8 a.m. pass.	9 a.m. pass.	10 a.m. pass.	11 a.m. pass.	12 a.m. pass.	13 a.m. pass.	14 a.m. pass.	15 a.m. pass.	16 a.m. pass.	17 a.m. pass.	18 a.m. pass.	19 a.m. pass.	20 a.m. goods.	21 p.m. pass.	22 p.m. pass.	23 p.m. pass.	24 p.m. pass.	25 p.m. pass.	26 p.m. pass.
m. ch.																					NS	S					S
... ...	West Kirby....dep.	...	...	...	...	...	...	7 57	...	8 32	...	8 57	...	9 32	...	9 57	...	1032	...	1127	1130	...	1230	1259	...	1 27	...
1 13	Hoylake { arr.	...	...	...	...	...	...	8 0	...	8 34	...	9 0	...	9 35	...	10 0	...	1035	...	1130	1134	...	1230	1 2	...	1 30	...
	{ dep.	...	...	...	...	...	...	8 1	8 36	...	9 1	...	9 36	...	10 1	...	1036	...	1131	1235	...	1231	1 4	*	1 31	*	
2 31	Meols......„	...	...	...	...	...	...	8 4	...	...	9 4	...	...	...	10 4	...	...	...	1134	...	...	1234	...	...	1 34	...	
4 12	Moreton......„	...	...	...	...	...	...	8 9	...	...	9 9	...	...	...	10 9	...	...	...	1139	1243	...	1239	...	...	1 39	...	
... ...	Bidston Jnct. pass.	...	...	...	...	...	...	8 13	8 45	...	9 13	9 45	...	...	1013	...	1045	...	1143	1247	...	1243	1 13	...	1 43	...	
... ...	Wallasey......dep.	...	...	7 24	...	7 54	...	...	8 24	...	8 54	...	9 24	...	9 54	...	1024	...	1124	...	...	1224	...	1 24	...	1 54	
... ...	Docks Goods...arr.																				1250						
6 49	Docks......dep.	6 46	7 16	7 30	7 36	8 0	8 6	8 16	8 30	...	9 0	9 16	9 30	...	10 0	1016	1030	...	1130	1146	...	1230	1246	1 16	1 30	1 46	2 0
7 43	B'head Park....arr.	6 49	7 19	7 33	7 39	8 3	8 9	8 19	8 33	...	9 3	9 19	9 33	...	10 3	1019	1033	1049	1133	1149	...	1233	1249	1 19	1 33	1 49	2 3

Distance from West Kirby.	STATIONS.	27 p.m. pass.	28 p.m. pass.	29 p.m. pass.	30 p.m. pass.	31 p.m. pass.	32 p.m. pass.	33 p.m. pass.	34 p.m. pass.	35 p.m. pass.	36 p.m. pass.	37 p.m. pass.	38 p.m. pass.	39 p.m. pass.	40 p.m. pass.	41 p.m. pass.	42 p.m. pass.	43 p.m. pass.	44 p.m. pass.	45 p.m. pass.	46 p.m. pass.	47 p.m. pass.	48 p.m. pass.	49 p.m. pass.	50 p.m. cars.	51	52
m. ch.		S		S	S		S				NS		NS	NS		NS											
... ...	West Kirby....dep.	1 59	...	2 27	...	2 59	...	3 27	...	4 27	...	4 55	...	5 29	...	5 57	...	6 29	6 59	...	7 27	8 27	9 27	1010		
1 13	Hoylake { arr.	2 2	...	2 30	...	3 2	...	3 30	...	4 30	...	4 58	...	5 32	...	6 0	...	6 32	7 2	...	7 30	8 30	9 30	1014		
	{ dep.	2 4	...	2 31	*	3 4	*	3 31	...	4 31	...	5 1	...	5 34	...	6 1	...	6 34	7 4	...	7 31	8 31	9 31	...		
2 31	Meols......„	...	...	2 34	...	...	...	3 34	...	4 34	...	5 4	...	...	...	6 4	...	...	...	...	7 34	8 34	9 34	...		
4 12	Moreton......„	...	...	2 39	...	...	...	3 39	...	4 39	...	5 9	...	...	...	6 9	...	...	...	...	7 39	8 39	9 39	1021		
... ...	Bidston Jnct. pass.	2 13	...	2 43	...	3 13	...	3 43	...	4 43	...	5 13	...	5 43	...	6 13	...	6 43	7 13	...	7 43	8 43	9 43	1025		
... ...	Wallasey......dep.	2 13	2 24	...	2 54	...	3 24	...	3 54	4 24	...	4 54	...	5 24	...	5 54	...	6 24	...	...	7 24	...	8 39	9 38		
... ...	Docks Goods...arr.																									
6 49	Docks......dep.	2 16	2 30	2 46	3 0	3 16	3 30	3 46	4 0	4 30	4 46	5 0	5 16	5 30	5 46	6 0	6 16	6 30	6 46	7 16	7 30	7 46	8 46	9 46		
7 43	B'head Park....arr.	2 19	2 33	2 49	3 3	3 19	3 33	3 49	4 3	4 33	4 49	5 3	5 19	5 33	5 49	6 3	6 19	6 33	6 49	7 19	7 33	7 49	8 49	9 49	1030		

Trains marked *S* run on Saturdays only.

Trains marked *NS* do not run on Saturdays.

The times under which a bar, thus ——, is placed, shew where the Trains in opposite directions are appointed to cross.

* These trains cross at Hoylake on Saturdays only.

The 8·38 p.m. and 9·38 p.m. trains ex Wallasey run to Docks only, and are in connection there with the 8·27 p.m. and 9·27 p.m. trains ex West Kirby.

The trains arriving at Wallasey at 8·57 p.m. and 9·57 p.m. run from Docks only, leaving there at 8·51 p.m. and 9·51 p.m.

This Working Timetable for the Seacombe, Hoylake & Deeside Railway was dated 1st February 1888, just a month since the opening of the extension to meet the Mersey Railway at Birkenhead and of the first section of the New Brighton branch as far as Wallasey. It may be assumed that this was a revision, which eliminated all the problems experienced in the first few weeks of the extended system. Note the 'clock face' timings and the Park-Wallasey hourly off peak service occupying only nine minutes, and also the references to Birkenhead North as Docks station. COURTESY JOHN RYAN

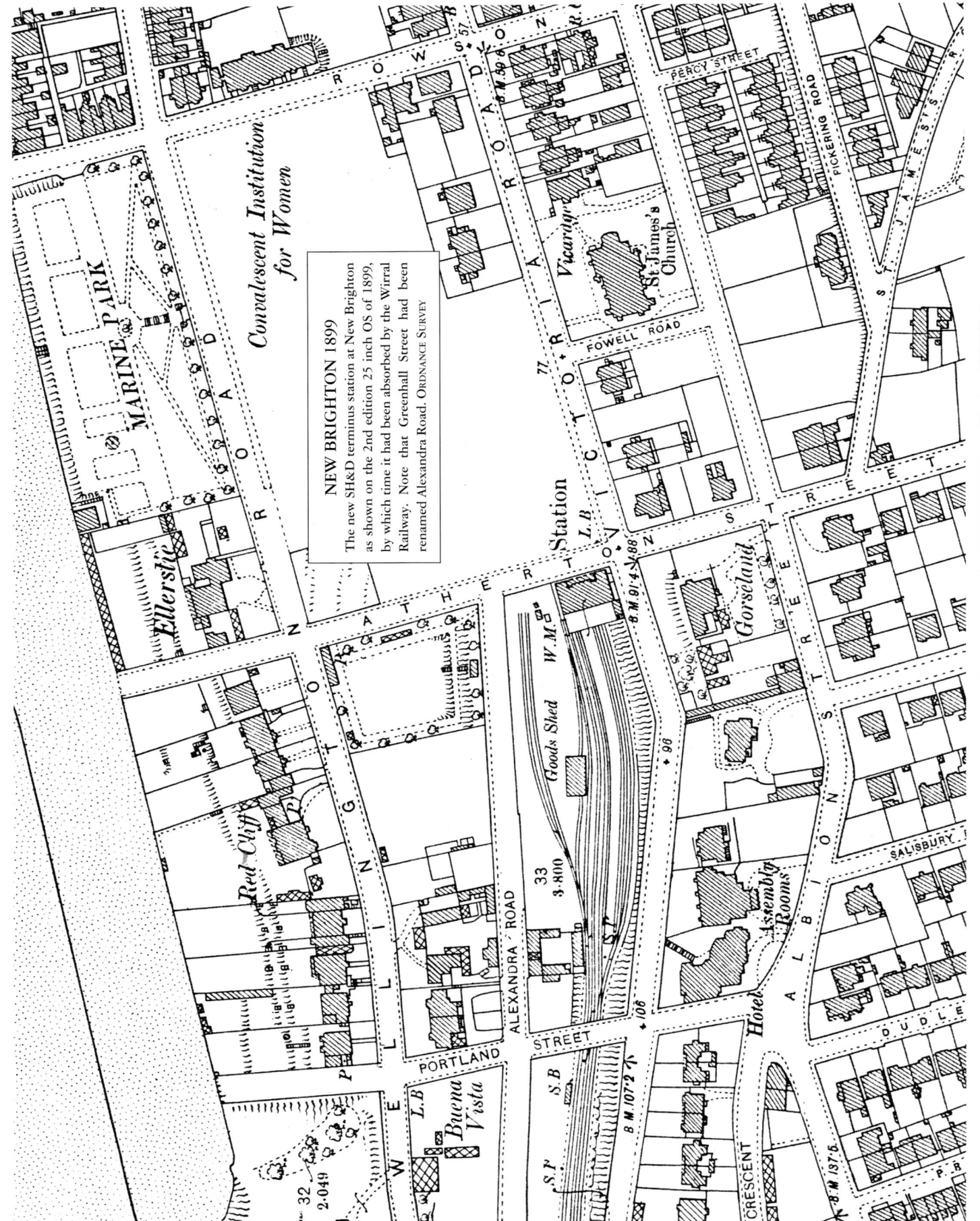

NEW BRIGHTON 1899
The new SH&D terminus station at New Brighton as shown on the 2nd edition 25 inch OS of 1899, by which time it had been absorbed by the Wirral Railway. Note that Greenhall Street had been renamed Alexandra Road. ORDNANCE SURVEY

The street frontage of the terminus at New Brighton, opened in 1888 and seen here in Wirral Railway days circa 1910. The termination of the New Brighton line at Atherton Street, instead of the original intended location at Rowson Street, put the company at a disadvantage, as it was inconveniently distant from the centres of attraction, so over the years various devices were tried to make people aware of the station's location. The Wirral Railway's 'Railway Station' sign was not visible from any distance and it was replaced by a massive illuminated sign erected in Victoria Road, New Brighton, in the hope that the crowds which massed in the lower part of the thoroughfare in the background would become aware of the existence of the railway. After the Grouping it was redesigned with the letters 'LMSR'. Note the sandstone blocks with carved Wirral horns on the gables either end of the building. JOHN ALSOP COLLECTION

the Wirral's line, was built by the SH&D.

As compensation for the loss of the Pool line, Vyner was given quite extraordinary privileges. Sec. 5(3) of the 1886 Act stated:

> 'Mr Vyner (and all persons and companies authorised by him) shall have an absolutely concurrent right with the company (and equal as regards time and convenience) to run over and use the company's railways (both now existing and hereby authorised) and the railway authorised by the 1881 Act to and in Mr Vyner's estate and also to all docks etc ... to the full extent of one half of the capacity of the railways for all commercial purposes provided that Mr Vyner shall not ... interfere with the passenger traffic of the company'.

Rate fixing was at the discretion of Vyner when part of a through running but the company was entitled to their mileage proportion. If the traffic passed only over the company's line, they were entitled to the rates usually charged. However, Vyner's dock was never built and his railway privileges never invoked. The 1886 Act also facilitated the making of working agreements with the Wirral and Mersey railways, the raising of additional capital and a slight change in the compensation to be paid to the Birkenhead Tramways Co., who were also to be compensated if the line were diverted to Birkenhead Park.

PARK AND NEW BRIGHTON BRANCHES OPENED

At their meeting on 1st November 1887, the directors fixed the opening of the new lines as not later than 12th December but, in the event, they were not ready and it was not until 2nd January 1888 that the Mersey Railway opened its branch from Hamilton Square to Birkenhead Park and the SH&D opened its branch thence to Wallasey, the last section to New Brighton still not being complete. Building of the branch, which started in 1886, had involved the construction of substantial embankments across the marshy Bidston Moss, an overbridge across Leasowe Road (the only one on the system) and the blasting of rocks on the approaches to New Brighton. There was also the problem of blown sand across the line between Wallasey and New Brighton, which cost the company £2,000 per year to remove; it found its way into the motion of the locomotives too. This section of line was exposed to westerly gales which could bury the tracks in the course of a single storm. A study was made of the Highland Railway's snow removal methods but the problem was finally alleviated, though not completely solved, by planting star grass in the sand dunes to stabilise them. During the 1914-18 War, German prisoners-of-war were used to clear the line.

Two sturdy station buildings, faced with red Accrington brick, were erected at Wallasey and New Brighton. They included accommodation for the station masters and in each gable a sandstone block was incorporated on which the Wirral horn had been carved. New Brighton station boasted a short clock tower mounted centrally on the roof and eventually housed the Wirral Railway head office, which was moved from Hamilton Square, Birkenhead. The stations at Birkenhead Docks and Hoylake were built in similar style.

With the opening of the new Birkenhead Docks station on 2nd January 1888, the old Hoylake Railway Docks station was closed. This date is worth quoting clearly because previous histories of the Wirral have not done so, whilst the relevant volume in the David &

Charles series *A Regional History of the Railways of Great Britain* (*Vol. 10, The North West*, Geoffrey Holt, 1978), gives an erroneous date of 1st April 1878. This is apparently based on misconceptions over the extension of the line into the docks area for goods traffic.

The West Kirby trains were run to and from Birkenhead Park and, initially, according to contemporary reports, through carriages were operated every half hour between Liverpool (James Street) and West Kirby, with a change of locomotive at Park, as the Wirral engines had insufficient power to tackle the 1 in 27 gradient in the tunnel and had no condensing equipment. The exact course of events has not come to light but it would appear that the level of service was soon found to be excessive and some reduction took place as early as June 1888. The line to New Brighton was opened on 30th March 1888 and there were some through trains for a time. A primitive station was built at Warren with access from Sea Road, which eventually bisected a nine-hole municipal golf course with no clubhouse. It was located ¾ mile east of Wallasey and ½ mile west of New Brighton. Maj-Gen Hutchinson reported on his inspection of Warren station on 16th August 1888. He wanted runaway points [*sic*] on the Down line a full train's length from the Down home signal, an exit from the Down platform and made other stipulations regarding the positioning of signals. The names of the signal boxes were to be painted on them. He nevertheless gave permission for it to open immediately and Douglas Fox wrote on 27th September to assure him that all his requirements had been met. Not surprisingly, it generated very little traffic and by 1911 only one train in each direction stopped there. It officially closed on 1st October 1915 but it is thought that trains had ceased to call just before the 1914-18 war. It remained in the RCH Handbook for several years.

Direct links with central Birkenhead and Liverpool, with or without through carriages, transformed the fortunes of the SH&D. Four new trains, each of six four-wheel carriages with vacuum brakes and gas light, were placed in service in 1888. There were other repercussions on public transport facilities. The Birkenhead Tramways Company was forced into bankruptcy by the loss of the railway traffic on the Docks route and competition affected the Wallasey Local Board's ferries. Because of ferry competition, fares on the New Brighton line were, for many years, cheaper than those for corresponding distances on the West Kirby line.

There was a serious dispute with the Mersey Railway about the through fares to be charged. That company being seriously in debt and being run by Receivers, was anxious to get the full local fare out of all the through rates, whereas the SH&D, knowing that new traffic had to be attracted by offering favourable rates, proposed that the Mersey should receive a lower proportion of some through fares. In view of the cost of construction of the tunnel, the Mersey believed that it should be entitled to charge additional mileage, a principle which had been conceded in the cases of the Severn Tunnel and Runcorn bridge, the latter being worth an extra six miles. Various proposed tariff schedules having been exchanged, on 21st November 1887 the Secretary was instructed to write to the Mersey in the following terms:

> '*The proposals of your Board as to fares were laid before the directors today and they gave them very careful consideration but they found that the principle of the authorised maximum of the Mersey Railway instead of the actual circumstances of each fare had throughout been adopted and my directors are unable to concede the principle. They considered that, as a through fare must be fixed by the question 'What can reasonably be obtained?' so the division must be fixed with regard to all the circumstances. My directors observe that you have adopted the through fares which they suggested but those through fares were only suggested with the expectation that, along with them, the proposed division of them would also be accepted. They have never contemplated your taking from a through fare a larger fare than your local fare but that, in making through arrangements, each company would concede something for the local fare ...*'

In March 1888 it was agreed that the matter would be settled by arbitration. On 28th August 1888, the limited company's Board reported as follows:

> '*In consequence of the division of through rates from Liverpool to New Brighton and West Kirby not having yet been settled with the*

A broadside view of 2-4-0T No. 3, delivered new from Beyer, Peacock in May 1884. No. 3 is seen here wearing Wirral Railway insignia and in lined black livery. Vacuum brakes were fitted in 1887, with No. 3 having her cylinders bored out and coal bunker enlarged at the same time. Withdrawal took place in February 1914 and the engine was sold for scrap to R. Smith & Son of Birkenhead soon after. JOHN ALSOP COLLECTION

RIGHT: Beyer, Peacock official photograph of Seacombe, Hoylake & Deeside Railway 0-4-4T No. 6, delivered new in April 1887 along with No. 5. Painting in matt works grey allowed the lining and the locomotive's details to stand out when photographed. No. 6 remained in active service until June 1921, after which it served with the Loco Department as a ballast engine for another year. JOHN ALSOP COLLECTION

BELOW: SH&D No. 5 photographed in Wirral Railway days, by which time it had been renumbered 2 following withdrawal in 1891 of the original engine to carry that number, No. 2 *Birkenhead*. The engine remained in service until November 1923 and was allocated LMS No. 6770 but was withdrawn without ever carrying it. Note the railwayman cycling off home on the left. JOHN ALSOP COLLECTION

Mersey Railway, the subsidiary question of the division between the company and the SH&D has been postponed. It has therefore been arranged that, for the purposes of the present half-yearly account, only such a sum shall be placed to the credit of this company by the SH&D as is required for the payment of Debenture Stock and the expenses of management. The Directors are glad to find that a considerable percentage of their traffic originated in Birkenhead and is independent of the Mersey Tunnel. The railways from Park to New Brighton and West Kirby give the inhabitants of Birkenhead, for the first time, a direct and cheap access to the sea and they have not been slow to avail themselves.'

The hands of the Wirral company were not entirely clean, however, as contemporary reports indicate that the train service was a regular source of controversy and complaint. In January 1888, fares had been increased by 25 per cent and trains were late because of *'changes in the system'*, presumably the exchanging of through carriages at Birkenhead Park. It was said that, because of the high fares, Moreton people were no longer travelling to Hoylake to shop.

Talks with the Mersey dragged on and an Agreement was at last signed on 30th April 1890 but the question was soon to rear its head once more.

THE SEACOMBE, HOYLAKE & DEESIDE LOCOMOTIVES

The SH&D era, which had commenced in 1881, ushered in a period of expansion and, in view of the fact that Henry Robertson, the chairman, was a founder member of Beyer, Peacock & Co., it is not surprising that all new engines were manufactured at their Gorton works. When the SH&D took over there were only four locomotives, *Comet* and No's 1-3, which were scarcely adequate for the line's needs. Indeed, No. 3, the erstwhile N&B No. 14A, was nearing the end of its working life on the rails. It was withdrawn in 1883 or 1884, but went on to serve as a stationary engine at the works at Birkenhead Docks for some years. During its time at Birkenhead, it had gained a saddle tank, a copper dome and, in line with the rest of the SH&D locomotive fleet, a copper ring round the top of the chimney.

An order was placed for two 2-4-0 tanks, No's 3 and 4, which

LEFT: No's 7 and 8 were delivered in August 1887. The latter is seen here probably circa 1920, shortly before Grouping. It was scrapped by the LM&S in October 1923. As can be seen from the official photograph of No. 6, the bunker coal rails were a later addition. JOHN ALSOP COLLECTION

BELOW: With traffic still on the increase, Beyer, Peacock were approached for a fifth 0-4-4T, to the same dimensions as the first four. No. 9 entered service in July 1888 and is seen here looking quite smart in Wirral Railway days, probably around 1910, shortly after it had been back to its manufacturers for a new boiler. The engine continued in service until the Grouping and was scrapped by the LM&S in April 1924. T.B. MAUND COLLECTION

were commissioned in May 1884 and August 1885 respectively. They had a slightly larger tractive effort at 8,850lbs, with a tank capacity of 820 gallons and they weighed 33 tons 18cwt in working order. On freight trains they were restricted to 290 tons on the West Kirby line and 220 tons on the Seacombe and New Brighton lines. They were both fitted with vacuum brakes in December 1887 and, at the same time, No. 3 had its bunker capacity increased from 1t 10cwt to 2 tons and its cylinders bored out from 15 to 16ins. No. 4 had its boiler pressure reduced from 140 to 120lbs per sq. in. in 1895. In the early years of the 20th century they were often used on the undemanding Seacombe-New Brighton passenger service and after that was withdrawn in 1910, they were only seen on ballast trains; both were sold for scrap in 1914.

In 1887, the company took delivery from Gorton of two identical pairs of 0-4-4 tank locomotives. The first pair, No's 5 and 6 (maker's No's 2826 & 2827), arrived in April, followed by No's 7 and 8 (No's 2863 & 2864) in August. They were bought on hire purchase, each pair costing £1,719 (£1,928 10s 0d with interest), the quarterly payments being spread over three years. The terms of the agreement enabled the company to pay off the balance at any time but also entitled the makers to repossess the engines if the company fell behind in their payments by as little as twenty days. They were purchased in expectation of greatly increased traffic when the New Brighton line opened and this was justified as a fifth engine to the same specification, No. 9 (maker's No. 2975), was placed in service in July 1888. The wheel arrangement was considered especially suitable for the tight curves and they were the most powerful engines to have been used on the railway, with a tractive effort of 11,790lbs and a tank capacity of 1,000 gallons. Several of these locomotives were reboilered, some by Beyer Peacock and others by Vulcan Foundry.

The SH&D chose a different livery scheme to the Hoylake Railway. The locomotives were painted black, with white, yellow and vermilion lining on the tank and bunker sides. The frames and the cab were adorned with a plain red line, whilst buffer beams were vermilion edged with black and with black buffer casings. Topping off this stylish scheme, the coupling rods were also painted, red on some engines, vermilion on others, and all edged in black with vermilion lining. Oval, polished brass number plates were fixed to the tank sides, bearing the letters 'S.H.& D. RY. Co.' at the top, the number in the centre and the year of manufacture at the bottom. The number was also painted on the buffer beams in gold shaded with black and the maker's plates were bolted to the bunker sides.

SIGNALLING

In the very early days, the line was worked on the 'one engine in steam' principle. Until well into the 1880s, trains were controlled by the 'time interval' method and, as the line was single apart from the passing loops at Moreton and Hoylake, there were no serious problems. Even though the number of train movements was approaching twenty daily in each direction, until 1887 the 'train staff and ticket' principle was used without block telegraph. Under this system, the driver would be handed a 'Train Ticket' at the beginning of a section specifying the train number and the point to which the train was authorised to proceed. On arrival at the end of the section, the ticket had to be surrendered to the stationmaster or other authorised person. The staff was handed to the guard on departure and similarly handed in at the end of the section. Tickets were kept in special boxes secured by an inside spring, the key to open the box being the staff for the same section, so no ticket could be issued unless the staff was present. Tickets and staffs were colour-coded, the colours in use being West Kirby-Hoylake – green; Hoylake-Moreton – red and Moreton-Birkenhead Docks – white. Should it be necessary to permit two trains travelling in the same direction to occupy a section, this would be entered on the ticket and the staff would be carried by the guard of the second train. The Birkenhead Park-Docks and Docks-New Brighton sections, being double from the outset, were worked on 'absolute block', though the West Kirby line continued to work on 'time interval' until 1889 when block working was introduced. Trellis type signals, made by Stevens & Co. of Southwark in the 1860s, survived at Hoylake station for many years. A lamp was hoisted up on chains and the wheel was still visible in 1951.

There was a serious accident on 7th February 1888, when a passenger train leaving Hoylake collided head on with a train travelling in the opposite direction. The fireman, William Stitch of Beckwith Street, Birkenhead, subsequently died of severe burns and several passengers were injured. In a letter to the Board of Trade dated 1st April 1878, the company's secretary had agreed that the railway would be run on the block system with train staff but this had not been done. If it had, the accident could not have happened. The train from Hoylake to Birkenhead at 7.04pm was in the station awaiting the arrival of the 6.45pm Birkenhead to West Kirby service. The latter was carrying a train ticket, the staff being carried on a special train which was following. The stationmaster was in the habit of making out a ticket before receiving the train staff and the Birkenhead-bound train left before the special carrying it arrived. The two trains collided about 900 yards north of the station and 80 yards inside the Down distant signal. Both were travelling at 12-20 mph on a curve of 80 chains radius with good visibility over the flat countryside. The engine of the special, No. 3, and the first coach were derailed, as were the first and second coaches of the Birkenhead-bound train, 60 yards of track being torn up. In later criminal proceedings, Stationmaster Wilmot of Hoylake was found guilty of culpable homicide and sentenced to six months' imprisonment. The stationmaster of Birkenhead Docks was bound over. This accident demonstrated how serious the consequences could be if the carefully laid down procedures were not carried out to the letter.

Proposed Purchase of Seacombe, Hoylake & Deeside and Wirral Railways

The SH&D's ambition to revive the long lapsed powers of the Hoylake Railway, to extend along the banks of the Dee from West Kirby to Parkgate, had been thwarted by the L&NW & GW

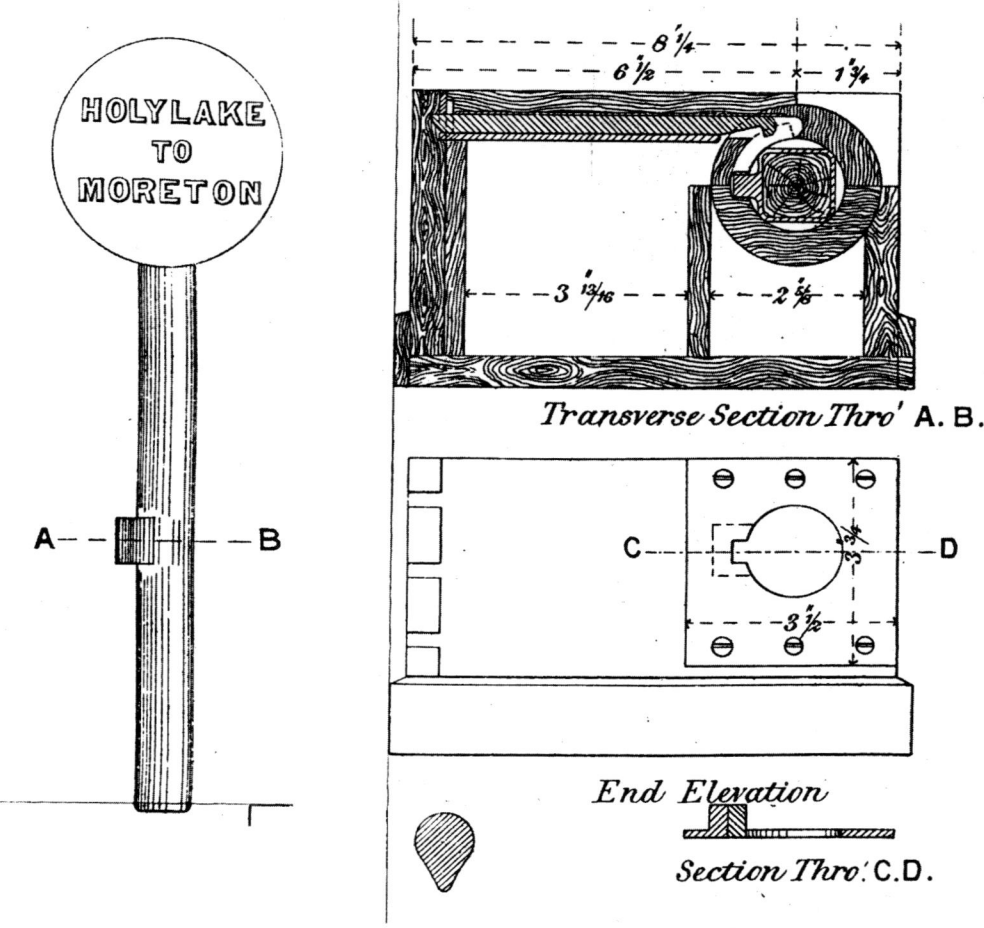

Diagrams of the staff and box for the Hoylake-Moreton section of single line. It is suspected that the misspelling of Hoylake occurred in the reproduction. T.B. Maund collection

Joint Railways, who had obtained similar powers and opened their line to West Kirby on 19th April 1886. The two stations were virtually side-by-side and there was a connection with the SH&D, which now had an outlet to the outside world that did not involve passage over the Dock Board lines. By the mid-1880s, the L&NW & GW Joint Railways' line between Chester and Birkenhead was reaching saturation point as freight traffic to the docks and the expanding town of Birkenhead increased but the single line between Hooton and West Kirby, on which the bridges and other infrastructure had been built to double track standards, was underused. The Joint companies planned to lay a new double track line from north of Ledsham to the West Kirby branch ('the Hooton Curve', which was authorised in 1889) and to double the branch through to West Kirby. Traffic could then be fed into the dock system from the west but they felt it was desirable to control the line between West Kirby and Docks rather than rely on the good offices of the SH&D to handle the traffic expeditiously. In 1888, heads of two Agreements were drawn up, the first covering the purchase of the Wirral and SH&D, which were to be worked as part of the Birkenhead Railway, the actual owning company of the joint lines which, since 1860, had been leased in perpetuity to the L&NW & GW. The parties to the other, signed on 14th June 1888, were the SH&D, Wirral and the WM&CQ. Mutual running powers were agreed with the latter on the Wirral's authorised, but not yet constructed, line up the centre of the peninsula from Bidston to Hawarden Bridge, where the MS&L line from Chester, which was under construction, was to be met. In yet a third Bill, the Mersey was to be given running powers over the Wirral and SH&D.

Anticipating the hostility of the MS&L, owners of the Dee crossing then being built, a clause was inserted to the effect that if they would not agree to the Wirral and SH&D running over the bridge, the latter companies could require the WM&CQ, who already held powers to run over the MS&L, to haul their trains to and from points on the Wrexham line. These draft Agreements were included as Schedules to the L&NW & GW Railways Bill, 1889 and the Wrexham, Mold & Connah's Quay and Wirral Railways Bill, 1889. A third schedule to the L&NW & GW Bill protected all the special rights to use the railway of Robert Vyner, who still apparently proposed to build a private dock, the companies having approached him to agree terms so that he did not oppose the acquisition.

The prospect of the mid-Wirral line falling into the hands of the L&NW & GW had been greeted with alarm, especially in the Wrexham area where manufacturers and traders desperately wanted to break the GW monopoly. An official petition was sent to Parliament by Wrexham council to the effect that '... *the Wirral Railway should not be permitted to sell any portions of their railway to the LNWR or GWR who have hitherto held the monopoly of the traffic.*'

The Bill was heavily opposed, particularly by the MS&L, and was thrown out on 20th August 1889. The Wirral, which was still unable to fund the mid-Wirral line, had meanwhile been approached by the MS&L and agreed to transfer its powers jointly to the WM&CQ and MS&L for a consideration. The transaction was authorised by the Wirral Railways (Transfer) Act, which received the Royal Assent on 12th August 1889. A sum of £210,850 was claimed, made up of Land £75,000, Additional Land £14,850, Purchase of Original Concession and Interest £21,000, Parliamentary, Engineering and Other Expenses £37,000 and Injury to the Constructed Railway (by depriving it of marshalling sidings, diversion of passenger and goods traffic and loss of profit and goodwill by taking the cheap part of the railway) £63,000. The matter went to arbitration, the award being £105,069. The date of transfer was 1st February 1892, interest of 6 per cent being payable if the amount was not paid by 28th February. This included the short length already constructed at Bidston.

Welsh Railways Union Act

On the same day the Transfer Act was passed, the Royal Assent was given to the Welsh Railways Union Act. This brought to a head a concept which had been developing since the 1860s and although it was promoted by a group of independent railway lines, it was strongly supported by the MS&L. The objective was to establish a route between South Wales and north-west England completely independent of the L&NW and GW lines. It was said that the capital of the Welsh railways was £15m, upon £9m of which no dividend had ever been paid and the implementation of the proposals was calculated to improve their financial prospects substantially. The Act authorised the making of Agreements between the eighteen companies and the appointment of a Joint Committee, the members of which would be drawn from the undermentioned companies. The MS&L agreed to work the through traffic.

Taff Vale Railway
Barry Docks & Railways Co.
Alexandra (Newport & South Wales) Docks & Railway Co.
Pontypridd, Caerphilly & Newport Railway
Swansea & Mumbles Railway
Neath & Brecon Railway (Neath to Brecon)
Brecon & Merthyr Tydvil Railway (Brecon to Talyllyn Jct)
Cambrian Railway (Talyllyn Jct to Ellesmere)
Wrexham & Ellesmere Railway (Ellesmere to Wrexham)
Wrexham, Mold & Connah's Quay Railway and Manchester, Sheffield & Lincolnshire Railway jointly (Wrexham to Hawarden Bridge)
Wirral Railway (Hawarden Bridge to Bidston)
Seacombe, Hoylake & Deeside Railway
Cheshire Lines Committee
Mersey Railway
Liverpool, Southport & Preston Railway
Southport & Cheshire Lines Extension Railway
West Lancashire Railway
Blackpool Railway Co. (?)

Although listed above, the Wirral (and of course the L&NW & GW Joint) opposed the Bill and the Act came to nothing as, one by one, the key participants fell into the L&NW or GW camps over the years. Thus the MS&L now accelerated its plans to create a link with Birkenhead, before any other legal measures might be devised to thwart its ambitions.

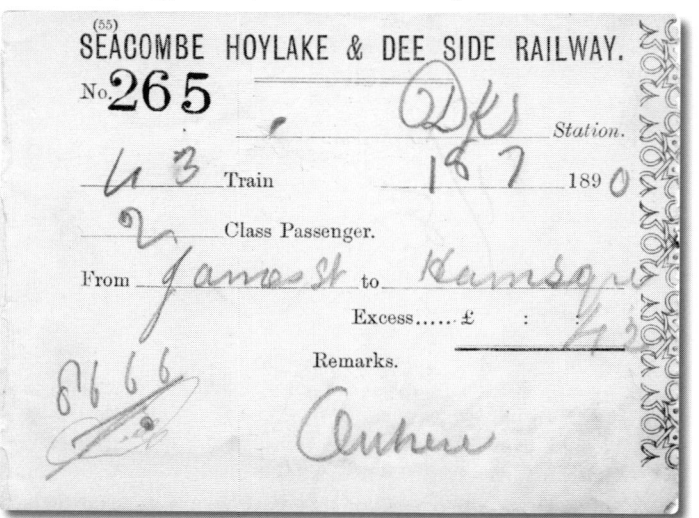

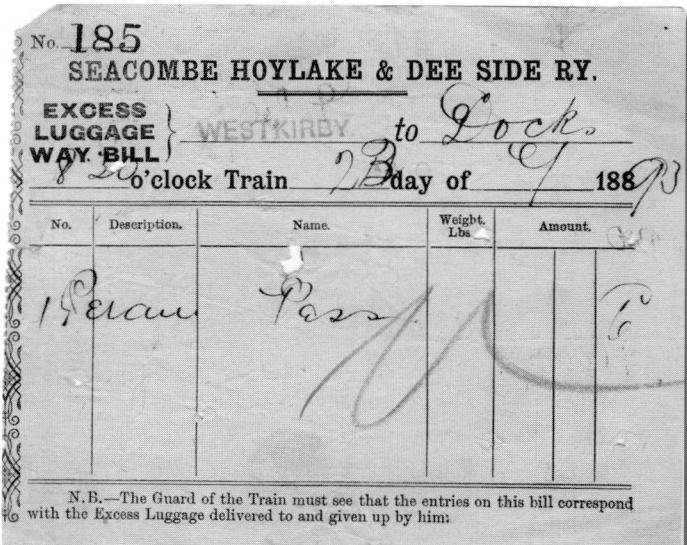

BELOW: An Excess Luggage waybill dated 23rd July 1893 acknowledges receipt of 6d (2½p). The Wirral Railway, founded in 1891, was still using up SH&D stationery. COURTESY MARTIN JENKINS

LEFT: A somewhat enigmatic SH&D Excess Fare voucher, issued at Birkenhead Docks station on 18th July 1890 in respect of a journey on the Mersey Railway between James Street and Hamilton Square. COURTESY MARTIN JENKINS

CHAPTER 2

THE WIRRAL RAILWAY

In 1891, the Wirral Railway Amalgamation Act brought together the SH&D and the remains of the Wirral Railway under the latter name, as had been planned seven years earlier. The original statutory Wirral company and the SH&D were liquidated, except for the payment of interest on mortgage and debenture stock up to 30th June 1891 but the Wirral Railways Co. Ltd remained in existence as a holding company. The new board of directors was T.H. Jackson (chairman), Sir Robert Egerton, Sir Henry Beyer Robertson, F. North, M.E. Burke Wood, John Davies and James Tomkinson. The company's office was at 2 Hamilton Square, Birkenhead and the Secretary was W.D. Haswell. An urgent task was the rationalisation of the limited company's capital structure. The share and loan capital authorised by the Wirral Railway Certificate 1883 and the Acts of 1884, 1885 and 1888 totalled £966,000 and of this £125,870 was paid up, £24,130 held for contingencies and £55,000 in debentures, a total of £205,000. Of this. 16,552 £5 shares not subject to any further call were converted into 8,276 £10 shares on a two-for-one basis. The balance of unissued authorised capital – £761,000 – was cancelled and extinguished by the Wirral Railway Act 1893. Soon after the amalgamation, the old SH&D engine shed on the south-west side of the line west of Birkenhead Docks station was replaced by a larger building on the north-east side of the line, the old shed becoming a carriage shed.

THE SEACOMBE BRANCH

The directors turned their attention to the Seacombe Branch and, in February 1892, cost estimates were prepared for its construction, for which a specification had been drawn up by Sir Douglas Fox & Partners (*below*). The Fox family had great influence on the railways of Merseyside and were engineers to many lines. Sir Charles Fox had worked for Ericson and drove his pioneer locomotive *Novelty* at the Rainhill Trials; he subsequently worked for Robert Stephenson. Douglas and Francis Fox followed their father into engineering consultancy and eventually the firm was renamed Sir Douglas Fox & Partners. Most railways of modest size had a Resident Engineer on their payroll but retained a Consulting Engineer to advise on major works; the Foxes acted for the Wirral in this capacity. Francis Fox was also knighted.

In 1880, 26 year-old George Andrew Hobson joined the firm as Chief Assistant to Sir Douglas. He became a partner in 1900 and retired in 1912. For thirty-two years, Hobson undertook all the bridge and structure design, and the station layouts which passed through the firm's hands, and was therefore responsible for the buildings and general appearance of the Wirral Railway. In the Liverpool area alone, he designed the structures for the Mersey Railway including the tunnel, much of the Liverpool Overhead, the Southport & Cheshire Lines Extension, the West Lancashire, the Hawarden swing bridge, the Snowdon Mountain Railway and the Wigan extension of the MS&L. 'Hobson's Flooring' was developed to deck the Overhead Railway and became a standard method for bridge decks.

G.A. Hobson M.Inst.C.E., 1854-1917. JOHN HORNE COLLECTION

	£
Single line 2 miles 24 chains (2.3 miles)	30,703 9 6d
Single line with excavations and bridges for double road	36,087 9 6d
Double line	40,530 5 6d
Improvements to stations	2,150 0 0d
Building bridge over River Birket and forming embankment	1,773 13 0d
In December 1892 an estimate was made of the revenue and working costs as follows:	
	£
Additional traffic accruing to Wirral Co. on Liverpool traffic based upon existing traffic via Mersey Tunnel	1,757
Season tickets	550
Additional excursion traffic that will be secured from Liverpool	1,000
Estimated traffic to and from Seacombe and Poulton including goods, Coal and passengers*	2,000
Gross Earnings	5,307
Less working expenses	1,612
Net	3,695
* including £1,000 dependent on opening of Dee Extension.	

An engraving from *The Graphic* depicting the Rt Hon. William Gladstone MP cutting the first sod of the original Wirral Railway near Hawarden Bridge in October 1892. Both spade and wheelbarrow were made of polished wood mounted with silver. Strictly speaking it was no longer the Wirral Railway, having been sold to the MS&L and WM&CQ on 1st February 1892. The Right Honourable gentleman had previously cut a first sod near Bidston, close to present day Gautby Road, on 16th October 1884.

However, these projects may not have loomed large in the memory of one who also designed the Zambesi Bridge at Victoria Falls, most of the railway structures in Rhodesia and the Cape, and the Rugby-Marylebone portion of the Great Central's London extension. George Hobson died aged 62 in January 1917.

Construction was entrusted to a Birkenhead contractor, Thomas Wilberforce Davies, on 11th August 1893, in the amount of £47,700, completion to be by 11th February 1895. It was to be a double line throughout and involved the excavation of a deep rock cutting in which the only intermediate passenger station, Liscard & Poulton, would be built. The branch was to leave the New Brighton line where it turned northwards on an embankment; this would be named Seacombe Junction and a triangular layout was specified so that trains could be run between Seacombe and New Brighton, as well as to West Kirby and Birkenhead Park. This resulted in an unusual if not unique layout, placing two triangular junctions with tight curves within less than half a mile of each other. Between Seacombe Junction and Breck Road the line ran close to the northern shore of the Wallasey Pool, where the ground was marshy and land consolidation was required. At one point it cut across a meander of the waterway, which was diverted. The rock cutting continued towards Gorsey Lane, beyond which the line occupied a low shelf before entering a final cutting, this opening up to accommodate Seacombe station with three platform roads and two storage sidings on the north side. There were no fewer than nine road overbridges – at Breck Road, Mill Lane, Sherlock Lane, Gorsey Lane, Oakdale Road, Wheatland Lane, Parry Street, Luke Street and Church Road. The contract included connection to the New Brighton and West Kirby lines. The way was to be 28 feet wide and embankments 30 feet clear. Rails were to be in 30 foot lengths and weigh between 74½ and 76 lbs per linear yard.

Work on the branch started at Gorsey Lane and proceeded in both directions. The first rails were soon laid and permission was sought from Wallasey Local Board (Urban District Council [UDC] from 1st January 1895) to lay temporary lines along the western side of Gorsey Lane and across Mill Lane on the level. The contractor sought permission to close Sherlock Lane while a bridge was being built and a sewer re-routed. Some delay must have been caused by the Council deferring decisions on this and other matters, and demanding that a formal Agreement be drawn up with the contractor regarding the bridges at Gorsey Lane, Sherlock Lane and Breck Road. In November, Davies requested authority to make a connection between the temporary lines and the Wallasey Gas Works siding, the other end of which was connected to the Dock Board railway. He offered to pay 3s 6d per wagon if the Gas Committee would collect consignments from the various railway stations and return the empties but this was rejected, the Committee charging 1s for way leave, the contractor to bear all other costs. This connection was valuable, as it enabled materials to be delivered by rail direct to the place where they were required.

Thereafter, construction appears to have gone quite smoothly until 4th December 1893, when the contractor's locomotive, an outside-

The Wirral Horn was the emblem of the Wirral Railway; it appeared on the rolling stock and was set in stone at the principal stations. The Wirral emblem was based on that of the Seacombe, Hoylake & Deeside Railway. Also shown are the emblems of the Wrexham, Mold & Connah's Quay Railway whose trains ran over Wirral metals to Seacombe. Although not strictly relevant to this work, the emblem of the Buckley Railway, which was leased to the WM&CQ for 999 years and was worked as part of it, is also included. JOHN HORNE COLLECTION (WR/SH&DR); JOHN RYAN COLLECTION (WM&CQR/BR)

cylindered Peckett 0-4-0 saddle tank named *Bristol*, was destroyed when its boiler exploded, resulting in the deaths of the fireman, E.A. Brown, and the driver, Oliver Edwards. An official enquiry found that the cause was shortage of water and the driver had previously been warned twice for the same thing. The locomotive, new in 1885 (Works No. 439), had been purchased by Davies from the Birkenhead contractors Meakin & Dean for £350 in August 1893; it had previously been retubed by the GWR at Chester in 1890. Davies is known to have owned at least one other locomotive named *Wirral*, which he tried unsuccessfully to sell to the Wallasey Gas Committee for £350 at the end of the contract, and there may have been others as he found it necessary to employ a locomotive foreman.

The original plan, as authorised by the SH&D Act 1881, was to continue the railway right down to the river's edge, north of the ferry terminal with a short covered passenger connection, but the land needed was owned by the trustees of Richard Smith, a former owner of the ferry, and was not yet in the possession of the railway company. It was decided to build a temporary station at the junction of Church Road and Victoria Road (later renamed Borough Road), which would enable the branch to open earlier and this was agreed with the Wallasey Local Board, though they were most anxious that the railway should extend down to the river as soon as possible. The station was always referred to as '*the temporary station*', a description which it richly deserved despite its eventual permanence. It comprised one platform on the south side and an island platform, constructed of wood and cinders; waiting facilities were minimal and there were no platform canopies whatsoever.

However, in late 1894, the directors announced a different plan, to extend the branch into new cattle lairages planned to be built between Seacombe ferry and Alfred Dock. This was a major scheme, as Birkenhead was then an important cattle importation centre and the existing facilities were inadequate. The main lairages were just to the north of Woodside ferry but a building known as 'the Black Shed' and the adjoining No. 3 shed on the north side of Alfred Dock had been used for cattle purposes from time to time. The proposal was for something much more extensive, with accommodation for 12,000 cattle, slaughterhouses and chillrooms. However, there was opposition, mainly on the grounds of the positioning of a new 1,000 foot long cattle landing stage, which it was felt would constitute a danger to shipping due to its proximity to Seacombe ferry landing stage and the Alfred Dock entrances. The Great Western Railway inevitably objected to the Wirral's plans to site a goods station at Alfred Dock.

The Wirral designed a scheme to extend the line from the temporary station, to connect with the Dock Board's railway in Birkenhead Road and to build a passenger station on the south side of Seacombe ferry terminal with a connecting pedestrian way. This was a very expensive scheme, which would have required the major diversion of public roads in Seacombe. No detailed costings have been found but the Wirral Railway Act 1895, which authorised these works, permitted the company to raise £60,000 additional capital. As a station to the south of the ferry terminal was just as convenient as one to the north and the railway would pay for the new street layout, the Wallasey UDC approved the scheme. The Act cancelled the power to build the line to the river bank on the north side of the ferry so the company had burnt its boats in that respect. The Mersey Docks & Harbour Board went before Parliament in March 1895 to raise money and get powers to carry out the work on the

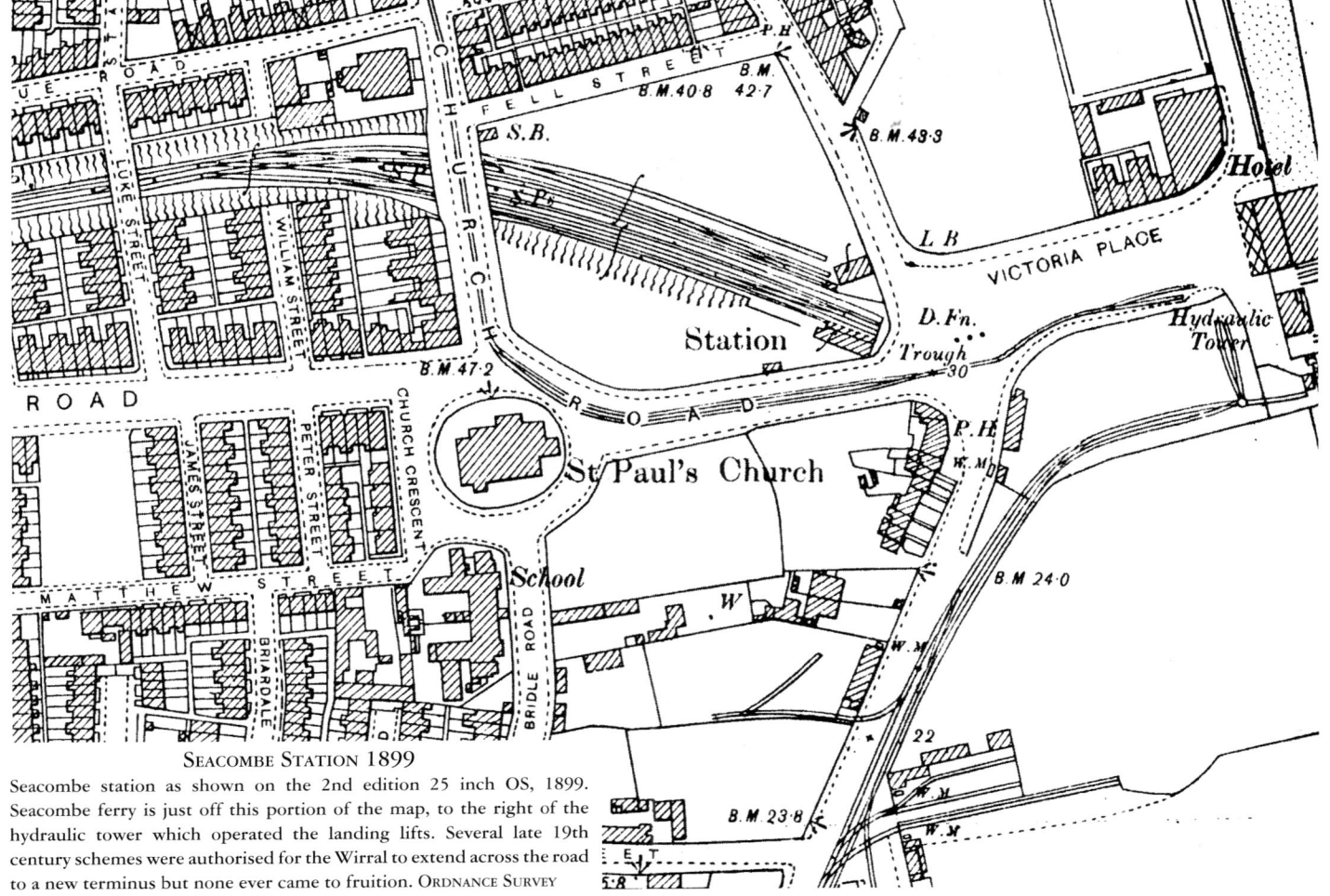

SEACOMBE STATION 1899
Seacombe station as shown on the 2nd edition 25 inch OS, 1899. Seacombe ferry is just off this portion of the map, to the right of the hydraulic tower which operated the landing lifts. Several late 19th century schemes were authorised for the Wirral to extend across the road to a new terminus but none ever came to fruition. ORDNANCE SURVEY

LEFT: Leasowe station and level crossing looking east towards Birkenhead around 1910. The house was provided for the stationmaster and the lever frame for the signals was inside the corrugated iron extension jutting on to the platform. JOHN ALSOP COLLECTION

BELOW: A fine early view of the Wirral Railway terminus at West Kirby, dating from circa 1905. The turreted clock tower can be seen in the centre but the mock Tudor buildings beyond are not part of the station. It was, however, faced in a similar style to complement these. WR 0-4-4T No. 7 simmers gently at the buffer stops on this bright sunny day and note also the station name in the glass of the gas lamp on the left of the picture. JOHN ALSOP COLLECTION

lairages but, mainly due to the Wallasey UDC objection regarding the danger to navigation, it decided to withdraw the Bill and the whole scheme was abandoned in favour of extensions to the existing lairages. The Wirral Railway, therefore, had no alternative but to cancel its plans for Seacombe.

There is every indication that the company's financial situation at this time was precarious and various loans were obtained from the Paris Banking Co. between 1887 and 1892. There is evidence of directors borrowing money on their own sureties so that they could lend it to the limited company to help finance the building of the Seacombe branch.

IMPROVEMENTS TO THE WEST KIRBY LINE

The gradual increase of traffic made it essential to double the West Kirby line. At first, it was proposed to double the line between Bidston Junction and Bidston station, where there was already a passing loop, and from the loop at Moreton station to the loop at Hoylake station. However this was amended to cover the whole line between the bifurcation of the New Brighton line and Hoylake, the contract being awarded to T.W. Davies, who was already busy on the Seacombe branch, for £10,634. Blown sand, which had already become a problem on the New Brighton line, was to be removed and used in the formation of the double line.

During the doubling of the Bidston-Moreton section, a new station, named Leasowe, was built at Reeds Lane. It was a simple affair comprising two brick-faced platforms and a pair of corrugated iron sheds but a brick-built cottage was added on the south side later. It opened on 5th May 1894. The completion date for the whole project was 23rd May 1895 which was met by the contractor, construction, however, continuing on doubling of the Hoylake-West Kirby section for which no contract has been found, though the estimate for the work was £2,217; this was completed during 1896.

At a board meeting on 28th October 1895, the manager was authorised *'to arrange with Mr Thorne [a Joint official] to at once run through trains between Seacombe and Hooton via West Kirby and to ask Mr Thorne to submit a proposition for a joint station at West Kirby'*. It is not clear whether this referred to passenger or goods trains but probably the latter. A joint station at West Kirby was seen as a desirable goal but agreement could not be reached on terms, the Joint accusing the Wirral of intransigence. Finally, though, it was agreed to handle goods jointly and the Wirral decided to build a new passenger station slightly to the north of the original, the site of which was then used for sidings. The new station was a red brick building, in the same style as the other principal stations, situated right in the town centre, with the added refinement of a short, turreted clock tower in diapered brick with lancet windows. A frontal mock Tudor gable echoed other buildings on the opposite side of the road. A seven-bay roof with furrowed awnings covered the head of the platforms and the concourse which gave shelter to waiting cars. However, the platforms remained unprotected from the weather, this refinement having to wait until 1938.

SEACOMBE BRANCH OPENED

The Seacombe Branch was opened to traffic on 1st June 1895, bringing the mileage for the Wirral Railway up to its final total of 13.75, all double track. On the same day, facilitated by track doubling on the West Kirby line, a new timetable for the whole system was introduced giving nineteen return trips between Park and West Kirby, twenty-seven between Park and New Brighton, and nineteen between Seacombe and West Kirby. On Sundays, there were six, nine and nine trains respectively. The new branch was well

This aerial view of Seacombe ferry terminal also shows the station centre left and, although it dates from circa 1930, it ties in neatly with the OS extract on page 35. The 'temporary' railway station had by now become permanent, whilst the land behind the hotel, purchased by the railway company for an extension which, if it had been built, would have reduced the distance passengers would have needed to walk to the ferry, remained undeveloped. To the left of the terminal is the ferry goods yard; an alternative scheme, authorised in 1895 but subsequently repealed, would have provided for the Wirral Railway to be linked with the docks lines and for the passenger station to have been sited here. COURTESY T.G. TURNER

used from the outset, a half-hourly service being given to West Kirby in the first weekend during which over 2,000 passengers were carried. It is thought that Liscard & Poulton station was not opened until September, as it first appeared in *Bradshaw* in October 1895. There was a short coal siding on the north-west side and an even shorter stub on the south-east side leading towards a stone quarry the product of which may have been used in the consolidation of the nearby embankments.

As doubling of the Hoylake-West Kirby section was not completed until 1896, it seems likely that there was some difficulty in maintaining this service at first. Goods traffic on the Bidston-North Wales line commenced on 16th March 1896, followed by passenger traffic on 18th May. The original Bidston station, a rudimentary affair with cinder platforms, which had been closed in June 1890 because of lack of traffic, was reopened with new buildings. Because of the very marshy land, it was stipulated that the buildings must be wooden as the foundations would not support a heavy brick or stone structure; it was well into 1896 before these were erected.

From 6th July 1895, the name 'Wirral Railways Committee', used in the Wirral Railways Transfer Act 1889 under which the line had been built, was dropped in favour of the Dee & Birkenhead Committee, a title authorised by the MS&L Railway Act 1895. The name was changed again to the North Wales & Liverpool Railway Committee on 7th August 1896. Then, on 1st August 1897, the Manchester, Sheffield & Lincolnshire Railway, which was behind the whole affair, retitled itself the Great Central. One of their first acts under the new title was to obtain judgement against the WM&CQR for payment of the latter's share of the Wirral Railway purchase money, resulting in a Receiver and Manager being appointed the following month. This enabled the GC to step in and absorb both the WM&CQ and the associated Buckley Railway, which was formalised by the Great Central Railway Act 1904. The term 'North Wales & Liverpool Committee' had to continue in use until the GCR finally absorbed the WM&CQ in January 1905. The GCR took over the working of Wrexham-Bidston trains in February 1901.

As originally envisaged, the Wirral statutory company's line would have run parallel to the SH&D line at Bidston and a linking curve about 420 yards long west of Bidston station had been authorised by the Wirral Railway Act 1890. The North Wales & Liverpool opened for goods traffic on 16th March 1896 and there was a special working from Hawarden to Liverpool Central Low Level on 28th March 1896, with an engine change at Birkenhead Park. The Wirral was prepared to allow GC passenger trains to run to Birkenhead Park and a few did so with through carriages to Liverpool on isolated occasions but the Mersey would not agree to a permanent arrangement. There was even talk of the GC becoming a member of the Birkenhead Park Station Joint Committee. The line having been consolidated, a passenger service over the NW&L began on 18th May 1896, using Bidston station as its terminus, although how trains reversed is unknown. Perhaps the triangle was used.

The Wirral then agreed to the extension of the Wrexham-Bidston passenger service to Seacombe and this was done from 1st May 1898, with restrictions on the carriage of local traffic between Bidston and Seacombe. This prohibited the carriage of local passengers except for the holders of specially endorsed contracts, which were issued at a slight premium. Initially, the situation was complicated by the MS&L not yet having powers to absorb the WM&CQ, nor having running powers over the branch, so that they were unable to work their share of the traffic. Instead they hired engines to the WM&CQ which had running powers. The MS&LR engines were relettered and renumbered for the duration, as detailed later in this chapter. This lasted only a few months, as the GCR, as the MS&L had become, obtained the necessary powers later in 1898.

In November 1897, the Wirral company announced its intention to apply for powers to build an embankment across the Dee and extend its line to Rhyl. There were to be intermediate stations at Trewelod, Gwespyr, Gronant, Llanasa, Prestatyn, Nant, Meliden, Dyserth, Rhydorddwy and Brynhedydd. Just what was behind this announcement is unclear, as the likelihood of the company being able to finance such a project was remote. On the Welsh side of the river the line would have been built some way inland from the existing Chester & Holyhead section of the L&NW. However, nothing further was heard of this grandiose plan.

Wallasey UDC persisted in its demand that the railway should be extended down to the river on the original alignment. The Wirral pointed out that it now had to approach Parliament for a new authority and that would take time. However, it went ahead and bought the land required from the Smith Trustees, conveyance of the 16,056 square yards plot being effected on 14th April 1896 for £8,547 6s 8d – rather less than the £9,300 estimate. The company had proposed to purchase the Seacombe Ferry Hotel's bowling green for £3,500 (presumably required for terminal buildings) and had

The end of the Mersey Docks & Harbour Board line in Birkenhead Road, Seacombe, probably in the mid 1920s. The line leads into the ferry goods yard, which was alongside the ferry workshop buildings seen in the background. The workshop was closed in the late 1920s and the land used for the building of a new ferry terminal, which opened in 1933. Seacombe ferry clock tower, a local landmark between 1880 and 1932, housed the hydraulic equipment which powered the goods lift. The floating roadway installed in 1926 replaced the lift and the high level bridge, which were demolished to make way for the new terminal. The Wirral's Seacombe station lay about 100 yards off to the left of this view. MARTIN JENKINS COLLECTION

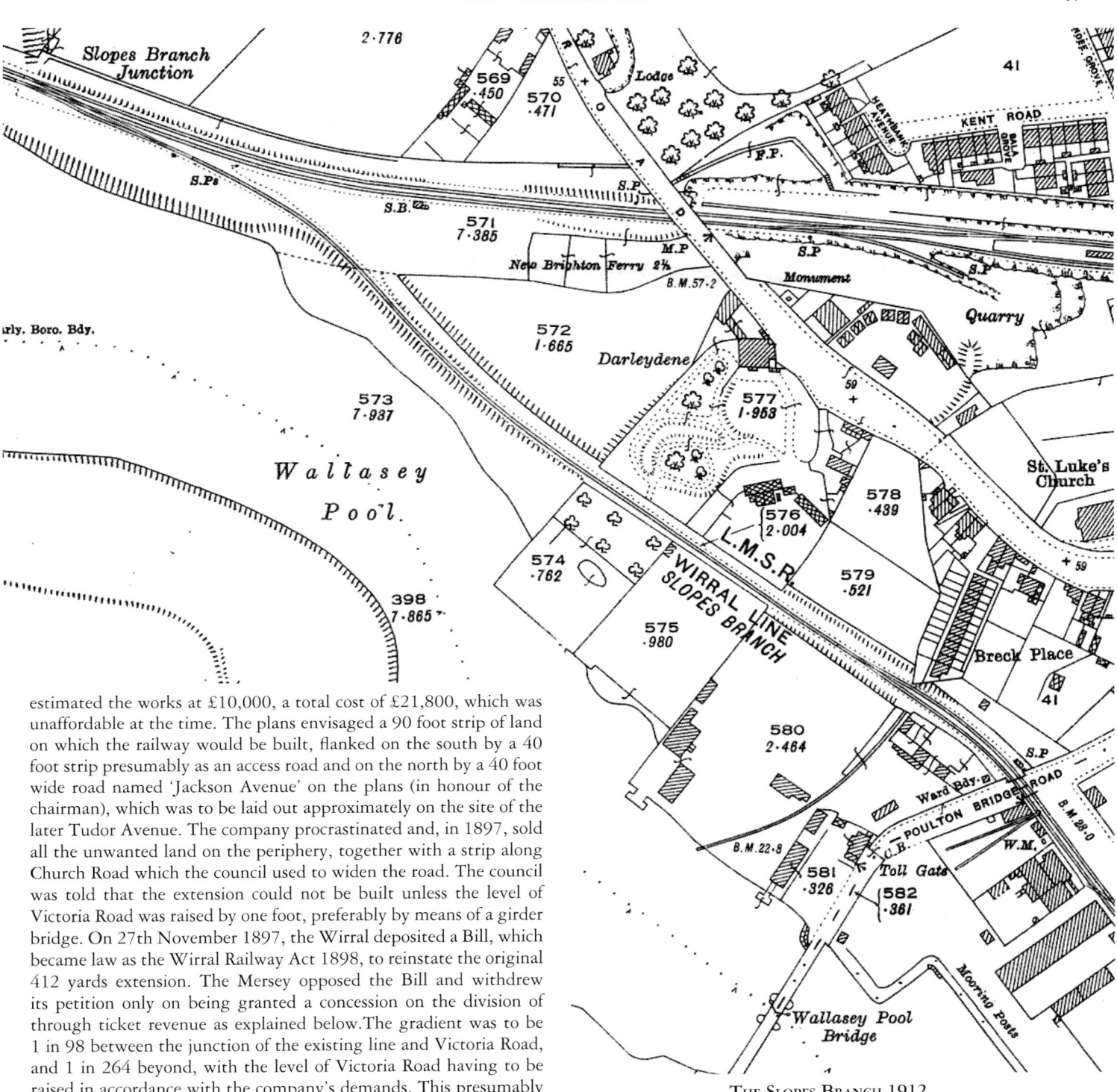

The Slopes Branch 1912

The Slopes Branch as shown on the 2nd edition 25 inch OS, 1912. It left the Seacombe Branch west of Liscard & Poulton station, the island platform of which appears top right. The branch was opened in 1906 (probably in October) and connected with the Dock Board lines at Poulton Bridge Road, its main function being to improve access to the Great Central and Cheshire Lines goods depots on the north side of the Dock Estate. Poulton Bridge Road level crossing was gated, although the dock lines were unfenced. Note the proximity to the line of the undeveloped Wallasey Pool, the marshy terrain having added to the construction cost. Wallasey Pool Bridge was commonly known as 'Penny Bridge'; its successor gave ships access to Bidston Dock, which was built on the west side and opened in 1933. East of the bridge is the West Float, part of the Great Float. Between 1952 and 1980, Bidston was the dock from whence thousands of tons of iron ore were railed to Shotton Ironworks but it has since been filled in. ORDNANCE SURVEY

estimated the works at £10,000, a total cost of £21,800, which was unaffordable at the time. The plans envisaged a 90 foot strip of land on which the railway would be built, flanked on the south by a 40 foot strip presumably as an access road and on the north by a 40 foot wide road named 'Jackson Avenue' on the plans (in honour of the chairman), which was to be laid out approximately on the site of the later Tudor Avenue. The company procrastinated and, in 1897, sold all the unwanted land on the periphery, together with a strip along Church Road which the council used to widen the road. The council was told that the extension could not be built unless the level of Victoria Road was raised by one foot, preferably by means of a girder bridge. On 27th November 1897, the Wirral deposited a Bill, which became law as the Wirral Railway Act 1898, to reinstate the original 412 yards extension. The Mersey opposed the Bill and withdrew its petition only on being granted a concession on the division of through ticket revenue as explained below. The gradient was to be 1 in 98 between the junction of the existing line and Victoria Road, and 1 in 264 beyond, with the level of Victoria Road having to be raised in accordance with the company's demands. This presumably was to avoid too steep a gradient. An agreement signed in 1901 has not been found and the details are thus unknown but to this day there is a rise in the level of the thoroughfare which is probably the result of this. The company continued to do nothing about the ferry extension on the grounds of cost; the powers were renewed by the Wirral Railway Act 1905 and the Wirral Railway (Extension of Time) Act 1909. A house, 1 Mersey Street, which was needed for demolition, was bought for £200 in 1910. However, the powers finally lapsed in 1912 and Seacombe 'temporary station' became very permanent, with no improvements whatsoever undertaken until after Nationalisation. Throughout its life, it compared very unfavourably with the other terminal stations on the line.

The 1899 Act also authorised the Slopes Branch, a 516 yards long

WIRRAL RAILWAY
SLOPES BRANCH JUNCTION
Redrawn from the Board of Trade Survey, 3rd September 1906

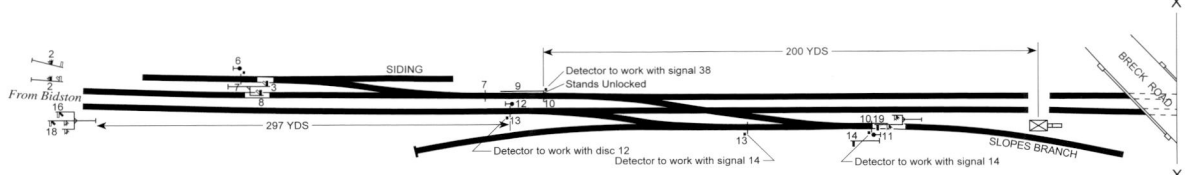

NOTE: The siding shown to the north of the line and the runaway siding at the end of the branch on the south side apparently had both been removed by the time of the circa 1920 photograph of the junction, shown below. This may have been carried out as a wartime economy measure, although there is little sign of any earthworks or redundant trackbed in the picture.

WIRRAL RAILWAY
LISCARD & POULTON STATION
Redrawn from the Board of Trade Survey, 3rd September 1906

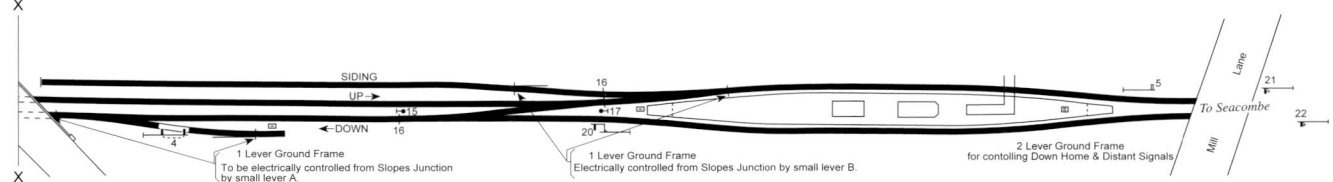

The only known view of Slopes Branch Junction, looking towards Seacombe and probably dating from around 1920. The signal box is just discernable to the left of the large house in the centre, which was originally named Slopes but later changed to Darley Dene; it was later destroyed in an air raid during the Second World War. The main line curved to the left to enter Liscard & Poulton station. TED LLOYD COLLECTION

Wallasey station looking east. The view is undated but the horse-drawn cab just visible in the forecourt suggests the early years of the 20th century. Note too the little wooden shelter with slated roof and internal heating for the benefit of waiting cabmen. The substantial accommodation on the Up platform and commodious covered footbridge are somewhat in contrast to the tiny shelter provided for waiting passengers on the Down side, tucked back against the fence. Unusually, the station name board reads 'Wallasey Station'. This photograph also provides good detail of the Down starter, a product of the Railway Signal Company across the water in Fazakerley. COURTESY ONLINE TRANSPORT ARCHIVE

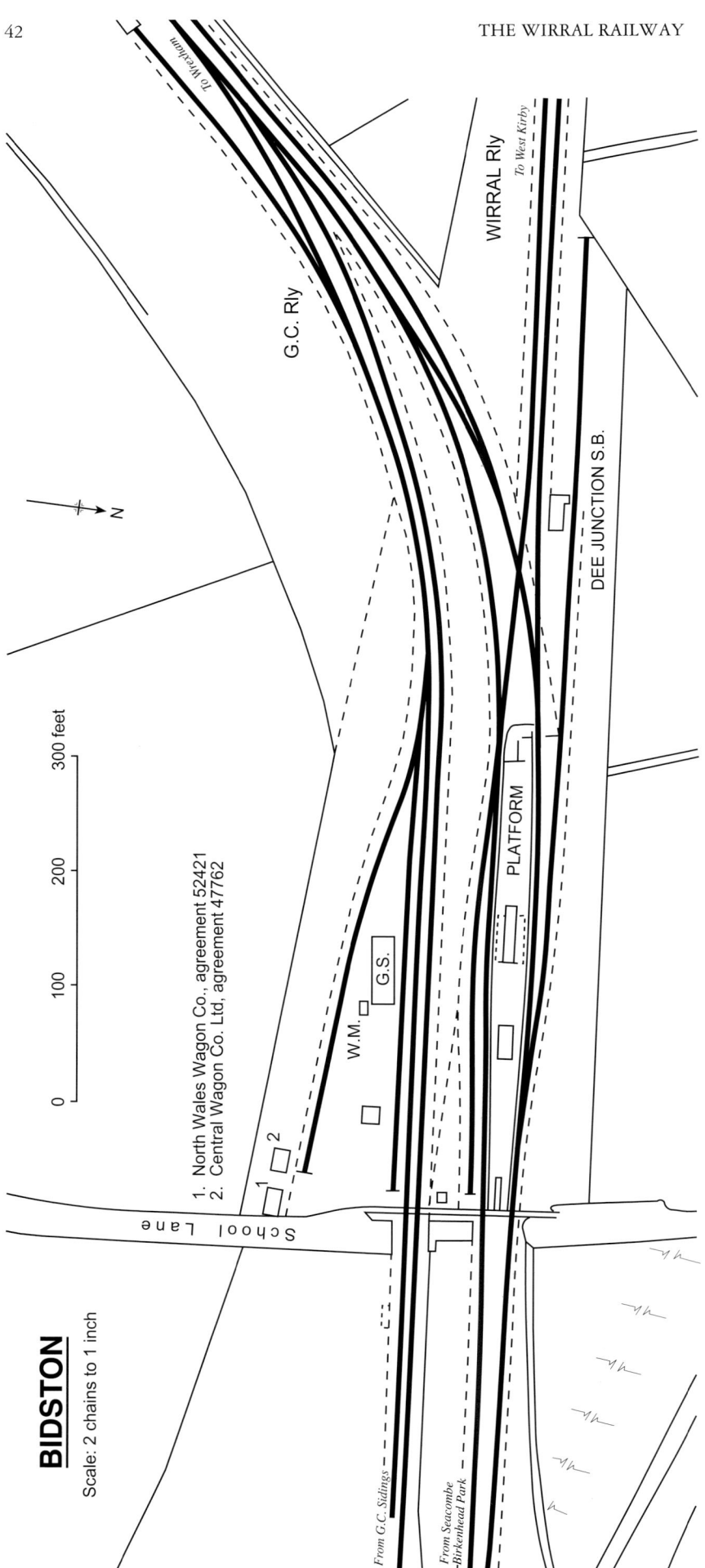

single track connecting the line west of Breck Road with the Mersey Docks & Harbour Board line at Poulton Bridge Road. The branch took its name from a large house, 'The Slopes' in Breck Road; it was later known as 'Darley Dene' and was destroyed by an enemy bomb in 1941. Authority to connect the Wirral Railway to the Dock Board tracks on the north side of the West Float had been contained in the 1895 Act but the line itself was not specified. The Slopes Branch was built mainly for the convenience of the Great Central, as it was to improve access to the Cheshire Lines' East & West Float goods depot, opened in November 1892 and the temporary GC depot on CLC land opened in 1900. Access to both of these had been over Dock Board tracks across Duke Street swing bridge, which had locomotive weight restrictions. The construction of the Slopes Branch took time, as the route was virtually lapped by the waters of the then undeveloped western end of Wallasey Pool, and the marshy ground had to be drained and consolidated. It finally came into use on an unrecorded date late in 1906; the GC's new Birkenhead (Dock Road) station, on the Kelvin Road site, was opened on 8th October 1906 and this may have been the date of both events. The line crossed Poulton Bridge Road on the level, the gates being worked by the train crew. A 560 foot-long siding on the north side, just inside the junction with the Seacombe Branch, was added at a later date; it served an electrical sub-station, being leased by Wallasey Corporation in 1922 and subsequently the Central Electricity Authority.

The transfer of wagons between the GC's Bidston sidings and points on the south side of the dock estate involved reversing on to the Wrexham line, across Dee Junction, through Bidston station and on to the Birkenhead Docks goods lines, sometimes causing delays to passenger trains. As a consequence, the Wirral and the GC agreed to an improved layout, which became Railway No. 4 of the Great Central Railway Act 1903. The GC's Bidston sidings were extended eastwards and a double line was laid from their east end which crossed the 'Great Drain' on a wooden trestle bridge, replaced by a concrete structure in 1957. It then passed over the Wirral main line on the level by a series of diamond crossings. The Wirral's Birkenhead Docks goods sidings on the north side of the main line were extended westwards almost to Bidston East Junction, where access from the main line was relocated. The new connection from the GC came into operation in 1907 and although the distance was short, revenue from GC traffic both via Birkenhead Docks and the Slopes Branch was important to the Wirral, which had apparently insisted on working GC trains from Bidston into the Docks up until this time (as indicated by the 1906 Working Timetable). The company was also empowered to purchase additional property, in particular strips of land on both sides of the railway between Oakdale Road and Gorsey Lane, and another parcel of land north of the line between Wallasey and New Brighton.

The remote location of Bidston station, looking west from the footbridge which spanned the line at this point, is clearly shown in this circa 1920 view. The West Kirby line runs straight ahead, whilst the GC line to Wrexham branches off to the left. The GC sidings are on the left, with the goods shed just out of picture. In the centre distance, the timber-built Bidston Dee Junction signal box watches over the junction. The two station buildings were also built of wood, as were the platform walls, as it was thought that the marshy ground would not support brick or stone-built structures. JOHN RYAN COLLECTION

THROUGH FARES

Disagreement with the Mersey Railway about through fares cropped up again and is contained in a letter dated 15th October 1891. Behind the dispute was the Mersey's strong objection to the construction of the Seacombe Branch, which they naturally saw as a threat to their traffic, a threat that increased as the atmospheric conditions in the tunnel deteriorated. The Wirral felt strongly about the 'bonus' being paid to the Mersey over and above the mileage payment, which was costing them £13,500 per year. They suggested terms for renewal of the existing agreement as follows:-

1. Traffic to and from the New Brighton line be divided as to actual mileage.
2. Traffic to and from the West Kirby line, the bonus to be not more than ¼-mile.
3. These proposals shall apply to the Mersey's Bold Street station (Liverpool Central Low Level, opened on 11th January 1892).

The Mersey described these terms as '*preposterous*' and announced that the existing arrangement would lapse from 31st July 1892. The Mersey was still hoping to get a substantial bonus on the mileage but continuing negotiations were in vain, except for the postponement of the termination until 31st October 1892. The Wirral then threatened to apply to the Railway & Canal Commissioners to adjudicate on the division of fares and this kept talks going. There was agreement that the bonus to the Mersey should be commuted to a sum of £1,660 per annum paid quarterly. Finally, the Mersey themselves applied to the Commissioners, the result of which was the passing of the Mersey Railway (Rates & Charges) Act 1894, which decreed that the tunnel was to be regarded as five miles long instead of the actual 4.1 miles. This was much less than the Mersey had hoped for but they were obliged to accept the ruling. However, the Wirral's determination to push on with the Seacombe Branch was viewed with keen concern by the Mersey's directors and was undoubtedly a factor in the decision to electrify the line. Their hostility was demonstrated by the cancelling of all through trains, which meant that all passengers to and from the Wirral had to detrain at Birkenhead Park, which soon became known as 'Pneumonia Junction'. The Mersey refused to issue through contracts via Park, saying that '*the Wirral traffic is not worth having*'. The end result was a further reduction in the Mersey's traffic, the benefits going to the Wallasey Council's ferry from New Brighton. When the Seacombe Branch opened, the Railway & Canal Commissioners awarded the Mersey compensation of £2,000.

A further agreement between the Wirral and the Mersey was signed on 27th May 1898 covering the train service, the 'bonus' for the added expense of the tunnel and the apportionment of revenue. The Mersey on their part withdrew their opposition to the Wirral's 1898 Bill. This agreement was terminated on 31st December 1899.

THE FERRY CROSSING

The most complex negotiations between Wallasey UDC and the railway company were those about the conditions under which railway passengers would be carried on the council's ferry to and from Liverpool. The Wirral Railway directors were fully appraised of the conditions which had been hammered out by the London & North Western & Great Western Joint Railway and Birkenhead Corporation governing the carriage of railway passengers on Woodside ferry in 1878 and were determined to secure equally good terms. The circumstances were not quite the same, as the Joint Railways had been carrying passengers across the river on their own ferry and, in effect, handed over a going concern to Woodside thus justifying a substantial discount on the normal tariff. The Wirral could argue, however, that

Seacombe landing stage from the river in the early years of the 20th century, with the goods ferry boat *Wallasey* unloading, showing both the goods lift, with its attendant hydraulic tower far right, and the goods bridge alongside it. The bridge was quite steeply angled and the laden carts coming off the boat are therefore queuing to use the lift. At one stage, there were plans to carry railway wagons across the Mersey and much money was spent developing and equipping the Seacombe terminal to this aim, despite the hostility to the scheme of the Mersey Docks & Harbour Board. If the 1894 proposals had come to fruition, the railway passenger station would have been on this side of the ferry terminal. PRIESTLEY & CO.

they could continue routing their traffic via Birkenhead Park on to the Mersey Railway but generous terms could result in much of this traffic choosing Seacombe ferry as an alternative free of the noxious fumes in the underwater tunnel. A formal Agreement was signed on 3rd August 1893, the main provision being a discount of one third on the ferry tariff for railway passengers, through tickets being issued from Liverpool landing stage to various railway stations. These were similar to the Woodside conditions. There were also provisions for passengers' luggage to be carried on the ferry free of charge, except for excess luggage which was initially charged at £50 per annum. Free passes on the ferry were issued to railway servants travelling on duty. A booking office was opened on Liverpool landing stage adjacent to that of the Birkenhead Joint. The Agreement became the Schedule to the Wirral Railway Act 1895. There were disputes from time to time. In 1895, when the railway started issuing contracts (season tickets) through to Liverpool, the Ferries department refused to make any reduction and at first there was a disinclination to make any concession for excursion traffic. However, these difficulties were soon overcome. The ferries, operating vessels with certificates for 1,000 passengers or more, realised that they could absorb a train load of passengers without incurring any additional cost and it was worthwhile accepting excursion passengers at very low fares. The GC ran excursions to Caergwrle for 1s return from Liverpool landing stage, which were enormously popular.

There were many relatively minor causes of disagreement between the parties and the Ferries department seemed to view whatever the railway company proposed with suspicion. In August 1899, the railway was complaining about the '*continuous unpunctuality of the boat service*' and of delays in sending parcels up the passenger bridge, using the goods bridge and the lifts instead. In 1902, the Dock Board created additional passenger shelter by removing part of the Wirral Railway booking office. In the same year, the ferries refused to issue discount family tickets for through bookings to New Brighton and later refused to issue any further rail/ferry contracts. Parcel handling difficulties seemed to be never ending as, in June 1910, the ferries management refused to allow the railway to convey parcels in lorries on the goods boat, saying that the passenger boats must be used. The legality of this decision under the 1895 Agreement was queried but, in the end, the railway paid for using the goods boats just to get the traffic moving expeditiously.

Optimistically, the Wirral's timetables included a table for a roundabout journey between Birkenhead Park and Liverpool Landing Stage, via Bidston, Seacombe and the ferry. It is doubtful, however, if many passengers took advantage of this facility, though a journey between Park and Liscard & Poulton or Seacombe might have been viable to the less active in the days before cross-docks bus services. To the average fit person, it would have been quicker to walk from Docks station to Liscard & Poulton across the toll bridge. JOHN RYAN COLLECTION

A fine study of No. 12, one of two 0-6-4 tanks built by Beyer, Peacock for the Wirral Railway in 1900, the other being No. 13. They were the only examples with this wheel arrangement on the Wirral system and, because of the many severe curves, they proved more suitable for freight than passenger duties. No. 12 is posed in front of the distinctive sausage shaped water tank, constructed from an old boiler mounted on brick piers, which featured in many of the locomotive portraits taken at Birkenhead Docks engine shed. T.B. MAUND COLLECTION

WAY AND WORKS

Apart from the principal stations, the buildings on the line tended to be rudimentary. The signal boxes were mainly wooden structures, most dating from the resignalling on the Sykes lock and block system in 1899. Much of the permanent way was relaid at the same time with 30 foot lengths of 85lbs rail. Leasowe station was not provided with a signal box, signals and the level crossing being controlled from a ground frame on the platform.

Water was obtained from local wells and from Birkenhead's River Alwen supply. It is apparent that hard water was taking its toll of locomotive boiler tubes and, in 1902, water samples were sent for analysis to Mather & Platt, who were asked what could be done to counteract the effect. It was found that Lake Vyrnwy water, as supplied to Wallasey, was superior and negotiations for a supply were commenced in August 1904. These were successful but whilst there was no difficulty in tapping into this supply at Seacombe, Wallasey and New Brighton, it is not clear how it was effected at Birkenhead Docks and other stations beyond Wallasey's borders. Unsuitable water could be devastating to steam engines and increase costs enormously but very little attention is given to this aspect by historians. There was a 4,500 gallon tank made from an egg-ended boiler at Birkenhead Docks locomotive shed and parachute tanks at Docks (2,200 gals), Park (3,000), and New Brighton (1,500) stations. Seacombe had a rectangular 1,500-gallon tank, whilst there was a column at West Kirby and a stand-pipe in Hoylake goods yard.

Leasowe station house in 1912, with the gates across Reeds Lane closed to allow the passage of a West Kirby-bound train. Staff and passengers pose for the photographer. The ground frame here controlling the gates and signals was finally replaced by a very small signal box in 1938. This was not a block post and only the signals protecting the crossing were controlled from here. JOHN RYAN COLLECTION

A fine selection of private owner wagons fill New Brighton sidings in this circa 1910 view, to the extent that even the goods shed road is completely occupied, suggesting perhaps that traffic in general merchandise was sparse. Of particular interest are the three Moreton Brick & Tile Company Ltd wagons in the rake standing at the platform. The GCR registered a dozen Chas. Roberts-built wagons for this concern in 1903 and their siding connection at Moreton was probably brought into use around the same time. The company began operations in the mid 19th century and continued until the late 1920s, being formally wound up in 1930. Next to them are two Haydock Collieries wagons, with the lettering in an arc; this changed in later years, with wagons simply being lettered HAYDOCK in a straight line along the top two or three planks. Towards the end of this rake, the two BC wagons are likely to belong to the Bredbury Colliey Co. Ltd of Stockport. Next to the goods shed entrance is a wagon belonging to Wallasey-based coal merchant James Langley, who was in business from 1902 to 1938 at least. In the same rake can also be seen two John Speakman & Sons wagons, who were colliery proprietors in Leigh and Bedford, Lancashire. In 1914, the business was registered as Speakman, John & Sons Ltd and in 1930 it joined with others to form Manchester Collieries Ltd. Finally, the wagon partly hidden by the water tower is thought to belong to the Lancashire Coal Company of New Brighton. Note the completely open platforms without any protection from the weather and the 'New Brighton Station' running in board.
MARTIN JENKINS COLLECTION

Goods Traffic

Because of the relatively isolated situation of the line, goods traffic on the Wirral Railway was always secondary to passenger traffic. Further, the district served was residential in character, so that its freight business was almost totally confined to domestic or 'landsale' coal for some years. Following a Board resolution of 3rd July 1876, coal yards were established at Moreton (on the south side) and Hoylake (on the north side). Gradually the company provided adequate facilities at all the principal stations, though at the smaller ones, such as Liscard & Poulton and Wallasey, only coal traffic was handled, merchants providing their own huts. However, with every household using solid fuel, there was a steady demand.

Wallasey, in particular, was known as 'the dormitory of Liverpool', yet stretching inland from Seacombe it had a significant industrial zone. Shipbuilding, cement, chemical manure, crane building and milling industries all thrived, along with gas works, coal yards and a small oil refinery. Sadly for the Wirral Railway, however, these industries were connected to the private railways of the Mersey Docks & Harbour Board long before the Seacombe Branch was built.

The Dock Board was obliged by an early Act of Parliament to provide railway access to its Birkenhead and Wallasey quays, in sharp contrast to its Liverpool docks where the cartage interests were influential. The Board did not provide haulage on the Wirral side of the Mersey but, for many years, levied charges 'per wagon' hauled over their lines. Those who wanted to run locomotives over the Board's lines typically paid monthly for a licence. Several industrial concerns had engines of their own but others employed haulage contractors, some of whom graduated from horses to steam power. When the Wirral's predecessors sought to connect their line to the Dock Board's system at Birkenhead North (Docks), they were treated as if they were just another trader who wanted a siding.

The Dock Board's lack of interest in the Wirral was probably because it had no significant goods traffic to offer. The Board had built a double track railway, which followed their southern boundary for almost two miles from Cathcart Street to a point very close to the original Docks terminus of the Hoylake & Birkenhead. At Cathcart Street, this railway made an end-on junction with the GW/L&NW Joint Lines and was therefore the potential freight link with the outside world which the proposed Mersey Railway could not be.

Negotiations began on 25th May 1877, when the directors and manager of the Hoylake & Birkenhead Railway & Tramway Co. attended a meeting of the Dock Board's Works Committee and asked for the Board's lines to be put in repair from Ilchester Road to the Township Boundary, so that a junction could be made. Apart from connecting themselves to the outside railway network, the Hoylake & Birkenhead wished to serve the factories which had been built between Beaufort Road (as it is today) and the Float. The Dock Board did not want this traffic on their rails but, on 25th January 1878, their Works Committee heard another request from the Hoylake Company that the tracks might be repaired '*for the benefit of those parties who are entitled to use them.*' This was tactless. The Committee stiffly replied that '*the Company be informed that it does not appear that the Company have any rights to use the line except with the permission of the Board.*' The H&B had to concede that this was so and humbly asked permission.

Having laid a short connecting line between the two systems, the Hoylake Company sought permission to pass wagons over the Dock Board's lines. This was granted on 19th July 1878, subject to a charge of 1s per loaded wagon which, in September was raised to 2s! The L&NWR wanted to send a number of loads of sanitary pipes through to the Hoylake lines and tried without success to have the 2s charge reduced; they were also told that the traffic was accepted on condition that no precedent was set and that no obstruction was

0-6-4T No. 12 passes the locomotive sheds at Birkenhead with coal empties from Seacombe on 19th April 1919. There are a number of private owners in the train but only the nearest is positively identifiable, belonging to Vauxhall Colliery at Ruabon. This pit began production in the 1850s, when it was named Kenyon Colliery, changing its name around ten years later to Vauxhall. It closed in 1928. In later years, their wagons seem mostly to have come from Charles Roberts Ltd at Wakefield. They were painted red with white lettering shaded black. JOHN WARD COLLECTION, COURTESY JOHN HORNE

LEFT: A circa 1910 view of Hoylake station, with a service arriving from Birkenhead behind 4-4-4T No. 11. The waiting passengers are mainly children and ladies in Edwardian summer dress, some of the latter carrying parasols to shield them from the sun. Behind the rather ramshackle collection of station buildings is Hoylake Gas Works, which was served by a private siding and provided reasonable traffic for the railway. T.B. MAUND COLLECTION

caused. In December 1878, the Plas yn Wern Fire Clay Company was told *'the [Dock] Board has no arrangement with the Hoylake & Birkenhead Railway & Tramway Co. as regards passage of traffic … and are not disposed to alter the practise'* (of charging 2s per wagon load). Although the railway company used firebricks for firebox arches, a likely destination for the wagon load from Plas yn Wern was the new gas works at Hoylake. Surplus land on the south side of the line at Hoylake had been let for a gas works and a private siding was provided. The several firms whose sidings connected to the Dock Board's line just east of Docks station were also tenants of the Board and succeeded in having the toll reduced to 6d per wagon. Thomas Brassey & Co., Edward Logan and Laird Brothers were among the firms concerned. There was still the matter of haulage to be paid for and one wonders whether the Hoylake Company had hoped to do this work. There is no record of them being granted authority to run locomotives over the Dock Board's line but it may have happened. Only when the Wirral Railway became a significant source of dock traffic did the Dock Board become cooperative, notably for coal and livestock transferred from the WM&CQ/GCR via Bidston. By 1928, and possibly for many years before, the Dock Board could claim that *'at Birkenhead the dock lines may be used free of charge for the conveyance of goods to and from the quays.'* However, whether this generosity applied to the use by railway companies of the double track line from Cathcart Street to Birkenhead North is doubtful.

Because of the lack of space at Seacombe passenger station, a quite separate goods station was built at Oakdale Road, with road access opposite Geneva Road some half a mile short of the line's terminus; this was often referred to as Oakdale Sidings. The first sidings were laid during the earlier months of 1899; they were extended in 1906 when a coal yard was established and again in 1913 when yard lighting was added. On 1st July 1901, both goods and passenger stations were renamed 'Seacombe & Egremont'. A facing siding led off the Up line and a crossover provided access to the Down line; a new signal box, 'Seacombe & Egremont Goods Yard', controlled train movements. In July 1904, Major Druitt inspected two new trailing connections with the Down line, the English McKenna Process Co's siding being situated east of Gorsey Lane and Wallasey Gas Works siding, to the west. It is not known why the gas works siding had not been connected earlier, as a temporary link had been made during the line's construction. As it was, it was still not fully ready at the time of the inspection but permission was given for it to open in about a month's time. McKenna's siding was controlled from the Goods Yard signal box but a single lever ground frame protected by an Annett's key controlled the gas works siding; it was interlocked with the levers from the box, which by then had 14 levers in use and four spare. Equipment was provided by the Railway Signal Company Ltd, Fazakerley, Liverpool.

The Great Western and London & North Western Joint Railways naturally dominated rail access to the docks on the Wirral side of the Mersey. A small dent had appeared in their monopoly when the Cheshire Lines reached Helsby in 1869. The CLC had running powers to Birkenhead (but paid the Joint Companies to do the necessary haulage) and opened goods depots in 1871 at Birkenhead and in 1896 on the north side of the docks. None of this benefited the Wirral Railway immediately. Even the Wallasey Gas Works relied on the GW/L&NWR Joint Lines to deliver their coal to Birkenhead. The Gas Department hired contractors whose horses, and later

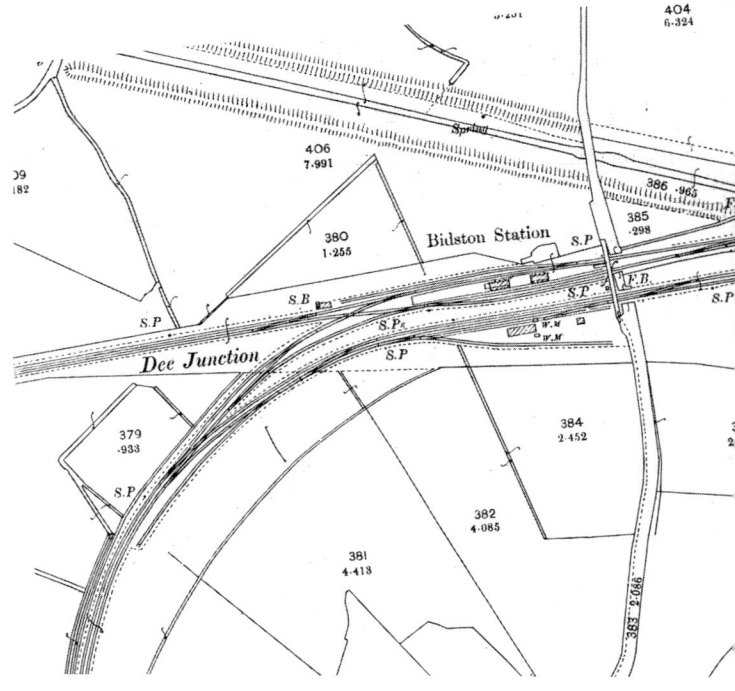

BIDSTON & SEACOMBE JUNCTIONS 1899

The array of junctions in the Bidston area as depicted on the 2nd edition 25 inch OS 1899 (Note: The map has been reduced by 50% to fit the page). The Wirral main line heads northwards to New Brighton from Seacombe Junction No. 3, whilst the branch to Seacombe swings eastwards from Seacombe Junction No. 1 and through Seacombe Junction No. 2. Southwards from Seacombe Junction No. 1, the main line runs past Bidston North Junction and Bidston West Junction, through Bidston station and thens heads westwards from Dee Junction towards Hoylake and West Kirby. The Wirral's Park Branch is seen running eastwards from Bidston station, past Bidston East and West junctions. At the edge of the map, this branch splits in two, with the northernmost line running to Birkenhead Docks Goods, whilst the main branch swings slightly south-east towards Birkenhead Park station, where the Wirral made an end on junction with the Mersey Railway. Bidston Sidings and the engine shed were Great Central property, their line heading away southwards from Dee Junction. ORDNANCE SURVEY

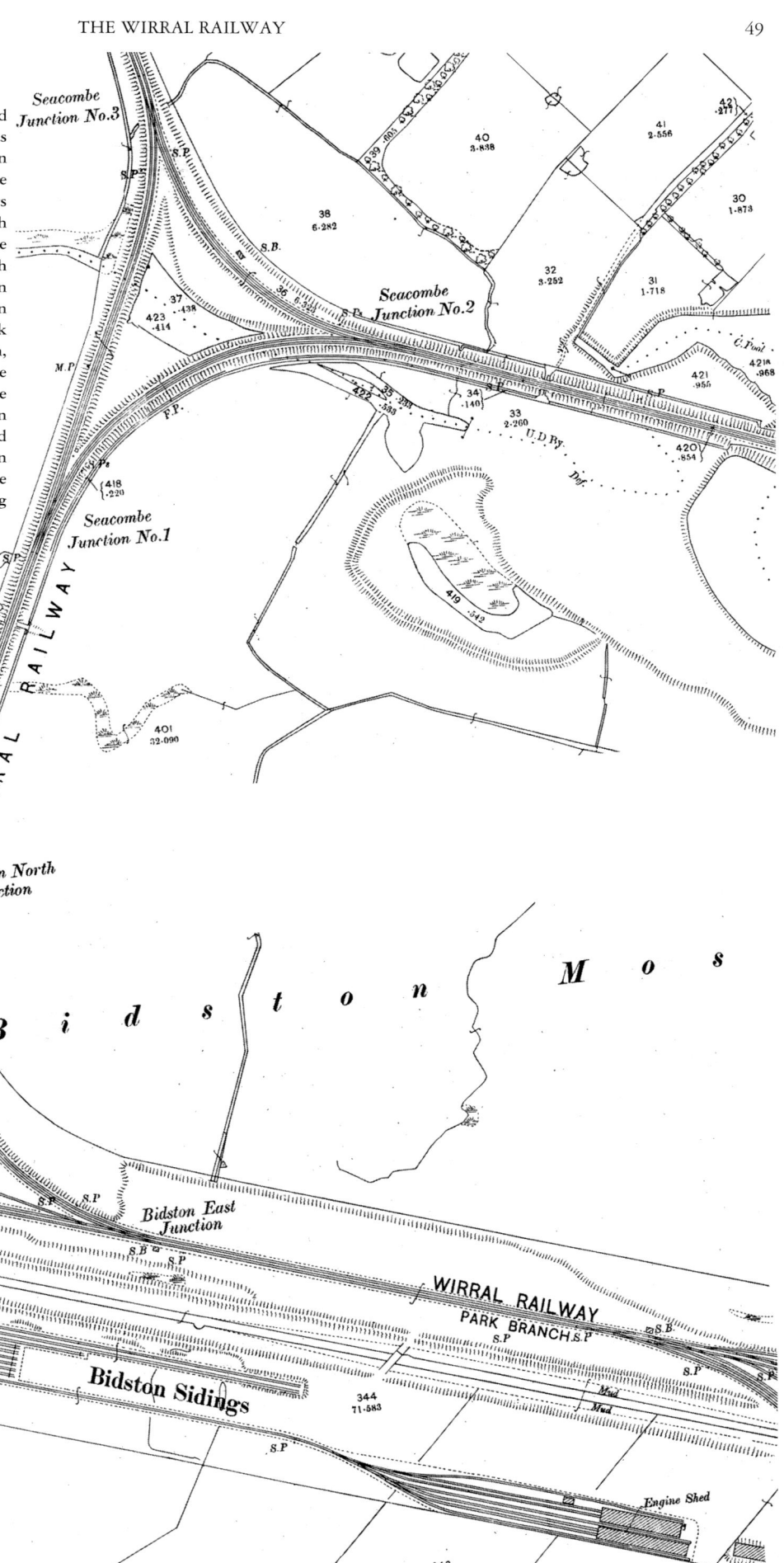

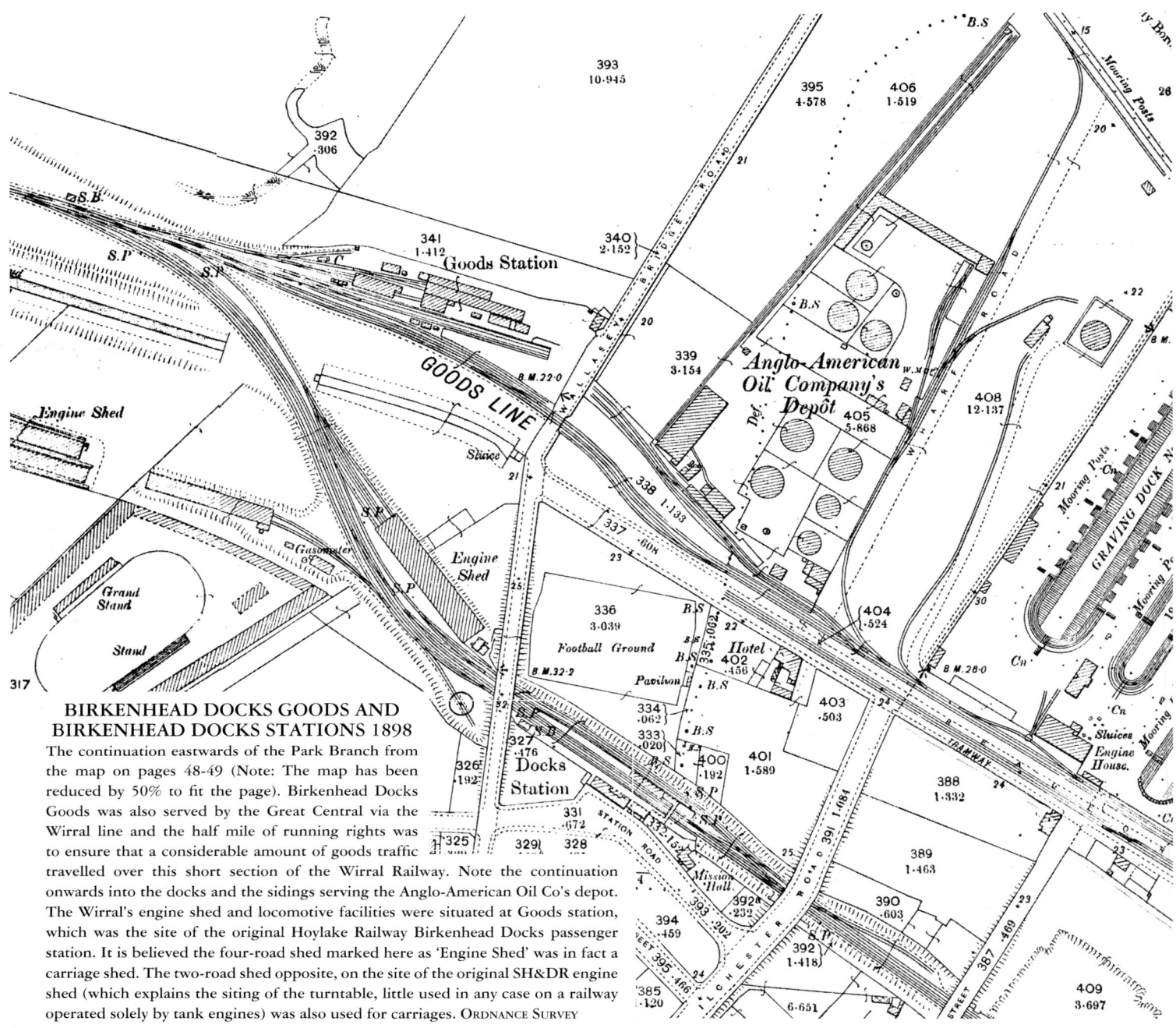

BIRKENHEAD DOCKS GOODS AND BIRKENHEAD DOCKS STATIONS 1898

The continuation eastwards of the Park Branch from the map on pages 48-49 (Note: The map has been reduced by 50% to fit the page). Birkenhead Docks Goods was also served by the Great Central via the Wirral line and the half mile of running rights was to ensure that a considerable amount of goods traffic travelled over this short section of the Wirral Railway. Note the continuation onwards into the docks and the sidings serving the Anglo-American Oil Co's depot. The Wirral's engine shed and locomotive facilities were situated at Goods station, which was the site of the original Hoylake Railway Birkenhead Docks passenger station. It is believed the four-road shed marked here as 'Engine Shed' was in fact a carriage shed. The two-road shed opposite, on the site of the original SH&DR engine shed (which explains the siting of the turntable, little used in any case on a railway operated solely by tank engines) was also used for carriages. ORDNANCE SURVEY

locomotives, pulled the wagons for three miles over the MD&HB lines to the gas works. However, the arrival of the Wrexham, Mold & Connah's Quay Railway (part of the GCR from 1905) at Bidston greatly increased the goods traffic transported over the Wirral. The distance over which this traffic was carried by the WR was small but it is significant because, even when extended over the double crossing at Birkenhead Docks South Junction, the GCR did not reach the dock lines but had to use a half mile of Wirral track.

The GCR ended between the River Birket ('the Great Drain') bridge and the diamond crossing, so that the ownership and maintenance of this unusual piece of trackwork was entirely Wirral Railway. The agreement which granted running powers to the GCR over this short length of Wirral line has not been seen but it probably allowed for rates rather higher than the usual 'per mile', just as the Mersey Railway was allowed to round-up its underground mileages when charging the Wirral for through passenger bookings. The GCR, and later the L&NER, ran special trains for Irish and overseas cattle traffic passing through the lairages at Birkenhead and Seacombe, and this could account for the 51,414 head of cattle carried by the Wirral in 1922. The same would apply to most of the merchandise tonnage quoted. The coal and coke tonnage, claimed by the Wirral chairman as 261,308 for 1922, would include GCR coal traffic to Cavendish Sidings, Birkenhead, where North Wales coal was tipped for export and for ship's bunkers. In this instance, it is possible that 50 per cent of the 261,308 tons was for consumption on the Wirral's own system, either for landsale or for gas and electricity works.

Wallasey Gas Works was almost certainly the Wirral's best freight customer. Annual coal and cannel* consumption reached 53,629 tons by 1914 and continued to increase for several years. Production ceased in 1961, after which cheaper gas came across from Liverpool.

---

* Cannel is a type of coal with a large amount of hydrogen, which burns easily with a bright light and leaves little ash. It was added to the mix to produce a higher candle power gas before the days of incandescent mantles – hence its other name 'candle coal'.

The original Duke Street swing bridge over the Great Float, photographed probably in the late 1920s; it was replaced by the present bascule bridge in 1931. This was not actually on the Wirral system but goods traffic to and from the WR made much use of it. The road was freely shared by road and rail traffic and one of the docks shunting locomotives is seen approaching the bridge; it is probably waiting for a clear road, with a horse and cart passing across the span the train will traverse, whilst a motor bus is crossing the adjacent span. Note how the dockyard rails were laid into the road surface in tram fashion. In the background, on the south side of the West Float, is Cavendish Sidings, which served the coaling berth for ships, part of the equipment of which can be seen on the far right, behind the building which is the Dock Master's Office. Numerous private owner wagons are in evidence, including several from Gresford Colliery, near Wrexham. In the foreground, a William Cooper & Sons Ltd lorry, possibly an ex-army WW1 surplus vehicle, loads sand alongside a Sentinel steam wagon belonging to W. Gray. Wallasey Gas Works lay behind the photographer's right shoulder. In a few yards the lines on the right of the picture will turn left and right to join the main line along the north (Wallasey) side of the dock estate, the line turning left ending in its junction with Slopes Branch of the Wirral Railway. *N.N. Forbes Collection*

LEFT: Oakdale Sidings was officially called Seacombe & Egremont Goods Yard, which name was later simplified to Seacombe Goods Yard as indicated by the nameboard on the signal box. This selection of photographs show the derelict yard after closure of the Seacombe Branch and this first view is looking towards the terminus.
A.S. CLAYTON, ONLINE TRANSPORT ARCHIVE

RIGHT: Seacombe Goods Yard signal box opened in 1901 and was a product of the Railway Signal Company of Liverpool. It also controlled access to the English McKenna works sidings, during the short time that firm was in operation prior to the First World War. It had been heavily vandalised by the time these photographs were taken.
BELOW: The connection to the sidings was from the Up line, so goods trains had first to travel to Seacombe, servicing the yard on the return journey by reversing back across the Down line. In the centre distance is Gorsey Lane bridge, with Wallasey Gas Works towering over it behind.
BOTH A.S. CLAYTON, ONLINE TRANSPORT ARCHIVE

THE WIRRAL RAILWAY

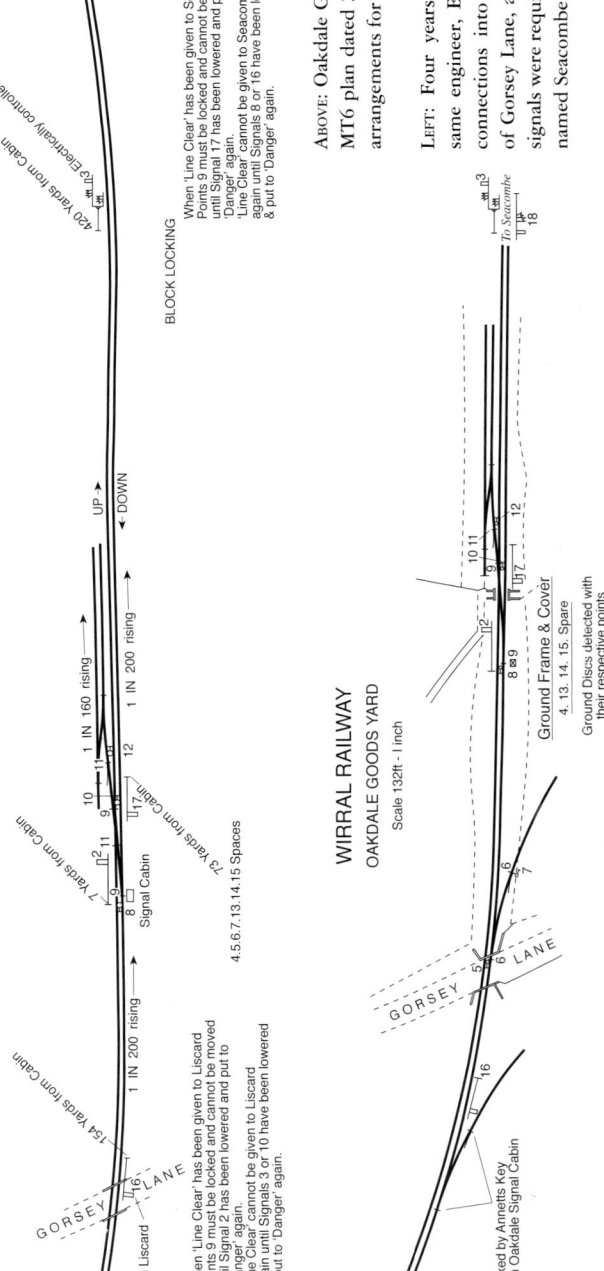

WIRRAL RAILWAY
GOODS YARD BETWEEN LISCARD & SEACOMBE
Scale 132ft - 1 inch

WIRRAL RAILWAY
OAKDALE GOODS YARD
Scale 132ft - 1 inch

BLOCK LOCKING

When 'Line Clear' has been given to Seacombe Points 9 must be locked and cannot be moved until Signal 17 has been lowered and put to 'Danger' again.
'Line Clear' cannot be given to Seacombe again until Signals 8 or 16 have been lowered & put to 'Danger' again.

BLOCK LOCKING

When 'Line Clear' has been given to Liscard Points 9 must be locked and cannot be moved until Signal 2 has been lowered and put to 'Danger' again.
'Line Clear' cannot be given to Liscard again until Signals 3 or 10 have been lowered & put to 'Danger' again.

ABOVE: Oakdale Goods Yard as first opened, redrawn from the MT6 plan dated 26th September 1900, showing the signalling arrangements for the new facility.

LEFT: Four years later, a new plan was drawn up, by the same engineer, Ernest Wilcox, to show the two new trailing connections into the English McKenna works, on the right of Gorsey Lane, and Wallasey Gas Works, to the left. Further signals were required, as the plan shows. The yard was officially named Seacombe & Egremont Goods Yard some time after.

LEFT AND BELOW: Although it had been attacked by vandals following closure of the branch, enough of Seacombe Goods Yard signal box still remained to determine its form and record it for posterity in these photographs. Note that the Board of Trade on their plan, above, refer to it variously as a Ground Frame & Cover and as Oakdale Signal Cabin. BOTH A.S. CLAYTON, ONLINE TRANSPORT ARCHIVE

Hoylake station around 1905, showing the piecemeal development which had led to rather a mish-mash of architectural styles using a range of different materials. It is not clear if the original Hoylake Railway terminus building had simply been demolished or incorporated into the farther building in the centre of the picture. In the right background, just beyond the platforms, this Edwardian picture postcard provides a rare glimpse of goods operations on the Wirral system, with a wagon apparently being shunted into the gas works siding. JOHN RYAN COLLECTION

By 1911, additional roads had been added at Oakdale sidings on the Up line, giving access to the private siding of the Seacombe Pressed Brick & Tile Co., which had a narrow gauge railway connection. Both the extensive gas works and McKenna's sidings were connected at the other end to the Dock Board railway but the connections were awkward and it is thought unlikely that the Wirral attempted to utilise them as a link.

McKenna's Birkenhead Steel Rolling Mill sidings were arranged approximately as an oval round the site. Shunting was carried out by a newly-built Hudswell Clarke 0-4-0ST named *Edwin Hale Abbott*. The expensively equipped American-style factory was engaged in re-rolling part-worn steel rails into rails of lighter section. However, production ended in 1909 and the factory was razed. After that, the only activity on the site was illicit gambling on greyhound racing by unemployed men. The police tried to stamp it out but the men always had lookouts who raised the alarm! Later the LMS & GW Joint Railway bought the site but did nothing with it. The Brick & Tile works siding was disconnected in the early 1920s.

Other sidings connected at an early date were those to the Hoylake & West Kirby Council's electricity works, situated to the east of the line at Hoylake station, close to the gas works. Here, there were eventually sidings parallel with the running roads on both sides, these sidings being accessed by trailing points on the Down line and a lengthy head shunt. The small gas works received 7,829 tons of coal by rail in 1914 and about 11,000 tons when it was gridded in 1954. Their steam locomotive was replaced by a petrol machine from Muir Hill in 1927. A small goods shed and coalyard, which was accessible to the public without using the level crossing, was provided on the west side of the line at Hoylake. At Moreton, a siding for the Moreton Brick & Tile Co. west of the station was in use by 1903. In October 1906, an agreement was made with a contractor, John Scott, for transport of the spoil from the new Vittoria Dock, which was being built on the south side of the East Float. This was loaded on the Dock Board lines and temporary sidings were laid to permit the spoil to be tipped into the triangle at Seacombe Junction and alongside Slopes Branch Junction, both sites being marshy. The 8½-acre dock was opened on 1st July 1909.

By 1913, the Wirral had laid the 'Sand Siding' on the north side of the line just west of New Brighton station. Initially, this was a single line leading towards the foreshore but ending above the high water mark. Its purpose was to load sand for use in railway works and for sale. Two more sidings known as 'Tip Sidings' were added and waste material from Birkenhead Docks was dumped there. The company had purchased the land under powers granted by the 1898 Act. About the same time, the Wirral was connected to further private sidings, notably those of the Anglo-American Oil Co. and the Vacuum Oil Co., leading off the dock line a few yards east of Wallasey Bridge Road, as well as sidings for a concrete company. The oil sidings were extended in 1917, a loop line being taken out at New Brighton station to provide the rails which were unobtainable new under wartime conditions. A milk dock had been provided at Seacombe and, in 1915, a siding was laid into Wallasey Corporation's generating station at Poulton, joining the Seacombe Branch slightly west of the gas works siding. After the 1914-18 war, the approach to these sidings was remodelled to provide only one junction for both the gas and electricity sidings. In the 1930s, the sand siding was extended to give access to a temporary contractor's railway used during the extension of New Brighton promenade. A land exchange deal was then made with the Corporation and the sidings were abandoned after construction ceased.

The working agreement between the Wirral and the MS&LR/Great Central no doubt caused the smaller company to be taken more seriously by the Birkenhead Joint Committee, not that there is any record of hostility or obstruction from that quarter. From 1907, if not earlier, it became normal for certain Joint Line goods trains to be worked from Hooton to Birkenhead Docks station and *vice versa*

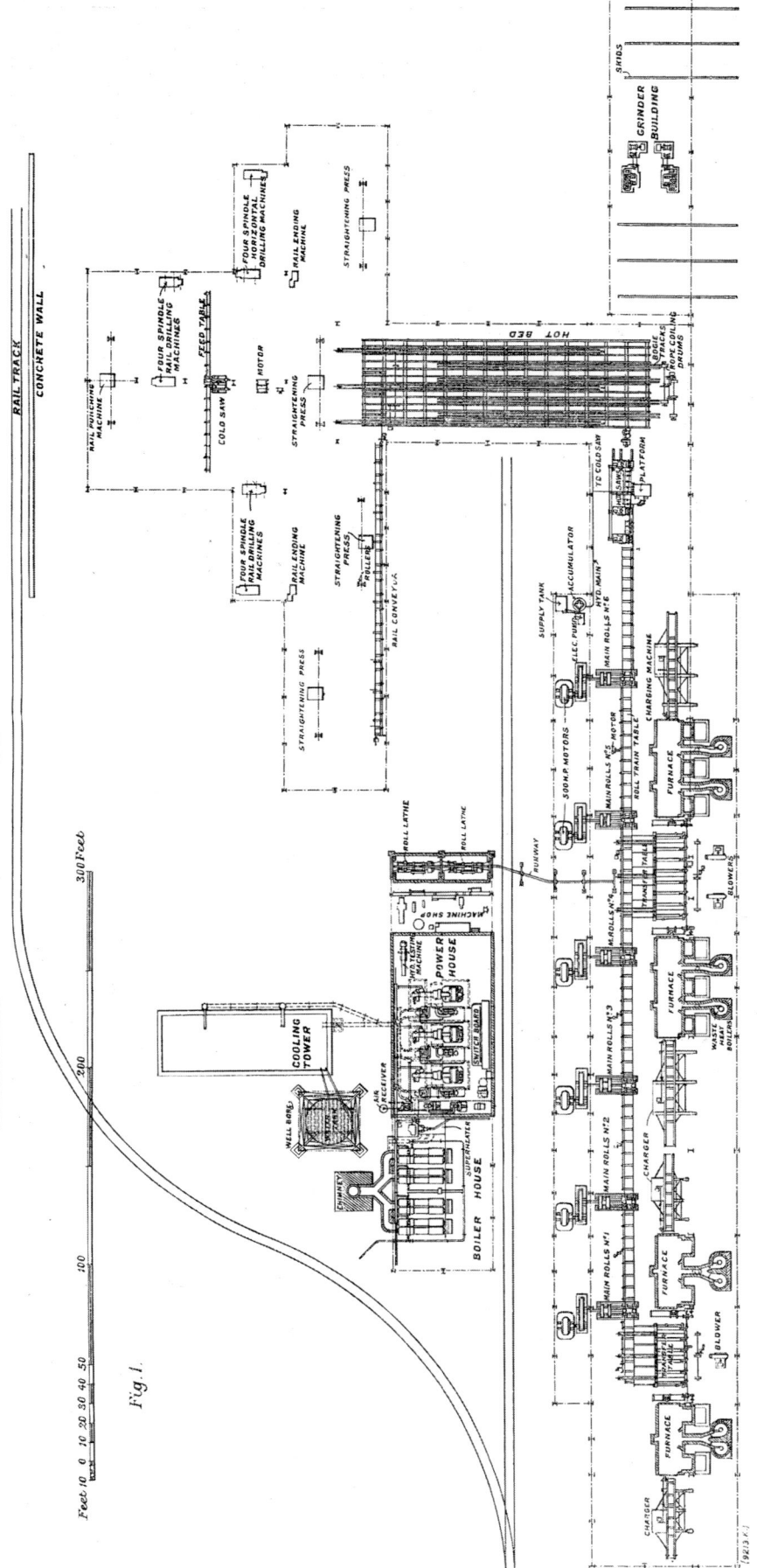

THE WORKS OF THE ENGLISH McKENNA PROCESS COMPANY, LIMITED, SEACOMBE, BIRKENHEAD.

Fig. 1.

via West Kirby, rather than via Rock Ferry and the Sough to the docks. A minute of the Joint Officers' Committee dated 19th March 1907 states that traffic would continue as though exchanged at West Kirby Junction, *'the Wirral Co. to pay 1s per mile (6d per mile Empty) for the service.'* From 10th August 1921 to the end of 1922, *'in view of the increased cost of engine power it was agreed to charge 2s 6d per mile for train working.'* After the Grouping, it was agreed to make no charge to the Joint Account for working trains over what was now the LM&SR from West Kirby to Birkenhead Docks station. Since this slightly disadvantaged the GWR component of the Joint Line, it might be guessed that some counter-balancing simplification was made elsewhere, the net effect being to reduce administrative costs.

The effect of the 1907 agreement between the Wirral and the Joint Lines was to deliver goods traffic to Birkenhead Docks station without having to use the MD&HB lines at Birkenhead. The Wirral granted the Joint Lines running powers over their 'main line' from West Kirby to Birkenhead Docks Station and paid the Joint Lines to deliver their traffic, without the use of Wirral engines. The Wirral had no 'goods engines' as such. It is not known if the Joint goods trains dropped off intermediate traffic at West Kirby for the Wirral to work forward but it seems likely. There is no mention of Joint Line engines shunting the yard at Hoylake, for example, nor of trains continuing on to the MD&HB line, though some trains (or light engines) may have done so. In the early post-Grouping period, some engines working the through New Brighton to Hooton (for London) coaches returned with goods trains and *vice versa*. The 'Night Goods' for Hooton left Birkenhead Docks (later 'North') at 10.32pm and, in LM&S days, was worked by a Birkenhead North engine.

In 1906, the Wirral Railway ran two goods trains daily, each visiting all the yards from Docks to West Kirby and Seacombe at least twice but only once along the New Brighton line. Train No. 1 left Docks at 6.00am but was back ten minutes later after a brief visit to Bidston. At 6.30am, it departed for Liscard (20 minutes allowed here), arriving at Seacombe & Egremont at 7.00am. Departure from Seacombe (presumably Oakdale) was not until 11.45, leaving plenty of time to shunt the coal yard, gas works and McKenna's sidings. The next stop was at Moreton (arrive 12.15pm, depart 1.20pm), followed by Hoylake (1.30 to 1.45pm), arriving at West Kirby at 2.00pm. After only 10 minutes at West Kirby, the train returned to Hoylake (the Up yard this time, no doubt, from 2.15 to 4.30pm), back to West Kirby (4.35 to 7.30pm), Hoylake again (7.25 to 8.25pm), followed by 20 minutes at Moreton, 10 minutes at Bidston and finally, arrival at Docks at 9.35pm. The Working Time Table dated 1st October 1906, from which these times are taken, makes no references to manning and it might be fair to assume that a single crew was at work for almost 16 hours.

Meanwhile, Train No. 2 was following a less strenuous circuit, leaving Docks at 9.00am to spend 5 minutes at Moreton, before running non-stop to West Kirby (55 minutes stay), then 10 minutes at Hoylake, a brief call at Moreton again and back to Docks at 11.15am. At 11.45am, Train No. 2 was away again, arriving at Wallasey at 11.55am after perhaps having glimpsed Train No. 1 coming off the Seacombe branch. After an hour at Wallasey, the train was at New Brighton from 1.05pm until it departed for Docks at 2.20, arriving there at 2.30pm. Twenty minutes were spent at Docks before Train No. 2 departed for Seacombe where, after a 10 minute pause at Liscard, it arrived at 3.15pm. Seacombe was left after 20 minutes and the duty ended following a 3.50pm arrival at Birkenhead Docks. Like all goods timetables, these paths were actually operated as the traffic required. However, their timings are more likely to have been adhered to than most goods workings, since they were designed to fit into the spaces of a fairly intensive passenger timetable. It should be noted that there was little variation in this time table until after Grouping

Less predictable were the Great Central goods trains, which had to be worked forward by Wirral engines from Bidston to Docks, although how far on to the MD&HB lines they travelled is not known. Instructions included:

'Traffic brought in by the Great Central Co. (North Wales Branch) Trains to Bidston will be worked to and from the Docks by Special Engines as required. Signalmen must therefore be on the look-out for these Trains at all times.'
'Mr. Jones, Docks, will provide a Yardman who will see the Trains through, and attend the Level Crossing Gates.'
'The up and down running lines through Birkenhead Docks Goods Yard must be kept clear for the passage of Goods and Coal Trains.'

It is assumed that Great Central engines worked through to Docks goods station and on to the MD&HB lines after the extension over the 'diamond crossing' was opened. The 'Coal Trains' mentioned above would be destined mostly for the coal tips around Cavendish Wharf.

Guards were provided with a rough ready-reckoner to help them calculate goods loads. The gross weight of a loaded coal truck was assumed to be 15 tons, bricks 10 tons, cement in bags 13 tons, and so on. The engines were listed with their permitted loads on each line. On the New Brighton and Seacombe branches the loads were about two thirds of those on the flat main line from Docks to West Kirby. Maximum trailing loads varied from 220 tons behind engines No's 3 and 4 on the branches, up to 620 tons for engines No's 12 and 13 on the main line. Apparently, any Wirral engine might have to take its turn on goods trains.

The goods sheds at New Brighton and Wallasey (Grove Road) were not much used for their intended purpose (an impression borne out by the photograph on page 46), although the Wirral seems to have carried a reasonable parcels traffic. The Grove Road building had space for letting, which gave rise to what, in modern jargon,

A view of Wallasey (Grove Road) station, looking towards Birkenhead and taken circa 1925, showing the goods yard which, like most stations on the Wirral lines in the later inter-war years, handled only coal and mineral traffic. Harrison Drive, on the left, had been slightly diverted during the construction of the New Brighton branch in 1887-88, with two dog-leg bends either side of the railway bridge. It was thronged in the summer with sun seekers walking down to the seashore. Note that wind-blown sand was something of a problem at this location and must have required regular clearing. TED LLOYD COLLECTION

might be called a seasonal intermodal traffic flow. On the shore near Harrison Drive there were a few bathing machines, popular with families who would rent one for a summer's day among the dunes. The 'vehicles' were taken to Grove Road for maintenance and storage during the winter months; whether they did so by rail is uncertain. However, the construction of the New Promenade did away with such things.

The Wirral lines were also involved in three major civil engineering projects which generated useful, if short-lived, goods traffic. Bidston Moss was a convenient dump for surplus material for over a century and the railway carried much of it, until the high embankments looked much smaller. The dock construction schemes at Vittoria and at Bidston also produced large volumes of surplus material from which the railway profited. Some of this material was probably dumped at the last rail-connected construction site, the New Promenade at New Brighton.

Private Sidings, Their Traffic and Locomotives

This section lists in more detail the known sidings which provided traffic for the Wirral Railway and includes details of their locomotives, although excluding engines which worked only on the Dock Board railways.

T.W. Davies, Contractor, Bidston-Seacombe Rly 1893-96

The Seacombe Branch was built from a point near Gorsey Lane, near the gas works, working in both directions. In November 1893, Davies wrote to the Wallasey Gas Committee asking if he could *'make a connection between his temporary roads and the siding at the new Gas Works for the purpose of hauling materials.'* He offered 3s 6d per truck for the privilege, provided the Committee would also haul the trucks from the several railway company depots and return the empties. He also offered to lay the roads and connect free of charge. The Gas Committee tooks its coal by rail but was paying haulage contractors to bring the wagons from the railway companies' yards on the Birkenhead side of the docks. Two of these contractors already had locomotives but most (including William Pugh, who was successful with a bid of 1s 6d per wagon) apparently did not. The Committee were interested in buying a locomotive so that they could undertake their own haulage and, in August 1893, had consulted the Dock Board, who replied with their usual list of charges and conditions. This left the Committee unsure of achieving cost savings and it was 1896 before they bought an engine. Without a locomotive, the Gas Committee could not perform Davies' haulage for him but, in November 1893, they offered him a simple wayleave of 1s per truck. There is no confirmation in the minutes that Davies accepted but it seems likely, and that his supplies and materials for building the Seacombe Branch were hauled through the gas works.

It is known that Davies' 0-4-0ST *Bristol* (Peckett 439/85) was employed on the Seacombe contract, because on 4th December 1893 it exploded, killing both driver and fireman. Davies had recently bought the locomotive from Meakin & Dean, contractors for the Park and New Brighton branches. In 1887, the Dock Board granted them permission for a locomotive to run on the dock railways. Which engine is uncertain but it may have been *Bristol*.

John Scott, The Vittoria Dock Contracts.

The contractor John Scott built this 8.5 acre Birkenhead dock from 1906 and it opened without ceremony on 1st July 1909. Unlike the Great Float, Vittoria had to be excavated from a dry-land site, so a great deal of spoil had to hauled away. On 3rd October 1906, Scott agreed terms with the Wirral Railway for siding connections near the northern triangle at Seacombe Junction and Slopes Branch Junction.

The surviving plan which records this agreement is unusually vague as to the precise location of the temporary connection to the triangle, so perhaps it was moved from time to time. More spoil was used to raise the ground level where McKenna's steelworks was under construction. Scott employed four six-coupled saddle tank locomotives on this contract. When bringing spoil to the Bidston tip they had a journey of several miles, presumably via Duke Street Bridge. It is not known whether these trains ran through to the tip sidings, or whether the Wirral Railway participated in their haulage. The Wirral had no suitable locomotive, nor would they have relished one of their own venturing on to the temporary tip lines, whilst the costs would have been much increased. It seems likely, therefore, that the 1906 agreements included permission for Scott's engines to work through to the tip sidings, including the steep climb up the new Slopes Branch. If so, the Wirral would have provided a pilotman, at least.

The locomotives used by Scott on the Vittoria contract were all 0-6-0STs:

Waskerley, Manning Wardle 1312/1896. Inside cylinders
Tynesider, Black Hawthorn 1116/1896. Inside cylinders
Sir William Black, Black Hawthorn 1115/1896. Inside cylinders
Butterley, Hunslet 617/1894. Outside cylinders

When the job was finished, the locos were sold with the other plant but two of them remained nearby. *Waskerley* went to Vernon's Mills at Seacombe, while *Tynesider* joined the hire fleet of Cudworth & Johnson, whose engines were usually to be found around Wallasey and Birkenhead. It was last on hire to William Johnson Lee, the haulage contractor. Scrapped by Cudworths in 1951, the locomotive's nameplates were transferred to another, even more venerable engine, which they sent back to Lee in its place.

English McKenna Process Co. Ltd, Seacombe (Duke St, Wallasey)

This complex and very modern factory operated only from 1905 to 1909. Its purpose was to take part-worn rails and, by re-rolling and heat treatment, to produce nearly new rails of a different or smaller section. Connections were made to both the Wirral Railway and the dock lines, the latter to take the output out for shipment abroad or coastwise. A new locomotive named *Edwin Hale Abbott*, an 0-4-0ST built by Hudswell Clarke (659/1904), was delivered in time to help with construction. The contractor, John Scott, had the permission of the Wirral Railway to dump spoil from Vittoria Dock on this site, which they owned, but access was almost certainly from the Dock Board lines. Permission for McKenna's locomotive to work over the dock lines and bridges was granted on 2nd July 1904, the charge being £25 per annum. A trailing connection from the Down (westbound) line of the Seacombe Branch was approved by Major Druitt of the Board of Trade. His report, dated 28th July 1904, describes how the necessary points and signals were worked from Oakdale goods yard cabin, which was known officially as Seacombe & Egremont Goods Yard signal box.

Despite success in the USA, the McKenna process found little favour here. The plant closed in 1909 and was so thoroughly retrieved that its site reverted to allotment gardens. The annual charge for using a locomotive on the dock lines was last paid on 2nd July 1911, so perhaps *Edwin Hale Abbott* was also employed on dismantling and shipping the plant. A 1930s plan shows the entire site as belonging to the LMS & GW Joint Railways. *Edwin Hale Abbott* was sold to Joseph Haigh Ltd, of Bruntcliffe Colliery in the West Riding of Yorkshire and the English McKenna company was wound up on 12th September 1911. Their office block on Dock Road proved more durable than the steelworks; it still stands and is known as 'McKenna's Buildings'. In recent years, some Vignoles rail on the Clay Cross-Crich tramway was found to have English McKenna roll marks when lifted for re-use on the Talyllyn Railway, where it remains.

Hoylake Gas Works

The Hoylake & West Kirby Gas & Water Co. was founded in 1877 and purchased by the UDC in 1926. Throughout this period, coal was delivered directly by the Wirral, the retort house being close to the railway. The works carbonised 4,400 tons of coal in 1908, rising to 8,976 in 1915. Its later history is dealt with in the next chapter.

Hoylake Electricity Works

The Hoylake & West Kirby UDC built its electricity works to the east of the gas works, commencing supply on 27th May 1901. The Council wished to oppose or control the gas company and saw this venture as a way of doing so. However, when the gas company proved commercially robust the UDC had to buy them out, which was a common situation in the north-west where municipal control

ABOVE: A rare view of the English McKenna works taken circa 1905. The private owner wagons in the picture all appear to belong to W.B. Dobell & Co. Ltd, who had offices in Seacombe and Birkenhead. The two nearest appear to be sandwiched between some internal user wagons, including a short wheelbase end tipping wagon. They are loaded with spoil or clinker and may have been temporarily pressed into use around the works pending despatch back to their owner. This view is contemporary with the plan of the works on page 55. JOHN HORNE COLLECTION

LEFT: Another early 20th century postcard view of Hoylake, which again shows the proximity of the gas works to the station. The building just behind the station was a carriage works, whilst the chimney in the centre right background belongs to Hoylake Electricity Works, which had its own private siding. NEIL PARKHOUSE COLLECTION

RAILWAY

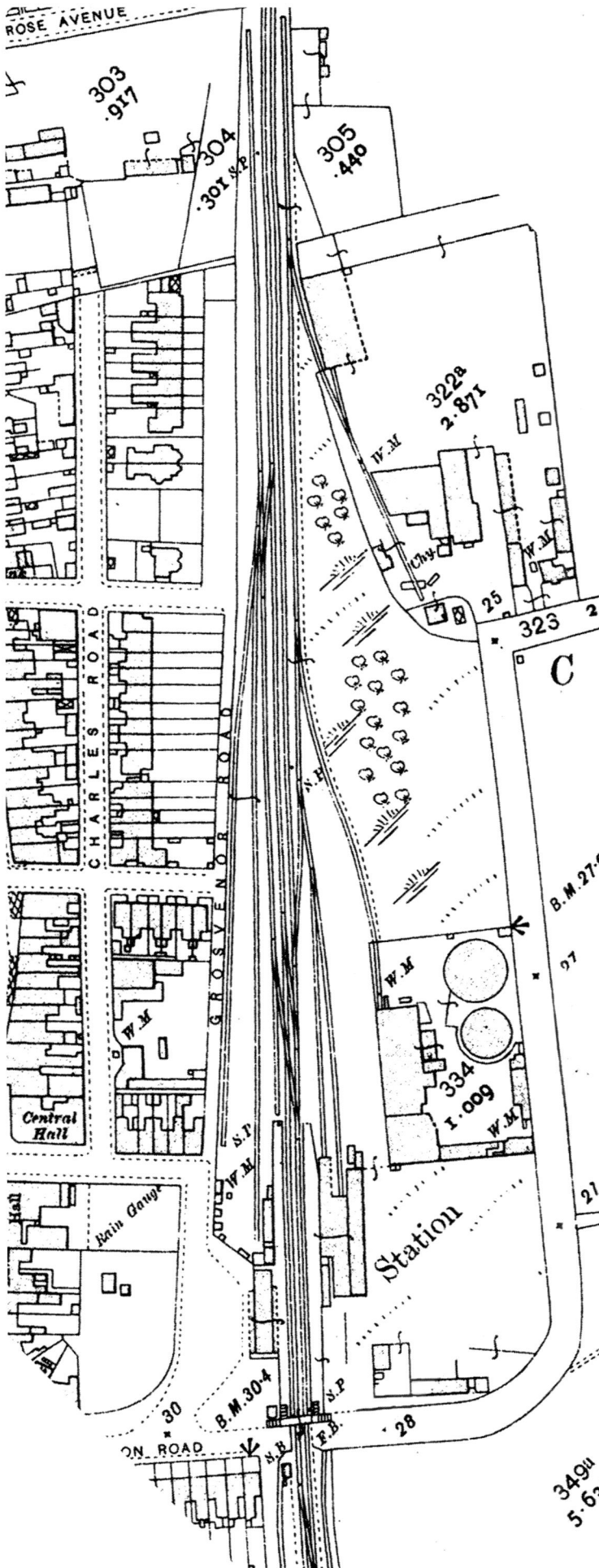

of utilities was favoured. The electricity works grew steadily and, by 1924, had no fewer than seven reciprocation steam engines driving alternators but no turbines. A row of five Lancashire boilers was served by a tall brick chimney, visible in some postcard views of the station. Unencumbered by any traction load, the undertaking was entirely a.c. from the first.

In 1924, about 4,800 tons of coal was burned, or roughly 440 railway wagon loads. The works ceased to generate electricity about 1930, or perhaps earlier, when a bulk supply was taken from Birkenhead. It must have been a source of some regret to the Engineer & Manager that, when the railway was electrified, the current came from Liverpool, even for lighting Hoylake station!

Wallasey Gas Works

Wallasey Gas Works was connected both to the Wirral Railway and the dock lines, the dock connection being far older. Coal for gas making and for the water works boilers came by rail, largely from South Lancashire and was delivered to Birkenhead via the GW/L&NWR Joint line. Haulage contractors used horses to bring the wagons over the Dock Board lines alongside Corporation Road and over Duke Street Bridge. A siding had entered the gas works since 1876 at least – on 3rd July 1876, the Dock Board resolved to charge £25 per annum for maintaining the associated paving where it crossed Dock Road. As already noted, it seems likely that, from about November 1893, the contractor T.W. Davies extended the gas works siding to give access to the temporary yard from which he constructed the Seacombe Branch. Davies suggested that the finished work could include a permanent connection from the branch into the gas works but it seems that direct 'main line' access was not then achieved. Nor did the new railway deflect the Gas Committee from their usual sources of coal. There was good gas coal in North Wales but none of it had found its way to Wallasey Gas Works by 1901, at least.

Parliamentary permission to lay a branch from the MD&HB lines was given in 1901 in a General Act obtained by the UDC. This was an additional connection *'at a point to the south of Gorsey Lane'*, for which the Dock Board's Works Committee gave consent on 31st May 1901. This further investment by the UDC confirms that they did not yet see the Wirral Railway as part of their coal supply line and, in fact, a trailing connection from the Wirral's Down line into the gas works was not made until 1904. A letter dated 28th May 1904 from Ernest S. Wilcox, Resident Engineer of the Wirral Railway, informed the Board of Trade that the gas works siding would be ready for inspection in about a month. There were other things overdue for inspection and Major Druitt approved the signal cabin controlling Oakdale Goods Yard, and the new connections to both the English McKenna steelworks and the gas works in his report dated 28th July 1904. A single-lever ground frame controlling access to the gas works was released by an Annett's key, which was interlocked with the locking frame in the cabin at Oakdale. All of this equipment was made in Liverpool by The Railway Signal Co. Ltd, Fazakerley.

HOYLAKE STATION 1912

Hoylake station, as shown on the 2nd edition 25 inch OS 1912. Immediately behind the station was a carriage works, with two sidings running into the buildings. To the right is the gas works and above that is the electricity works. These were both served by private sidings running back off the same headshunt, so neither could be accessed directly from the main running line. The main line heads north eastwards off the top of the page to Birkenhead and Seacombe, and curves south in the other direction bound for West Kirby. Hoylake goods yard was on the Up side of the line. ORDNANCE SURVEY

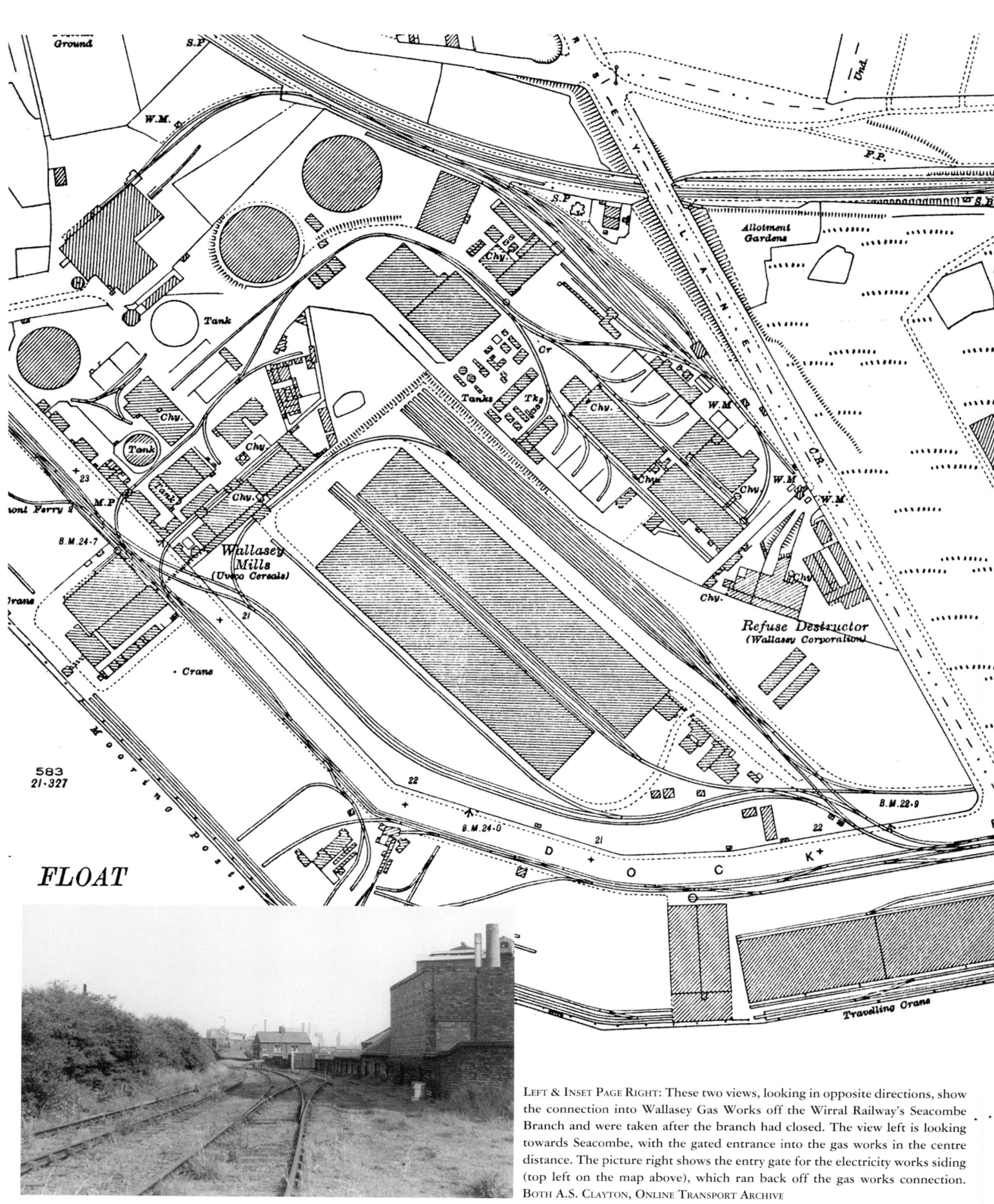

LEFT & INSET PAGE RIGHT: These two views, looking in opposite directions, show the connection into Wallasey Gas Works off the Wirral Railway's Seacombe Branch and were taken after the branch had closed. The view left is looking towards Seacombe, with the gated entrance into the gas works in the centre distance. The picture right shows the entry gate for the electricity works siding (top left on the map above), which ran back off the gas works connection. BOTH A.S. CLAYTON, ONLINE TRANSPORT ARCHIVE

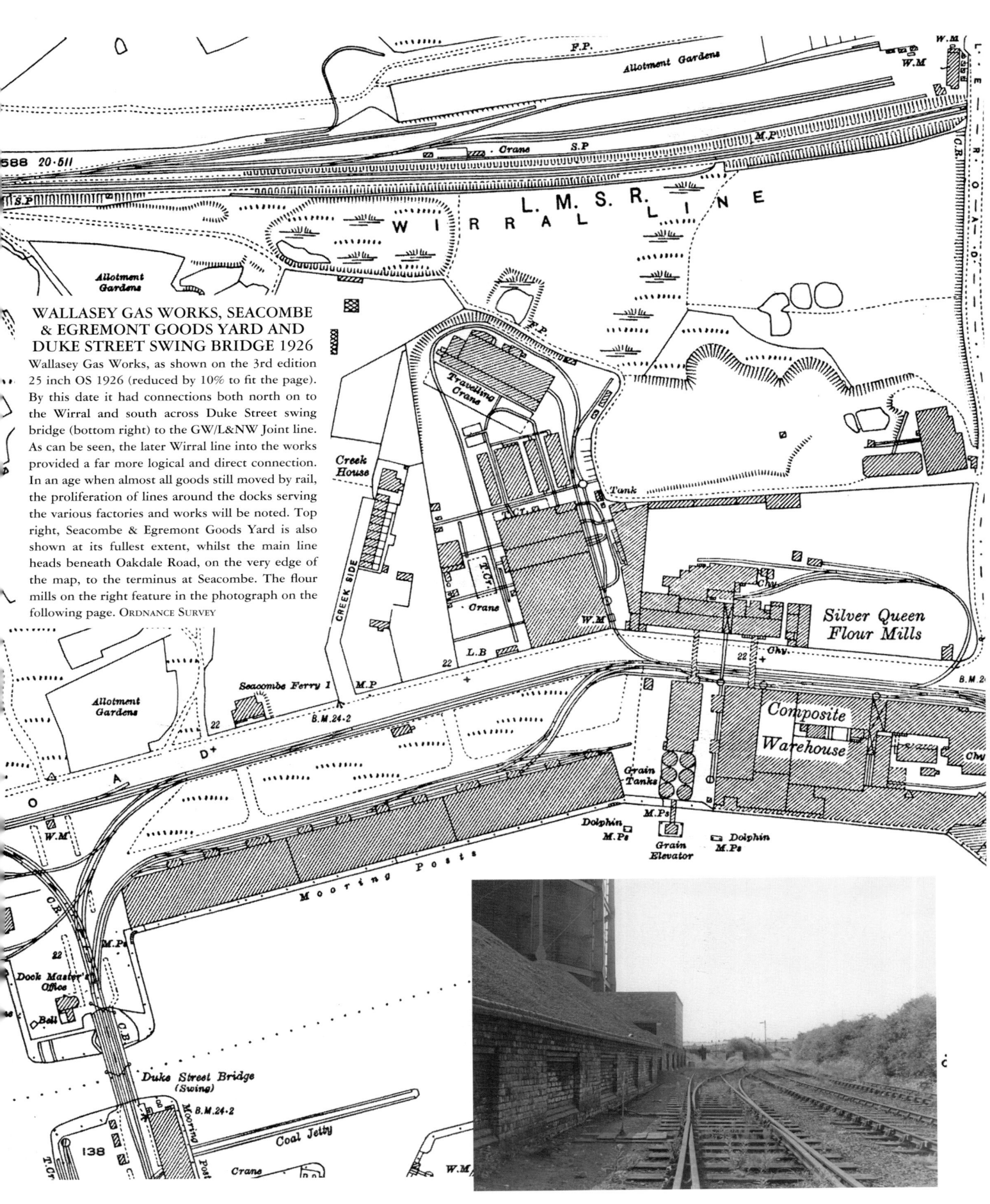

WALLASEY GAS WORKS, SEACOMBE & EGREMONT GOODS YARD AND DUKE STREET SWING BRIDGE 1926

Wallasey Gas Works, as shown on the 3rd edition 25 inch OS 1926 (reduced by 10% to fit the page). By this date it had connections both north on to the Wirral and south across Duke Street swing bridge (bottom right) to the GW/L&NW Joint line. As can be seen, the later Wirral line into the works provided a far more logical and direct connection. In an age when almost all goods still moved by rail, the proliferation of lines around the docks serving the various factories and works will be noted. Top right, Seacombe & Egremont Goods Yard is also shown at its fullest extent, whilst the main line heads beneath Oakdale Road, on the very edge of the map, to the terminus at Seacombe. The flour mills on the right feature in the photograph on the following page. ORDNANCE SURVEY

Wallasey Gas Works in Gorsey Lane, looking south towards Birkenhead on 16th July 1925, just fifteen months after it was opened as an all-weather highway. The road is descending from the bridge over the Seacombe Branch and the sidings run at a lower level behind the wall on the right. The Dock Board railway runs from left to right across the foot of Gorsey Lane and the short length of road visible to the left here leads to Duke Street Bridge, giving road and rail access to the Birkenhead side of the Dock Estate. The former English McKenna steel rolling mill with its sidings occupied the land to the left. COURTESY WIRRAL ARCHIVE

ABOVE: A panoramic view of the Seacombe Branch between Gorsey Lane and Seacombe & Egremont Goods (Oakdale Sidings). The signal box controlling movements to and from the goods yard and other adjacent sidings (on which the four wagons are standing) can be seen centre right. The principal buildings in the background are Buchanan's Flour Mills though there were a few small engineering works in the complex. The long low building to the right is the transit shed for Berths 1 and 3 Duke Street, on the East Float Dock. The pointed tower just visible over the taller buildings is the hydraulic tower of the Mersey Docks & Harbour Board, which provided power for bridges and capstans; the building, minus the top of the tower, still exists in a somewhat derelict condition, though preservation is being considered. It is of interest to note that whilst some of the flour mill buildings were destroyed in air raids, others are currently being converted into luxury flats. The picture dates from the 2nd June 1917 and the land in the foreground is in use as allotments. Gorsey Lane was not opened as an all weather road until April 1924. COURTESY WIRRAL ARCHIVE

LEFT: Gorsey Lane bridge and the gas works connection head shunt, with the entrance gate just showing on the right. The Home signal for the gas works connection, seen in both of these views, was mounted on a low post to aid sighting through the bridge. Neatly framed in the arch is the distinctive outline of the Liver Building, on the other side of the Mersey.

BELOW: Part of the gas works complex showing one of the holders, again after closure of the Seacombe Branch. The gated entrance can just be made out to the right of the buffer stop. Note the coal piled up behind the boundary wall. BOTH A.S. CLAYTON, ONLINE TRANSPORT ARCHIVE

More modern plant in the gas works relied much less on cannel and the rich coals of South Lancashire. A wider choice of coals could be carbonised, including Yorkshire and North Wales, especially after vertical retorts were installed in 1912. The Great Central/Wirral route for incoming coal was no longer at a disadvantage and there was no compulsion to haul gas coal across the Dock Estate. Having a direct railway connection also made it easier to get the best value from by-product tar, ammoniacal liquor and (especially) coke, whenever the local merchants could not absorb it. However, there was a tar distillery on the other side of the Great Float, while the Dock Board and the GW/L&NW Joint were both coke users, so some outgoing traffic to the dock lines was likely to have continued. When the docks were very busy, for example during the two World Wars, local coal traffic must have been a nuisance and might be expected to arrive via the Wirral lines. Certainly it did so throughout the 1950s.

The annual tonnage of coal carbonised at Wallasey had reached about 19,000 tons in 1896, which equates to approximately 2,500 wagon loads depending on the mix of 8-ton and 10-ton wagons received. The chosen haulage contractor, Willam J. Lee, reduced his price to 1s per wagon, perhaps because he was now using locomotives as well as horses. His example may have persuaded the Gas Committee to carry out their own haulage using steam. Having rejected the offer of the second-hand locomotive *Wirral*, used by Davies on the Seacombe Branch contract, tenders were invited from nine manufacturers. Andrew Barclay & Sons were successful at £725, providing a new 0-4-0ST which was named *W.G. Ellery* (Works No. 783/1897). The reason for the delayed delivery is unknown; perhaps Lee's contract could not be cut short.

W.G. Ellery spent some years crossing and recrossing Duke Street Bridge hauling loaded and empty coal wagons over the Dock Board's lines. After 1904, when the gas works made a connection to the Wirral Railway, the need to cross the dock system must have declined until *W.G. Ellery* and its successors were confined to the boundaries of the gas and electricity works. A second 0-4-0ST, Barclay No. 1304, named *Eastwood*, was delivered new in 1912.

PRIVATE OWNER WAGONS ON THE WIRRAL SYSTEM

The great majority of the non-passenger traffic consigned to Wirral Railway destinations was coal for local consumption, either as house coal or in the gas and electricity works of Hoylake and (especially) Wallasey. As the former declined, the latter increased. 'Wagon Hire' was a significant proportion of the total cost of railway freight. Some coal dealers and merchants found it cheaper to acquire their own railway wagons, although many of them were actually on hire from companies which specialised in providing and maintaining such vehicles rather than purchased outright. Privately owned wagons avoided demurrage charges but still had to pay Siding Rent, unless they had a private siding on which to take refuge. The railway companies were not obliged to provide wagons for this traffic.

Almost every station on the Wirral lines had its own coal yard until the 1950s, together with a small fleet of wagons which 'belonged' there. From 1939, all coal wagons were 'pooled' by Government decree; the coal merchants were paid a rental for their use and, finally, compensation when the wagons were nationalised in 1948. The wagon pool put an end to the homing instincts of most wagons, few of which were seen again by their pre-1939 owners.

Only a minority of coal merchants had their own wagons and

This enlargement from a postcard view of Hoylake station (the full view can be found on page 125), looking north circa 1906, shows an interesting array of wagons in the small goods yard behind the Birkenhead-bound platform. The left-most wagon belongs to E.F. Beddard & Co., coal merchants at Hoylake and West Kirby. Numbered 31 and looking quite new, the wagon's lettering is white shaded black and the strapping is also painted black. The background colour is probably grey but could also be red. Behind it can be seen the office of S. Parr, coal merchant, who it is believed also owned a few wagons as he appears on Railway Clearing House lists. On the right, the two end wagons belong to the Shelton Iron, Steel & Coal Co. Ltd and to Hanley Collieries, both from the Stoke-on-Trent area. To the right of the Shelton wagon is a Moreton Brick & Tile Co. 3-plank open, with a wagon belonging to Crompton & Shawcross, coal factors of Wigan, next to that. Behind, coupled to the Hanley wagon, is one lettered for Winstanley, also from Wigan. Finally, and perhaps most interesting of all, on the right is one of the Wirral Railway's own open wagons, lettered WR, the only glimpse we have other than a brake van of their small goods fleet. The livery was dark grey, with black underframe and also black strapping by the look of this view. JOHN RYAN COLLECTION

some also used colliery owned vehicles in addition. A wide variety of non-Wirral wagons were also to be seen, therefore. Several large collieries had branch offices in New Brighton or Wallasey and, although their wagons did not carry local names, they were certainly part of the local scene for many years. The railway itself was a major consumer of coal, much of which came from the North Wales field. For example, the Wirral Railway consumed about 3,500 tons of Bettisfield coal in 1892. In 1893, the contract was won by Messrs Barnes & Co., whose location is uncertain but their bid was accepted subject to the coal being from Bersham Colliery. Both pits were near Wrexham and both had substantial fleets of wagons which, for a year or so, would have been a regular sight at Birkenhead Docks station. However, photographs which show private owner wagons in WR goods yards indicate a lot of housecoal for the Wirral was also coming from the Lancashire and Staffordshire coalfields.

The wagons employed in certain special traffics were not pooled and this minority continued as 'Private Owner' through the British Railways days. Today, almost all railway wagons are again 'Private Owner'. The notable examples of non-pool wagons on the Wirral were the large bogie hoppers which shuttled between Bidston Ore Dock and John Summers' works at Shotton. Others were mostly oil tankers but these were seldom seen on the Wirral lines except for Slopes Branch traffic to the petroleum stores and to the Anglo-American Oil Company's depot at Wharf Road, Birkenhead. These will be dealt with in more detail in Chapter 4.

The businesses, colliery owners and merchants known to have run railway wagons and which were served by the Wirral Railway are examined in the following paragraphs. The references to 1926 and 1933 relate to the Railway Clearing House lists of wagon operators which appeared in those years, the latter being significantly shorter. It should be stressed that much detail work, outside the scope of this volume, remains to be done on this particular aspect of Wirral Railway history but the information included here will give an introduction to those businesses using private owner wagons on the system.

The *Liverpool Trades Directory* for 1900 places Edward Frederick Beddard & Co. at Station Yard, Grange Road, West Kirby. However, Beddard appears to have begun trading around 1886; on 26th February that year, the Midland Waggon Co. records one 10-ton wagon leased to him at £7.10s per annum for one year, then on 23rd December, the lease-purchase of one new 10-ton wagon at £8 per annum for seven years. In 1909, Beddard was included in the L&NWR's 1909 list of coal merchants who had a Ledger Account with them. They were listed as coal merchants in the 1928 *Colliery Year Book* at the Railway Yard, Hoylake but are back at Grange Road, West Kirby in the 1938 edition. E. Beddard & Co. of Albert Road, Hoylake, appear in both the 1926 and 1933 RCH lists.

Kelly's Directory of Liverpool for 1894 lists fourteen separate office addresses for Jonathan Blundell & Son around Bootle, Waterloo, Walton, Seaforth and West Derby, as well as at Seacombe (this was before the branch had opened). The company name later changed to Blundell's Pemberton Collieries of Wigan, Lancashire. However, whilst they were obviously receiving significant supplies of coal, no evidence of them having their own wagons has yet been discovered.

Richard Evans & Co. Ltd, Haydock, St Helens, Lancashire were a large and long standing firm whose wagons were regularly seen on the Wirral. They featured heavily in *Kelly's Liverpool Directory* of 1894 and the company seems to have been much involved in the retailing of its own coal. There were a large number of local coal offices listed in the Liverpool area, as well as at 13 Railway Yard, Abbey Street, Birkenhead and Poulton Bridge, Wallasey. Presumably Evans' wagons could usually be seen nearby. A similar list appeared in *Gore's Directory* of 1900 but added Dock Road, Seacombe station, Moreton and the Station Yard, Atherton Street, New Brighton on the Wirral system, and Upton station on the GC line. By 1938, four large collieries were being operated by the company: Golborne, near Newton-le-Willows, where a total of 730 men were employed,

New Brighton station circa 1905. The station buildings housed the Wirral Company's head office for many years. The goods yard is on the left and again a good selection of PO wagons are on view, with identifiable ones including Sneyd Collieries Ltd (Burslem), John Speakman & Sons, Chatterley Whitfield, Haydock Coal and Moore, with a Cannock Chase wagon visible on the siding behind. New Brighton Tower in the right background was 100 feet taller than its Blackpool counterpart but became unsafe following a lack of maintenance during WW1 and was demolished in 1920-21. As originally planned the line would have continued approximately to the group of buildings in the left background. Note the station name on the platform seat. JOHN ALSOP COLLECTION

plus Lyme Pits (employing 1,370), Newton (755) and Old Boston (1,100), which were all situated in Haydock. They also supplied coal to other local merchants in the Liverpool area, advertising the fact on the back of commerically produced picture postcard views. At least one is known for a merchant on the Wirral Railway (see below).

In the 1901 census, James Britland, coal merchant, (aged 48 and born in St. Helens) was living in the parish of Poulton cum Seacombe. His son, Robert Britland, aged 19, was a coal carter. There had been a small coal yard at Liscard & Poulton station from the opening of the Seacombe Branch in 1895 but, if there were similar facilities at Seacombe & Egremont (the terminus), they were short-lived. In 1901, as previously mentioned, a coal and goods yard serving Seacombe was opened at Oakdale, with road access from Oakdale Road. It seems likely, therefore, that Britland's wagons would have been seen there and perhaps also at Liscard & Poulton yard. A further possibility is that Britland used one of the yards in Birkenhead Road in the early years and was therefore supplied over the Dock Board lines. Britland is known to have run six wagons (at least) built by the Midland Railway Carriage & Wagon Co.: Wagon No's 1 and 2, both 10-ton, were registered by the Great Central on 1st November 1898; further 10-tonners were registered on 17th February 1899, 9th April 1900, 21st February 1901 and 14th November 1901. The North Wales coalfield is likely to have been Britland's major source and his wagons would have spent much of their lives on WM&CQR and GCR metals but they were 'at home' on the Wirral Railway, not the GCR. Although the Wirral is said to have registered wagons, apparently they were not doing so in 1899-1901, nor has a register been found. Britland was not listed among Coal Merchants in the 1938 *Colliery Year Book*. The source of these notes is James Britland's great-grandson.

W.B. Dobell & Co. appear in *Gore's Directory* 1900 edition but not in the 1894 *Kelly's*. They had two offices in Liverpool and also at 61 Hamilton Street, Birkenhead and Birkenhead Road, Seacombe. Their wagon No. 768 appears in a photograph of McKenna's works at Seacombe and had probably arrived via the Wirral connection rather than the dock lines. The firm were not listed among Coal Merchants in the 1938 *Colliery Year Book*.

The Lancashire Coal Company's yard at Seacombe was probably that previously occupied by R. Evans & Co. Ltd. in East Street, which was connected to the Dock lines rather than the Wirral. They took over from Evans on 2nd July 1913. One of their six-plank wagons is partly visible in a postcard view of New Brighton station yard. The top two planks carry the lettering 'LANCASHIRE COAL COMPY.' and the bottom right quarter plank carries 'NEW BRIGHTON', with all the initial letters slightly enlarged. The body colour is dark, possibly black, and the white letters are probably unshaded. They were still listed as trading in the 1938 *Colliery Year Book*, from addresses in Wallasey, Liverpool and London NW10.

Three of the Moreton Brick & Tile Co. Ltd's 3-plank wagons appear in the view of New Brighton yard on page 46 and another at Hoylake (opposite). Their private siding was in use by 1903 and the firm appears in the 1926 RCH lists but not in 1933.

Now is just the time to lay in Coal before prices change.

Haydock Coals are the best

Prices from our Local Agent—
Mr. D. WILLIAMS,
Grange Road, WEST KIRBY.
And Station Yard, HOYLAKE.
Telephone No. 6; Birkenhead.
Agent - Mr. JOHN WILLIAMS,
74, Argyle Street, BIRKENHEAD.

Richd Evans & Co., Limited.

WR No. 14, one of the 4-4-4 Tanks new in 1903, is seen approaching Birkenhead Docks station with a service for Birkenhead Park, in a view taken just prior to the Grouping. The train comprises a motley assortment of Wirral Railway coaching stock. The leading carriage is a 6-wheeled vehicle, probably one of the Third class coaches built by Cravens in 1894, followed by two of the 4-wheeled carriages supplied by Falcon of Loughborough in 1888, a 5-compartment Third and a 3-compartment Brake Third. The three bogie carriages are likely to be those built by the Wirral themselves at Hoylake, using old Falcon 4-wheeler bodies on new frames and bogies the company had specially purchased. Just out of picture, another Brake Third will be bringing up the rear. The wagons on the right are standing at the entrance to Birkenhead Docks goods station and the train has just passed Birkenhead North No. 2 signal box. The GC wagon alongside the Clay Cross private owner gives a hint to the large amount of traffic from the Great Central which was worked over this short section of the Wirral. T.B. MAUND COLLECTION

Passenger Services: The 1906 Working Time Table

As would be expected for a railway serving a largely suburban hinterland, the Wirral's passenger services were quite intensive. In 1906, departures from New Brighton consisted of one to West Kirby and thirty-seven to Park, from West Kirby there were sixteen to Seacombe and twenty-two to Park, whilst from Seacombe there were thirteen GCR trains to Chester, Wrexham, etc. and sixteen WR to West Kirby. Almost all were balanced by return workings.

New Brighton

On weekdays, the first movements on the Wirral were the light engines which left Docks at 4.50am for New Brighton and 4.55am for West Kirby, respectively. The West Kirby engine took 14 minutes for the 6.5 miles and one wonders if the various crossing keepers were awake so early or were their gates left closed to road traffic in the small hours? The New Brighton engine next worked the 5.07am train (stabled at New Brighton overnight) to Park, where it was left to be brushed out by the Carriage Department. The engine then worked the 5.47 from Park to New Brighton where it was the first passenger arrival of the day at 5.56am. Four minutes later, at 6.0am, it left for Hoylake and West Kirby direct, the only such working of the day, primarily to carry the mail although passengers were admitted.

On Sundays, the New Brighton line did not really open until the 9.28am from Park arrived at 9.39. However, the GPO required an earlier service and Sundays saw the only officially-designated Mail Trains on the system, leaving Park at 5.47am for New Brighton and then 6.0 from New Brighton to Hoylake and West Kirby direct. Passengers were probably allowed to travel on these trains and apparently a full train set was employed. Reverting to weekdays, New Brighton saw a further thirty-six departures after the early morning West Kirby, all of them to Birkenhead Park and mostly on the hour or half hour. After the last arrival in New Brighton, the engine left its carriages and departed light engine to Docks. Almost the only perturbations in this rhythm were the 10.30am from New Brighton, which paused two minutes later at Warren, and a return departure from Warren to New Brighton at 3.44pm. On Sundays, Warren had one Up train but no Down!

There were two empty carriage workings, one from Birkenhead Park which arrived at New Brighton at 7.53am and, unusually, one from Seacombe which arrived at 9.8am. The latter seems to have been the only regular train to use the curve between Seacombe Junctions 2 and 3 (also known as New Brighton Junctions 1 and 2) in an east-to-north direction, with nothing to polish the rails travelling the other way.

A view along Victoria Road, New Brighton, circa 1920, with the large projecting sign advertising the Wirral's station on the left. Note the substantial structure required to support it. JOHN RYAN COLLECTION

A strengthened rush hour train leaves Birkenhead Docks station for West Kirby or New Brighton headed once again by 4-4-4T No. 14. Note the two large ships visible in Birkenhead Docks in the left background. JOHN RYAN COLLECTION

An unidentified 4-4-4T (either No. 11, 13 or 14) departs bunker first from West Kirby station around 1910 with a train for Birkenhead. Note the 4-wheeled Brake leading; one of these vehicles was permanently attached to each end of a rake of passenger stock. The curve connecting the Wirral to the LNW/GW Joint line to Hooton leads off to the left. The Joint line had a separate terminus here, the platform of which can just be made out through the steam in the left background. T.B. MAUND COLLECTION

West Kirby

Weekday departures from West Kirby to Park began with the 5.20am, its engine having arrived light. This train skipped Leasowe, Bidston and Docks but made a two-minute connection at Park, which brought its passengers into Liverpool Central at 5.47am. Several morning trains skipped Meols or Leasowe, or both, and few called at Docks until mid-morning. In all, some twenty-two trains daily left West Kirby for Park, many on or about the hour. The last left at 10.55pm, after which there were two engines which stabled their trains before leaving light for Docks engine shed.

Interspersed between these twenty-two trains for Park and the Mersey Railway were sixteen for Seacombe and the ferry to Liverpool Pier Head. It was almost an hourly service, half the trains leaving at quarter past the hour, from 7.0am until the last three at 7.30, 9.00 and 10.30pm.

In 1905, three fast trains were provided morning and evening between West Kirby and Park, bringing West Kirby within 1½ hours of Manchester via Liverpool Central and the Cheshire Lines.

However, the two changes *en route* prevented the growth of a high class commuter traffic to Manchester, such as existed from Southport and the Fylde coast, and these trains were short-lived, *Bradshaw* of February 1906 showing no trace of them. In fact, at that time the best morning trains from West Kirby at 8.33 and 9.13am, not stopping at Moreton and Leasowe, ran to Seacombe in 20 minutes.

On Sundays, the Mail Train came and went early but otherwise the first passenger arrival at West Kirby was the 9.53am, returning to Park at 10.0. A total of only seven trains served Park, plus seven to Seacombe on a Sunday.

Seacombe

Departures from Seacombe had the added variety of Great Central trains but these were not supposed to carry local passengers. Up GCR trains only stopped at Bidston and Liscard to set down, and Down trains only did so to pick up. Inevitably, there was an exception; they could pick up '*specially endorsed contract ticket holders from Bidston to Seacombe, who will require to give notice to the Bidston Station Master as*

Wirral Railway No. 1 passes Seacombe No. 2 Junction (sometimes referred to as Seacombe West Junction) with a service for Seacombe on 19th April 1919. The train comprises a half rake of 4-wheeled stock with two bogie carriages, a compartment Third and a compartment Brake End, on the rear. T.B. MAUND COLLECTION

The 'temporary' sleeper-built platforms at Seacombe & Egremont are clearly discernible in this circa 1908 view, looking west and one of a number of photographs of similar scenes taken at this station. Perhaps the postcard photographer responsible hoped to sell copies to some of the passengers alighting from the trains featured; many of them would have been tourists or visitors and the likelihood is that he would hand out cards advertising his premises, where copies would be displayed for sale within a few hours of the pictures being taken. The train seen here, from West Kirby, is headed by 1894 Beyer, Peacock-built 0-4-4T No. 7, whilst the stock on the right is Great Central. The roof of the signal box can just be glimpsed over the top of the coaches. Note the barrier dividing platforms 2 and 3, the purpose of which appears to have been to keep apart arriving and departing passengers on busy days in the holiday season. The barrier does not appear in later pictures of the station. Note, too, the milk churns on all three platforms, indicating a healthy traffic at this time. Church Road bridge is in the background and straw boaters are the order of the day. JOHN ALSOP COLLECTION

ABOVE: No. 15 with the 5.43pm Seacombe to West Kirby service near Hoylake at 6.07pm on 13th August 1923. Although, strictly speaking, following the Grouping and now into the LM&SR period, it will be noted that little has changed and the train formation remains the same.

BELOW: No. 15 again, this time approaching Birkenhead Docks with the 2.15pm service from New Brighton on 20th April 1919, which includes two bogie coaches but only one 4-wheeled brake. Note the weighty but decorative cast iron bracket supporting the platform holding the bracket arm of the signal, another Railway Signal Company product. BOTH JOHN WARD COLLECTION, COURTESY JOHN HORNE

ABOVE: An unidentified 4-4-4T hauling a single standard set comprising three bogie coaches with a 4-wheeled brake at each end. This view was the work of well known railway photographer H. Gordon Tidey. JOHN ALSOP COLLECTION

BELOW: The forest of signals facing locomotive crews as they approached Bidston East Junction, although the pair seen here on the footplate of WR No. 1 seem more interested in acknowledging the presence of the photographer. The train is the 3.06pm from Birkenhead Park and the date is again 20th April 1919. The bracket signal the train has just passed indicates that it is bound for West Kirby. JOHN WARD COLLECTION, COURTESY JOHN HORNE

An overall view of Seacombe station circa 1920, with the rather inconsequential station building the Wirral provided here, another legacy of the station's 'temporary' status, in the right distance. On the left, a Great Central train in the charge of an unidentified 4-4-2T waits to depart platform 3 with a train for Wrexham, whilst one of the Wirral's 0-4-4 tanks stands at platform 2 with a service for West Kirby. It is not clear why there should be a check rail on the line serving this platform; it does not appear in the earlier view and was still in place in the 1930s but had apparently been removed by the 1950s. Note the tall wooden hoarding for advertisements, facing away from the station. The site of the intended terminus lay beyond this fence and to the left of the hotel, the roof of which can be seen above it. J.F. WARD COLLECTION, COURTESY JOHN HORNE

necessary'. 'Contract' was the usual term on Merseyside for a season ticket.

The first GCR train on weekdays started at Bidston, departing for Chester Northgate at 6.50am. There followed thirteen daily GCR departures from Seacombe between 7.50am and 8.55pm, of which seven were for Wrexham, five for Chester and one for Buckley Junction. Only on Saturdays was there a late train for North Wales, the 11.15pm for Chester via Connah's Quay. On Sundays, the GCR ran only two trains from Seacombe to Chester and three to Wrexham. The Wirral ran sixteen Seacombe to West Kirby trains each weekday and there were also two empty carriage trains, the 9.0am to New Brighton having already been described. The other, leaving at 9.34am, ran to Park and was the only train in the timetable described as 'Parcels'.

To fill a gap on Sunday mornings, a Wirral train left Park at 8.55am for Seacombe, to work the 9.30am from Seacombe to West Kirby. Passengers booked from Park or Docks to West Kirby and the GCR line were *'conveyed via Seacombe & Egremont'*. The timetable footnote ended with the remarkable phrase *'North Wales passengers change at Liscard'*. The first Down train of the day, the GCR's 9.0am from Seacombe, picked them up two minutes after they stepped out of the Wirral's first Up (eastbound) train of the day.

Connections

The importance of the ferry connection at Seacombe was emphasized by the 'Telephonic Communication' which the Wirral Railway set up between Seacombe station and their 'Landing Stage Office', which comprised a hut (with gas lamp) rented from the MD&HB on George's Landing Stage, Liverpool Pier Head. The Clerk-in-Charge could book through tickets from this office to the Wirral Railway and beyond, which included the six-minute ferry crossing. Another, rather grander office offered the same for the Joint Lines via the Woodside ferries and Birkenhead Woodside station. Beneath their floating pontoon ran the Mersey Railway, whose booking offices were well stocked with through tickets to both systems and even to London. Ordinary ferry passengers paid at turnstiles on the Wirral side of the water but those with through tickets by rail would pass through the 'Contractor's Gate'.

The Wirral Railway Clerk-in-Charge of the Landing Stage Office was instructed: *'In all cases where the time between the arrival of the Ferry Steamer at Seacombe and the departure of the Train is less than 10 minutes, telephonic notification must be given by the Clerk-in-Charge ... to Inspector at Seacombe, of late departure of the Boat.'* There was no suggestion of the ferries reciprocating in any way; most of their passengers reached Seacombe by the Council's own trams, not by train. The trams and later buses carried clock-face indicators showing the boat with which they connected.

The Wirral's timetables showed the ferry departures and arrivals with which Seacombe trains connected. Some were as close as four minutes, which required agility, but most were around eight or ten minutes. However, as the ferries ran every 10-15 minutes, these connections were largely irrelevant. Similarly, the connections at Birkenhead Park always showed the times into Liverpool Central (LL). The connections at Park mostly allowed between two and four

RIGHT: An interesting early 20th century rear view of Wirral passenger stock passing over Carr Lane Crossing, between Meols and Moreton. As this view illustrates, the Wirral system had little in the way of gradients to tax its locomotives. JOHN RYAN COLLECTION

BELOW: A classic view of a typical Wirral passenger train, with a brake composite at each end of a set of three bogie carriages, headed by No. 12, a Beyer, Peacock 0-6-4T new in April 1900. The service is an Up New Brighton train and the location is near the site of Warren Halt, where the line skirts the sea and is surrounded by sand dunes. JOHN RYAN COLLECTION

minutes but this was a simple cross-platform exchange, although passengers found it irksome, especially in winter.

The '*Change at Liscard for North Wales*' idea has already been mentioned; it is a reminder that the Wirral consistently referred to the GC as the '*Great Central (North Wales Branch &c.)*'. As for the Joint Lines service from Hooton to West Kirby, this does not appear in the Wirral's Working Time Table for 1906 and it would seem there was no co-ordination of passenger timings.

Saturdays

Given that Saturday mornings were part of the working week, the basic Saturday timetable was not very different from other weekdays but it did change with the seasons. When the July 1906 timetable was replaced on 6th October 1906, the changes included the withdrawal of six afternoon and evening departures from West Kirby, together with their return workings. Five of the six had been 'Saturdays Only'. The cancellations and changes were spread evenly between the Seacombe and Birkenhead Park lines; New Brighton was hardly touched, except that almost all Sunday timings were revised.

SIGNAL CABINS

The October 1906 timetable shows the signal cabin at Slopes Branch Junction to be open, although no trains are listed for the new branch. Perhaps the cabin was supervising spoil trains from the Vittoria Dock contract. Liscard & Poulton box was listed but had been ruled through as if recently closed, probably replaced by Slopes Branch. West Kirby cabin was the first to open, at 4.50am and the last to close at 11.50pm but Birkenhead No. 2 and Dee Junction were continuously open on weekdays. Meols and Wallasey cabins

LEFT: WR 0-6-4T No. 12 pauses at Hoylake station around 1910 with a West Kirby train. The view provides a close study of the decorative barge boarding to the signal box, on the left. There appears to be no record of the colour scheme for Wirral Railway structures but this view shows the boxes were painted a dark colour, possibly green or brown, with a lighter hue for the barge boards. The wooden footbridge behind looks to be painted the same dark colour. JOHN ALSOP COLLECTION

BELOW: Leasowe station probably circa 1920; compare with the pre-WW1 view on page 36. The level crossing and its attendant signalling, all controlled from the ground frame in the lean-to cabin on the platform, is nicely shown. Although the cabin is 'non-standard', it has been fitted with the same decorative barge boarding. JOHN ALSOP COLLECTION

were closed all day on Sundays; Wallasey and Seacombe Goods Yard opened only *'When required for Goods Trains'* even during the week. The eighteen signal cabins listed in 1906 were: Birkenhead Docks No. 1, Seacombe Junction No. 1, Birkenhead Docks No. 2, Seacombe Junction No's 2 & 3, Bidston East Junction, Slopes Branch Junction, Bidston West Junction, Liscard & Poulton, Dee Junction, Seacombe Goods Yard, Meols, Seacombe & Egremont, Moreton, Wallasey, Hoylake, New Brighton and West Kirby.

PROPOSED ELECTRIFICATION

At the turn of the century, when electrification of the Mersey Railway was under active consideration, there was serious debate about electrifying the Wirral and discussions took place between the two companies. The Wirral Railway Act 1900, passed in July of that year, granted powers to work the railway by electricity either separately or jointly with the Mersey Railway Co.; provision was made for the joint ownership of power stations, subject to agreement between the two companies and a body corporate, the Mersey & Wirral Electrical Joint Committee, was to be established to control power generation. Three sites for sub-stations were designated, at Birkenhead Docks goods station, on the triangular piece of land at Seacombe Junction and at Meols station. The Mersey Railway Act 1900 gave powers to establish the 'Mersey & Wirral Committee', a body comprising three directors from each company with an alternating chairman, the function of which would be to manage a joint undertaking. There was to be no casting vote and voting was to be by companies, not individuals. The existing body of the same name was to be renamed the 'Birkenhead Park Station Committee'.

The Wirral's adviser was Mr S.B. Cottrell, engineer of the Liverpool

LEFT: Wirral Railway advert from the *Railway Magazine*, 1914

An interesting early 20th century postcard view showing the complicated pointwork at the throat of West Kirby Wirral station, with the link to the GW/L&NW Joint line station curving off to the left. At the near end of the island platform, the locomotive at the head of a Birkenhead Park or Seacombe working is taking water prior to departure. Another engine is shunting the goods sidings in the left background, whilst in the left foreground, the passenger stock is stabled in one of the GW/L&NW Joint sidings. On the right, West Kirby signal box is positioned so as to have a clear view over all proceedings, although all the lower panes of glass, as well as some on the second level on this side, have been blanked out. Presumably, this was to cut out some of the effects of the sun on hot days. Note the wooden platform in front of the box protecting the linkage to the point rodding and the pulleys for the signal wires. The signalman appears to be leaning out of one of the far side windows, chatting to a mate at ground level reading a newspaper. Just behind him is another wooden platform, which appears to hold a coal supply for the box. The box is again in a dark colour scheme, which here seems to include the barge boards. JOHN RYAN COLLECTION

LEFT: Birkenhead Park station from the Mersey Railway sidings, with MR No. 7 *Orion* in residence. Built by Beyer, Peacock in 1864 for the Metropolitan Railway, it was rebuilt at Neasden in 1921, when it gained its cab, before migrating north to the Mersey. Plans to electrify the Wirral were never implemented, which meant passengers bound to and from stations west of here always had to change trains. No. 7 was broken up here at Birkenhead Park in September 1939. TED LLOYD COLLECTION

BELOW: Wallasey Village station, seen here prior to rebuilding for the 1938 electrification, was originally provided for the 'Seacombe Dodger' service. Each platform was reached by separate stairs from street level below. Note the corrugated iron structures and the notice boards devoted to the facilities of the Mersey and LM&S companies respectively. The smaller frame to the left of the lamp appears to contain a Crosville bus timetable, presumably as a result of the Rail/Road Liaison Committees set up from about 1930. TED LLOYD COLLECTION

Overhead Railway, who made an optimistic report. The chairman, T.H. Jackson, told shareholders in 1900 that the cost would be about £180,000 and this amount was authorised by the 1900 Act. This amount was later increased to £250,000 and then reduced to £225,000; these very large sums for the day deterred the directors from making a decision and the issue remained live for several years, so much so that, in its issue of 13th June 1903, *The Locomotive* magazine announced that a contract had just been signed with British Westinghouse for the complete electrification of the Wirral Railway on the same lines as the recently finished Mersey Railway. At the shareholders' meeting in May 1908, the chairman said:

> 'In our opinion it was necessary to prepare ourselves for such an eventuality and we have been very carefully watching the results of electric working in this country. I do not think that anyone can say that such a result is satisfactory from an investor's point of view even when large populations exist at each end of the line as well as at intermediate places and, as the population at one end of our line is very small (some 12,000), it is evident that before electric working becomes commercially possible, there must be cheaper installation and the working expenses must be covered. From time to time we hear of this being done but we are waiting for a satisfactory demonstration of it.'

Whilst remarking that no money had been made by other electric railways, the directors gave cautious approval but only in principle and consequently nothing was done. Half a century later, completely unused slip rings on the Mersey Railway's generating plant at Shore Road, Birkenhead still bore witness to plans for supplying the Wirral Railway with power if it had been able to finance electrification.

The Mersey Railway was the first British steam railway to be converted to electric working and one of the first in the world to employ a form of multiple unit control. The contract for electrification was awarded to the British Westinghouse company in July 1901 and electrical working commenced on 3rd May 1903. This brought to an end the possibility of through carriage working to Liverpool. The elimination of noxious fumes in the tunnel, the novelty of riding on an electric train and the acceleration of services brought an immediate increase in traffic, some of which flowed on to the Wirral, though T.H. Jackson complained that the additional traffic was less than expected.

THE SEACOMBE DODGER

The chord between the Seacombe and New Brighton lines at Seacombe Junction enabled a Seacombe-New Brighton service to be run, an eventuality which Wallasey councillors had obviously not foreseen when they gave the Wirral Railway through booking facilities to and from Liverpool landing stage via their ferry. At that time, the various districts later welded together to form the borough of Wallasey were separate and there were no public transport facilities between Seacombe and Wallasey Village. From 1897, the company made concerted efforts to develop local traffic between Seacombe and New Brighton on a seasonal basis. It seems strange in the circumstances that no firm timetable was decided upon and nothing ever seems to have appeared in *Bradshaw*, nor was it shown in an attractive timetable and guide issued in 1908. At their meeting on 2nd January 1899, the directors agreed to the running of the service in the afternoons and evenings during the coming season and, at Easter 1899, the return fare from Liverpool to New Brighton was 9d (3.75p), of which the

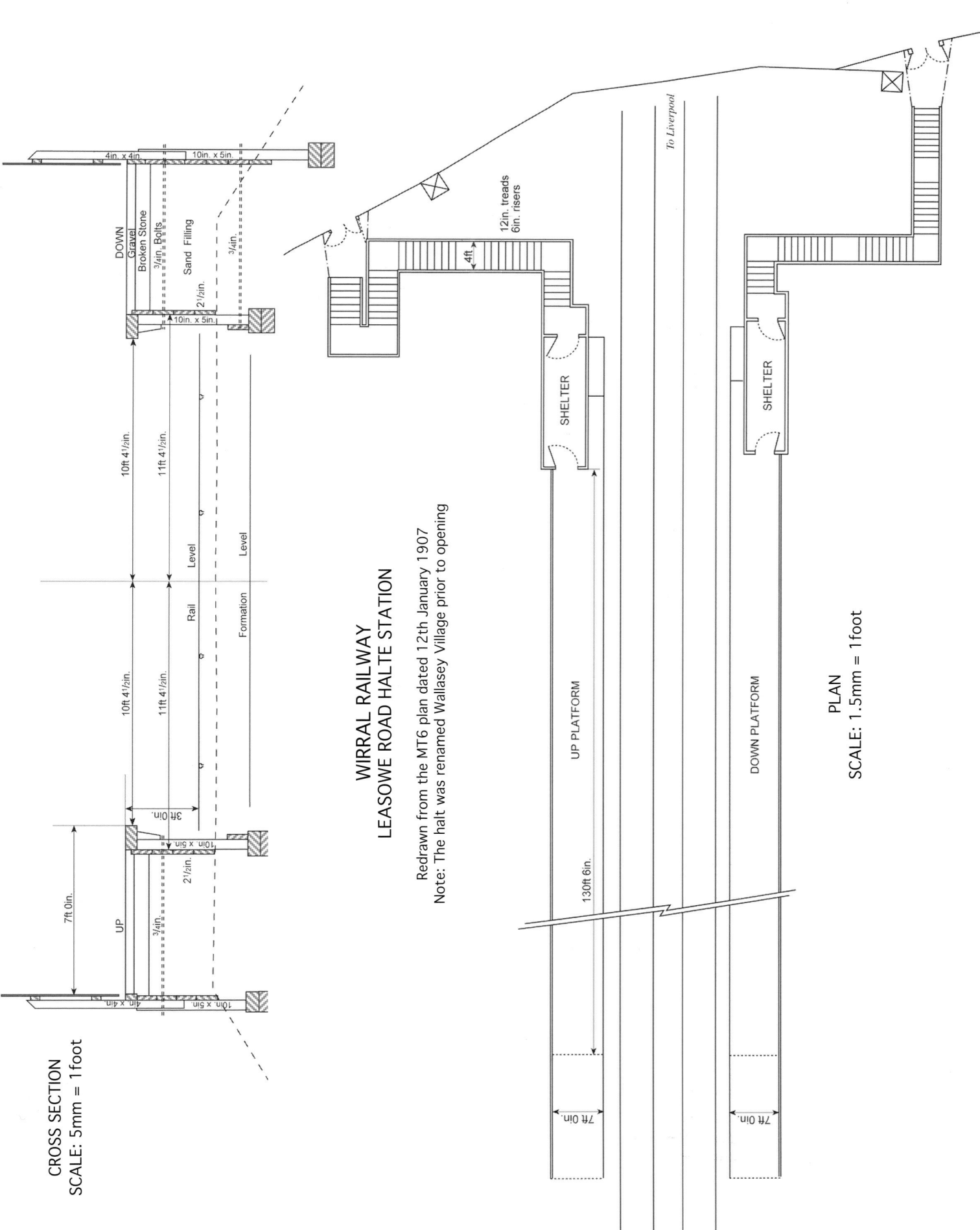

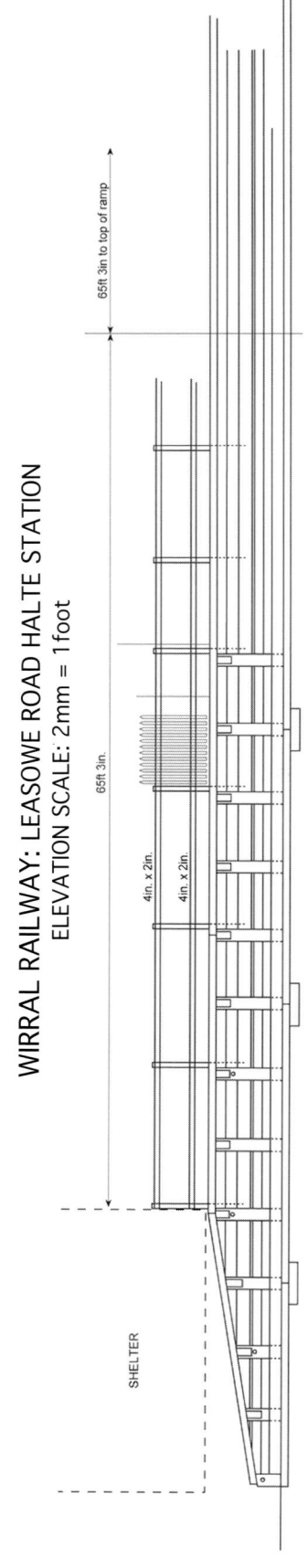

WIRRAL RAILWAY: LEASOWE ROAD HALTE STATION
ELEVATION SCALE: 2mm = 1 foot

ferries took 2d; this included admission to the Tower. Cheap tickets were also issued for journeys wholly within Wallasey.

Tramway electrification in 1902 had a serious effect on local railway traffic and, at the end of the 1905 season, it was decided to run the 'Dodger', as it had become locally known, only on Bank Holidays. However, in 1906, the railway management, possibly influenced by Wallasey Council's failure to extend their tramways to Wallasey Village, decided on special measures to win back the traffic. In September, they announced that the 'Dodger' was to be reinstated daily and a frequent service provided. A new station was built where the New Brighton line crossed Leasowe Road, on the only overbridge on the system; originally this was intended to be called Leasowe Road with platforms only 135 feet long and this name may indeed have been carried briefly. However, its name was changed to Wallasey Village either before or within a very short time of it opening on 1st March 1907 with 250 foot platforms, long enough for a seven-coach train. For many years this station was open only from 8.0am to 7.0pm on weekdays. It was intended to purchase three lightweight centre gangway coaches for the service but only one was obtained. If the service was successful, it was intended to build three new halts at Oakdale Road, Gorsey Lane and a point described as 'Breck Road', which was very close to Liscard & Poulton station, to which there was at that time access only from Mill Lane. An agreement giving access to 'Breck Road station' was signed with a landowner on 30th July 1906. As Wallasey Council had obtained powers to extend their tramways to Poulton and Wallasey Village, the logic was to intercept would be passengers as they walked along Breck Road before they reached the tramway. The problem was that the proposed halts were to be located away from areas of substantial population and the service was not sufficiently successful to justify their provision. In 1910, the tramways reached a point very close to Liscard & Poulton station and the following year were extended to Wallasey Village and New Brighton. The 'Dodger' was discontinued on an unrecorded date, probably at the end of the 1910 season, and the east-west chord at Seacombe Junction was disconnected in July 1914, the rails being removed in 1915 for reuse during the war. One result of this episode was the provision of a somewhat precipitous footpath giving direct access from Breck Road to Liscard & Poulton station.

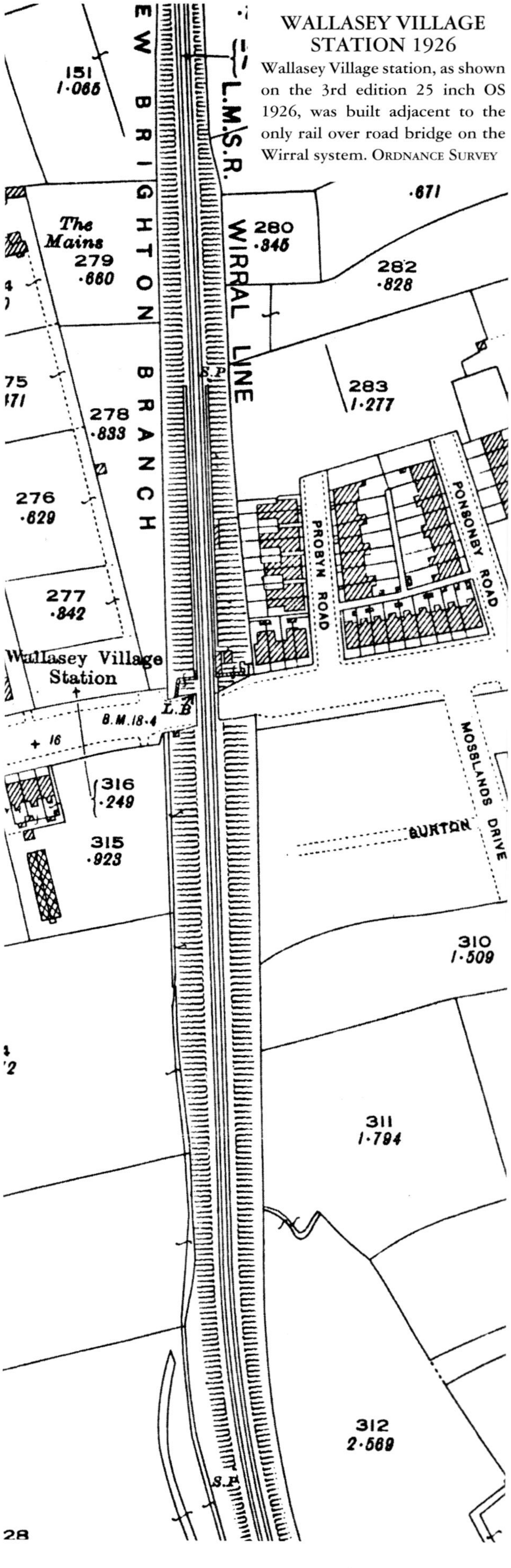

WALLASEY VILLAGE STATION 1926

Wallasey Village station, as shown on the 3rd edition 25 inch OS 1926, was built adjacent to the only rail over road bridge on the Wirral system. ORDNANCE SURVEY

Wallasey station circa 1912, with a train headed by No. 5 arriving from New Brighton *en route* for Birkenhead Park. Note the 'Wirral horn' emblem on the gable and the typical Wirral nameboard inscribed 'WALLASEY STATION' at length, and also the large clock mounted in the gable window. The main building was of an unusual design and, indeed, no two stations on the Wirral seemed very much alike. The wooden pillars supporting the semi built-in canopy are of particular note. The building on the second platform had a more traditional style awning. This station was renamed Wallasey (Grove Road) by the nascent British Railways on 31st May 1948 in order to emphasise the difference between Wallasey and Wallasey Village stations. JOHN RYAN COLLECTION

An unsolved mystery is a report in *Tramway & Railway World* of 7th January 1907, to the effect that an application would soon be made for a Light Railway Order for an electric line between Birkenhead and New Brighton, and that the contract for building the line and the power station at New Brighton was to be given to a local firm, Hickman & Sons. Nothing more was heard of this and it seems to have had no connection with the Wirral Railway which, if the application had been made, would no doubt have strongly opposed it.

INCREASED TRAFFIC

The growing popularity of the Wirral peninsula, both as a residential area and for recreation, was to some extent the result of its increased accessibility by rail and the railway, in turn, benefited from the increased patronage. The population of Wallasey in 1881 was 21,192 but it more than doubled to 53,579 by 1901 and continued to grow to 78,504 in 1911 and 90,809 in 1921. Other districts grew in population at a less spectacular rate. A high proportion of Wirral residents worked in Liverpool and, whilst the municipally owned ferries of Birkenhead and Wallasey carried much of this traffic, there was a steady increase in railway commuters from the districts which benefited most from the railway. Even allowing for the change of trains at Birkenhead Park, Wallasey was only 20 minutes from the centre of Liverpool and West Kirby half-an-hour. New Brighton's amusements and attractions largely drew day trippers from the Liverpool area but the catchment area was widened by the running of railway excursions, particularly by the Great Central. The Traffic Manager, Mr Burns, frequently complained that Wallasey and Hoylake councils did not do enough to publicise the undoubted attractions of the resorts and so encourage staying visitors, whereas the company had a relatively large publicity budget.

In February 1898, the directors decided to reduce fares to 1½d per mile for First class and 1¼d per mile for Second class but the latter class was abolished from 31st December 1898. The matter had been first suggested in 1895 and the Wirral complained that the Mersey continued to book Second class passengers who, of course, had to be carried in First class.

In April 1904, the directors decided to form an additional three-coach train to run between Birkenhead Park and New Brighton, so as to provide a half-hourly service from 1st July until further notice. This marked the beginning of seasonal augmentation of this service, on which overcrowding had become a problem as the popularity of the resort grew.

In 1906, the Wirral promoted a Bill in Parliament, the main provisions of which were the renewal of powers for the Seacombe station extension and building of the Slopes Branch, neither of which were opposed. However, the company also sought powers to run motor buses, similar powers being sought by the Mersey, which was soon to be forced to withdraw its buses because of legal action by Birkenhead Corporation. Both companies' Bills were similarly worded:

'... *to provide, own, work and use in any district or to and from any place situate upon the railways owned, worked or used by the company, omnibuses, coaches, cars and other road vehicles to be drawn or moved by animal or mechanical power and to convey therein passengers' luggage and parcels ... Not to run any railway omnibus in any city,*

borough or urban district other than to or from a station or hotel without local authorities' consent as to route and times. Refusal to be subject to appeal to the Board of Trade.'

In evidence, it was said that motor buses would meet the requirements of golfers at less expense than construction of a new station and would give accommodation to districts at some distance from the railway. Buses would be used only as feeders to the railway. The Wirral's powers were granted but they were subject to approval by the local authorities. The directors then had second thoughts and, assured of strong opposition from Birkenhead, Wallasey and Hoylake councils, lost interest in a scheme which would probably have involved the company in considerable financial loss.

Following discussions between the Wirral and the GW/L&NW Joint management, the Wirral had run a through excursion to Parkgate via West Kirby for the steeplechases on 29th April 1893 and this became an annual event. However, it was not until 17th July 1908 that a regular excursion was inaugurated from Seacombe to Parkgate

ABOVE: This eye-catching poster extolling the virtues of the Wirral peninsula was distributed to other companies for display at their stations by the Wirral Railway in the first decade of the 20th century. Note the emphasis on golf. MARTIN JENKINS COLLECTION

RIGHT: Traffic Manager Burns left no stone unturned in an effort to attract recreational traffic to the railway. This page comes from a brochure titled *Walks in the Wirral* published, complete with maps, in 1907. Note the facility to travel to Bidston, Leasowe or Moreton on the West Kirby line and return from Wallasey or New Brighton. COURTESY JOHN HORNE

RIGHT BELOW: The Wirral Railway derived much traffic from golf as there were several golf courses in close proximity to the line including the Royal Liverpool at Hoylake. This extract from the timetable dated 1st October 1913 shows how the issue of cheap tickets was confined to members of the various clubs. JOHN RYAN COLLECTION

FAR RIGHT: This notice of excursion tickets in October 1913 shows that their availability was restricted to a very small number of trains. Tickets were issued at the railway booking office on Liverpool Landing Stage as well as at stations. JOHN RYAN COLLECTION

for 1s 1d (5.5p) return, starting at 2.45pm and returning at 8.43pm, arriving back at Seacombe at 9.38pm. This was run every Saturday for about ten weeks; it was resumed for 1909 and continued into the war years. Excursion traffic to New Brighton from the GW/L&NW Joint line via Hooton and West Kirby, and from the GC via the CLC and Bidston, became important and caused some embarrassment on very busy days, as there was difficulty in stabling the stock during the day. At one stage, the Wirral asked the GC for financial assistance for the provision of extra sidings. The company also came to an agreement with the GC regarding the running of occasional excursions from Wrexham to Birkenhead Park, in some cases with through tickets to Liverpool. These discussions, which also involved the Birkenhead Park Station Joint Committee, continued sporadically from 1904 to 1909.

Total passengers carried reached 2,794,781 in 1904, 3,142,345 in 1908 and 3,444,595 in 1913, an increase of 23.25% over nine years or an average of 2.58% per annum. Results for five corresponding first half-years in 1905-09 showed a steady increase, earnings being £27,332, £29,066, £29,731 and £30,073. More season tickets had been issued and earnings per train mile in 1909 were 35.6d, compared with 34.75d in 1908. The profit per train mile rose from 14.82d to 15.81d. From about this time, the number of first class passengers fell slightly but this was compensated by the increase in third class travellers. There was a substantial increase in season ticket holders in 1908 (when there were 2,749) and again in 1912.

The problem was that expenses ate up so much of the receipts there was little left for the shareholders. During the railway strike of 7th-20th August 1911, the engineer and locomotive foreman manned trains, maintaining a service between Park and West Kirby, the Seacombe and New Brighton branches eventually being closed, though the GC ran Seacombe-Caergwrle excursions on Sunday 13th August. The subsequent adoption of the eight hour day necessitated the employment of more staff and the impact on the Wirral was severe as it needed men to cover short peaks, making it virtually impossible to get full productivity from the employees. The seasonal nature of the traffic usually resulted in no interim dividend in the first half of the year but a small payment in the second half of the year. From 1914, the preference shareholders were paid in full but there was nothing for the ordinary shareholders.

During the 1914-18 war, the company came under the control of the government and there was a temporary increase of traffic, to the extent that six carriages were hired from the GC and, later, another four from the same company, plus four from the L&NW. However, between 1913 and 1919, there was an overall 9.2% reduction in the number of passengers due to a combination of circumstances such as reduced normal economic activity and restricted train services. The latter was caused by shortages of coal, train services being reduced in February 1915 to save two engines. As Seacombe was most affected, there was some concern that Liverpool traffic would be diverted to the 'tunnel route'. Off-peak services were further reduced to two-hourly on each line from 1st October 1918. The 1913 passenger figures of 278,566 first class and 3,166,029 third class had fallen by 1919 to 266,191 first and 2,861,700 third. It will be noted that the fall in third class passengers (9.2%) was much greater than first class (4.4%). Only preference shareholders were paid in 1919 but in 1921 government compensation of £8,658 was paid for special services rendered during the war and this enabled the ordinary shareholders to be paid a dividend of 2½%.

At the outbreak of the war, the railway suffered some difficulty as men rushed to enlist. Eventually, fifty-three Wirral employees had enlisted in the armed services, of whom nine were killed in action. A Wirral Railway Comforts Fund was organised which raised and distributed £236. It was wound up at a special dinner in New Brighton in September 1919 attended by subscribers and about thirty returned soldiers.

Management

The Wirral Railway's first manager was Samuel Joseph Carr, who died at New Brighton on 5th August 1898. His replacement was John Henry Burns, who had spent the first nineteen years of his railway career with the Manchester, Sheffield & Lincolnshire Railway. He then served for nine years as Accountant and Chief Assistant to the manager of the West Lancashire & Liverpool, Southport & Preston Junction Railways at Southport. Although he was occasionally referred to as the General Manager of the Wirral in the technical press, that position was formally held by the Chairman, T.H. Jackson, and Burns was usually described as the Traffic Manager. He worked assiduously in the development of the company and was eventually aided by Mrs G. Harris as Assistant Manager and Mr T.D. Jones, as Outdoor Assistant Manager.

E.G. Barker left the Wirral's service in 1902 and was replaced as locomotive superintendent by Thomas B. Hunter, who joined the company from the Mersey in 1903. He persuaded the Board to spend £600 on new tools and machinery, and converted the former tramway stables in Wallasey Bridge Road into a machine shop, complete with wheel lathe (the timber structure at one end of the shed had been Spiers & Parks refreshment room from 1866-88). This made it unnecessary to send work out, heavy jobs having been done by the Mersey in the past and also by Beyer, Peacock. Hunter remained with the company until Grouping.

These portraits of Wirral Railway personalities appeared with the article on the company in the July 1914 issue of the *Railway Magazine*:

Far Left: J.S. Wilcox, Chief Engineer.

Left: J.H. Burns, Traffic Manager.

Right: T.B. Hunter, Locomotive Superintendent.

ABOVE: The second locomotive to carry the number 1 was this Beyer, Peacock 4-4-2T, built in 1892 and here photographed at Birkenhead around 1910 with a backdrop of colliery wagons. It was the first engine purchased by the new consolidated Wirral company and the only Wirral Railway locomotive built to this wheel arrangement. It is shown soon after entering service, although after bunker rails had been fitted to enable extra coal to be carried. In service it was found to be less than ideal for the company's traffic but nevertheless survived until Grouping, being withdrawn in February 1924. JOHN ALSOP COLLECTION

RIGHT: Wirral Railway No. 2, seen here circa 1907, began life as SH&DR No. 5 in 1887. It was renumbered by the Wirral following the withdrawal of the original No's 1 and 2 in 1891. JOHN WARD COLLECTION, COURTESY JOHN HORNE

LOCOMOTIVES

The locomotive specifications of the Wirral Railway and its predecessors were determined by the line, with its curves, frequent stops and gradients, of which the 1 in 88 section between Wallasey and New Brighton was the most arduous. As the population and the passengers carried increased, the need to achieve quick turn rounds, particularly at Birkenhead Park, became an important factor. In 1891, the fleet inherited by the Wirral comprised a total of nine locomotives; No's 1-4 were 2-4-0s, whilst No's 5-9 were 0-4-4Ts and only No's 1 and 2 had not been built by Beyer Peacock.

The two Yorkshire Engine Co. 2-4-0 side tank engines delivered new to the H&BR in 1877, No. 1 *West Kirby* and No. 2 *Birkenhead*, had a tractive effort of only 8,050lbs and a tank capacity of only 625 gallons. These locomotives were no doubt valued additions to the fleet in the relaxed days of the late 1870s but they soon became inadequate as traffic expanded. This probably explains their short lives with the Wirral Railway, as they were both withdrawn in June 1891, going on to see further service with Staffordshire collieries. No. 2 carried colliers between Bradwell Wood pit and Chatterley Whitfield on the North Staffordshire Railway until 1904. It was then dismantled and the frames, valve gear and cylinders were used in the construction of a stationary winding engine at Crackley Colliery, working until 1922.

Of the rest, the two Beyer, Peacock 2-4-0s, No's 3 and 4, were really only suitable for light passenger or goods trains, or shunting duties, although they continued in use until February 1914 and January 1913 respectively. The 0-4-4Ts, however, were up to the job and a couple of them were renumbered by the Wirral Railway in 1894, tidying up the number sequence following the disposal of No's 1 and 2, and the arrival of a new No. 1. No. 5 was renumbered 2 and No. 7 then became 5. No. 6 was withdrawn in June 1921 but was subsequently numbered 6B and used as a ballast engine in the locomotive department until January 1922; the other four passed into LM&S ownership in 1923, becoming LM&S No's 6770-3.

Locomotive No. 1 was a 4-4-2T, designed by Beyer, Peacock to

ABOVE: WR 0-4-4T No. 10 and 2-4-0T No. 3 face to face at Birkenhead circa 1908. It would appear that Broughton & Plas Power collieries at Wrexham were regular suppliers of loco coal to the Wirral. No. 3 remained in service until 1914. JOHN ALSOP COLLECTION

LEFT: WR 2-4-0T No. 4, sister to No. 3, was photographed on shunting duties on 15th August 1902, looking in distinctly uncared for condition. Note the dumb buffered wagon. No. 4's career came to an end in early 1913. JOHN WARD COLLECTION, COURTESY JOHN HORNE

BELOW: WR 0-4-4T No. 5, originally No. 7, with a passenger working at Birkenhead Park around 1905. JOHN WARD COLLECTION, COURTESY JOHN HORNE

ABOVE: No. 7, seen here at Birkenhead shed circa 1908, was built in 1894 and proved a reversion to type for the Wirral following the construction of 4-4-2T No. 1. Incidentally, it will be noted that No. 6 is missing from this photographic survey of the Wirral's locomotives. The only view of it so far discovered is the Beyer, Peacock official which appeared in the first chapter. JOHN RYAN COLLECTION

LEFT: A three quarter view of WR No. 8 outside Birkenhead shed on 28th June 1902. JOHN RYAN COLLECTION

BELOW: No. 9 was new in 1888 as an add-on to the order which produced No's 5-8 in 1887. It is seen here circa 1910 with very worn looking paint on the tank side and coupled to a WR brake van. JOHN ALSOP COLLECTION

the Wirral Railway's specification, which entered service in March 1892 (Works No. 3465). It was effectively a heavier version of the five 0-4-4Ts, with many dimensions in common and the same tractive effort but slightly larger tanks with a capacity of 1,030 gallons. It seems to have had an uneventful life, receiving a new Beyer, Peacock boiler in February 1914 and survived to be allocated an LM&S number, No. 6830, although it never got to carry it, being withdrawn in February 1924.

However, the search for the ideal locomotive wheel arrangement for conditions on the Wirral continued and there was a reversion to 0-4-4T for two engines, No's 7 and 10 (Works No's 3605 and 3606), delivered in April 1894. They had a similar wheelbase to the earlier 0-4-4s but 17ins (instead of 16) by 24ins cylinders. Boiler pressure was raised from 140lbs per sq. in. to 160lbs, increasing the tractive effort to 15,210lbs. Tank capacity was increased to 1,900 gallons. In later years, No. 10 worked goods trains when either of No's 12 or 13 was not available. Again their tenure under the LM&S was short, as they were scrapped in January and April 1924 respectively, and again they never wore their allotted numbers of 6774 and 6775.

In March 1896, No. 11 appeared, which was the first locomotive

on a mainland British railway to have the unusual 4-4-4T wheel arrangement. This was built to the design of Mr E. Barker, the Locomotive & Carriage Superintendent, who had joined the company in January 1892, having trained with the MS&L under Charles Sacré and also served with Dübs & Co., locomotive builders of Glasgow, and the North British Railway. He took over the

Two views of No. 10, new with No. 7 in April 1894, taken at Birkenhead shed around 1908 and illustrating both sides of the engine. They also show the pleasing lines of these 0-4-4Ts and the higher coal bunker rails eventually fitted. ABOVE: JOHN ALSOP COLLECTION; BELOW: T.B. MAUND COLLECTION

additional responsibilities as Permanent Way & Signalling Engineer in 1894. Both the leading and trailing bogies of No. 11 had 4½ins side play. In all other aspects, however, the locomotive was similar to No's 7 and 10. Although it was said to have been very successful on the Wirral, running very steadily through the tight curves, some with a radius of only ten or eleven chains, no further examples were ordered for several years. One reason may have been its very heavy coal consumption, though it had other compensations, running 121,000 miles before needing new tyres, compared to an average of 80,000 for the other engines. Although No. 11's riding qualities were good and the engine benefited on the many sharp curves from its rigid wheelbase, anecdotal evidence suggests that there was some fear amongst footplate crews that at some stage it would end up in the River Birket, which ran parallel to the line between Docks station and Bidston. No. 11 was withdrawn from regular service in June 1919 and served as a ballast engine for six months, before being broken up in February 1920. There were a few other locomotives built subsequently with this wheel arrangement for use on British railways: two were built for the Midland & South Western Junction Railway, connecting Cheltenham with Southampton, by Sharp Stewart in July 1897; forty-five for the North Eastern, to the design of Vincent Raven and built from 1913; and finally, the eight 'H'

WR No. 11 of 1896 was the first 4-4-4 tank engine built to run on a standard gauge British railway. Although considered a success, seven years were to elapse before the Wirral ordered two more of these nicely proportioned engines. No. 11 was withdrawn in 1919 and is seen here at Birkenhead circa 1908. Note the Wirral horn emblem on the upper cabside and the Beyer, Peacock work's plate on the bunker side. JOHN ALSOP COLLECTION

Class locomotives of the Metropolitan Railway, built by Kerr Stuart in 1920. In addition, S.W. Johnson proposed a 4-4-4T design for the Midland but none was built and there were a few narrow gauge examples in Ireland.

The next two locomotives, No's 12 and 13 (Works No's 4120 and 4121), arrived in April/May 1900 and introduced yet another wheel arrangement, 0-6-4T, to the line. They were designed by Mr Barker for use on the increasingly heavy goods trains, the specification put to Beyer, Peacock being a capability of hauling thirty loaded wagons up a gradient of 1 in 100. The cylinder dimensions were increased to 18ins by 26ins stroke; tractive effort, at 19,230lbs, was the highest on the line and they were delivered at a cost of £5,144 each. They were the first Wirral locomotives to have Belpaire fireboxes and, like No. 11, were supplied with screw reversing gear and Gresham & Craven's combination injectors. The working timetable showed the permitted load on the Seacombe and New Brighton branches as 440 tons, with 620 tons permitted on the main line from Docks to West Kirby. Their use on passenger trains was confined to very busy summer days. Allotted LM&S numbers 6848 and 6849, their life under their new owners was once more brief, the two engines being withdrawn in February 1924 and October 1923 respectively. The LM&S obviously thought little of the Wirral's fleet, their standardisation policy condemning all bar one of the Wirral locomotives built since 1894 to short lives.

Then, following an interval of seven years, it was decided to order two more 4-4-4T engines, these arriving in June 1903 as No's 14 and

After the 4-4-4T, there followed two 0-6-4Ts, No's 12 and 13, in 1900. No. 12 was photographed at Birkenhead Docks on 23rd September 1923, by which time it had been allocated LM&S No. 6948. Note the open wagon, right, which has already been lettered LMS. JOHN RYAN COLLECTION

RIGHT: These broadside views of 0-6-4T No. 13 provide a nice comparison. The first shows the locomotive when new and photographed in works grey. There is no evidence that the areas outside the lined panels on the tank and bunker sides, here shown as a darker shade, were ever painted a different colour in service. JOHN WARD COLLECTION, COURTESY JOHN HORNE

BELOW: No. 13 outside Birkenhead shed circa 1910. Note the tank filler lid has been left open. The evidence from many of these pictures shows the Wirral worked their engines hard and there was seemingly little time and effort spent on cleaning and polishing. No. 13 here looks particularly dirty below the footplate. JOHN ALSOP COLLECTION

15. Although generally similar to No. 11, a number of improvements were incorporated in the design. All wheels were 1 inch in diameter greater than their predecessors, the driving wheels being 5 feet 3 inches. The cylinders were identical but working pressure was 170lbs, which gave a tractive effort of 15,910lbs. The boiler diameter was increased from 4 feet to 4 feet 2 inches and the engines were given Belpaire fire boxes. Spiral springs were fitted to the coupled wheels, which resulted in a rather bumpy ride and tyre thickness was increased from 2½i to 3 inches.

The final new engine of the Beyer, Peacock era was an 0-4-4T numbered 3, which entered service in February 1914, taking the place of the recently withdrawn 2-4-0T No. 3. The boiler was similar to those of No's 12 and 13, though the water capacity was 1,500 gallons. The tractive effort was 17,360lbs, making this the second most powerful locomotive on the line. At the Grouping, the LM&S renumbered it 6776 and it survived until 1928, becoming the only locomotive new to the Wirral to carry an LM&S number.

No. 13 in later years on the Wirral, fitted with bunker coal rails and coupled to a Broughton & Plas Power Colliery wagon from the Wrexham area. It has also gained standard 3-link couplings in place of the screw link type originally fitted, a modification which may have been carried out in later years on locomotives no longer used for passenger work. JOHN RYAN COLLECTION

A selection of views of the interesting 4-4-4 tank locomotives, beginning with three of No. 14 on this page. In the top two pictures it is seen circa 1903 without bunker rails; indeed, its immaculate condition suggests No. 14 was probably quite new when photographed alongside the water tank at Birkenhead shed above. The third view, left, is later, probably circa 1920 and shows the locomotive after the fitting of bunker rails. JOHN RYAN COLLECTION; T.B. MAUND COLLECTION; JOHN ALSOP COLLECTION

RIGHT: This official works photograph of No. 15 was published in the Pouteau series of railway postcards. Again the engine is seen as delivered without coal rails to the bunker. JOHN ALSOP COLLECTION

BELOW: Two views of No. 15 in service. The bunker coal rails were seemingly fitted to the two locomotives after a few years service, as indicated by the circa 1906 view of No. 15 in the large title page picture, where it is seen still without them. No's 14 and 15 were new in 1903 and both were withdrawn by the LM&S in 1924. JOHN ALSOP COLLECTION; T.B. MAUND COLLECTION

ABOVE: Official works photograph of 0-4-4T No. 3, the last locomotive built for the Wirral in February 1914. It would seem likely the use of the darker shade was to highlight the shape of certain features for photography. JOHN WARD COLLECTION, COURTESY JOHN HORNE

RIGHT: This is believed to be a view of No. 3 in service, circa 1920. It was the most powerful of the Wirral's 0-4-4Ts, being fitted with 18ins by 26ins cylinders by the builders Beyer, Peacock. T.B. MAUND COLLECTION

BELOW: No. 3 had a very short life, running only from February 1914 to July 1924, when it was scrapped as LM&S No. 6776. It is seen here shortly after Grouping and carrying its new number, shunting redundant ex-L&NWR stock at an unknown location. JOHN WARD COLLECTION, COURTESY JOHN HORNE

SECOND-HAND LOCOMOTIVES

At various times during its existence, financial constraints forced the company to turn to second-hand purchases for essential locomotive replacements and augmentation of the stud to meet increased traffic. Ironically, in two instances, the replacements were older than the engines withdrawn. A Webb 2-4-2T side tank, No. 2282, built at Crewe in December 1877, was bought in February 1913 from the L&NWR to replace 1885-built No. 4, the number of which it took. This having proved satisfactory, two slightly newer locomotives of the same type were acquired as additions in 1919; L&NW No's 969 of 1886 and 889 of 1884 took the numbers 11 and 16 respectively. A fourth similar engine, L&NW No. 284 of 1883 was added in January 1921 as No. 17. The Wirral's final acquisition was ex-Lancashire & Yorkshire Railway 2-4-2T No. 1041, built at Horwich in July 1890, which replaced and was numbered No. 6 in June 1921.

No photograph has been discovered showing No. 4 in WR days, the first L&NWR Webb 2-4-2T bought by the Wirral Railway in 1913 and which took the guise of the recently withdrawn 2-4-0T No. 4. However, it obviously proved useful and two more similar locomotives were bought from the L&NW in 1919. The first of these, No. 969 of 1886, became the Wirral's second No. 11, taking over the number (and numberplate) from the first of the 4-4-4Ts, which was taken out of service in the same year. On Grouping, No. 11 became LM&SR No. 6759 and it continued to run on the Wirral lines until April 1927, when it was scrapped. It was photographed at Birkenhead around 1920. T.B. MAUND COLLECTION

RIGHT: A Wirral period view showing the fourth ex-L&NWR 2-4-2T, as WR No. 17, has also not been found. However, this post-Grouping photograph of the locomotive at Llandudno Junction, probably taken circa 1925, shows the painted Wirral number still clearly visible on the tank side. TED LLOYD COLLECTION

BELOW: The second Webb 2-4-2T purchased in 1919, ex-L&NW No. 889, became Wirral Railway No. 16. As this was a new number to the Wirral, no numberplate was available, so the number was painted on the side tanks. With the livery of the two companies being very similar, it is unlikely that these engines were repainted on arrival. JOHN RYAN COLLECTION

LEFT: The last locomotive to be acquired by the Wirral was 1890 Horwich-built ex-Lancashire & Yorkshire Railway 2-4-2T No. 1041, which came into the fleet as No. 6 in June 1921. It is seen here passing over the water troughs at Walkden in its L&Y days, circa 1900. Note the rake of colliery wagons on the line passing over the bridge behind. JOHN WARD COLLECTION, COURTESY JOHN HORNE

BELOW: No. 6 at Birkenhead, probably shortly after arrival. Note it has retained the L&Y lining, with scalloped corners, which further supports the suggestion that these second-hand locomotives were not repainted. No. 6 became LM&S No. 6762 in the L&NW series at Grouping, although No. 10638 in the L&Y series had originally been allocated on paper. The locomotive enjoyed a long life, eventually being withdrawn in February 1952 as British Railways No. 46762. T.B. MAUND COLLECTION

Two of the second-hand locomotives together in Birkenhead Docks sidings circa 1921, providing a contrast in pre-Grouping locomotive styles. On the left is the chunky ex-L&YR 2-4-2T No. 6, whilst behind is the more graceful ex-L&NWR Webb 2-4-2T No. 11. JOHN WARD COLLECTION, COURTESY JOHN HORNE

Wrexham, Mold & Connah's Quay and Great Central Locomotives on the Wirral Railway

The first locomotives to appear at Bidston from the south were, of course, working for the contractors Monk & Newall, who built the 15-mile line of the North Wales & Liverpool Railway. The Wrexham, Mold & Connah's Quay Railway had prepared for the opening of this line by ordering two 0-6-2T engines from Beyer, Peacock. These were identical to the Manchester, Sheffield & Lincolnshire Railway's '9F' Class of goods radial tank engines, many of which Beyers had already produced and which worked through to Wrexham. These two, numbered 17 and 18, were insufficient for the expected traffic and, because the MS&LR had no authority to work the line, three more of the same design were hired to the WM&CQ by the MS&L. These were MS&L No's 754-756, the first two having been built by Beyer, Peacock in January 1896 and the third by the MS&L themselves a few weeks earlier. All three had the letters 'W.M.& C.Q.' added to their side tanks and the new numbers 19, 20 and 23 respectively. Goods traffic commenced with these five engines.

These 0-6-2Ts were powerful and successful. Their Belpaire fireboxes distinguished them from Parker's original 0-6-2T engines and, having combined steam and vacuum brakes, they were suitable for passenger traffic also. However, the MS&L provided five further locomotives for passenger services, which were also disguised as WM&CQ property for their new duties. In contrast to the goods tanks, these were 2-4-0 tender engines with outside frames and among the oldest in service on the MS&L. It was not one of these ancients but the similar No. 89 which hauled the special train of saloon coaches which carried Mr and Mrs Gladstone from Hawarden to Liverpool Central (Low Level) for the formal opening of the line to Bidston on 28th March 1896. No. 89 was replaced by a Wirral engine at Bidston, which in turn gave way to a Mersey locomotive at Birkenhead Park. Lunch at the Midland Adelphi followed.

The five MS&L 2-4-0 tender locos which adopted WM&CQ identities were No's 55, 56, 57, 59 and 153, becoming WM&CQ No's 21, 22, 24, 25 and 26 respectively. All had been built at Gorton in 1867. This Class '24' design was by Charles Sacré and had first appeared in 1865. They were good enough for Robinson to rebuild some with more modern boilers.

When the five 2-4-0s opened the passenger service on 18th May 1896, they ran to Seacombe, not Park, as the Mersey Railway refused to agree terms for through running to Liverpool. In 1898, the Great Central, as it now was, negotiated running powers over the Wirral Railway from Bidston Dee Junction to Seacombe and the eight hired engines were able to revert to their true numbers and the new company name. The WM&CQ still existed and the locomotives were still on hire.

Further engines hired from the GCR for use on the North Wales & Liverpool line – and probably kept at Bidston shed – were: No. 152, Class '24' 2-4-0, built Gorton 1867, scrapped 1904; No. 409, Class '24', built Gorton 1877, scrapped 1904; No. 940, 0-6-2T radial goods tank, Class '9F', built Beyer, Peacock, July 1900; and No. 596, 2-4-2T radial passenger tank, Class '3', built Neilson, March 1891.

The Great Central took over the working of the North Wales & Liverpool and most of the associated Seacombe trains in February 1901, when the hiring arrangement ceased. The WM&CQ continued to work two return trips from Wrexham to Seacombe and one from Seacombe to Chester, usually with their 0-6-2 radial goods tank No. 17. After the Great Central finally absorbed the WM&CQ in January 1905, engines No's 17 and 18 lost their livery of Indian red, lined black with a fine amber line. The Great Central painted their goods engines black with red and white lining; the '9F' tanks were regarded as goods, despite their often appearing on passenger workings. Passenger engines were green.

There had been a great shortage of engines on the GCR from 1900, leading even to imports from America but, by 1902, this had been overcome and the work of the elderly 2-4-0s on the Seacombe trains proved a swan-song for most of them. The five which had carried WM&CQ numbers were withdrawn for scrapping between 1902 and 1907. Enginemen, who had had to work them cab-first, must have been glad to see them go.

Many railway companies dabbled with steam-powered railmotors in Edwardian times but only the GWR and the L&Y judged them a success. The Great Central built only three, two at Gorton in 1904 and a third in 1905. They had a vertical boiler on the motor bogie and were totally enclosed in a smart coach body. Either one car or two ran

ABOVE: WM&CQR 0-6-2T No. 17, one of two engines built by Beyer Peacock in 1896 specifically to work North Wales & Liverpool Railway trains from Wrexham to the Wirral. They were mixed traffic engines and three more of almost identical design were hired from the MS&LR, through the WM&CQR.

RIGHT: WM&CQR 2-4-0 No. 26 was one of five of this type of engine hired from the MS&LR for working passenger services on the NW&LR to Seacombe. They were given new WM&CQ identities for this purpose, No. 26 seen here having previously been MS&LR No. 153. BOTH THE LOCOMOTIVE MAGAZINE

There are no known photographs showing the Great Central steam railmotors on the Wirral. This is the official works photograph of No. 1 when new at Gorton in late 1904. The vehicle was 61ft 6ins in length and could seat 12 First class and 44 Third class passengers, with a separate compartment for luggage. The *Locomotive Magazine* of 15th March 1905 recorded that it was '*now running in regular service between Seacombe and Wrexham, after making an extended trial trip from Gorton works to Marylebone and back.*' Railmotor No. 2 is noted as having joined it later in the year. NEIL PARKHOUSE COLLECTION

on the Wrexham-Seacombe and Wrexham-Brymbo lines when they were new; they were also used in North Lincolnshire. Among their novelties was electric lighting; the Great Central usually employed compressed oil gas, as did the Wirral Railway.

The GC steam railmotors do not seem to have remained very long on the Seacombe branch and it is not thought they ventured elsewhere on the Wirral system. However, a couple of letters discovered in the National Archives at Kew indicates the Wirral Railway themselves certainly had the use of steam railmotors under consideration for a short while. On 3rd November 1903, J.H. Burns was writing to the Board of Trade to inform them:

'*I am instructed by my Directors to inform you that they are considering the desirability of introducing a Motor Car service similar to that now in operation between Fratton and Southsea on the Joint Railways of the LB&SC and L&SW Companies, and I am to inquire whether*

(a) It is necessary to obtain your assent to the introduction of such Cars manned and driven in the same way as the Car referred to above, without any alteration being made in the Stations or Signals, providing such cars are worked in the same way as the ordinary steam locomotive trains.

(b) Whether if such a consent is necessary you will give it for a service between Park Station, Birkenhead, and New Brighton; and Seacombe Station and New Brighton Station on this Railway.'

Burns wrote further on 11th November in reply to questions asked by the BoT. He informed them that there was no intention of stopping to pick up passengers between stations and also that there was no intention of turning the Cars at the termini. Rather, '*the driving arrangements, electric communication, brake appliances etc shall be provided at the rear of the Coach*', likening this to the similar cars running on the L&SWR between Fratton and Southsea, and also on the GWR between Stonehouse and Chalford. The lengths of railway involved were 4 miles 9 chains between Birkenhead Park and New Brighton, and 4 miles 25 chains between Seacombe & Egremont and New Brighton. There were no level crossings involved bar one occupation crossing.

It is not known if the BoT actually granted the Wirral permission for these services. Certainly permission would have been required by the Directors before they committed capital to building a steam railmotor or two. Nothing further is heard of the proposal and it may well be that, following the GCR's experiment with railmotors on the Seacombe line, it was realised they would not be suitable and the idea was quietly dropped.

LIVERY

The basic livery of Wirral Railway locomotives was all-over black, with bunkers, tanks, etc. being lined out in vermilion, yellow and white. The cabs and frames carried a plain red line and the cab interiors were green on some locomotives and vermilion on others. Coupling rods varied, some being plain red, whilst others were lake with black edging and vermilion lining. The locomotive numbers were carried in gold on a scarlet background on brass plates, which were transferred from the old engines to the replacements, the exceptions being No's 16 and 17 which were painted, these numbers not having been used previously.

No. 5 at West Kirby around 1905, with the low angle and bright sunlight showing off some of the lining and livery details nicely. JOHN WARD COLLECTION, COURTESY JOHN HORNE

PASSENGER STOCK

There is very little information about rolling stock in the early years of the line and it is thought that the four-wheel stock used was purchased second-hand from an unknown source. However, with the re-interpretation of the early photograph of Hoylake station (page 12) as dating from 1866, there is now at least an illustration depicting a number of these vehicles. The photograph indicates there were at least eight carriages in use at this date, a wooden shed being constructed at Hoylake to house some or all of them. They are typical of their period, with metal chimney pots on the roofs, whilst inside they were divided into compartments by partitions which only rose part-way to the ceiling. They were recorded as having hard, narrow, wooden seats with no coverings, which forced pasengers to sit very straight-backed. Whilst they were no doubt out-moded compared to new main line stock of the 1860s, they were a perfect match for *Ashton*, the ancient locomotive with which the Hoylake Railway commenced its operations. Indeed, such was the pace of railway development at this time that these coaches were probably less than fifteen years old when they arrived on the HR in any case.

These carriages seem to have sufficed for some years and the next passenger stock known to have been purchased were the horse-drawn tramcars for the H&BR&T Co. However, it is unlikely that any of these were ever operated on the railway, particularly as they were soon converted from single to double deckers. When more carriage stock was required, the railway turned again to Locomotive Superintendent J. Medley, who acquired some second-hand from the Neath & Brecon Railway and these may have arrived at the same time as No. 3, the ex N&BR No. 14A, in early 1879.

The first new coaching stock known to have been purchased was by the SH&DR in 1888, from the Falcon Engine & Car Works Ltd of Loughborough, which became the Brush Electrical Engineering Company the following year. Four sets of stock, each comprising six 4-wheeled carriages with a wheelbase of 15 feet 6 inches, were obtained for the opening of the extensions to Birkenhead Park and New Brighton. These were equipped with Pintsche's gas lighting as through running to Liverpool required all-day illumination. A retort house, gas holder and compressors were built on the south-west side of the line near the turntable at Birkenhead Docks. They also had vacuum brakes fitted and the shed at Hoylake was turned into a paint shop for the coaching stock.

By 25th March 1890, all SH&D passenger stock had been fitted with continuous brakes, except vehicles used only on Bank Holidays. These comprised five Composites, two First class, two Second class, seven Third class and four Break [*sic*] vans.

The amalgamated company was keen to improve its rolling stock as soon as possible and, on 7th July 1891, the directors accepted a tender from the Ashbury company, whose quotation had been as follows:

1 First class four compartment	£ 575
1 Third class five compartment	£ 370
1 Composite, 4 second 1 first	£ 540
1 Composite, 4 third, 1 first	£ 450
1 Second class Brake, 3 compartment	£ 460
1 Third class Brake, 3 compartment	£ 400
TOTAL	£2,795
Extra for Vickers tyres and axles	£ 102
Fitting with Pintsche's gas lighting	£ 229
TOTAL	£3,126

A Second class carriage was deleted from the original draft order, which suggests that abolition of this class was being contemplated as early as 1891, though it was not actually abolished until 31st

Falcon Engine & Car Works official photograph of Seacombe, Hoylake & Deeside Railway Brake Third No. 27, new in 1888. The vehicle is seen in the Wirral livery of all-over lake with yellow lining but with SH&DR crests. Although the Wirral Railways Co. Ltd had been formed in 1884 to take over the SH&D, it was not until 1891 that this was finalised. The guard's ducket can just be made out to the left of the door lettered 'GUARD'; note also the lamp, flush with the top of this ducket. COURTESY, LEICESTERSHIRE, LEICESTER & RUTLAND RECORD OFFICE

RIGHT: Official photograph of SH&DR Composite Third No. 29, displaying destination boards for running between Liverpool and West Kirby.

BELOW: SH&DR Compartment First No. 30, complete with Park Branch destination boards. Note the Pintsch gas cylinder beneath the solebar, with pressure gauge mounted on the solebar and the Falcon maker's plate alongside. Both of these coaches were also part of the order completed in 1888. BOTH COURTESY, LEICESTERSHIRE, LEICESTER & RUTLAND RECORD OFFICE

December 1898. The specification for the above stock was quoted as *'same as carriages being built for Mersey Railway'*, suggesting that, as stock was running through between the two companies' lines, the directors thought there was a need for a measure of uniformity to avoid critical comparisons being made.

An invitation for tenders for the supply of fourteen Third class carriages, two Third class Brakes and two First class carriages, *'of similar construction to those now in use'*, brought forth offers from eleven suppliers as follows:

Ashbury Railway Carriage & Wagon Co.	£6,660
Birmingham Railway, Carriage & Wagon Co.	£7,007
Bristol Wagon Co.	£7.120 10s 0d
Brown, Marshall & Co.	£6,796
Craven's Ltd.	£6,234
Falcon Engine & Carriage Co.	£7,936
Gloucester Railway, Carriage & Wagon Co.	£7,152
Lancaster Railway, Carriage & Wagon Co.	£6,862
Metropolitan Railway Carriage & Wagon Co.	£8,525
Midland Railway Carriage & Wagon Co.	£7,561 16s 0d
Oldbury Railway, Carriage & Wagon Co.	£7,349 12s 6d

These were 6-wheeled carriages and, not surprisingly, Cravens were given the order in August 1893, subject to an agreement being drawn up for deferred payment over seven years, the company to have the option of paying the balance at any time. However, in September 1894, the Board was complaining about the late delivery of twelve coaches. The directors approved the sale of six old carriage bodies at not less than £5 each, the company retaining wheels, axles and springs. Eventually two were made into cabins for drivers and cleaners, whilst a third became a shelter for the gateman at Leasowe crossing, although this appears to have gone by the early years of the 20th century.

In January 1896, the tender of the Birmingham Railway, Carriage & Wagon Co. was accepted for the supply of further rolling stock as follows:

2 x Third class Brake @ £413 each	£ 826
2 x five compartment Third class @ £433 each	£ 866
2 x four compartment First class @£499 each	£ 998
TOTAL	£2,690

The above, quoted from official records, was the precise specification for contemporary Mersey Railway 4-wheeled stock but photographs show that these were bogie coaches; Third class carriages had eight compartments and there were Composites with two Third class and four First class compartments, so it appears that the specification was altered. These vehicles were 50 feet 6 inches long and weighed about 20 tons. One is obliged to assume that either there is an error in the records or there was a last minute change of mind in favour of ordering bogie carriages.

Apart from an unknown number of coaches made redundant by electrification and bought from the Mersey in 1903, there were no more additions to the passenger stock until 1906, when a special coach was ordered from Brush for the Seacombe-New Brighton 'Dodger' service. At first it was intended to have three such vehicles

WR No. 8 pauses at Hoylake station with a train for West Kirby around 1905. Immediately behind the engine is a 4-wheeled Third class Brake, most likely an ex-Mersey Railway vehicle bought from that company following the conversion of their line for use by electric trains, which brought with it new bogie stock. Note also that as well as having its number painted on the bufferbeam, this view clearly shows the engine lamps as carrying the number '8' as well, which would suggest the lamps were allocated to each locomotive and not part of a common pool. However, this feature has not been noted in any of the other Wirral locomotive views which have been seen, so this suggestion cannot be confirmed. JOHN WARD COLLECTION, COURTESY JOHN HORNE

ABOVE: First Third Brake Composite No. 78 was purchased from the Brush Electrical Engineering Company (formed by an 1889 amalgamation of the Falcon Engine & Car Works with the Brush Electric Light Corporation) in 1906 specially for the Seacombe-New Brighton service, which it was hoped to develop, but orders for two more seem not to have been placed. Pintsch gas lighting was once more provided, with the pressure gauge again visible on the solebar in the centre, just above the gas cylinder. The coach looked very smart with its white tyred Mansell wheels. Note the two Smoking sections were placed in the centre and the coach carried two Wirral horn crests on each side.

LEFT: The interior view taken from the First class section with the Third class beyond, shows a level of appointments which was rather excessive for a journey lasting, at most, about ten minutes. The service was a failure, lasting only two years and the carriage was subsequently disposed of but its fate is currently unknown. BOTH COURTESY LEICESTERSHIRE, LEICESTER & RUTLAND RECORD OFFICE

Wirral Railway coach No. 41 was one of three rebuilds carried out using two of the old Falcon built 4-wheeled coach bodies, mounted by the company on new bought-in frames and bogies, the work being undertaken circa 1910 in the Carriage Works at Hoylake. Each bogie coach appears to have utilised one five compartment Third and one four compartment First but, in the case of No. 41 seen here, the end Third class compartment was then converted to a First, thus leaving the split the other way; it is not known if the other two bogie coaches had the same compartment ratio. JOHN ALSOP COLLECTION

but it seems certain that only one was ordered. It was a 56 foot long centre gangway coach, divided into four compartments (First and Third, Smoking and Non-Smoking), each seating 16 passengers. It had Mansell wheels and rubber cushioned seats; there was also a Brake compartment. An agreement with Brush was signed on 28th May 1906, allowing for payment of £1,030 over five years at 5% interest. Its ultimate fate, following the demise of the 'Dodger' service is unknown and exhaustive enquiries have failed to trace it. In 1908, the company bought two coaches from the Midland Railway and converted them into one bogie coach at a cost of £170 for materials. The success of this venture led to the Wirral converting six of their 4-wheelers into three bogie carriages. Underframes were obtained from the Consett Iron Co. and bogies from Pickerings. The bodywork was done in the Hoylake carriage works and the metal work at Birkenhead Docks.

The Wirral Railway had one item of Non-Passenger Carrying Stock (NPCS), a 4-wheeled Mail Van of unknown build which was in use for many years. When it was eventually withdrawn, the body

A rare photograph of the Wirral Railway Mail Van, with various members of staff. Fortunately, they were positioned so as not to obscure the lettering. The mail was brought over from Liverpool to Seacombe by the ferry and conveyed by train to various stations on the West Kirby line. JOHN RYAN COLLECTION

was removed from the underframe and sited at Moreton, where it became the home of an elderly Wirral railwayman and his wife for many years.

In 1916, the company turned down an offer of rail motors by the London & South Western Railway. About 1919, four First class and two Third class 6-wheeled coaches of some considerable age were hired from the Great Central, followed by a further four First class from the same source and four from the L&NWR.

Passenger rolling stock was painted dark lake with yellow lining, lettering and numbers, very similar to those of the Mersey Railway, with the company name on a garter containing the Wirral horn. Underframes were black and train ends scarlet.

The relative unimportance of goods traffic on the line is indicated by the small fleet of goods vehicles owned. At the time of the amalgamation in 1891, there were just fifty goods vehicles. By 1913, this had increased to eighty-three open wagons, three covered wagons, three Brake vans and three rail & timber trucks. In 1919, there were seventy-eight open wagons, whilst a breakdown crane, eleven ballast wagons, two Loco Coal wagons and a travelling crane were also listed in the annual report. Four open wagons and a rail & timber truck were scrapped in 1921 but two ballast wagons added. It is believed that there were no more than seventy-two open wagons when the LM&S took over in 1923. Goods stock was painted grey, with white lettering and numbers, and black underframes. Photographs showing any of the goods stock are particularly rare.

Ancillary road vehicles in 1913 included one motor vehicle and there were six horse drawn carts. By 1919, the motor had been replaced by another horse drawn cart, presumably as a result of wartime petrol supply difficulties. By that time the horses were hired from a jobmaster.

The Final Years

Post-First World War inflation created financial difficulties for all railway companies and in 1921, the Mersey, which had reached the limit of its statutory charging powers, promoted a bill to raise fares, which included the through fares on to the Wirral lines. There was considerable opposition from contract holders and the following examples will show the reason why:

To and from James Street station – First class annual

	Existing	1st Proposal	Amended Proposal
Wallasey Village	£9 3s 10d	£13 4s 6d	)
Wallasey	£9 4s 1d	£13 14s 6d	) £12 0s 9d
New Brighton	£9 5s 0d	£17 0s 6d	)

The Mersey was, of course, applying for new maxima above current statutory levels but the 49% increases went down like a lead balloon and brought forth strong organised opposition from local councils.

Suggested New Brighton Extension

The situation of the station at New Brighton, so far from the commercial and entertainment centre, was a considerable drawback, as it was possible for trippers to visit the resort yet be unaware of the existence of a railway. The steep climb up to the station after a tiring day out was a serious deterrent to travel by rail. A large 'Railway Station' sign was mounted on the station façade but as this was not visible from any distance, the company erected a lattice work tower at the corner of Victoria Road and Atherton Street and placed upon it an enormous 'STATION' sign, visible from the lower reaches of Victoria Road where the crowds circulated. A letter written by Mr Burns, the Traffic Manager, on 3rd August 1922, puts forward an interesting scheme which does not seem to have received a public airing. As part of the letter is missing it is not known to whom it was written but most likely it was the chairman, Thomas Jackson. By this time, the company's destiny under the Grouping would have been known. Burns refers to the '*L&NW Company's suggestion scheme*' which seems to signify that the L&NWR had invited the smaller companies to be absorbed to propose changes and improvements. Burns mentions the financial weakness of New Brighton Amusements Ltd, the owners of the Tower, the steel structure of which had been dismantled allegedly because of wartime neglect. The remaining building housed a ballroom and theatre, standing in 35 acres which were not being fully exploited. Burns believed that the Amusements company would make land available for a station at a very reasonable rate. The plan envisaged a line deviating at the western end of the cutting leading to New Brighton station, passing through the sandstone rock by means of a tunnel 600yds long and terminating on the north side of the Tower buildings. Burns proposed four entrances to the station from Victoria Road, Egerton Street, Seabank Road and the Promenade. However, nothing more has been discovered about this interesting scheme.

Hoylake's Complaints

The railway company was constantly criticised by the Hoylake & West Kirby Council. In 1919, the company agreed, under pressure, to reinstate the 7.0am train from West Kirby as a convenience to local workmen. However, arrears of maintenance and attempts to economise on staff to offset higher wages and the effect of the eight hour day resulted in a general deterioration in service standards. On 18th January 1921, the Council, having lost patience with the company, passed a Notice of Motion:

> '*That having regard to the inefficiency of the Wirral Railway and its long continued failure to meet the needs of the district ... with serious inconvenience and loss to a large community ... 15,000 population ... this Council do petition the Ministry of Transport to consider with the management of the Great Western, London & North Western and Great Central companies, the desirability of taking over the Wirral Railway or including it in one of the proposed groupings.*'

The Council eventually got its wish when, on 30th June 1923, the Wirral Railway's independent existence came to an end.

The End of the Wirral Railway Company

At the 35th Ordinary General Meeting of the Wirral Railway Company on 7th February 1923, the directors voted themselves £3,220 as compensation for loss of office. At this stage, the company was still in existence, as final terms had not been agreed with the LM&S, and Sir Henry Beyer Robertson and R.W. Egerton were re-elected as directors. The formal date of transfer was 1st July 1923 and the final Extraordinary General Meeting took place at the Queen Hotel, Chester on 3rd July 1923, when the terms of settlement with the LM&S were approved. By a Special Resolution of the Wirral Railways Co. Ltd on 13th November 1923, the capital was reduced from £600,000, of which 24,753 shares at £10 each had been issued and paid up, to £49,506. The limited company owned several properties which were eventually sold to the LM&S and was not liquidated until 29th May 1936.

At the time of the handover the 91-year old chairman, Thomas Hughes Jackson, was the oldest serving railway director in Britain.

He was the third son of Sir William Jackson, MP, Lord of the Manor of Claughton, and lived in the Manor House in Manor Hill which has since been demolished. His father who, in the past, had been described as the richest man in Birkenhead, had been intimately concerned with the Chester & Birkenhead Railway. He was a partner in the firm of Peto, Betts, Brassey & Jackson, which carried out many railway contracts throughout the world, the largest of which was for the Grand Trunk Railway across Canada, for which Canada Works on the West Float, Birkenhead had been built. The young Thomas went to Canada with Robert Stephenson, who was engineer for the Grand Trunk scheme. Later in life he travelled extensively, visiting India which, at the time, possessed only six miles of railway, and South Africa and South America which had none at all.

The Wirral Railway had a proud safety record and it was tragic that in its last month of independent existence it should have suffered its one and only passenger fatality. An accident occurred at 4.26pm on 6th December 1922 at Birkenhead Park station. The 4.18 service to West Kirby was eight minutes late departing. The 4.0pm train from West Kirby passed a signal at danger and collided with the departing train, half of which had cleared the platform. A 68-year old invalid travelling in a wicker bath chair in the guard's van subsequently died and twelve other passengers were hospitalised. The driver, also 68, had forty years of exemplary service but both he and the fireman were demoted.

The trading results for 1922, the Wirral's last independent year, were as follows:

Passengers	Tickets	£
First class	215,662	8,395
Third class	2,700,158	58,249
Workmen	623,752	7,359
	Season Tickets	£
First class	1,295	13,031
Third class	2,078	12,081
TOTAL	3,542,945	99,115
Goods	Tons	£
Merchandise	186,639	17,632
Coal & Coke	261,308	10,123
Other minerals	35,454	2,303
Livestock	51,414	375
TOTAL	534,815	30,433
GRAND TOTAL		£129,548

It will be noted that goods traffic brought in only 23.5% of receipts, a fairly typical result for the line.

No. 5 passes Bidston West Junction on 21st April 1919 on the 11.18am Birkenhead Park to West Kirby service, with the normal six-coach set strengthened by the addition of a couple of extra carriages. These were stopping services, calling at all stations, with this train preparing to stop at Bidston as indicated by the signal, with the Home arm being 'off'. The splitting distant for Dee Junction is also 'off' (although not very well 'off'!), confirming that just west of Bidston station, the train will take the diverging route towards West Kirby. The lines on the left head off to New Brighton and Seacombe, via Bidston North Junction and the bracket signals behind the first carriage applied to trains from Seacombe and New Brighton round this side of the triangle. This was the final day of photographer Ken Nunn's three day visit to the Wirral (the first since he had visited Birkenhead shed to photograph the locomotives in 1902) and it would appear that footplate crews and passengers were all now well aware of his presence. TED LLOYD COLLECTION

Birkenhead Park Joint station frontage in either late Victorian or early Edwardian days, with a fine horse-drawn Landau waiting for passengers. The station was named after the nearby Birkenhead Park, opened in 1847, the first municipal park in Great Britain and reputedly the model for Central Park, New York. Notice the unmade nature of the road. IAN BOUMPHREY COLLECTION

THE ROUTE DESCRIBED – PRE-GROUPING
BIRKENHEAD PARK TO NEW BRIGHTON

The jointly owned Birkenhead Park station eventually grew to comprise three pairs of double tracks separated by two island platforms. There were four platform faces, the outermost tracks on each side being loops used for running round and shunting. The northern pair were electrified on the third and fourth rail principle and were used exclusively by Mersey Railway trains. The centre and southern pairs of tracks were available for use by the Wirral, the former providing a cross-platform interchange between the two companies' trains. As the OS maps show, the connections at the eastern end were removed in the early years of the 20th century and these lines then became a terminus for Wirral trains. The southern loop was added at the same time. The station buildings were situated above, at street level in Duke Street. All train movements were controlled from Birkenhead Park box, a Mersey Railway cabin which was situated on one of the platforms.

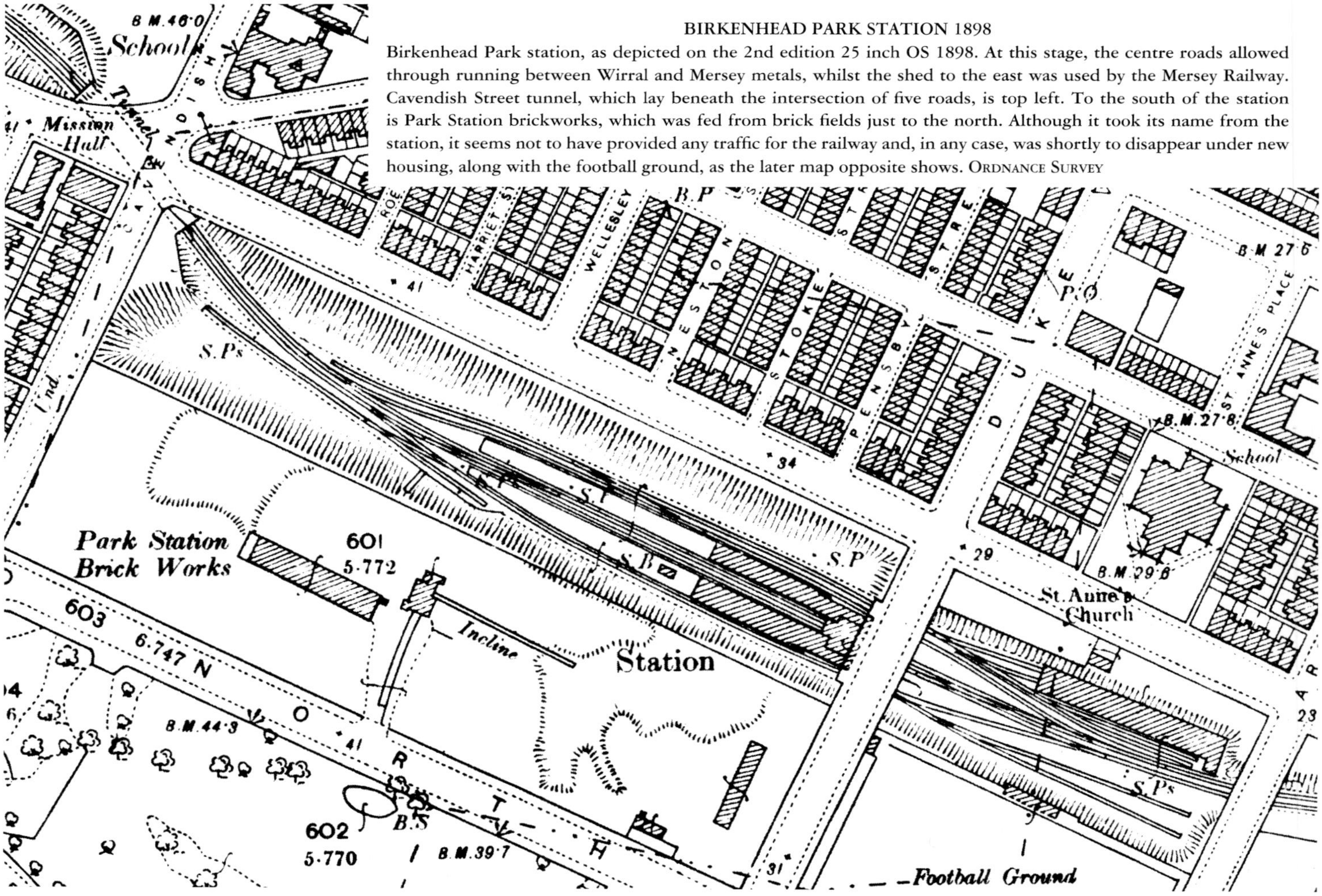

BIRKENHEAD PARK STATION 1898
Birkenhead Park station, as depicted on the 2nd edition 25 inch OS 1898. At this stage, the centre roads allowed through running between Wirral and Mersey metals, whilst the shed to the east was used by the Mersey Railway. Cavendish Street tunnel, which lay beneath the intersection of five roads, is top left. To the south of the station is Park Station brickworks, which was fed from brick fields just to the north. Although it took its name from the station, it seems not to have provided any traffic for the railway and, in any case, was shortly to disappear under new housing, along with the football ground, as the later map opposite shows. ORDNANCE SURVEY

Birkenhead Park station circa 1910, looking east towards Liverpool, with the Wirral Railway platforms to the right and a train of Mersey Railway electric stock waiting on the left. Note the station buildings straddling the tracks and facing on to Duke Street in the background. Interestingly, although Birkenhead Park box, on the right, was situated on the platforms used by the Wirral, it was a Mersey Railway structure. The box had been substantially enlarged in 1902, in connection with the Mersey electrification, and it was replaced by the LM&SR in 1938. NEIL PARKHOUSE COLLECTION

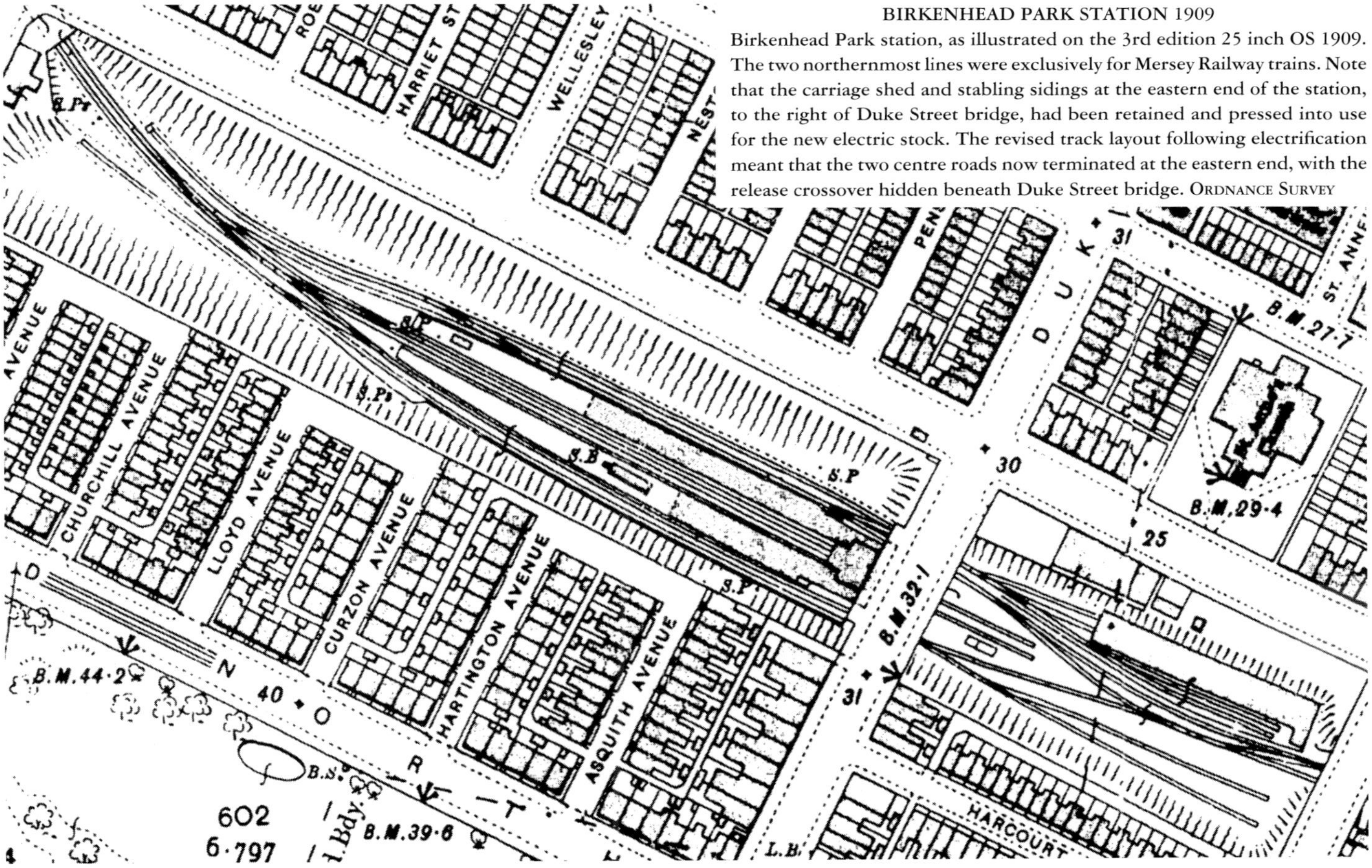

BIRKENHEAD PARK STATION 1909

Birkenhead Park station, as illustrated on the 3rd edition 25 inch OS 1909. The two northernmost lines were exclusively for Mersey Railway trains. Note that the carriage shed and stabling sidings at the eastern end of the station, to the right of Duke Street bridge, had been retained and pressed into use for the new electric stock. The revised track layout following electrification meant that the two centre roads now terminated at the eastern end, with the release crossover hidden beneath Duke Street bridge. ORDNANCE SURVEY

A slightly later view of the imposing road frontage to the station, which sat atop the bridge carrying Duke Street across the railway. As the sign on the facia board indicates (which has been repainted since the earlier view), this was a joint station between the Mersey and Wirral railways. Note that the road surface also appears much tidier. Some of the staff have come out to pose for the photograph but the pony and 2-wheeled cart in the foreground have been 'added' by the publisher of this circa 1905 postcard. A later version of the card had this cart removed and a couple of early motor cars substituted instead! JOHN RYAN COLLECTION

ABOVE: The eastern portal of Cavendish Street tunnel, photographed in LM&SR days on 17th October 1937. The signal gantry is interesting; placed close to the tunnel mouth, it attests to the cramped nature of the station site and sighting for arriving trains was limited. Note the crossover just inside the tunnel does not appear on the 1909 OS, suggesting it was a later addition. TED LLOYD COLLECTION

LEFT: The only glimpse of Birkenhead Docks station in Wirral Railway days is this view from the *Railway Magazine* of July 1914. Note that it was simply Dock Station on the running in boards (it was renamed Birkenhead North by the LM&SR in 1926), whilst the RCH Handbooks always referred to it as Birkenhead Docks. The station photographs accompanying the article were credited to local photographer Arthur Shaw of Seacombe and included a view of Wallasey, which was also published as a postcard and which appears on page 113. It is likely, therefore, that this view of Dock Station was also published as a postcard but a copy is yet to be found.

RIGHT: This view of Birkenhead North No. 1 box dates from later British Railways days. The box was at the west end of the station, with Wallasey Bridge Road crossing over the railway behind. GLYNN PARRY

BELOW: Wirral Railway No. 3, a Beyer, Peacock 0-4-4 tank, was the last new engine to be built for the company, entering service in 1914. It is seen here circa 1920, having just departed Birkenhead Docks station, with Birkenhead North engine shed and the Docks Goods station yard just featuring in the left background. The composition of the train was typical of this period, two rakes having been joined for peak hour traffic with a mixture of 4- and 6-wheeled stock, along with a couple of the bogie coaches. T.B. MAUND COLLECTION

Immediately beyond the western end of the platforms, trains enter the 71 yards Cavendish Street tunnel, followed after a quarter of a mile by the 64 yards Corporation Road tunnel. A siding on the Down side heralds the approach to Birkenhead North station, which has three platforms and is sited slightly to the south of the original Birkenhead Docks station which it replaced. The station architecture bears similarities to that at Wallasey, particularly the semi-enclosed wooden posted canopy as part of the main building. Birkenhead North No. 1 signal box stands at the western end of platform 1.

Beyond the station, the line passes under Wallasey Bridge Road, with a four-road carriage shed to the right and another two-road carriage shed, to the left. Beyond the latter can also be seen the Great Central engine shed, though there is no physical connection between the two. There is also a little used turntable to the left. The Goods station, which was the original passenger station until 1888, can be seen away to the right. Wirral sidings lead off to the right and Birkenhead Docks No. 2 signal box stands at the junction for the Goods station. The train crosses the connecting line between the Great Central sidings to the left, and the goods and the dock lines, with its several diamond crossings. Between the Wirral line and the extensive Great Central sidings is the 'Great Drain', the culverted River Birket, which has greatly assisted the drainage of this naturally

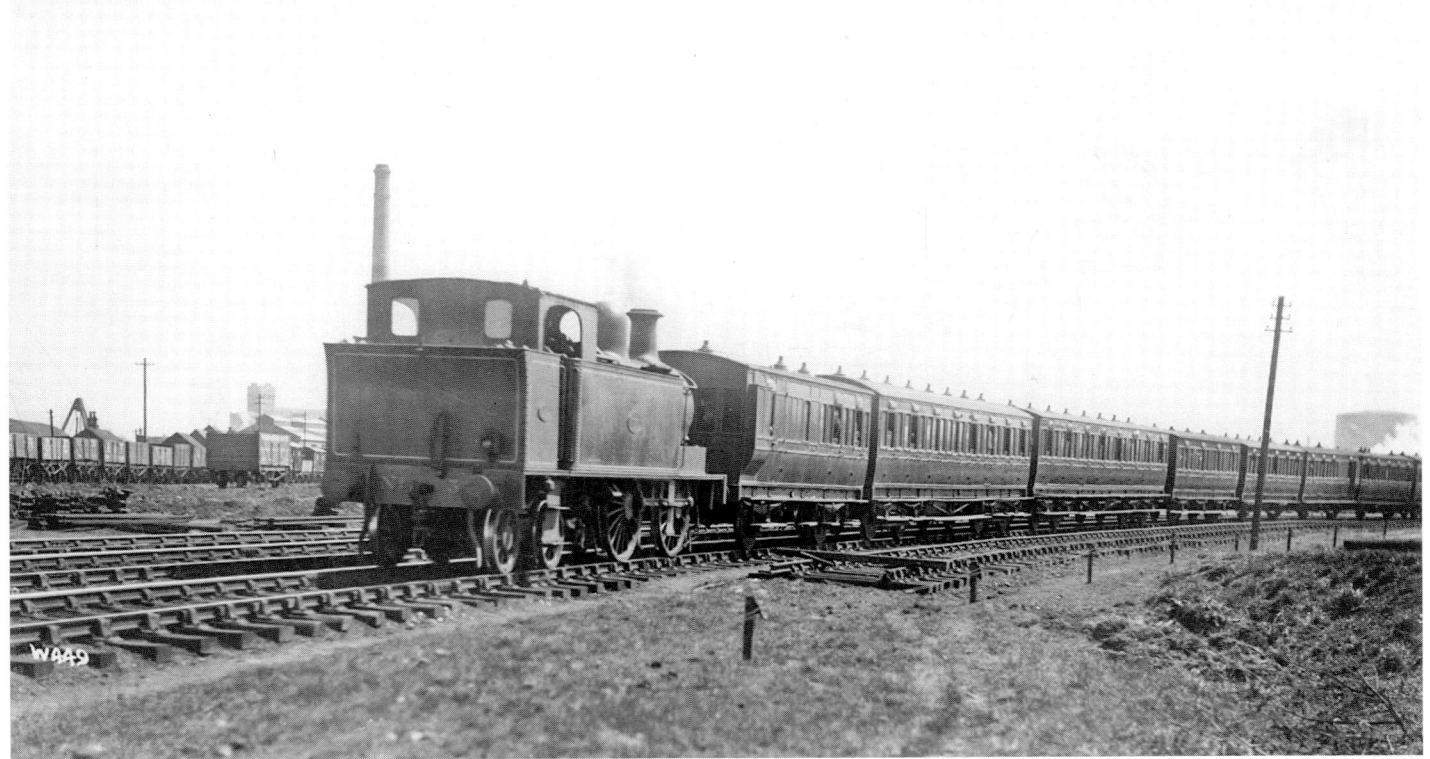

A circa 1910 view of the Wirral's rather ramshackle engine shed and locomotive repairing facilities at Birkenhead Docks. Alongside the coaling stage on the left are 0-4-4T No. 8 of 1887, which was eventually broken up in October 1923, and No. 10 of 1894, which lasted until April 1924. Behind the engine shed is the Wirral's locomotive workshop, where general repairs and heavy servicing was carried out. The independent nature of the company meant that it had to be capable of looking after its own engines and it is recorded that much good work was undertaken here, including a heavy repair to No. 7 following an accident in December 1922. Following his appointment as Locomotive Superintendent in 1903, Thomas Hunter spent around £600 over the next four years on new tools and better machinery for the workshops, including the provision of a wheel lathe. On a line blessed with numerous sharp curves, this would undoubtedly have been a most useful piece of equipment. T.B. Maund collection

These two studies of Wirral engines on shed provide further detail of the locomotive servicing facilities. The crew of 4-4-4T No. 14 pose carefully for the photographer, as they wait to move off shed in the view ABOVE. The picture BELOW is from a more unusual angle and gives a glimpse of the covered coaling stage behind WR No. 16, one of the ex-L&NWR 2-4-2Ts acquired in 1919. The appearance of a Renwick Wilton wagon here is worthy of remark. They were a large coal factor based in London, Birmingham and Torquay, and operating over much of the country but the wagon seen here seems to be one of their West Country ones, with the 'TO' of Torquay not quite obscured by No. 16's buffer. BOTH JOHN RYAN COLLECTION

WIRRAL RAILWAY
BIDSTON LOOP AND SEACOMBE JUNCTION
Redrawn from the Board of Trade Survey, 1894

New signals and cabins erected by the Railway Signalling Co., December 1894, in connection with the new line to Seacombe, and the new loop line between the Liverpool & New Brighton line and the Liverpool & Hoylake line. Provisional sanction granted 27th December. Existing box at Bidston East Junction has 10 levers in use with 6 spare, the new Bidston West Junction box has 13 levers in use with 6 spare and the new Seacombe Junction box has 29 levers in use with 5 spare. All are block posts and Sykes electrical apparatus is used for interlocking.

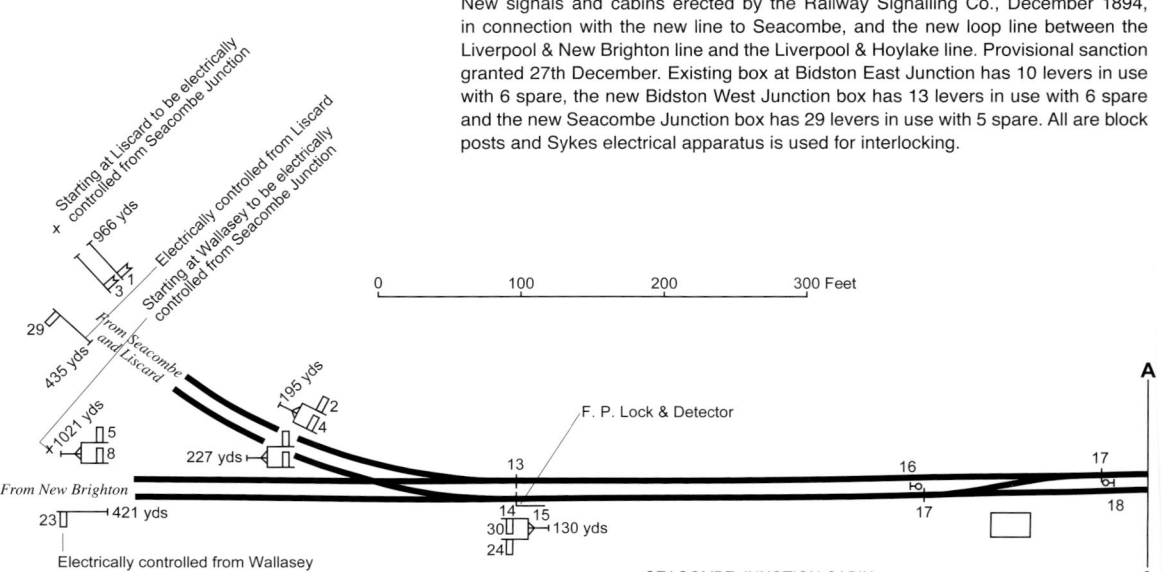

SEACOMBE JUNCTION CABIN
11.12.22.26.28.Spare

When 'Line Clear' is given to Liscard, Points Nos 13, 17 to be locked until Signal 2 or 4 is lowered & put to Danger again.
'Line Clear' to Liscard cannot be given again until 7 or 10 or 18 is lowered & put to Danger again.
Before 'Line Clear' is given to Wallasey, Points 13 must be pulled over and when 'Line Clear' is given 13 Points must be locked in the pulled over position and 17 Points locked normal until 6 or 9 has been lowered and put at Danger again.
'Line Clear' to Wallasey cannot be given until Signal 7 or 10 or 18 has been lowered and put to Danger again.

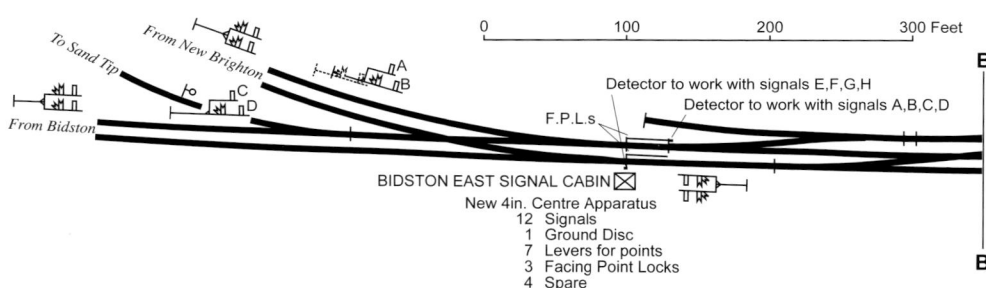

BIDSTON EAST SIGNAL CABIN
New 4in. Centre Apparatus
12 Signals
1 Ground Disc
7 Levers for points
3 Facing Point Locks
4 Spare

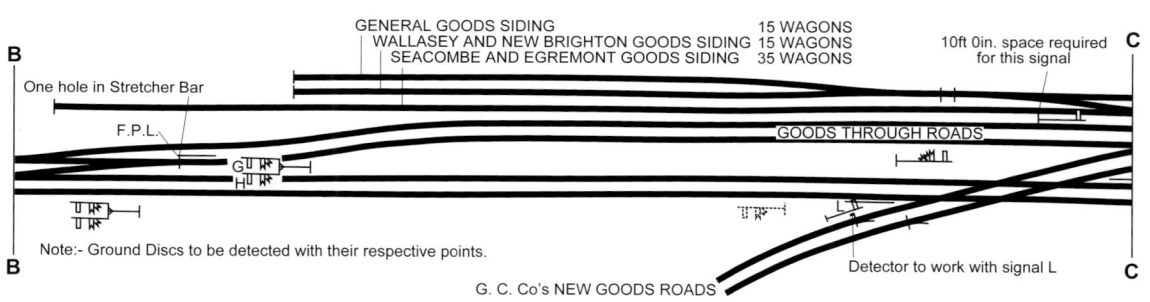

Note:- Ground Discs to be detected with their respective points.

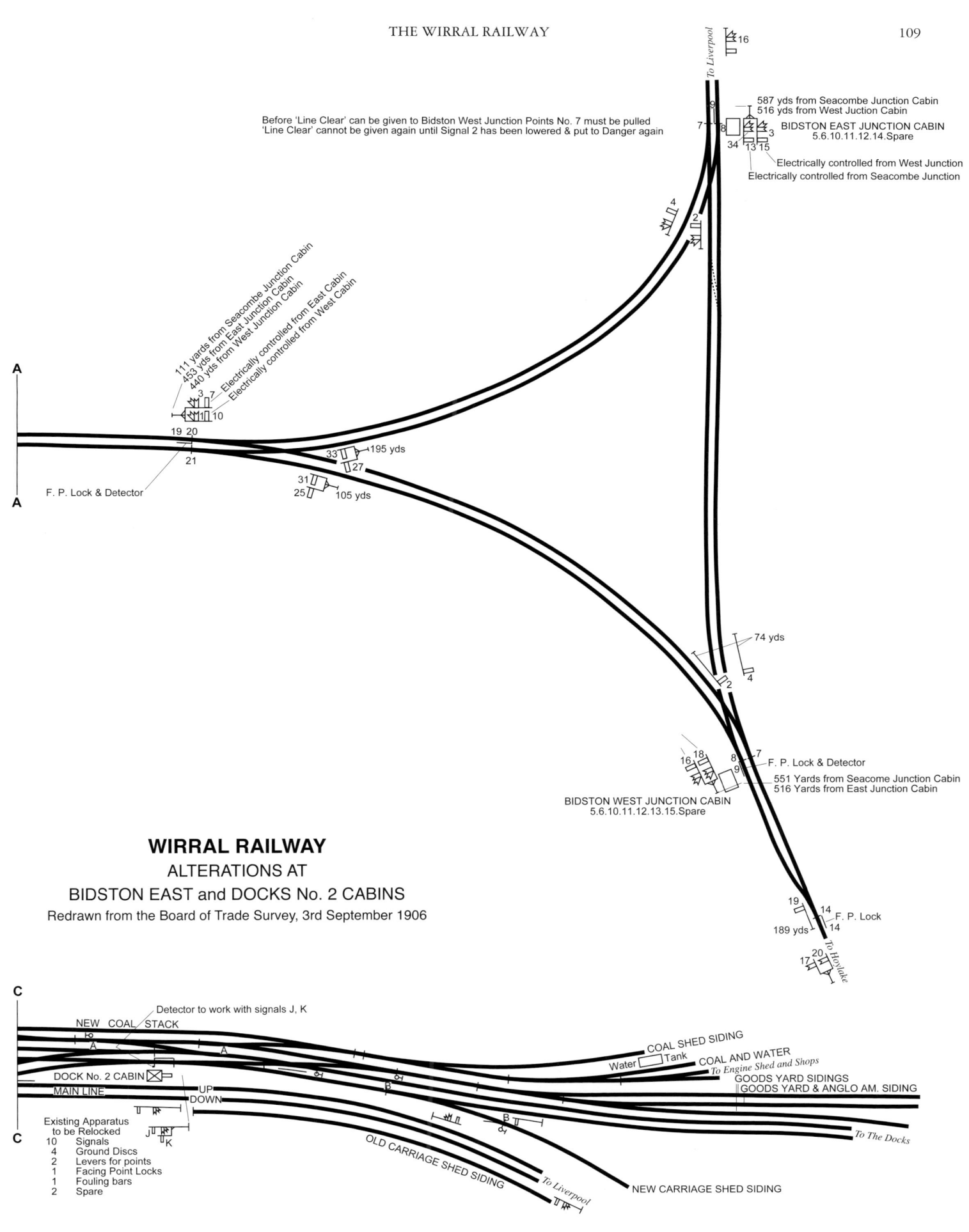

The marshy nature of the ground made it necessary for the lines to cross Bidston Moss on an embankment. This pre-WW1 view shows the chord between Seacombe No's 1 & 2 Junctions, with the branch to Seacombe curving round to the right. The pair of bracket signals are presumably the home signals for Bidston North Junction; the one on the left would control trains heading to Bidston station and points west, whilst the one on the right would be for trains heading east onto the Park Branch towards Birkenhead. Just right of centre is a rare glimpse of Seacombe Junction No. 2 signal box, which was closed and demolished when the chord was removed. The Bidston footpath, a popular walk for Wallasey people, follows the line and still exists though it had to be diverted when the Bidston Dock reception sidings were built. The top of New Brighton tower can just be seen peeping over the top of the hill; the line to New Brighton headed off behind the platelayers' hut, before curving right around the hill to terminate just beneath the tower. WALLASEY TRAMCAR PRESERVATION GROUP

ABOVE: Seacombe No. 1 Junction, with a train coming off the Seacombe branch, probably circa 1925. The photographer has his back to the signal box but nothing will have changed in this view from Wirral Railway days. The church on the skyline is St. Hilary's at Wallasey.

RIGHT: The one major change at this location, which occurred in Wirral Railway days, was the closure in July 1914 of the connecting chord between the Seacombe and New Brighton lines, as shown on the MT plans on the previous pages. This was an obvious economy, following the failure of the 'Seacombe Dodger' passenger service, and enabled the closure of two signal boxes, Seacombe Junction No's 2 & 3. The rails were lifted in 1915 for the war effort. This view is looking from the site of Seacombe Junction No. 2, with the bare alignment of the chord curving off to the right. BOTH C.E. HEYWOOD COLLECTION

marshy area.

At Bidston East Junction, where there is another signal box, the train takes the right hand curve, negotiating the eastern sector of the Bidston triangle, joining the Seacombe-West Kirby line on an embankment at Bidston North Junction. Almost immediately, the Seacombe line goes off to the right at Seacombe Junction No. 1. There was formerly another triangular layout here but the north-east sector was removed during the 1914-18 war.

The line now gently curves north-westwards and soon crosses Leasowe Road, via the only overbridge on the system, to reach Wallasey Village station, catering only for passenger traffic. A short straight section in urban surroundings leads to Wallasey station (later to be renamed Wallasey Grove Road), which has substantial buildings, including a stationmaster's house, a small two-road goods yard with shed and a coal siding. Wallasey signal box stands to the left beyond the station.

After passing under Harrison Drive, the line runs between golf links with views of the open sea to the left. It climbs steadily at an average 1 in 88, the steepest gradient on the line, heading eastward with the urbanised high ground of Wallasey and New Brighton visible to the right. This part of the route suffers from sand blowing on to the line, a problem which has not been completely solved by the planting of star grass. It was also the site of the little used and relatively short lived Warren halt. This first appeared in the timetables for November 1888 but for much of its life, the service consisted of just one train each way per day, although there were occasional

This pre-First World War view of Wallasey, from the sand hills on the edge of the town, is looking west towards Birkenhead, which lies beyond the low hill on which St Hilary's church stands in the left background. Wallasey station can be seen in the centre, with a Seacombe-bound service, which has skirted the edge of the hill to the right of the picture, waiting at the platform. Notice how the station was built in a hollow and was consequently slightly below the level of much of the village. The large house on the left is the Vicarage. JOHN RYAN COLLECTION

WALLASEY STATION 1926
Wallasey station, as shown on the 4th edition 25 inch OS 1926. The entrance to the station is at the junction of Groveland Road and Harrison Drive. ORDNANCE SURVEY

An Edwardian postcard view of Wallasey station, showing the handsome brick-built station building and the footbridge, a hybrid of timber, iron and glass, which abutted on to the stone built bridge carrying Groveland Road across the line. However, there was no direct access to the road from the footbridge, so prospective passengers had to reach the platforms through the station building. Above the entrance to the footbridge is a Wirral Railway notice exhorting passengers to cross the line only by the bridge. The station nameboard is unusual; few locations in the British Isles carried the word 'station' on the nameboard, much less the full stop! Note, too, that the station name is also proclaimed in painted shaded letters on the front of the canopy. The view is looking in the Birkenhead direction; the small goods yard here was to the left of the photographer, Arthur Shaw of Seacombe. This is the only one of the station views published in 1914 by the *Railway Magazine* of which an original has been found. JOHN ALSOP COLLECTION

WARREN HALT 1899
Warren halt, which was termed as 'station' on the 2nd edition 25 inch OS 1899. Perhaps it was hoped that the grand new homes being built in Warren Drive would provide custom for the line. ORDNANCE SURVEY

Warren halt, looking towards New Brighton when it was still in very limited use. The bridge over Sandcliffe Road (then called Jockey Lane) is in the foreground, with the homes (many of them newly built) of the well-to-do in Warren Drive in the background. COURTESY G. PARRY

LEFT: This view of Warren halt, looking west towards Wallasey and with the Irish Sea in the background, shows sand drifting over the platforms. However, the dress of the little girl on the left would suggest this is pre-WW1, when the halt was still open. MARTIN JENKINS COLLECTION

LEFT BELOW: Warren halt after closure, probably taken around 1930 and looking towards New Brighton. The second platform had been removed at an unknown date, sometime after closure. JOHN RYAN COLLECTION

times of extra use. It was used mainly by golfers and walkers but was closed from 1st October 1915, presumably as a war time economy measure. However, it was left *in situ* and remained in the RCH *Station Handbook*, and may have seen the odd special call from time to time. The halt was substantially built, with proper brick-faced, cinder-filled platforms and there were brick buildings on both platforms. Obviously, the traffic the railway expected to be generated never materialised.

The train now enters a rock cutting and, on the approach to New Brighton station, the sand siding can be seen leading off to the left. The station comprises a single curving island platform with a line each side, each with its own run-round. To the north is the goods yard with two sidings and a shed, and beyond that there are two coal sidings. The two-storey station buildings house the Wirral company's head office. From the station exit there is an attractive view over Liverpool Bay and the estuary of the River Mersey.

The distance from Birkenhead Park to New Brighton is just 4.13 miles.

RIGHT: This view of New Brighton terminus is another of the pictures which accompanied the *Railway Magazine* article of 1914. In common with the other pictures, it has not been possible to get a good reproduction from the pages of the magazine but the view is nevertheless sufficiently unusual to merit reproduction here. This is a passenger's eye view of the station from the island platform, with the tower in the background and it is to be hoped that a good photographic copy turns up eventually.

WR No. 6 prepares to run round its carriages having disgorged another trainload of passengers at Seacombe station around 1910, whilst a second train, probably Great Central, which has arrived with engine bunker first, empties on to the adjacent platform the other side of the fence. These would be services from West Kirby and Wrexham respectively, whilst the stock for an outward bound train can be seen on the right. JOHN ALSOP COLLECTION

SEACOMBE TO WEST KIRBY

Seacombe station lies at the junction of Church Road and Borough Road, about 200 yards from the ferry terminal buildings. The minimal buildings provided here comprise a covered waiting area alongside the booking office. The three platforms are made of sleepers and cinders, and there is also a small waiting room on platform 1, which runs parallel to Church Road. Three sidings run parallel to the island platform on the north side of the station. The signal box is located in the station throat and several crossovers facilitate the movement of trains to and from the platforms and sidings.

From Seacombe, double tracks run due west, passing under four overbridges. Beyond the fourth, which carries Oakdale Road, the goods depot and coal yard with its four sidings, can be seen on the north side. The line now runs on a low embankment and, after passing the junction for the goods depot, there is a vista of the dock sheds and Duke Street bridge on the south side. There is a further siding on the north side giving access to the narrow gauge railway of the nearby Brick & Tile works. Seacombe & Egremont Goods Yard signal box, controlling the various siding junctions, stands on the south side, close to the siding connection which led to the Birkenhead Steel Rolling Mills; this company's sidings were linked at the other end with the dock lines but had been closed and cleared in 1911-12. Beyond Gorsey Lane is the junction giving access to the Wallasey Gas & Electricity works.

The line curves first to the right and then to the left through a

Liscard & Poulton station, taken circa 1914 by Arthur Shaw of Seacombe. Situated in a rock cutting, it was also little photographed. The point in the foreground gave access to the coal siding. MARTIN JENKINS COLLECTION

ABOVE: This 1920s view of the station gives a good impression of its cramped site, with the minimum clearance afforded either side of the waiting rooms on the island platform, Access was by the enclosed staircase running down from road level behind. Note the signal placed high up on the embankment for sighting purposes beyond Mill Lane road bridge. The approach road to the second Mersey road tunnel now occupies this cutting. The quarry and its siding was slightly behind and to the right of the photographer. JOHN ALSOP COLLECTION

LEFT: Ironically, although it generally received little in the way of attention from photographers, Liscard & Poulton station featured on one of the best known and most widely distributed postcards of the Edwardian era. This comic design was used by resorts and towns across the country for overprinting with local place names, this example reading *'Arrived Safely at Colwyn Bay'* – which it patently isn't! The porter looks genuine and the young lady, probably a local lass, a friend of or regular model for the photographer. The side of the rock cutting is visible on the left, with Breck Road bridge in the background. The card is postmarked 20th May 1908, which gives a good indication of the date of the original picture. Note the 'WIRRAL RAILWAY' name is quite clearly seen on the noticeboard. G. PARRY COLLECTION

rock cutting, which eventually widens out to accommodate Liscard & Poulton passenger station with its solitary coal siding. The station is reached by a private road from Mill Lane and comprises an island platform with waiting room and inspector's office. A short siding on the south side leading into a quarry was dismantled around the time of the First World War.

After passing under Breck Road bridge, the line passes Slopes Branch signal box and the junction for the Slopes Branch, which connects with the Dock Board lines on the north side of the dock system. The proposed Breck Road station was to be built nearby. The surrounding land is now low-lying and the line runs on a shallow embankment, with the western extremity of the Wallasey Pool (which will be converted into Bidston Dock in 1933), beyond. A gentle left-hand curve brings the route to Seacombe Junction, where it joins the Park-New Brighton line for a few yards, before taking the right hand curve at Bidston Junction North and entering Bidston station.

LISCARD & POULTON STATION 1898

Liscard & Poulton station, as shown on the 2nd edition 25 inch OS 1898. The short siding serving the quarry is still *in situ*, as it is on the portion of the 1912 OS, on page 39. The quarry is believed to have fallen out of use and the siding removed during the First World War. There was a crossover at the western end of the station only, which was presumably installed to facilitate shunting of this siding at the same time as the coal siding. ORDNANCE SURVEY

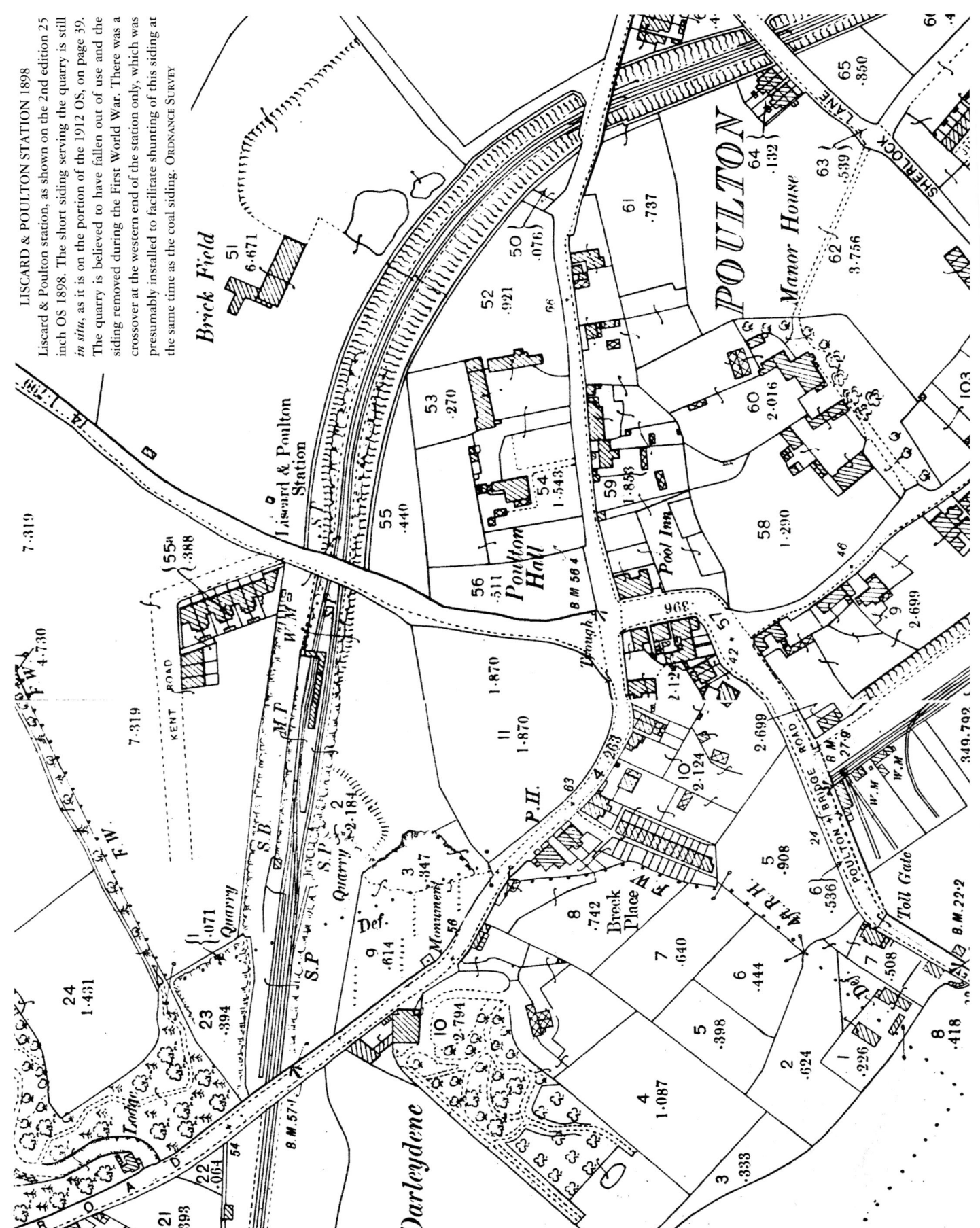

LEFT: Looking east towards the site of Seacombe Junction No. 2. This picture corresponds with the lower view on page 111 and is taken from the trackbed of the abandoned Seacombe-New Brighton chord.

BELOW: The view from Bidston station footbridge to Bidston West Junction around 1925, with the line to New Brighton and Seacombe swinging away to the left and that to Birkenhead Park curving off to the right. Bidston East Junction box can just be discerned around the curve to the right. The single line on the right leads to the Great Central's engine shed. The abandoned route to the left, running behind West Junction box and marked by the remains of a single track bridge, is presumed to be the original alignment of the Hoylake Railway. BOTH C.E. HEYWOOD COLLECTION

This is a rather primitive island platform affair, built entirely of wood because of the marshy ground. To the south is the simple goods depot and the extensive Great Central sidings, linked to the Wrexham GC line which leaves the Wirral tracks at Dee Junction, a few yards beyond the station. Bidston Hill with its observatory and windmill rises to the left.

The line now follows a dead straight course for almost a mile to Leasowe station, with its level crossing and hand-operated gates. There are no goods facilities here.

A journey of a further 0.64 of a mile over straight track then brings the line to Moreton station, where there is a short coal siding on the south side. The station buildings stand on Pasture Road bridge, beyond which, on the north side, is the entrance to the Brick Works siding.

On leaving Moreton, the line curves gently over a distance of 1.82 miles on the level to reach Meols station, passing over two unmanned crossings on the way. Meols has no sidings and the station offices are situated on the bridge crossing over the line at this point.

Still curving gently to the left, the line continues to Hoylake, an important station and originally the terminus of the route. Just before reaching it, sidings lead off to the left successively to the Electricity Works, Gas Works and Carriage Works. The Company minutes of 28th October 1874 record the invitation for tenders to construct an engine shed but there is no evidence of one being built. To the right, there is access to a small goods depot and coal yard. Departure from Hoylake station is over a level crossing controlled from the nearby signal box.

The line continues its slightly curved progress to West Kirby, where an island platform is flanked by carriage sidings on both sides. To the east there is a three road goods depot with a shed. At the approach to the station, there is a double track connection to the GW/L&NW Joint line, with its separate passenger station only a few yards away to the east. The Wirral's West Kirby signal box stands close to this junction.

Another variation on the 'classic' view of Leasowe, this one dating from circa 1908 and including a horse and cart posed on the level crossing. The poster board on the Down platform is lettered London & North Western Railway and note the photographer's addition of 'station' below the running in board; the backward 'S' was quite a common error when such wording had to be painted on the reverse of the glass negative! JOHN RYAN COLLECTION

A slightly more elevated viewpoint for this photograph of WR No. 17 arriving at Leasowe with a train for West Kirby, comprised of two of the 5-coach sets, around 1910. Note the arrival of a Down train is also signalled. JOHN ALSOP COLLECTION

ABOVE: An early 20th century view of Moreton station and Pasture Road bridge, looking west towards West Kirby. Note the tall starter signal, on a slender, tapering lattice post, unusual for the Wirral which generally seemed to be equipped with wooden-posted signals. The crossover just beyond the bridge matched one at the east end of the station, which also connected to the single siding in the yard on the south side of the station. The Moreton Brick & Tile Company's siding led off to the right just under the bridge; the end of the point can just be made out.

RIGHT: Moreton station staff (plus possibly some local carters or coal merchants) in 1912. The wearing of railway uniform seems to have been somewhat 'open to interpretation'. BOTH JOHN RYAN COLLECTION

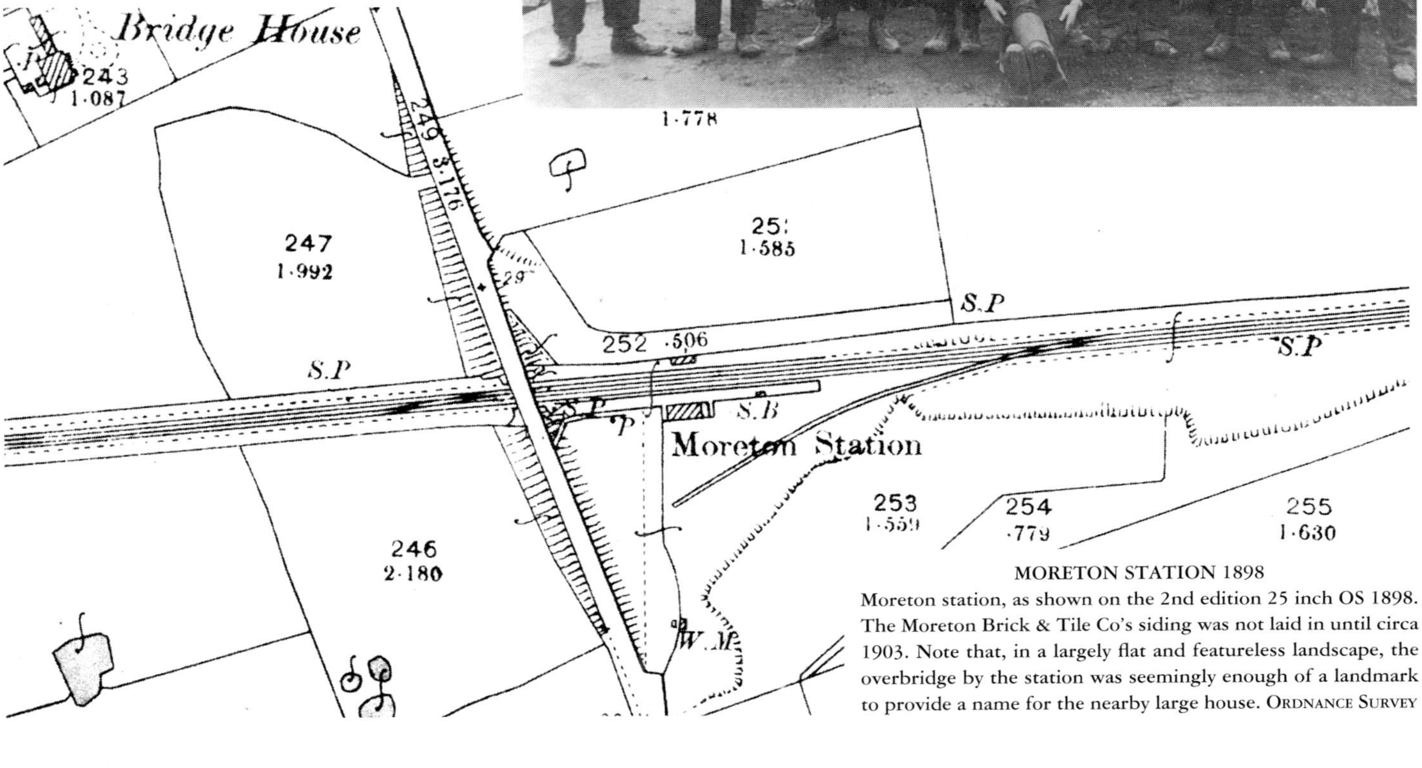

MORETON STATION 1898
Moreton station, as shown on the 2nd edition 25 inch OS 1898. The Moreton Brick & Tile Co's siding was not laid in until circa 1903. Note that, in a largely flat and featureless landscape, the overbridge by the station was seemingly enough of a landmark to provide a name for the nearby large house. ORDNANCE SURVEY

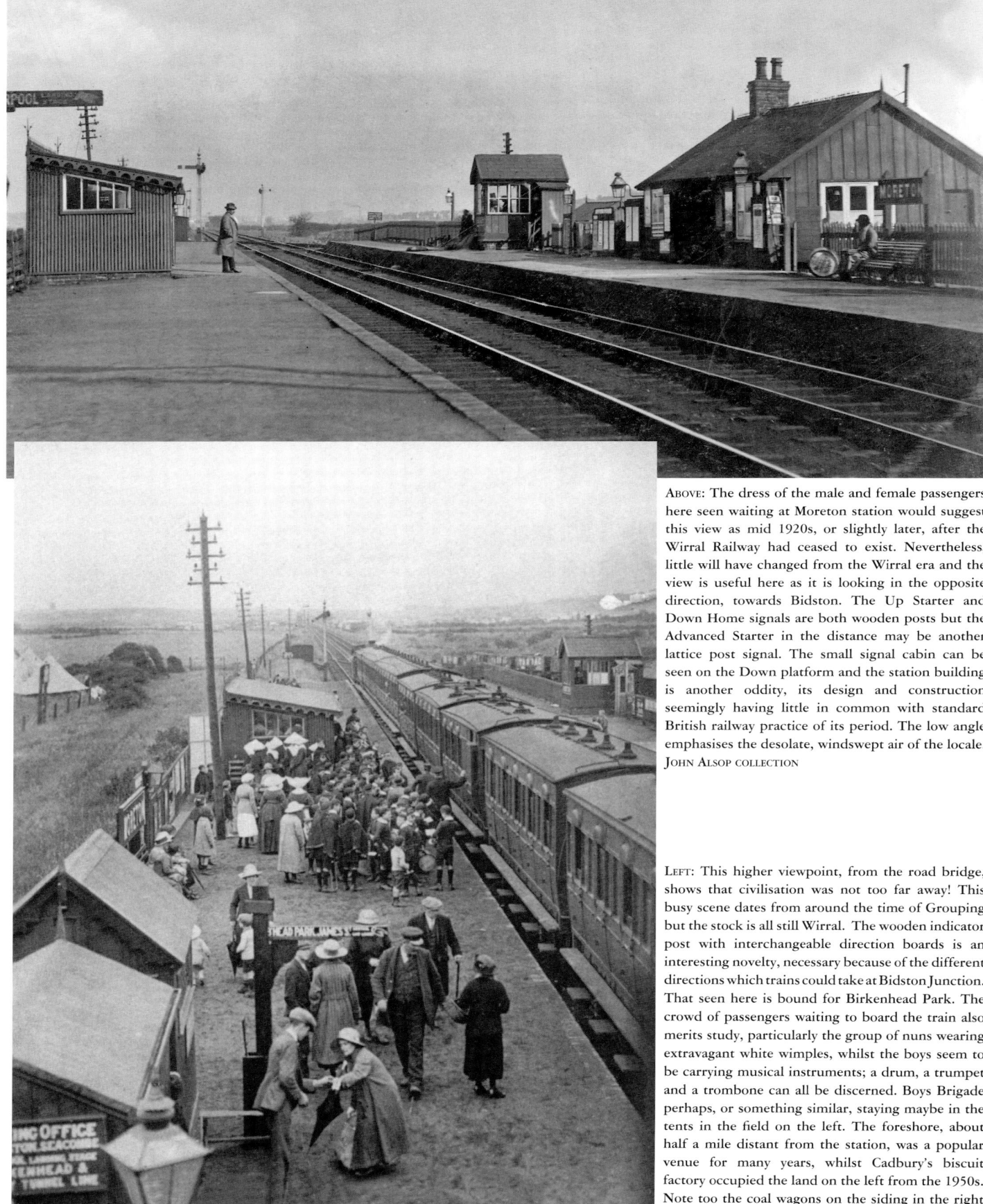

ABOVE: The dress of the male and female passengers here seen waiting at Moreton station would suggest this view as mid 1920s, or slightly later, after the Wirral Railway had ceased to exist. Nevertheless, little will have changed from the Wirral era and the view is useful here as it is looking in the opposite direction, towards Bidston. The Up Starter and Down Home signals are both wooden posts but the Advanced Starter in the distance may be another lattice post signal. The small signal cabin can be seen on the Down platform and the station building is another oddity, its design and construction seemingly having little in common with standard British railway practice of its period. The low angle emphasises the desolate, windswept air of the locale. JOHN ALSOP COLLECTION

LEFT: This higher viewpoint, from the road bridge, shows that civilisation was not too far away! This busy scene dates from around the time of Grouping but the stock is all still Wirral. The wooden indicator post with interchangeable direction boards is an interesting novelty, necessary because of the different directions which trains could take at Bidston Junction. That seen here is bound for Birkenhead Park. The crowd of passengers waiting to board the train also merits study, particularly the group of nuns wearing extravagant white wimples, whilst the boys seem to be carrying musical instruments; a drum, a trumpet and a trombone can all be discerned. Boys Brigade perhaps, or something similar, staying maybe in the tents in the field on the left. The foreshore, about half a mile distant from the station, was a popular venue for many years, whilst Cadbury's biscuit factory occupied the land on the left from the 1950s. Note too the coal wagons on the siding in the right background. IAN BOUMPHREY COLLECTION

RIGHT: Meols was another under photographed station in Wirral Railway days and generally only appears because postcard photographers were intent on capturing the lake next to it – or 'pond' as the publisher of the postcard view at the bottom of this page termed it! The locomotive of this train, *en route* to West Kirby, is obscured by the platform shelter. In the foreground is Meols Lake, which is said to have been created by the Hoylake Railway for boating and skating, in order to stimulate traffic. JOHN RYAN COLLECTION

LEFT: There is little evidence of any craft for prospective boaters in any of these views, so it is presumed that no such traffic was ever seriously developed. However, this vista of the lake includes part of the waiting shelter on the West Kirby platform on the left, as well as the pedestrian entrance to this platform from the road bridge.

BELOW: The rear of Meols signal box and the main station building as seen from the far side of the lake. Interestingly, the signal box was tinted a dark green on this hand coloured postcard, suggesting this was indeed the colour the Wirral painted their wooden structures. The deck of the road bridge looks to be steel girders. BOTH JOHN RYAN COLLECTION

WIRRAL RAILWAY
MEOLS STATION
Redrawn from the Board of Trade Survey,
17th February 1914
Showing new crossover and associated signalling

Whilst many of the Wirral Railway's stations seemed to be largely ignored by Edwardian photographers, Hoylake, by comparison, enjoyed an inordinate amount of coverage, which is doubly odd when its distinctively shambolic appearance is taken into account. The photograph above dates from 1906 and the viewpoint emphasises the low platforms. The view below is possibly a year or two later and shows the buildings on the Up platform in some detail. There is what appears to be a large clock attached to a wooden post at the far end of the main building, an unusual arrangement for a small station. However, it may be a manually operated train arrival indicator – useful on what was largely a suburban passenger route – rather than a working clock. Just beyond that, a cloth awning juts out from the centre of the next building, which rather looks to be an on-platform greengrocer's shop; were the Wirral ahead of their time in maximising station rents? Note too the Great Northern Railway and Midland Railway noticeboards on the left. BOTH JOHN ALSOP COLLECTION

Hoylake station, looking north circa 1906. The goods and coal yard is behind the Birkenhead-bound platform, whilst in the left foreground can be seen part of the carriage works, with a rude wooden fence used to screen it from the platform. The impressive array of enamelled advertising signs and noticeboards serve only to emphasize the station's untidy appearance rather than disguise it. JOHN RYAN COLLECTION

A service for West Kirby, headed by an unidentified 0-4-4T, arrives at Hoylake station circa 1912. The standard set of six 4- and 6-wheeled carriages has been strengthened by the addition of a single bogie coach in the centre. JOHN McROBERTS COLLECTION

LEFT: Ex-L&NWR 2-4-2T No. 889 as WR No. 16 is seen poised at the throat of West Kirby Wirral station, with the driver carrying out a spot of oiling as they wait to run back into the platform to couple up to an eastbound service. The GW/L&NW Joint line platform is in the background. The view was taken, around the time of the 1923 Grouping, from Bridge Road on the embankment leading up to the bridge, with the signal box just off to the right. JOHN RYAN COLLECTION

ABOVE: The road frontage of West Kirby station probably in the early 1920s, around the time of the Grouping, with a selection of motor taxis on view. The passenger access to the platforms is just out of view to the left. It is obviously a quiet time between trains, so the drivers have gathered in the street for a chat whilst they await their next fares. The raised viewpoint suggests the photograph was taken from the window of a house or hotel opposite. Grange Road rises to cross over the GW/L&NW Joint line in the right background. The brick-built goods shed is prominent in the yard and note the coal merchants' offices clustered around the entrance, with that of the Cheshire Coal Co. nearest. JOHN RYAN COLLECTION

RIGHT: Another poor but otherwise rare view of the terminus circa 1914, which again comes from the *Railway Magazine*. The last of the station pictures accompanying the article, it was the also work of Seacombe photographer Arthur Shaw.

WEST KIRBY STATION 1899 & 1909

Development at West Kirby station, as shown on the 1st and 2nd edition 25 inch OS maps for 1899 (below) and 1909 (right). As originally built, the station had limited siding accommodation for both goods and carriage stock. By 1909, an enlarged island platform had been built on some of the spare land just to the west of the station and space created for three carriage storage sidings and three extra goods sidings. The line into the station was double-tracked, as was the connection to the GW/L&NW Joint's West Kirby station immediately to the east. Note this latter was also equipped with a small turntable; Joint line passenger services terminated here and it may have been used for turning Brake vans. Extensive building development had also taken place to the west of the Wirral station and to the north of Bridge Road. ORDNANCE SURVEY

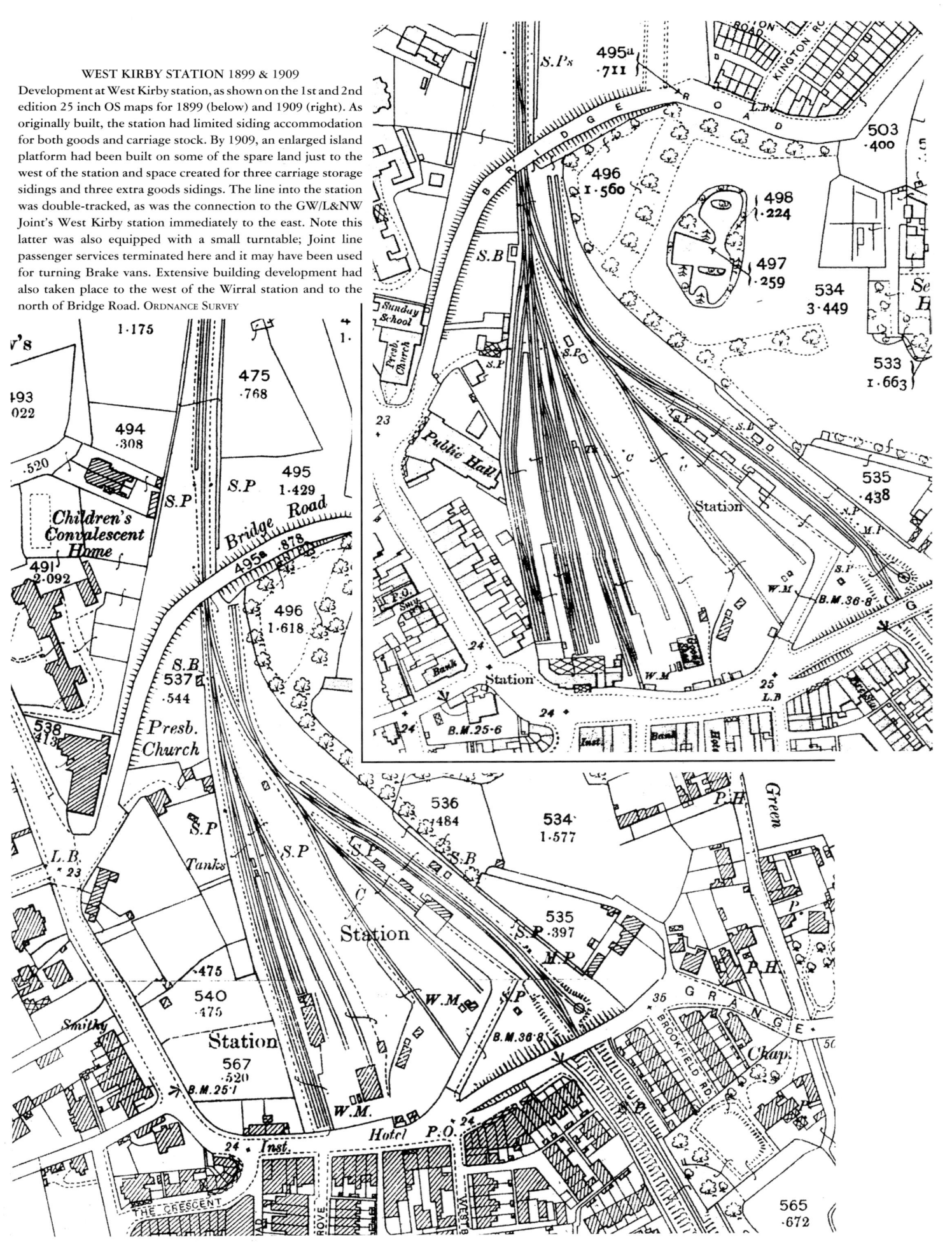

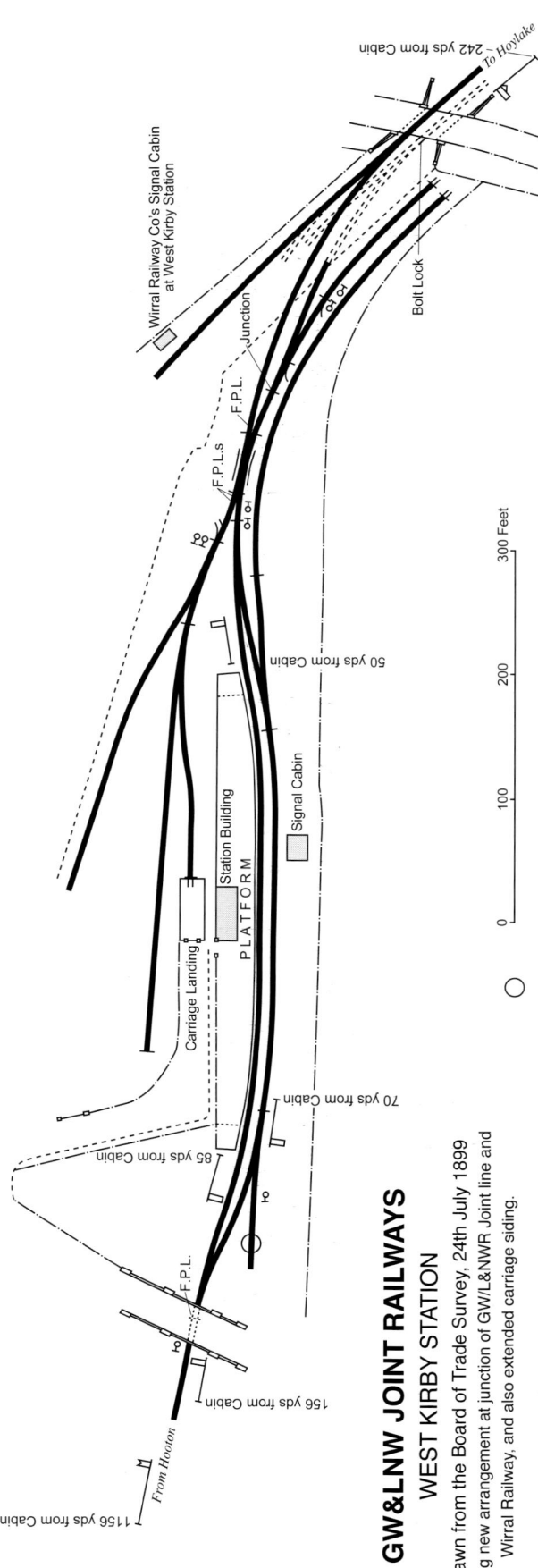

GW&LNW JOINT RAILWAYS
WEST KIRBY STATION

Redrawn from the Board of Trade Survey, 24th July 1899
Showing new arrangement at junction of GW/L&NWR Joint line and Wirral Railway, and also extended carriage siding.

ABOVE: This 1899 track plan shows the new layout of the junction between the GW/L&NWR Joint line and the Wirral Railway at West Kirby. Note the turntable at the southern end of the loop. Although strictly not of interest here, as this station was not used by Wirral trains, the turntable scales to less than 20 feet in diameter, which begs the question what was it for? It is shown on both OS extracts on the previous page, which clearly indicate it was not connected to anything else, so is not a wagon turntable. However, it is too small to be for locomotives, other than the smallest tank engines which would not have required turning.

LEFT & FAR LEFT: These memoranda from the general manager (Carr) to Mr Jones, stationmaster at Birkenhead Docks, cast light on operational matters in the last years of the 19th century. The first, dated 15th March 1895, complains of the absence of a signalman at Seacombe Junction, resulting in the early Seacombe to West Kirby mail train having to divert via Birkenhead Docks and reverse, as the points at Bidston Junction could not be changed. The second, dated 4th August 1896 demands an explanation for a Birkenhead Park-New Brighton train being delayed by three minutes. JOHN RYAN COLLECTION

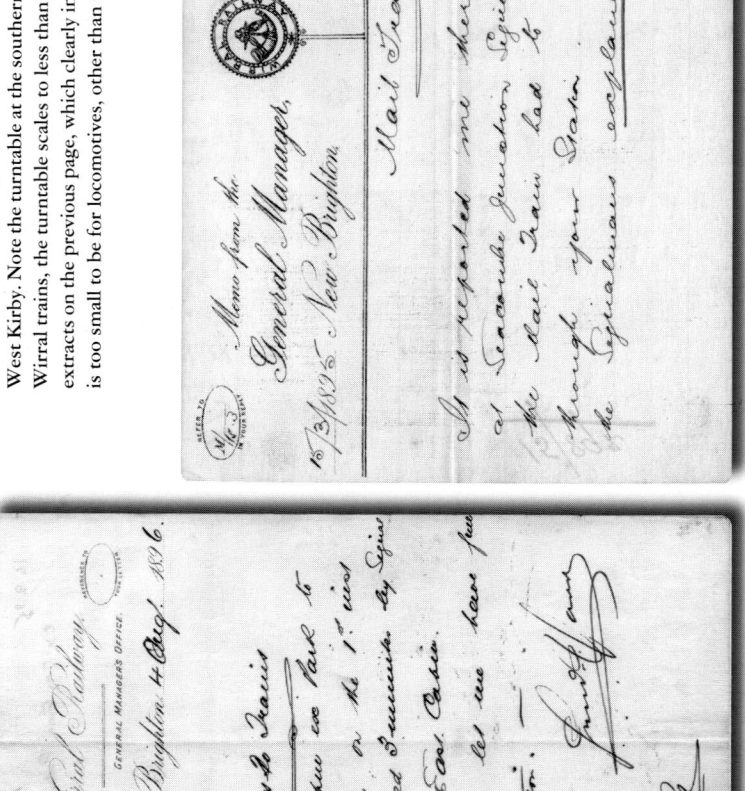

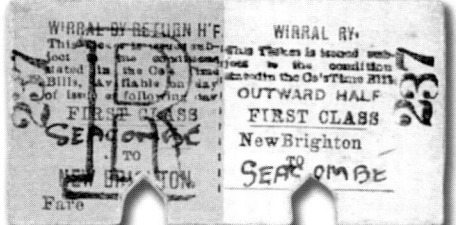
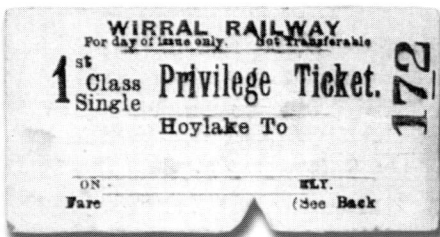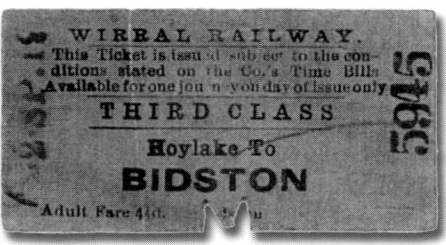
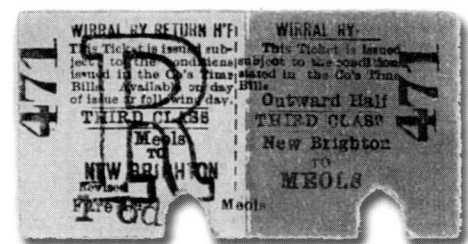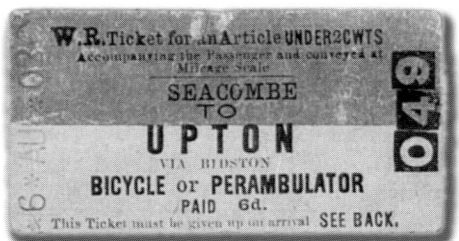

ABOVE: A selection of Wirral Railway tickets. Note there was no pre-printed ticket for the First Class return journey between Seacombe and New Brighton, so the clerk had to hand write Seacombe on the ticket – already an indication that the direct chord linking the Seacombe and New Brighton lines was underused. However, other journeys off the Wirral system were more common and merited their own printed tickets, such as to Spital and Upton, and from Chester.

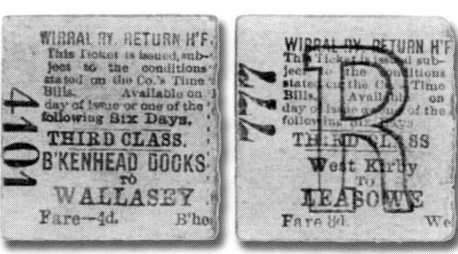

RIGHT: A Wirral Railway parcels way bill covering a parcel addressed to W.D. Haswell, the company secretary, whose office was in Chester. It was sent 'OCS' (On Company Service) on 14th January 1918.

LEFT: The reverse of the Wirral Railway official postcard, the map on the front of which is reproduced on the front title page. This extremely rare and collectable postcard was issued in 1907 for use as a correspondence card by Company officials, and is the only postcard design so far known to have been published by the Company. Indeed, there is only one other recorded Wirral Railway official postcard but this is an overprint of a card issued by another publisher, something which was common practice amongst the larger railway companies. JOHN ALSOP COLLECTION

LEFT: A Wirral Railway Summary of Cash Receipts – Goods, for April 1892.

BELOW: A Wirral Railway memo re stopping at Warren halt for a Submarine Mining Engineers Camp between 8-20th June 1896.

ABOVE: A Wirral Railway telephone message form, used on 13th April 1896.

RIGHT: A Wirral Railway porters' bill of July 1908, regarding boxes of fish from Grimsby Docks.

CHAPTER 3

THE WIRRAL IN LM&SR DAYS

The Railways Act, 1921, had the objective of creating a more modern railway system for Great Britain. During the First World War, the railways had been under government control and operated as one system controlled by a Railway Executive Committee. There was no appetite for nationalisation either politically or economically but it was realised that some of the layers of Victorian legislation, much of it designed to prevent monopolistic railway companies holding industry to ransom, needed to be swept away. There were still over 120 separate railway companies with a tremendous range of sizes, from the gigantic London & North Western Railway to the tiny Mersey and Wirral concerns. Based to some extent on wartime experience, it was decided to group the railways into four large regional companies, a process which became known as 'the Grouping' and was set for 1st January 1923. However, the London & North Western and Lancashire & Yorkshire railways were combined from 1st January 1922. The new companies were named the Southern (SR), Great Western (GWR), London & North Eastern (L&NER) and London, Midland & Scottish (LM&SR) railways. The latter was formed from eight principal companies and twenty-seven minor ones, of which the Wirral was one. The transfer was made under the LMS Railway Absorption [No.1] Scheme, 1923. It was the statutory Wirral Railway Company that was taken over, the Wirral Railways Co. Ltd, which held most of the shares, remaining in existence.

By virtue of the location of its major activities, the Great Central became part of the L&NER, which led to the anomaly of giving this railway of eastern England a presence in Wirral and North Wales. However, illogical outrunnings of this kind were allowed to persist and were not eliminated until well into the post-nationalisation years.

INTEGRATION OF THE WIRRAL LINES WITH THE LM&SR

The LM&SR found the Wirral in a very run down and, in some respects, almost derelict condition. Shortage of manpower and materials during the war had contributed to this state of affairs but the financial position, accentuated by restricted wartime traffic, shorter working hours (adding to labour costs) and post-war inflation had limited the management's ability to take the necessary action. As explained in Chapter 2, cash flow problems had forced the company to resort to the purchase of second-hand engines and carriages, and the poor condition of the rolling stock and infrastructure affected the company's performance, whilst ruling out modernisation. Despite the ingenuity of its officers, the company's small size imposed disproportionately high overhead costs.

The small, poorly equipped workshops were closed and work transferred to Crewe, Derby and Horwich. As described below, the locomotive stud was replaced by ex-L&NW or L&Y machines, some of which were older but nevertheless in better condition. Birkenhead Docks locomotive shed was designated No. 12 in the Western Division. The antiquated passenger carriages were all removed for scrapping, being replaced by ex-L&NW bogie stock, which carried its former owner's livery for some time before it was repainted into LM&S maroon. Carriages were made up into permanently coupled rakes of four, labelled on the ends as 'Wirral Section No. 1' etc. Two-coach strengthening sets were added at peak hours. The Hoylake carriage and paint shop was closed down and several lower-quadrant signals on wooden posts were replaced by L&NWR equipment. The LM&S, which had inherited responsibility for track and signalling on the adjacent Joint lines, could easily adapt its existing organisation

The LM&SR closed the Wirral's carriage and paint shops at Hoylake soon after taking over, having also removed the company's antiquated and worn out passenger stock from service. The buildings remained extant however, albeit with the track truncated short of the entrance doors, as this view taken on 26th February 1938 shows. The carriage shop is on the left and the paint shop on the right. TED LLOYD COLLECTION

LEFT: The new order on the Wirral after Grouping. Ex-L&NWR 'Watford Tank' No. 27664 departs Moreton with a train for West Kirby. The date is uncertain but is probably in the later 1920s. TED LLOYD COLLECTION

BELOW: Webb 'Coal tank' No. 7583 passes Bidston West Junction with a West Kirby-bound train shortly after Grouping. The coaches look to be the Wirral bogie stock. TED LLOYD COLLECTION

to include the Wirral lines. The turntable at Birkenhead Docks was removed in 1925; on the rare occasions when it was necessary to turn a locomotive, the Bidston Junction triangle was used.

CHANGES TO MOTIVE POWER

At the Grouping, the LM&SR inherited 10,400 locomotives and set about allocating numbers in what had been the L&NWR series to its acquisitions from other companies. The Wirral engines were allocated numbers as follows:

```
No. 1 .... .... .... .... .... .... .... 6830
No's 2, 6, 8, 9, 7,10, 3 .. .... .... .... 6770-6776
No's 12-15 .... .... .... .... .... .... 6848-6851
No's 4,11,16,17, 6... .... .... .... .... 6758-6762
```

It is thought that No. 6 was originally allocated No. 10638 in the L&Y series but it is extremely unlikely that it carried it. It is known to have been painted in LM&S red with crest by June 1924.

The LM&S, having found that the Wirral Railway's locomotives had not been maintained to a satisfactory standard, took steps to assess the whole fleet and draft in replacements. A policy of standardisation was adopted and locomotives which did not fit in were scrapped, irrespective of age. Furthermore, any engine requiring a major repair of any kind was withdrawn and scrapped. Most of the Wirral engines were replaced by Webb Class '1F' 0-6-2 'Coal Tanks', of which No's 7744 and 7759 were fitted with side and bunker tanks several inches wider than standard, so as to be able to carry enough water for a 24-mile trip from New Brighton to Park, then to West Kirby and back, before returning from Park to New Brighton. With their tall chimneys and H-section spokes, these engines, built between 1881 and 1896, handled both passenger and freight workings until the arrival in the late 1920s of standard locomotives. Meanwhile, the Wirral locomotives were rapidly scrapped, the only ones to receive LM&S numbers being No's 3, 6 and 17. A report in *The Locomotive* of October 1924 records the recent repair at Crewe works and return to service of No. 3 (6776), which had the distinction of being the last genuine Wirral engine to run in service, lasting until 1928.

The second-hand purchases were similarly disposed of, with the exception of the ex-L&Y No. 6762 (Wirral No. 6), which was transferred first to Warrington and then to Preston, where it remained for many years. In 1952, carrying No. 46762, it was still acting as station pilot at Preston or working the Southport-Preston line, covering 1,000 miles every week in its last days. Webb tank No. 1032 was specially drafted in for use on the new London train between New Brighton and Hooton, returning with a goods service. It worked another goods train to Hooton at about 7.25pm, returning at 9.25pm with the coaches for New Brighton. This duty was taken over by one of four 0-6-0T Johnson Class '3F' engines, built by the LM&S to a Midland Railway design between 1924-31. They had Belpaire fire boxes, extended smoke boxes and a ventilator

fitted in the cab roof. Originally numbered 7100-49 and 16400-64, they were later renumbered 7260-7681 and No's 7353, 7503, 7504 and 7507 were allocated to the Wirral section. Several of the Webb tanks were withdrawn and this trend continued in the early 1930s, when, from May 1930, another LM&SR standard design made an appearance, in the form of a number of Fowler Class '3F' 2-6-2T locomotives originally numbered from 15500 but later renumbered 1-70. The original five allocated (No's 15500-4) had increased to thirteen by 1934 (No's 2-5, 12, 42, 44, 48-51, 55 and 70). The four 0-6-0 tanks remained and at the beginning of 1938 there were still five Webb tanks (No's 7711, 7759, 7780, 7841 and 27664), which mainly hauled engineering trains in connection with electrification work. They were augmented by Birkenhead North shed's first tender locomotives, No. 421, a Midland Class '2P' 4-4-0, and No. 2954, an LM&S Stanier-designed 2-6-0 'Mogul'. The Fowler 2-6-2Ts were not renowned for their pulling power but were reliable in service, and they helped to improve timekeeping and public confidence in the trains in preparation for the electric services to come.

There was no doubt some public expectation for through passenger services across West Kirby, where a short walk along the street between the two stations was necessary for anyone desirous of travelling from Seacombe or Birkenhead Park for instance, to Heswall or Parkgate. Some envisaged a Seacombe-Woodside facility, amalgamating the Seacombe-West Kirby and Birkenhead (Woodside)-West Kirby services but the joint ownership of the latter was a stumbling block, as the Great Western stood to lose revenue if a shorter and more convenient route was established over the Wirral to stations on the Joint branch. In 1926, the LM&S considered the use of Sentinel-Cammell steam rail coaches on lightly trafficked branch lines and a service using these was suggested between New Brighton and Heswall but nothing came of it. The only exception was the operation of through carriages between New Brighton and London (Euston) from 1st October 1923. Consisting of two carriages, this train left New Brighton at 9.58am, used the west curve at Bidston Junction and stopped at the Joint station in West Kirby, before continuing via Heswall and Neston to Hooton; it stopped at all stations between New Brighton and Hooton except Bidston and Kirby Park. The carriages were then attached to a Birkenhead (Woodside) to Crewe train, from where they went forward as part of the 11.15am Liverpool (Lime Street) to London (Euston) train, the whole journey taking 5½hrs. The Down train left Euston at 5.20pm, arriving at New Brighton at about 10.25pm. Times varied slightly at different dates. The train was well used by people who were not in a hurry or disliked the inconvenience of making the journey to Liverpool Lime Street, encumbered by luggage. The LM&S issued special timetables in the aftermath of the 1926 General Strike. The coal shortage resulting from the miners' strike, which continued for many months after everybody else

TOP: The only Wirral-owned engine to survive the 1920s was the ex-L&YR 2-4-2T No. 6762, which had been numbered 6 in the WR fleet following its purchase in June 1921. It is seen here on station pilot duties at Preston in June 1949, its service days finally coming to an end here in February 1952. JOHN WARD COLLECTION, COURTESY JOHN HORNE

CENTRE: As previously noted, Wirral Railway No. 3 was the last new locomotive to be bought by the company, in 1914. It was also the only genuine Wirral engine to run with its LM&S number (6776), albeit briefly, being withdrawn in July 1928. TED LLOYD COLLECTION

BOTTOM: Two of the Webb Class '2F' 0-6-2 'Coal Tanks' at Birkenhead Docks on 10th January 1925. They still retained their L&NW numbers 652 and 3720 but were eventually allocated LM&S numbers 7707 and 7664 respectively. The latter eventually became No. 27664 and enjoyed a long life, being withdrawn from Shrewsbury shed in December 1947. GLYNN PARRY COLLECTION

LEFT: The through London carriages, mentioned in the text and here with an unidentified Webb tank in charge, prepare to depart a wet and miserable looking New Brighton station in the later 1920s.

BELOW: Seacombe & Egremont station's 'temporary' status is highlighted by this view of the platforms from the mid 1930s, with workmen engaged in replacing some of the wooden sleepers which formed the deck. It must have been a trial to walk along them, particularly in the wet. No. 10638, an ex-L&YR 0-6-0T built in 1890 as number 1041, waits to leave with a train for West Kirby. J.F. WARD COLLECTION, COURTESY JOHN HORNE

had gone back to work, required strict economy but the Wirral lines seem to have come off lightly, the main service reductions being on the New Brighton line.

The distinction between the LM&S (ex-Wirral) and the GW/LM&S Joint lines was not apparent to the railway passenger but was important to the accountants, as witness the following memorandum dating from 1926:

'Mr Williams, Joint Superintendent at Shrewsbury, pointed out that the Joint staff at Birkenhead were being requested almost daily by the LM&S Company to haul wagons from South Reserve and Duke Street [on the Dock estate] to the Wirral Section of the LM&S Railway and for this he was getting no recompense whatsoever. The LM&S Company were requested to review the matter with the object of making payment to the Joint Companies for this service. It was, therefore, suggested to the LM&S Company that a charge of £1 per trip should be made for hauling the LM&S empties from South Reserve and Duke Street to the Wirral Section, the distance being 1½ miles and ¾ mile respectively. The number of empties hauled averaged 30 per trip and from January to August 1926 39 trips *were made. The time occupied in running the empties to the Wirral Section and the light engine back is about one hour and no question of shunting or standing time is involved. Mr Collett agreed that the charge of £1 per trip was a reasonable offer and the Chief General Superintendent of the LM&S Company arranged for this payment to be made as from January 1st 1926, and the LM&S Accountant had been asked to credit the Joint Account accordingly.'*

One wonders what traffic required so many empties and how the supply of empties was handled in Wirral days.

In accordance with an LM&S policy of renaming stations with duplicate or confusing names, Birkenhead Docks was renamed Birkenhead North from 1st May 1926. The Docks name was inappropriate as it was situated at the western extremity of the dock system and was likely to be confused with the L&NER's Birkenhead Dock Road goods station, which was not in Birkenhead at all but in Seacombe! Some road bridges were strengthened and rebuilt, in particular that by Meols station in June 1927, a bus operator, the Crosville Motor Co., paying £1,140 towards the cost, and also Pasture Road bridge, Moreton in 1935.

Service Levels

The LM&S continued, with slight modifications, the timetables worked by the Wirral until summer 1929, when an improved time interval service was introduced on the Park-West Kirby and Park-New Brighton lines, along with an hourly Seacombe-West Kirby service. There were further improvements in 1933-34, when half-hourly services were increased to every 20 minutes with 15-minute peak hour frequencies. On summer Saturdays and Sundays, there were two diagrams for the New Brighton line for 'favourable' or 'unfavourable' weather. If, by noon, 3,000 or more passengers had travelled towards New Brighton, the 'favourable weather' service was put on, giving a 10-minute service, otherwise a 20-minute service was provided. On August Bank Holiday 1936, 47,400-passengers were carried. The turn-round at Park was very smart, four minutes being allowed but it was normal practice to uncouple vacuum and heater pipes and screw coupling, run ahead over the points, set back through the loop and couple up in 2 minutes 50 seconds. Passenger rolling stock was made up in four-coach sets, with two-coach strengthening sets for peak hours.

An unusual feature on busy days was the practice of working engines which had finished their turns back to Birkenhead North on the front of passenger trains. This was done because the close-interval services left little scope for spare train paths. The sight of three locomotives heading a six-coach train was startling to onlookers, who might speculate about the condition of the engines to make such practice necessary.

Top: Seacombe in the late 1920s with a West Kirby train. Note the Seacombe ferry hydraulic tower in the background. T.B. Maund collection

Above: Birkenhead Park station, with a Wirral Railway steam hauled service contrasting with the coaches of one of the Mersey Railway electric trains. John Alsop collection

Below: Webb 0-6-2 'Coal Tank' No. 7841 pauses with a West Kirby train at Birkenhead Park station in May 1934. W. Potter, courtesy Martin Jenkins

The Fowler Class '3P' 2-6-2Ts became the mainstay of the Wirral section motive power in the last days of steam and the photographs on these two pages show a number of them hard at work and on shed. New into service in 1930, by 1934 thirteen of these nicely proportioned 'Prairie' tanks were stationed at Birkenhead North shed. They were very successful and their performance helped to bolster the confidence of the travelling public in preparation for electrification of the Wirral system.

LEFT: Fowler Class '3F' 2-6-2T No. 15501 (second of the class) posed outside Birkenhead North shed with footplate crew and cleaners in 1930-1, when the type was first allocated to the line. This engine became No. 2 after the class were renumbered 1-70 in 1934. JOHN RYAN COLLECTION

OPPOSITE PAGE TOP: Mirroring some of the views from Wirral Railway days some two decades earlier, No. 12 leans to the curve between Birkenhead North and Bidston in October 1937. F. HEWITT, COURTESY MARTIN JENKINS

LEFT: No. 42 is seen passing Birkenhead North carriage shed *en route* to Birkenhead Park in June 1936. Note the new-looking LM&S suburban stock in the train, much smarter in comparison to the older coaches that Wirral passengers were used to. W. POTTER, COURTESY MARTIN JENKINS

OPPOSITE PAGE BOTTOM: No. 51 works bunker first past Birkenhead North box with a New Brighton-Birkenhead Park train in October 1937. Note the third rail in place on both lines in preparation for the electrification of passenger services. F. HEWITT, COURTESY MARTIN JENKINS

BELOW: No. 12 is seen in close up with a West Kirby train passing Birkenhead North shed in June 1936. W. POTTER, COURTESY MARTIN JENKINS

RIGHT: An unidentified Webb 'Coal Tank' heads an eastbound train strengthened to five coaches near Moreton in 1936. The 0-6-2T is one of those which was fitted with widened side tanks especially for working on the Wirral system but, as the photographs below show, Webb tanks with standard side tanks still featured routinely working passenger trains on the system. TED LLOYD COLLECTION

LEFT: Webb tank No. 7841 heads a train at Birkenhead Park station in the 1930s. Five of these engines were still serving on the Wirral section up to electrification. JIM PEDEN COLLECTION

BELOW: An eastbound train arriving at Hoylake in warm summer sunshine, on 16th August 1933 behind Webb 0-6-2T No. 7791. This train is comprised of a standard four coach set as used by the LM&S up to electrification. Note the fire iron stowed on the tank top and the substantial Hoylake Station Cabin wooden nameboard on the front of the box. E.R. MORTON, COURTESY TED LLOYD COLLECTION

Stanier Class '2P' 0-4-4T No. 6406 heads a West Kirby-Birkenhead Park service in October 1937. The train has just passed Bidston East Junction signal box, visible in the left background. The three coach composition is unusual as passenger stock was usually made up into rakes of four. These engines were push-pull fitted but were never so used on the Wirral lines. Note the third rail in place on both running lines. F. HEWITT, COURTESY MARTIN JENKINS

At the time Moreton was absorbed into the County Borough of Wallasey in 1928, hundreds of these shanties, caravans and huts had been built, with only rudimentary sanitation, on the land between the railway and the shore. The new authority eventually succeeded in clearing them all away and new housing was constructed which provided additional traffic for the railway. However, this circa 1930 view, with a Webb 2-4-2 tank heading a West Kirby train, shows the area which was to be occupied by Cadbury's biscuit factory from the 1950s. JOHN RYAN COLLECTION

New Brighton station looking west in the 1920s, with a Webb tank running round its train which has just arrived from Birkenhead Park. The viewpoint gives a glimpse of the eastern end of the goods shed, in the centre of the picture but the yard again appears to be occupied mostly by coal wagons. Note in the foreground, the locomotive release point at this end of the loop was worked by a hand lever and not from the signal box. JIM PEDEN COLLECTION

The ticket-collector's barrier at Seacombe & Egremont station, with Church Road bridge in the background, probably in the later 1930s. Note the rustic roofed archway, which afforded some protection from the elements for the ticket collector. Wirral Railway passengers, however, were afforded little in the way of such luxury, with few awnings being provided at any of the stations. Also worth a second look is the Nestlé's chocolate vending machine, handily positioned and once a familiar sight on station platforms all over the country. MARTIN JENKINS COLLECTION

A Sunday working trundles through the remains of Warren halt on 3rd October 1937. Fowler 2-6-2 tank No. 51 is in charge of the 3.26pm New Brighton-Birkenhead Park service. Commencement of electric services was less than six months away by this date and the third rail is in place on both lines. TED LLOYD COLLECTION

A wintry scene at Meols station on 17th January 1936 with a West Kirby train drawing into the westbound platform. It will be noted that the station boasted a small kiosk inside the main building, operated by Finlay & Co. Ltd, which must have been very useful for passengers. The viewpoint, off the road bridge crossing the line at the western end of the platforms, illustrates well the flat nature of the terrain the Wirral traversed, whilst from Bidston to Hoylake, the line was straight for much of the way. The tall combined home and distant signal, with repeater banner for starting trains lower down the post, was to aid sighting over the bridge for eastbound trains. T.G. TURNER COLLECTION

Birkenhead North Engine and Carriage Sheds

Birkenhead North engine shed was established on the site of the old Hoylake Railway's Birkenhead Docks station which, after final closure in early 1888, became Birkenhead Docks Goods station. It is rumoured that a temporary two-road shed was built by the SH&DR just to the south-west of the new Docks station, opened on 2nd January 1888. They certainly provided a turntable here, which remained in existence until removed by the LM&S in 1925. However, no evidence has been uncovered as to the existence of such a shed, although a two-road carriage shed was later built on the site, whilst the rather odd siting of the turntable, some way from the rest of the locomotive depot, must remain a conundrum.

As the Wirral Railway's only locomotive depot, facilities at Birkenhead North grew to include a two-road engine shed, a repair depot, a distinctive sausage-shaped water tank and a covered coaling

A general view of Birkenhead North sidings and engine shed in October 1937, with an end perspective of the sausage-shaped water tank and the new coaling stage. LM&S built Class '3F' No. 7353 is prominent, with Webb tank No. 7759 visible in the background. MARTIN JENKINS COLLECTION

The gloomy and decidedly draughty interior of the engine shed in February 1936, with Webb tanks much in evidence. Note only one of these has the extended side tanks. The front end of a Fowler 2-6-2T is on the right and there is another visible at the far end of the row. TED LLOYD COLLECTION

This line-up at Birkenhead North shed on 3rd October 1937 illustrates the partial transition from ex-L&NWR motive power to LM&S types, steam hauled services on the Wirral coming to an end before the process was completed. In the upper view, looking west, LM&S-built Class '3F' 0-6-0T No. 7353 is buffered up to Fowler 2-6-2T No. 55, in front of which are two Webb 0-6-2Ts and another LM&S 2-6-2T. Behind, the rebuilt coaling stage can be seen, with its distinctive curved roof and three ventilators. The picture below shows the same line-up from the opposite direction, revealing the Webb tanks to be No's 7780 and 27664, with No. 7759 in the background. The building in the background, above, with the curved roof and smoke chimneys, was the covered coaling stage. The shed building, seen below, had an interesting hybrid roof, curved at one end and pitched at the other! It is not clear whether this was the result of a repair or the building having been extended at some stage. BOTH F. HEWITT, COURTESY MARTIN JENKINS

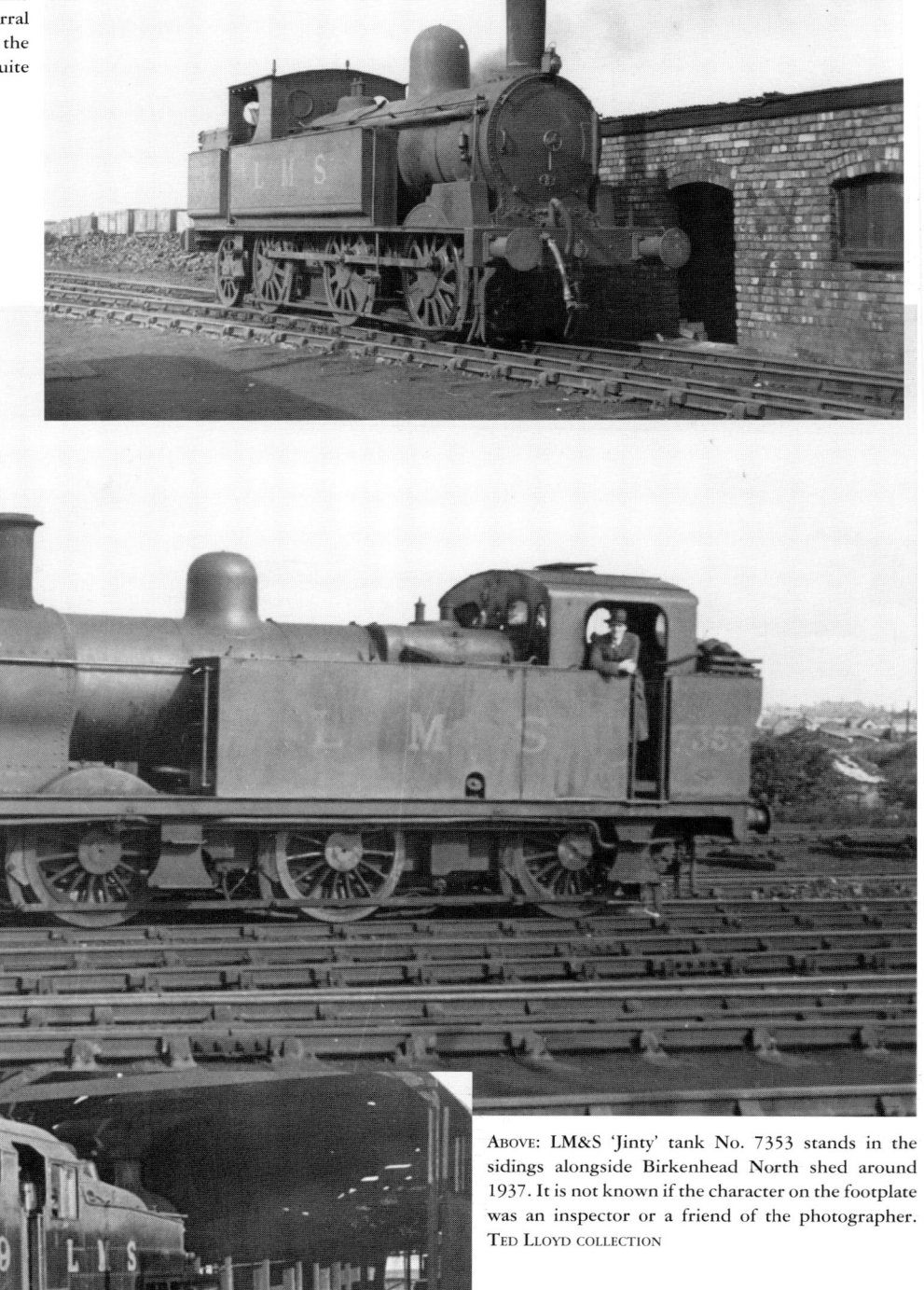

RIGHT: One of the ex-L&NW 'Coal Tanks' poses at Birkenhead North shed in the mid 1930s. In careworn condition, its painted number is too indistinct to read but again the extended side tanks fitted to a number of the engines used on the Wirral system are very noticeable. Note the coal piled on the ground behind; servicing facilities here were quite labour intensive. TED LLOYD COLLECTION

ABOVE: LM&S 'Jinty' tank No. 7353 stands in the sidings alongside Birkenhead North shed around 1937. It is not known if the character on the footplate was an inspector or a friend of the photographer. TED LLOYD COLLECTION

LEFT: The gloomy interior of the shed, with Stanier 2-6-2 tank No. 159 hovering outside on the last day of steam, 12th March 1938. These 'Prairie' tanks were introduced by Stanier in 1935, being a taper boiler version of the earlier Fowler design. With their sloped side tank tops and raised bunkers, they were easily distinguishable from their predecessors. JIM PEDEN COLLECTION

The near derelict condition of Birkenhead North shed is again seen in this photograph of 3rd October 1937. Webb tank No. 7711 appears to have been cleaned up a little, in contrast to Fowler 2-6-2T No. 48 standing under the sheerlegs, which apparently still saw occasional use right up till closure of the shed. F. HEWITT, COURTESY MARTIN JENKINS

RIGHT: Fowler 2-6-2T No. 42 alongside the water tank just a month before the end of steam services, on 13th February 1938.
BELOW: A bleak view of the decaying buildings on 7th March 1937. The two 2-6-2Ts are No's 55 and 70, whilst also recorded as being on shed or in the yard that day were No's 4, 5, 12, 48, 50 and 51, along with Webb tanks No's 7504, 7507, 7658, 7711, 7759, 7780, 7838 and 7841. The sheerlegs and hut were all that remained of the repair shed, which was dismantled in the mid 1920s BOTH TED LLOYD COLLECTION

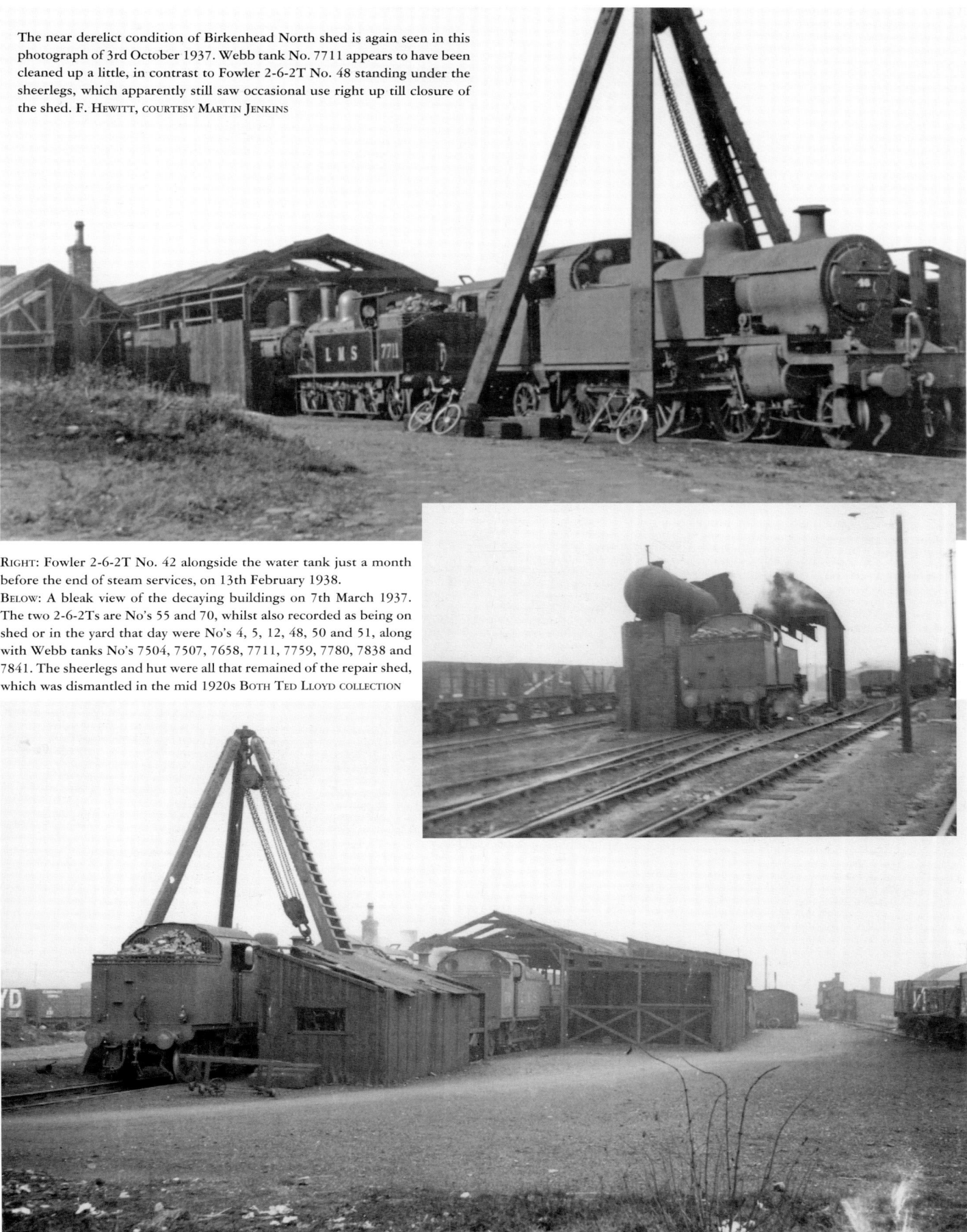

Webb 'Coal Tank' No. 7759 and footplate crew pose for the photographer just in front of the water tank. This was another of the class fitted with extended side tanks. The photograph is undated but is circa 1930. Behind the engine, the coaling stage is minus its roof but whether it disintegrated due to old age or was destroyed somehow is unknown. It obviously caused some inconvenience because the LM&S were forced into providing a new facility around 1935 which, with electrification pending, must have been something of an annoyance. The new covered coaling stage had a ramped siding leading into it, raising wagons up so that coal could be loaded directly into locomotive bunkers. This siding is clearly seen through the shed in the bottom picture, opposite page. TED LLOYD COLLECTION

Fowler Class '3P' 2-6-2T No. 4 basks in sunshine outside the shed in July 1935. Although 'parked' at the end of the siding, the bunker is piled high with coal. It appears locomotives were coaled as soon as they arrived on shed, in readiness for their next turn of duty, whenever that might be, as almost all of these photographs show engines at rest with full bunkers. TED LLOYD COLLECTION

Somebody still took a bit of pride in the job! Whilst the photographic evidence seems to indicate that Wirral engines were generally kept in a rather grimy state through the 1930s – unsurprising perhaps, given the state of the locomotive depot – this close up study of Webb 'Coal Tank No. 7711, outside the shed on 3rd October 1937 shows it in near immaculate condition. Coaled and ready for its next duty, the less charitable possibility is that the engine had just returned from a heavy overhaul, as its condition certainly differs from that of the other locomotives on shed that day.
F. HEWITT, COURTESY MARTIN JENKINS

A panorama of the shed and sidings on 7th March 1937, with two Webb tanks and a Fowler 'Prairie' tank on view. Note the Loco coal wagons on the right. TED LLOYD COLLECTION

Almost exactly a year later, on 13th March 1938, the shed is empty following the withdrawal of its allocation of steam locomotives with the start of the new electric services. By the end, the building was little more than a skeleton. Note the ramped siding leading up to the coal stage in the background. This facility remained in use following closure of the shed, to service locomotives used on goods workings in the area. TED LLOYD COLLECTION

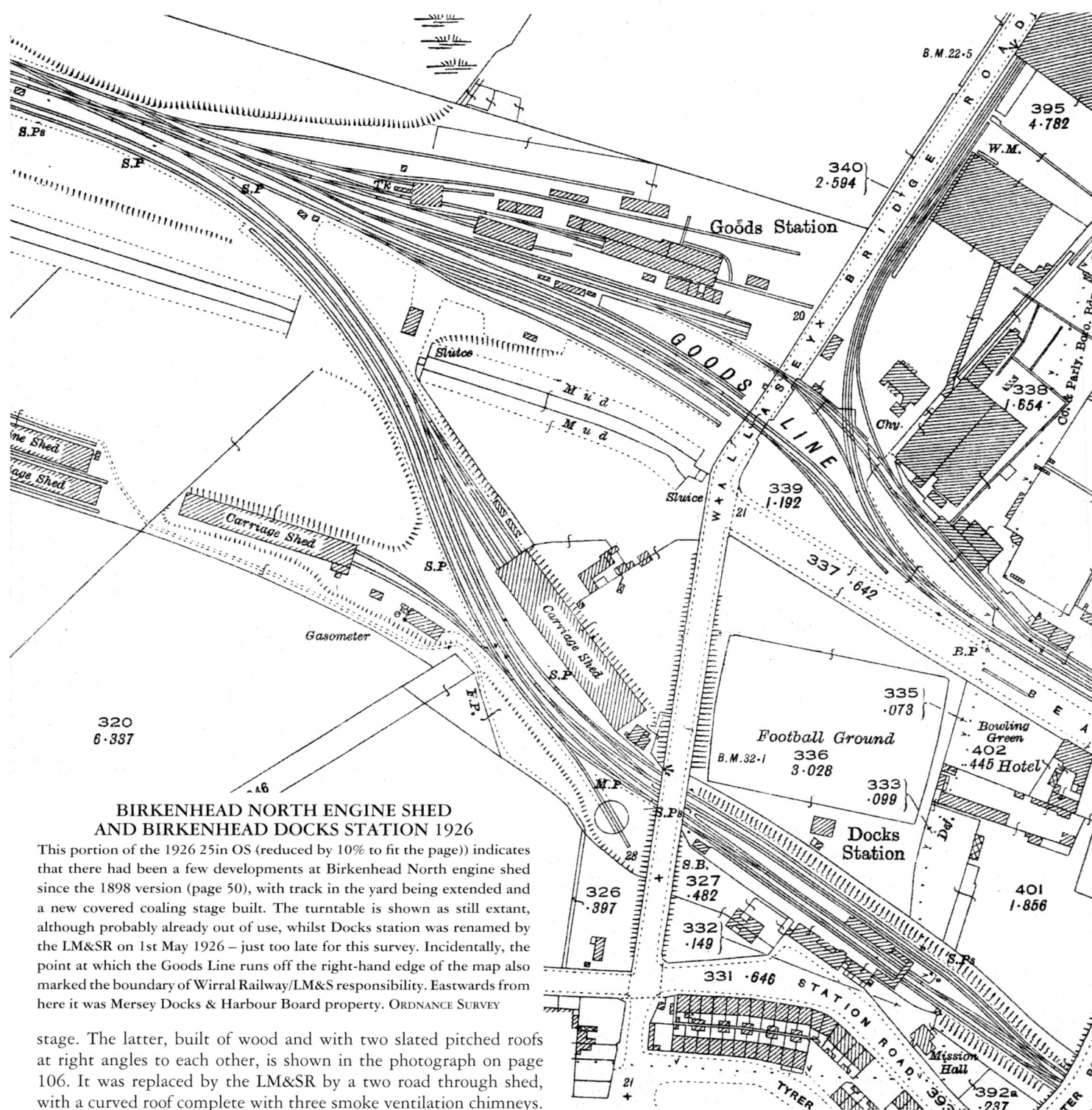

BIRKENHEAD NORTH ENGINE SHED AND BIRKENHEAD DOCKS STATION 1926

This portion of the 1926 25in OS (reduced by 10% to fit the page)) indicates that there had been a few developments at Birkenhead North engine shed since the 1898 version (page 50), with track in the yard being extended and a new covered coaling stage built. The turntable is shown as still extant, although probably already out of use, whilst Docks station was renamed by the LM&SR on 1st May 1926 – just too late for this survey. Incidentally, the point at which the Goods Line runs off the right-hand edge of the map also marked the boundary of Wirral Railway/LM&S responsibility. Eastwards from here it was Mersey Docks & Harbour Board property. ORDNANCE SURVEY

stage. The latter, built of wood and with two slated pitched roofs at right angles to each other, is shown in the photograph on page 106. It was replaced by the LM&SR by a two road through shed, with a curved roof complete with three smoke ventilation chimneys. This was the first investment in the depot since the early 1900s when T.B. Hunter, newly appointed to the post of Locomotive Superintendent, authorised the expenditure of some £600 on new tools and machinery. At the same time, the old stable block of the Hoylake & Birkenhead Rail & Tramway Co. was gutted and fitted out as a repair shop, after which the Wirral were able to carry out much of their heavy maintenance in house. This included such jobs as straightening the frames and fitting a new cylinder to No. 7 after it had been involved in a collision.

The depot had little in the way of other investment by the Wirral Railway and thus reached LM&SR ownership in generally very run down condition. As something of an outpost in the LM&S empire and with the Wirral's fleet of locomotives being replaced initially with equally ancient (although rather better looked after) ex-L&NWR Webb tanks, there was little incentive to make many improvements in the early years of its new ownership, apart from the aforementioned new coaling stage, whilst the turntable was taken out of use in 1925 and removed a year or two after. Then, as the prospect of electrification of the Wirral system gathered momentum, there was even less reason to spend money on the steam depot and its final years were characterised by extreme dilapidation, with the shed

LEFT: LM&S Stanier Class '2P' 0-4-4T No. 6406 heads past Birkenhead North sidings in October 1937 with a Birkenhead Park-New Brighton train. Class '3F' 0-6-0T No. 7353 appears again in the left background. MARTIN JENKINS COLLECTION

BELOW: This view of Fowler 2-6-2T No. 15501 heading round the curve to the west of Birkenhead North station is the only one found so far showing the site of the Wirral's turntable. It was regarded as unnecessary by the LM&S as engines could easily be turned on the Bidston triangle but quite how much use it got even in Wirral days is a moot point. It is also the only clear view of the large shed on the right, marked on the 1898 OS as an 'Engine Shed'. Equipped with four roads and of some length, it was almost certainly a carriage shed (fully enclosed, it was also without roof ventilators which further suggests locomotives were not admitted), providing additional accommodation to the two-road shed in the left distance, of which this is also the only known view. The photograph dates from circa 1931. COURTESY GLYN PARRY

RIGHT: Another unusual view, dating from probably late 1937, with a west-bound passenger train hauled by an unidentified 'Jinty' tank passing the newly built electric car sheds on the left. These were built on the site of the four-road carriage shed seen above. The modern design and pristine interiors are in marked contrast to the conditions prevailing at the steam shed and whilst enthusiasts no doubt mourned the passing of steam on the Wirral system, it is unlikely that footplate crews, shed staff or passengers did! TED LLOYD COLLECTION

A typical Wirral passenger train in the last days of steam, the conductor rails already being in place. The locomotive is Fowler 2-6-2T No. 4 and the train is pictured on the straight section between Moreton and Leasowe, heading eastwards. JOHN RYAN COLLECTION

itself providing very little protection from the elements. It may have been given a partial roof repair at some stage because it ended up with a strange hybrid of curved roof one end and pitched the other, although both were covered with corrugated iron. The LM&S coded Birkenhead North 6D and the depot was closed on 12th March 1938 with the commencement of electric train services. However, whilst the buildings were quickly razed, the coal stage and water tank were retained to service the locomotives working local goods trains. Indeed, the water tank was not demolished until 1969.

The two carriage sheds are very similar in appearance and most probably date from the same time. A pointer to this is given in a Board minute of 24th December 1894: *'New Carriage Sheds – rails to be taken from sidings in Wallasey station yard.'* This seems to indicate they were built together, whilst a further minute of 27th July 1896 records *'Carriage shed to be extended'* but unfortunately does not indicate which one. The four-road shed was closed and demolished in the mid 1930s to make way for the new electric car sheds.

THE ELECTRIFICATION

In the early 1930s there were few rail routes outside London which offered better prospects for electrification than the Wirral. Short, close-interval services, with frequent stops and heavy peak hour and summer loadings, were ideal for electric multiple unit working and there were prospects for better utilisation of stock and very considerable manpower savings. Add to this the attractions of accelerated services and the elimination of the tiresome change to and from the Mersey's electric trains at Birkenhead Park, and the potential for increased traffic was enormous.

Although electric trains had been running in Liverpool since 1893 and in Wirral since 1903, they were by no means a familiar sight to the majority of the Wirral populace because the Mersey's trains were

A rather hazardous viewpoint at Bidston station, with the photographer standing in the four-foot of the west-bound line to get this shot of Class '2P' 0-4-4T No. 6405 which has paused with the 12.18 West Kirby-Birkenhead Park service on 17th October 1937. Note the stovepipe chimney with which this class of ten engines were fitted and which were replaced in the 1940s. The class were also renumbered, this engine becoming 1905. TED LLOYD COLLECTION

LEFT: Stanier 'Prairie' tank No. 159 heads into Seacombe in the mid 1930s with a train from West Kirby, which is comprised of an ex-L&NWR three-coach set coupled with an LM&S suburban carriage. TED LLOYD COLLECTION

BELOW: The same train waiting to depart Seacombe a while later, with No. 159 having run round its carriages to head bunker first back to West Kirby. TED LLOYD COLLECTION

BOTTOM: West Kirby station on 25th March 1936, with Fowler 2-6-2T No. 3 waiting to depart. This train consists of a three-coach LM&S suburban set with an older pre-Group carriage at the rear. Although still two years before the commencement of electric services, the third rail is in place. E.R. MORTON, COURTESY TED LLOYD

out of sight in their tunnels for most of the time. Non-users might catch a glimpse between Rock Ferry and Green Lane but otherwise they were concealed from public view. Electric trains were novel and somewhat charismatic, and these were qualities which could be exploited. A high proportion of the working population of the county borough of Wallasey commuted daily (some twice) to Liverpool and was firmly wedded to the municipally owned ferries. There were three of these, the main one, Seacombe, providing a 10-minute frequency throughout most of the day, fed by a very comprehensive network of municipal tramway (until 1933) and bus services. In only the north and north-western parts of the borough proper and the then lightly

LEFT: Fowler 2-6-2T No. 3 runs round its train at West Kirby in early 1938, with Bridge Road forming the backdrop to the picture. This was close to the end of steam-hauled passenger services and the work installing the third rail on all tracks for electric trains appears to be complete.

BELOW: No. 3 backs down onto its train a short while later, prior to departing for Seacombe. On the left, an unidentified classmate is about to leave with a train to Birkenhead Park. The large building in the left background is the Dee Hotel. BOTH TED LLOYD COLLECTION

BOTTOM: LM&S 2-6-2T No. 55 heads eastwards from Hoylake in late 1937 or early 1938 with a four coach train composed entirely of ex-L&NWR stock. It has just passed a westbound train arriving at Hoylake station. The siding on the left gave access to both Hoylake gas and electricity works, whilst the line on the far right was the headshunt for the small goods yard. TED LLOYD COLLECTION

populated areas of Leasowe and Moreton, absorbed into the borough in 1928, did the railway offer competition to the ferries. Nevertheless, season ticket rates on both modes tended to be fixed with the competitor's rates in mind and rail commuters on the New Brighton line tended to pay less per mile than those on the West Kirby line. In those days, many workers went home to lunch even if this meant crossing the Mersey twice and acceleration of the service, especially by eliminating the change at Birkenhead Park, could extend this option to those who lived slightly further afield and might be tempted to change from ferry to rail. The West Kirby line also presented some opportunities of this kind from Moreton, where the residential development had followed the main road to the south of the railway. Birkenhead Corporation, whose buses served Birkenhead Park station, had made a through ticketing agreement with the Mersey from Moreton, Leasowe and Bidston in August 1923.

The Mersey's directors had always been disappointed that the Wirral had never exercised the electrification powers obtained in 1900 and the absorption of the Wirral into the LM&SR in 1923 seemed to offer some hope of progress. The Mersey Railway's general manager, Joshua Shaw, raised the matter in 1926 and the LM&S chairman, Sir Josiah Stamp, gave his approval in principle. There followed a lengthy period of wrangling over detail. The LM&S electrical engineer, Cortez Leigh, had sat on a committee which had advocated the adoption of the 1,500v DC overhead wire system for all future electrification schemes; he was adamant that this should be used and wanted the Mersey to change over from its existing third and fourth rail system. Shaw, pointing out the chaos that would be caused by overhead wires coming down in the tunnel and the cost of creating an overhead line department, was uncompromising in his opposition. The overhead option was ruled out when it was realised that the road overbridge at the south end of Green Lane station was too low to accept overhead equipment and could not be raised as it ran under the adjoining GW/LM&S Joint line; the Mersey line could not be lowered as a main sewer ran below. There was a further wrangle about the design of rolling stock. The LM&S wanted compartment stock on the grounds of maximum seating but the Mersey was firmly wedded to open saloons, through which their travelling ticket collectors could inspect a whole train in motion, collecting excess fares far exceeding their wage cost.

There was further argument about

the technical specifications. New three-car compartment stock on the Euston/Broad Street-Watford line was powered by four 328hp motors, approximately three times the power of the existing Mersey trains and the LM&S wanted similar stock on the Wirral. Shaw wanted to know why it was necessary to provide power equal to the output of a main line 4-6-2 express steam locomotive to propel a relatively low speed six-car electric train. He was regarded as 'difficult' by the LM&S but his arguments were sound and he refused to give ground. It was not until the retirement of Cortez Leigh and the appointment of C.E. Fairburn as his successor as LM&S chief electrical engineer that the impasse was broken. Fairburn's early career had been with the Midland Railway, where he had been a pupil of Henry Fowler at Derby works in 1910 but his recent experience had been with the English Electric

Wirral Railway signal boxes were of a distinctive design with timber sides, hipped slated roofs and decorative barge boards. They were supplied by the Railway Signal Company Ltd of Fazakerley, Liverpool but many were replaced by LM&SR cabins in the inter-war years.

ABOVE: West Kirby Cabin stood facing the junction of the Wirral and Joint lines and its large nameboard partially obscured the two locking room windows.

LEFT The small cabin on the platform at Moreton, was replaced by an orthodox box on the north side of the line in 1932. Unusually, the station name was painted on the front of the cabin.

BELOW Meols Signal Cabin was abolished when the crossover was removed. ALL JOHN RYAN COLLECTION

RIGHT: A West Kirby train departs Hoylake in 1937 beneath the newly built concrete footbridge. This was provided as part of the modernisation of the station carried out in readiness for the new electric train services. Whilst the station was entirely rebuilt, Hoylake box was to survive, not closing until 1994, with the installation of the new central control system. Note Hoylake Post Office in the background.

BELOW: An undated view of the interior of Hoylake box. Note the gate wheel in the background. BOTH JOHN RYAN COLLECTION

Co., latterly as manager of the Traction Department. By 1934, he had been involved in the electrification of forty-nine different railways and in modern parlance he was 'head hunted' by the LM&S. One of his first priorities was to come to an early agreement with the Mersey and electrify the Wirral as soon as possible. Technically, it is hard to imagine a more suitable candidate for the job and the financial aspects were taken care of by a government subsidy under the Railways (Agreement) Act 1935, which also covered the cost of necessary adaptations to the Mersey.

Shaw got his way and it was agreed to adopt the 650v DC third rail system for the Wirral, and to retain the Mersey's third and fourth rail as their running rails were used for track circuits. The LM&S agreed to run open saloons and the Mersey agreed to re-upholster their rather spartan rolling stock and to reposition their third rail to the British Standard, 16 inches from the running rail instead of their existing 22 inches. The electrification scheme, which was aimed at achieving a significant increase in traffic, was to be not just a changeover of motive power but a total refurbishment of the line. Reballasting and relaying of track was, of course, central to the project but one new station was planned and five others were to be totally rebuilt, with improvements made to several more. Numerous wooden Wirral Railway signal boxes were scheduled to be replaced by new brick structures and alterations made to the signalling at various places. A new maintenance facility was to be erected at Birkenhead North and various logistic problems tackled. The Seacombe Branch was excluded, as it was considered that, in view of the roundabout nature of the route, it was unlikely much Liverpool traffic would be won from the direct ferry service. The L&NER service to Wrexham would continue and could adequately serve the local traffic, whilst also providing connections at Bidston for the West Kirby line.

RIGHT: The nameboard dominating the exterior of Seacombe station during the inter-war years. Beneath it are a selection of timetables and railway posters. Whilst the purpose of the large sign was obviously to advertise the train service to passers-by, one cannot but help feeling that it also served to hide the rather dismal terminal station behind. GLYNN PARRY COLLECTION

BELOW: An unidentified Fowler 2-6-2T exits Birkenhead Park Tunnel on the approach to the station, probably circa 1936. There were no goods facilities at this station, so the wagon glimpsed on the left in the headshunt may have belonged to the permanent way department. Work on the third rail electrification has yet to be commenced, however. TED LLOYD COLLECTION

BELOW: Another Fowler 2-6-2T sits in the headshunt at the western end of Birkenhead Park station, waiting for the points to be changed in order to complete running round its train. Electrification work is imminent; note the new ballast on the right and the new point rodding and signal wire pulleys on the left. The headshunt was to disappear with electrification, the new track layout seeing the main running lines sweep through the centre of the station, making a straight connection between Wirral and Mersey metals for the first time. The odd skyline is caused by the photographer having masked out the station buildings above the bridge parapet for some reason, whilst leaving the Birkenhead Corporation bus shelter in place! TED LLOYD COLLECTION

Birkenhead Park just prior to electrification, with Wirral tracks on the right and Mersey tracks on the left. The cross-platform interchange is clear, with an LM&S train on the right and a Mersey train opposite. The new signal box in the foreground was built by the LM&SR in 1938 (it appears to be awaiting fitting out and painting here), replacing the Mersey Railway box behind, which served both lines from the station's opening in 1888. GLYNN PARRY COLLECTION

PREPARATION OF THE LINE

Work on reballasting and relaying the whole of the track, along with installation of the conductor rail, started during 1936 and continued until late 1937. Flat bottomed conductor rails weighing 105lbs per yard in 60ft lengths were used. One side of the Bidston triangle was extended so that a complete train could be held on it, whilst between Bidston station and Seacombe Junction, the track was realigned to provide a separate line for the L&NE trains, which used the electric lines only for 100 yards whilst crossing to the Seacombe branch. As the triangle was on embankments, this involved much tipping and the extension of culverts. A long redundant refuge siding and Bidston West Signal Box were removed and new signal cabins built at Bidston East Junction and Bidston Dee Junction. New brick signal boxes were also erected at Seacombe Junction and West Kirby, whilst a small 10 foot box at Leasowe replaced the ground frame which controlled the level crossing. At Birkenhead Park, where the Wirral and Mersey trains had used separate tracks, the signal box was rebuilt, the stop blocks were removed and the track layout changed to facilitate through operation.

The carriage shed on the Up side west of Birkenhead North was dismantled and a much larger shed and office block was erected. This was used for washing and daily maintenance, and could accommodate a six-car train on each of its four roads. Overhead trollies with jumpers enabled trains to run in and out under power. Adjoining was the 325 foot long repair shop, with pits on two of its three roads and a 15 ton electric overhead travelling crane. The two-road carriage shed on the Down side was retained but was destined to be destroyed by a bomb in 1941.

Semaphore signals were retained throughout, although lower quadrant signals on timber posts were replaced by upper quadrant

The new electric car shed at Birkenhead North under construction in 1937, on the site of the old 4-road carriage shed. GLYNN PARRY COLLECTION

signals on steel tubular posts. Many of the ex-L&NW type signals installed by the LM&S in the 1920s were retained and some had very long lives, two lower quadrants at Hoylake lasting into the 1970s. To enable a more intensive service to be run, track circuiting was installed throughout.

Current Supply

In 1935, the LM&S invited tenders for the supply of electricity for the Wirral line. Liverpool Corporation quoted £2 15 0d (£2.75) per kW per annum and 0.182d (0.075p) per unit at 11,000v AC, 50 cycles, the supply not to exceed 4,000 kW. Birkenhead Corporation quoted £3 1 10d (£3.09) per kW and 0.20d (0.08p) per unit, the supply to be 6,600v, 3-phase, 50 cycles. The LM&S asked Birkenhead for an 11,000v supply but they were not in a position to supply it. The Liverpool supply was to be delivered from Harrington Street sub-station, to a site leased from the Mersey Railway at James Street station, where it was metered and then taken through the tunnel by LM&S owned cables to Birkenhead North, for an annual wayleave of £50.

Liverpool Corporation's quotation for a 4,000 kW supply was less than Birkenhead Corporation had to pay the Central Electricity Board for a 17,000 kW supply. It was obviously the best deal so the LM&S asked Liverpool Corporation to apply to the Minister of Transport under Section 47 of the Electricity (Supply) Act, 1926, for his consent for the supply to be given by them. Section 47 permitted power to be supplied outside the normal area of supply, if current was being provided for haulage or traction within the normal area of supply. Current for the former L&Y electrified lines in Liverpool was supplied by the LM&S Formby power station, so Liverpool Corporation was not supplying any traction current to the LM&S. The applicants relied, therefore, on a very wide interpretation of the term 'haulage', quoting particulars of various capstans and traversers at Great Howard Street, Sandon Dock, Edge Hill, Stanley, Bank Hall Locomotive Shed and Garston, which were powered by municipal current (*see Appendix 3*). The wagon movements facilitated by this equipment fell within the general railway use of the word 'haulage' but it seems unlikely that Parliament had intended such an interpretation.

Birkenhead Corporation applied for a Court Order restraining Liverpool Corporation from supplying current to the Wirral line. A Ministerial Inquiry was held on 20th October 1936 and the Minister, no doubt mindful of the much lower cost of the Liverpool current, gave his consent on 1st February 1937. The Birkenhead action therefore failed and the Liverpool supply was quickly installed through to the main control centre and sub-station at Birkenhead North, using two feeders each of 0.25 sq. ins per phase cross section. Each cable was approximately 3 miles 520 yards long and the underground section, where the cables were lead covered and jute served, was for the most part laid on battens supported by brackets close to the tunnel roof. There was also a pilot cable comprising the pilots for the feeder protective relays and the pilot for transmitting the kW demand metered at James Street to a repeating instrument at Birkenhead North.

Technical details given here are based on the official hand-out distributed in 1938. The EHT feeders, consisting of stranded copper conductors, were mainly carried overhead using special anti-fog insulators, with the earth wire below the conductors. The clearance between the nearest power wire and the telegraph and telephone wires on the opposite side of

Top: An interior view of Birkenhead North sub-station when new.
Centre: The Control Room at Birkenhead North.
Bottom: The interior of the new electric car shed at Birkenhead North in 1938.
All *The Locomotive Magazine*, 15th April 1938

the track was, in general, 35 feet, with a reduction to 30 feet in a few places. The traction sub-stations converted the 11kV supply to 650v DC by transformers and rectifiers, and fed it out on the track through high speed breakers. With the exception that Bidston and Birkenhead North had additional tracks to feed, all six sub-stations were alike as far as conversion and DC distribution was concerned. The arrangement of high tension switchgear and auxiliaries was identical at Meols, Hoylake, Bidston and Wallasey, consisting of an oil circuit breaker controlling the supply to the rectifier and a switch-fuse controlling the supply to the ancillary services transformer. It was a restriction of the Liverpool supply that two feeders should not be paralleled, so alternate sub-stations were fed from alternate feeders with provisions to bring all on to one feeder subject to the necessary interlocks. The form of sub-station was such as to give a direct route for the current through them, resulting in long narrow structures which fitted well into the available sites. The Crompton Parkinson switchgear was solenoid operated for remote control from 50 volt batteries, with separate leads for operating, tripping and indicating. It was compound filled vertical isolation type, rupturing capacity being 250mVA at Birkenhead North and 150mVA at the other sub-stations. The Metro-Vickers relays and kilowatt hour meters were fitted with a contacting device operating a printer to record the input to a rectifier.

Each set of 600kW Hewitt Electric Co. rectifiers were arranged for six phase connection to three bulbs, the fourth cubicle containing DC smoothing equipment. The cubicles were interlocked with the rectifier oil switches, making it possible to obtain access to them only when the transformer oil switch was open. The busbars were enclosed in the lower part of the cubicle. A portable 3-ammeter set was provided to check sharing of load by the bulbs. The BTH DC switchgear was arranged for solenoid operation held in by the main current. One breaker in each sub-station was arranged for closing off the track.

The remote control apparatus was manufactured by the Automatic Telephone Company and gave an indication of all breakers from the Control Room at Birkenhead North. The layout of the railway required two sets of pilots, one for Bidston and Wallasey sub-stations, and the other for Moreton, Meols and Hoylake sub-stations; in each case, a spare pilot was provided with facilities for changeover from one to the other. The pilots were continuously proved and an alarm was activated if one became defective. The DC breakers were arranged so that those at both ends of one track section could be closed simultaneously. The time required to perform an operation, including automatic check back without which no operation could be carried out, varied from three to ten seconds. The adoption of voice frequency metering enabled one meter reading to be obtained from each sub-station simultaneously and provision was made for obtaining the DC output of the rectifier in amperes, or its voltage or the voltage at the end of any track feeder.

Each sub-station contained an ancillary services transformer supplied through a switch fuse with limiting resistances. The BTH transformers stepped down to 420 volts were specially insulated to resist surges. The Birkenhead North transformer was of 100kVA capacity, as it also served the car shed and repair shop, whereas the other sub-stations were of 25 kVA capacity. In addition, sub-stations provided for station lighting, sub-station services and signal supply. The LT output was controlled by English Electric switch fuses, the single phase loads being approximately balanced. Two similar transformers were installed at Leasowe and Wallasey Village; they and their switch fuses were of the outdoor type but were otherwise similar and supplied station lighting at those stations. Each sub-station contained one battery, trickle

The new larger signal box at Bidston East under construction prior to electrification in 1937, alongside the smaller timber-built Railway Signalling Company cabin it was replacing. GLYNN PARRY COLLECTION

Rebuilding the culvert which took the River Birket under the line just east of Bidston station in 1937, as part of the preparations for electrification. This tributary of the Mersey emptied into the Wallasey Pool and was bridged further east to carry the GC goods lines across the Wirral. Bidston West signal box and the signal controlling the junction to Seacombe and New Brighton are visible in the background. COURTESY GLYNN PARRY

charged by Westinghouse rectifiers, used for tripping and closing, for remote control apparatus and emergency lighting. Current for signal lamps was given at 240 volts single phase from Hoylake and Bidston sub-stations, where they were fed direct from the ancillary services board. The feeders ran to the nearest signal box, where an automatic contactor facilitated changing over to an emergency supply, from the public network, in the event of a failure in the sub-station supply. The supply from Hoylake sub-station covered West Kirby to Moreton, whilst that from Bidston covered New Brighton to Moreton and Birkenhead North. The signal supply for the North-Park section was provided by the Mersey Railway.

The retention by the Mersey of their third and fourth rail system required special arrangements at Birkenhead Park. To allow operation over the LM&S three-rail system, the Mersey Railway motor coaches were fitted with electro-pneumatic earthing switches, which had to be switched off when leaving Park on Wirral tracks and on when leaving Park on Mersey tracks. LM&S motor coaches were, of course, fitted with similar equipment, enabling them to run on the Mersey lines. Elaborate devices were fitted to ensure that the changeover was made. All tracks on the Wirral-bound side of the station were fed from the LM&S supply, whilst those on the Liverpool-bound side were fed from the Mersey supply.

MODERNISATION OF THE STATIONS

The less important wayside stations on the Wirral had always been somewhat primitive, with plenty of wood and corrugated iron in evidence. After the Grouping, the LM&S had carried out basic repairs and applied some paint but the image presented to the public was poor and an ambitious rebuilding programme was central to the electrification project. The buildings at Hoylake, Meols, Moreton, Leasowe and Wallasey Village were completely replaced to a common theme, using reinforced concrete frames with brick filling. New concrete footbridges were installed at all these stations and also at Bidston, where the bridge was of exceptional length as it spanned the four Wirral and L&NE tracks. In addition, concrete platform awnings were erected at West Kirby and New Brighton. At New Brighton, the enormous 'STATION' sign on the corner of Victoria Road and Atherton Street was replaced by one announcing 'LMSR'. The two separate wooden buildings at Bidston were joined by a new roof section, thus increasing the covered waiting area. Many station platforms were raised, repaved and faced with concrete, though the Seacombe branch was not included. Numerous of the oil and gas lights were replaced by electricity.

The work at Hoylake, arguably the most ramshackle of the Wirral stations in any case, was the most extensive, with a new 175 foot long Up platform building being reached through a concourse with an impressive circular clerestory. At Meols and Moreton, the buildings were at street level with staircases to each platform; at Meols, they were built alongside the roadway embankment, with a basement cycle store and heating chamber, the 42 foot girders for the footbridge being cast *in situ* and hoisted into position by a mobile crane. With the exception of those at Leasowe, buildings were all 10 feet wide with 10 foot of clear platform width. The cantilever platform awnings were of interest, being supported by cantilever beams above, leaving clear soffits beneath. The overturning effect of

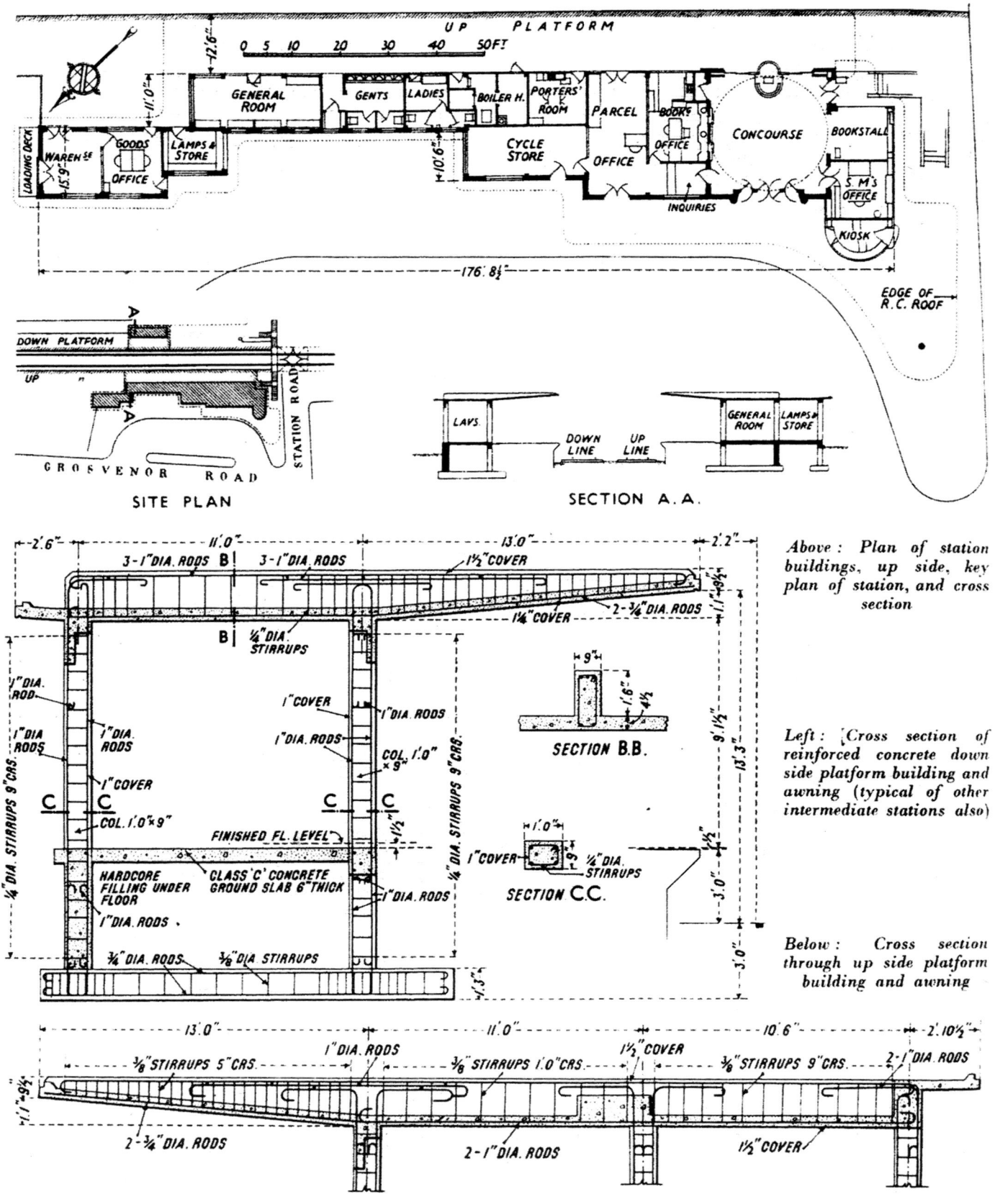

A detail drawing of Hoylake station as rebuilt shortly before the 1938 electrification. Whilst this was the most elaborate rebuild, the same principles were followed in the reconstruction of the other selected stations. FROM *THE RAILWAY GAZETTE*, 18TH MARCH 1938

An interesting view of Hoylake, taken almost certainly in January 1938. Reconstruction of the station is almost complete, with new platform seats to match the 1930s 'art deco' style buildings and canopies but the old gas lighting is still in use. The steam hauled service on the left is in contrast to the brand new, all steel, three-car electric train on a driver training run on the right. Note, however, that Driving Car No. 28678 is showing the wrong destination on its indicator board, as the train is coming from West Kirby and is bound for Birkenhead North. TED LLOYD COLLECTION

the awnings was resisted by a balance wall along the back of the buildings, supporting the brickwork and floor. The 230 foot long awnings at West Kirby and New Brighton were respectively 35-40 feet and 21 feet wide, the latter being on a sharply curved platform. Each projected one foot over the platform coping and there were expansion joints.

THE CHANGEOVER

The rail infrastructure was substantially finished by December 1937 and trial trips for instruction of motormen began on 3rd January 1938, between Birkenhead North and West Kirby (17 minutes) and New Brighton (9 minutes). LM&S stock was tested for clearances over the Mersey lines after normal services ceased on 11th January and familiarisation of LM&S drivers began three days later. Mersey trains were tested over Wirral lines and driver familiarisation started on 17th January; all clearance tests were finished by the end of the month and training continued each Sunday during February. It was agreed that all train staff must be familiar with all lines, including the Mersey's Rock Ferry line. To maintain this familiarity, the LM&S trains were to operate the West Kirby line on all weekdays, and the New Brighton and Rock Ferry lines on Sundays. The Mersey trains ran the New Brighton and Rock Ferry services on weekdays and West Kirby on Sundays.

The last Seacombe-West Kirby steam train ran on Saturday 12th March 1938 and, on Sunday 13th, a 'dress rehearsal' electric service

The newly built concrete platform canopy at New Brighton in 1938, a first for the station, whose passengers had not previously been afforded any such protection from the elements. *THE LOCOMOTIVE MAGAZINE*

was run more or less to the steam timetable but running through to and from Liverpool. It was decided that all locomotives should be clear of Birkenhead North shed by 12.30am on Sunday 13th and all possible coaching stock removed. On Saturday, 2-6-2Ts No's 2, 3, 4, 5, 42, 44, 49, 50 and 51, 0-6-0T No. 7503 and 0-6-2T No.

Reconstruction underway at Hoylake in 1937. In the foreground, the reinforced concrete footbridge is part completed, as are the platforms, which were rebuilt with new surfaces and facings; note the new benches on the Up platform awaiting distribution. The old level crossing gates are still in place however. W.S. WHITEHEAD

This view from the new footbridge at Hoylake in late 1937 or early 1938 shows the roofs of the concrete canopies, with the integral bracing beams on the outside or top as a feature of the design. East and west bound passenger services are just passing and the tiny goods yard is chock full mainly with coal wagons. Note the underslung bracket starter signal for Down trains, which has appeared since the previous view was taken. It was presumably installed to allow better sighting due to the new station canopy. TED LLOYD COLLECTION

Looking east through the new level crossing gates after completion of rebuilding. The low viewpoint emphasises the lack of platform supports for the concrete awnings, which were effectively suspended off the roof beams. Note the new concrete post platform lamps in the right distance and the enamelled station sign on the left. COURTESY THE LENS OF SUTTON ASSOCIATION

RIGHT: Meols station was also substantially rebuilt, complete with a new entrance situated on the road bridge, previous access having been at track level. The entrance, seen here shortly after completion, included a new bookstall for Finlay & Co, replacing their old one in the original station building on the platform, seen in the picture on page 141. The design was similar to London suburban stations of the period but note the stylish pre-cast concrete LMS signs on the roof.

RIGHT: The eastbound station buildings at an early stage of their construction, revealing the reinforced concrete framework prior to the addition of brickwork.

BELOW: Men at work constructing the new platform on the westbound line. Note the opportunity was taken to raise it at this time to standard height. A temporary booking office was provided.
ALL COURTESY GLYNN PARRY

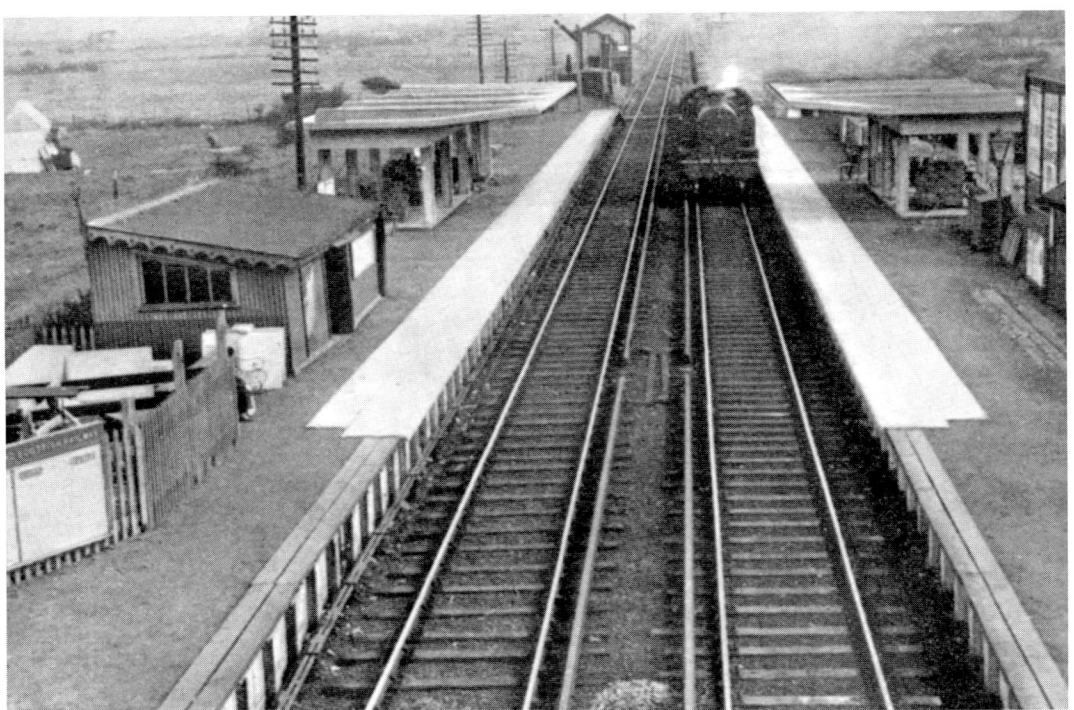

LEFT: The new facilities at Moreton under construction in 1937. The platform facings have been replaced but the new edging and surface stones are only partly laid. The shelters on both platforms were identical in design to the one on the Up platform at Hoylake. The old buildings were cleared once the new ones were open. PHOTO H.A. ROBINSON

BELOW: Bidston station circa 1938, showing the new platform facings and edging stones, and the section joining the previously two separate station buildings. Apart from the addition of the third rail, little else changed here, however, with the old platform seats, enamelled advertising signs and Wirral Railway running in boards with cast-iron letters all remaining in place. JOHN ALSOP COLLECTION

7841 were working passenger services, No. 55 was spare engine and 0-6-0Ts No's 7503, 7353 (Seacombe branch), 7780 (West Kirby) and 7404 (Bidston-Birkenhead North transfers) worked the goods services. No's 12, 48 and 7507 were away at Chester, Derby and Crewe respectively, 2-6-2T No. 159 was on loan from Chester and an ex-Midland 0-6-0T, No. 1818, allocated to Birkenhead (Mollington Street) was on ballast work.

The first movements commenced on Saturday afternoon, with No. 7711 working empty stock to Hooton followed by No. 44 with the coaches from the 4.30pm Park-West Kirby train. These were coupled together and went on to Crewe, followed by No's 5, 42 and 55 coupled together to Mold Junction. After midnight, there was a wholesale exodus, No's 7759 and 27664 leaving for Crewe, No. 3 working the last passenger train from Park to West Kirby at 11.22pm and then proceeding with No. 4 on empty stock to Crewe. No's 2 and 7841 worked another empty stock train to Crewe whilst No's 70 and 159 went coupled together to Birkenhead shed via Hooton. The last West Kirby to Seacombe train at 10.19pm was headed by No. 51, which then worked empty stock to Birkenhead North, before proceeding with No's 49 and 50 to Chester. No. 7780 worked the 10.32pm Birkenhead North-Hooton goods train, then proceeded to Birkenhead shed. The three remaining 0-6-0Ts,

RIGHT: The terminus at West Kirby 'before and after' electrification. This picture dates from circa 1930 and shows the trackwork leading in to the platforms from ground level. JOHN RYAN COLLECTION

BELOW: This second view, taken in early 1938, shows the new West Kirby signal cabin on the right. Like the other new boxes built for the Wirral at this time, it had a brick base with timber upper storey. The more elevated viewpoint for this photograph indicates that the trackwork had not been altered apart from the installation of the third rail. However, a concrete awning is being built on the island platform, which has also gained a new bracket starter signal. Two of the 3-car sets of new electric stock (in use on training runs) can be seen stabled in the carriage sidings, whilst the goods yard looks relatively quiet. The GW/LM&S line curves off to the left, to the Joint station just out of sight. TED LLOYD COLLECTION

LEFT: Part of the 230 foot long concrete awning built over the island platform at West Kirby, showing the method of support and the skylights. Note even the advertising hoarding, seen end-on in this view, is in keeping with the new modern design. TED LLOYD COLLECTION

No's 7353, 7503 and 7504, went the short distance to the Bidston L&NE (ex-GC) shed, where they remained based to work the goods services on the Wirral and the New Brighton-London passenger train to Hooton. No. 7841, heading the 10.56pm West Kirby-Park service, was scheduled to work the last public steam service but, because of late running, the 11.08pm New Brighton-Park service was allowed to precede it from Bidston East Junction. So, it was No. 7503, working the 11.30pm to New Brighton 15 minutes late, which took the honour. This was the only late working of the day.

The official opening took place on Monday morning, 14th March. The official party, led by Sir Josiah Stamp, President of the LM&S, boarded a train made up of the latest Mersey Railway stock at Liverpool Central Low Level and travelled non-stop to Birkenhead Park, where they were met by the Mayor of Birkenhead and other local dignitaries. They then crossed the platform to board a five coach train of new corridor stock headed by 2-6-2T No. 200, newly outshopped, which had been brought in specially the previous day. This train left at 10.10am non-stop to West Kirby, where the party detrained to be greeted by the Chairman of Hoylake UDC, Selwyn Lloyd, who was destined to become, some years later, MP for the town and Foreign Secretary. The ever-increasing party then boarded an electric train which carried them to New Brighton, where the Mayor of Wallasey and his entourage boarded. The train then ran non-stop through to Liverpool Central Low Level, to be met by the Lord Mayor of Liverpool. The whole party then walked the short distance to the LM&S-owned Adelphi Hotel for lunch and speeches. No. 200 and its coaches returned empty from West Kirby to Hooton and Crewe. The ramshackle engine shed was demolished but the unusual water tank, which figured in so many photographs of locomotives, remained and continued in use by steam locomotives on goods turns.

Destination blind as fitted to the 1938 Wirral Section electric stock. This one came from Driving Trailer No. 29288. COURTESY T.G. TURNER

The public electric service started with the first trains on 14th March 1938, two Mersey Railway trains having spent the night at New Brighton to make the inaugural departures. There was a 20 per cent increase in the number of trains over the Wirral lines, frequencies on each line being 10 minutes in the peak hours and 15 minutes during the day. Midday commuting was encouraged by a slight augmentation of the service between approximately 12.30 and 2.00pm, Mondays to Fridays. Parallel bus services were immediately affected; Wallasey Corporation reported a loss of £20 per day, which they attributed to passengers using the faster rail service to come home for lunch, though this was soon recovered as economic conditions improved. The running time from Liverpool Central to West Kirby was reduced from an average 36 to 29 minutes and to New Brighton from 24 to 21 minutes. The service was very reliable and quickly became popular with the travelling public.

In an age when accountants are king and the cost of everything is constantly emphasised, it will seem strange that the cost of the Wirral electrification was not even mentioned in any of the detailed and comprehensive accounts which were featured in the technical press of the time. The only monetary figure which was mentioned was a global £30 million for all the projects financed under the Railways (Agreement) Act.

ELECTRIC ROLLING STOCK

The heavyweight electric stock as used on the Watford line and which had been proposed for the Wirral electrification was rejected, and it was announced in 1936 that three-car articulated sets, with an overall length of 181 feet and seating for 24 First and 176 Third class passengers would be used. The articulation was said to be an unusual type, *'with two pivots on the articulation bogies instead*

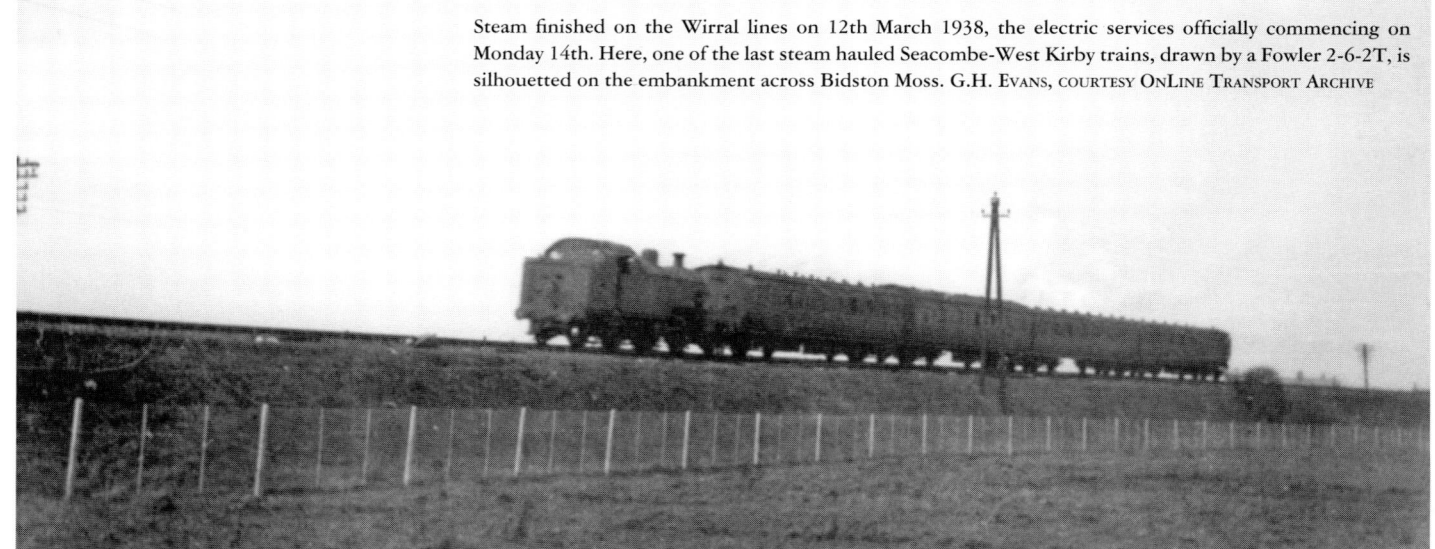

Steam finished on the Wirral lines on 12th March 1938, the electric services officially commencing on Monday 14th. Here, one of the last steam hauled Seacombe-West Kirby trains, drawn by a Fowler 2-6-2T, is silhouetted on the embankment across Bidston Moss. G.H. EVANS, COURTESY OnLine Transport Archive

THE WIRRAL RAILWAY

of the normal one'. However, articulation was dropped at an early date and an order was placed for nineteen all-steel three-car sets, comprising a Third class Motor Coach with motors on all four axles, a Composite Trailer and a Third class Driving Trailer, arranged for multiple unit operation in two or more rakes.

The order was divided between the Metropolitan-Cammell Carriage & Wagon Company, who built the Motor Coaches, and the Birmingham Railway Carriage & Wagon Company, who built the Trailers and Driving Trailers. The coach bodies were welded to the underframes, whilst the bogies were also of welded construction and fitted with 36 inch diameter wheels. The outer ends of each unit were equipped with 'buckeye' type centre couplings, whilst the three cars were coupled by a single slotted link, connected through pin joints to drawbars pulling on rubber springs. Buffers were fitted along with these couplings but not at the outer ends of each three-car unit, where the centre coupling also acted as a buffer. It was expected that the normal make-up of a train would be two units or six carriages.

Seating capacity was for 40 First and 141 Third, the latter being provided in 3+2 formation with wide aisles and a roomy circulating area adjacent to the two pairs of 3 foot 9 inch air-operated sliding doors, which were electrically controlled by the guard. However, push buttons for passenger use at certain stations were also fitted, the circuit for these also being controlled and therefore made operable by the guard. It saved all the doors being opened at lightly used stations, exposing travelling passengers to the elements. All opened doors had to be closed by the guard on departure and the local opening circuit cancelled. Ventilation of the carriages was by sliding lights and heating was thermostatically controlled.

Traction motors were of 135hp 650 volts, axle hung and nose suspended, all electrical equipment being supplied by BTH. Standard Westinghouse electro-pneumatic and straight air brakes were fitted and all trains were equipped with trip cocks. The Westinghouse air compressor also provided for operation of the control and door gear. The control equipment was of electro-pneumatic operation, arranged into four groups of individual electro-pneumatic contactors. There were four traction motors in each Motor Coach, each rated at 93hp for continuous use. They were self ventilated, with air being drawn through ducts in each coach and a louvred opening in the coach side. The Trailers and Driving Trailers were permanently coupled but the electrical connections were arranged to allow easy removal of the Motor Coach from a unit. There was no provision for one three-car unit to be connected to another but a power receptacle was fitted to each unit to enable it to be 'plugged in' and moved when on shed, where safety precluded the use of conductor rails. A negative shoe was also provided, required for use on the fourth rail when running on the Mersey Railway system.

The dimensions of the three-car units were as follows:

Centres of Bogies: Motor Coach & DT Car	41ft
Centres of Bogies: Trailer Car	39ft 6ins
Bogie Wheel Base	7ft 6ins
Width over Body	8ft 8ins
Length over Body: Motor Coach & DT Car	58ft
Length over Body: Trailer Car	56ft
Height from Rail to Top of Roof	11ft 5ins
Weight of 3-car unit tare incl. equipment	77 tons
Seating: Motor Car 3rd Class	58
Seating: Trailer Car 3rd Class	15
Seating: Trailer Car 1st Class	40
Seating: Driving Trailer Car 3rd Class	68
Total Seats	181

However, this was not the only electric stock which would operate

One of the LM&SR three-car electric trains photographed when new in 1938. Nearest the camera is Driving Trailer No. 29279, with Trailer No. 29709 in the centre and Motor Coach No. 28679 at the far end. JOHN HORNE COLLECTION

One of the 3-car units posed outside the new shed, with Motor Coach No. 28683 to the fore. The train was photographed in early 1938 when it was still engaged on driver training duties. The third rail ended outside the shed, so trains had to coast inside. They could be moved around once in the shed by plugging the Motor Coach into the depot mains supply. NEIL PARKHOUSE COLLECTION

LEFT: In contrast to the brand new all steel units built by the LM&SR, a Mersey Railway six-car train is seen at Birkenhead North station soon after the electrification. The end car is either No. 13 or 14, a Cravens car of 1923/25, whilst the rest are Milnes 1903 stock. The train is destined for New Brighton. J.C. GILLHAM

BELOW: Although this view of Birkenhead Park station is pre-electrification, it serves to illustrate the Mersey tracks, on the left, with their third and fourth rails. Both the old and the new stock had therefore to be capable of working from the Wirral Section's third rail system and the Mersey Railway's fourth rail and of switching between the two. GLYNN PARRY COLLECTION

No. 7838, one of the ex-L&NWR 'Coal Tanks', passes Moreton signal box on 20th October 1937 with a lengthy goods train from Birkenhead, which will stop at West Kirby and points beyond on the GW/LM&S Joint line to Hooton. Note the ex-L&NW ground signal in the foreground, controlling the exit from the tiny yard here at Moreton. In the 1950s, the Cadbury's factory was built on the land to the left of the signal box. TED LLOYD COLLECTION

on the Wirral Section. The New Brighton-Liverpool (Central) service was to be worked by Mersey Railway stock, which was refurbished to bring it more in line with the standard of the new units. New upholstered seating was fitted for the comfort which passengers would rapidly get used to with the new stock, along with electric heaters. These were a necessity now the trains would be running in the open instead of mostly in tunnels. They were equipped with motor driven air compressors in place of storage reservoirs and a change-over switch arrangement for switching between the Mersey fourth rail system and the running rail return on the Wirral.

GOODS TRAFFIC

The pattern of general goods workings on the Wirral barely changed after the Grouping, with most of the stations seeing little more than deliveries of coal and parcels traffic. Such larger tonnages that were handled were to and from the docks and to various industrial concerns which were connected to the Wirral, and they will be dealt with separately. The Slopes Branch was busier during both World Wars but was otherwise very quiet. By 1934, there were usually only three trains per week, sometimes fewer. The trips were 'as required' and were performed by engines working the Oakdale coal trains. It might be thought that the L&NER would have used the branch to access its yards on the north side of the docks but

this was seldom the case. They had a few Sentinel locomotives for such duties but these were kept at a sub-shed in a corner of the CLC yard on Shore Road, rather than at Bidston. There were gates where the branch crossed Poulton Bridge Road, worked by the train crews, and a Wirral Railway plan shows Wirral ownership ending immediately west of the gates.

Ex-L&NW Class '1F' Ramsbottom 'Special Tank' No. 7287 (formerly L&NW No. 3215) shunts at Birkenhead North sidings in the 1930s. No fewer than 258 of this class were built between 1870 and 1880 and the last was not withdrawn until 1959. JOHN RYAN COLLECTION

An L&NER goods train being shunted at Bidston in July 1930, prior to heading over the short section of Wirral metals to Birkenhead North. The train includes a number of private owner wagons belonging to Llay Main Collieries Ltd near Wrexham. The company was part of the Yorkshire-based Carlton Main empire and the coal was probably bound for Rea Ltd at Birkenhead Docks for bunkering, although the colliery also supplied gas coal. Rea's had shares in Llay Main, whilst Carlton Main in turn held shares in Rea Ltd. The shunting engine, Ivatt '1201' Class 0-6-0ST No. 4206 (ex-68810), built at Doncaster in 1897, survived into BR days, being withdrawn in late 1955. JOHN WARD COLLECTION, COURTESY JOHN HORNE

Liscard & Poulton station lay in a cutting hewn out of the local sandstone rock. This view, looking towards Seacombe, shows the single coal siding and the approach road from Mill Lane, up on the left. A Seacombe-West Kirby train headed by 0-6-2T No. 7841 is seen departing on 12th February 1938. In earlier days, there was a short siding serving the quarry on the right, possibly in connection with the laying of foundations over the marshy ground on which the Slopes Branch was constructed in 1906. The cutting now carries the approach road to the second (Wallasey) Mersey road tunnel. TED LLOYD COLLECTION

The railways of the Mersey Docks & Harbour Board are not the business of this book but Bidston Dock was uniquely associated with the ex-Wirral lines and has to be included. The Board had bought all that portion of Bidston Moss, some 170 acres, east of the Wirral line, with no clear plans for its development. Work began in February 1924 on a 100-foot water passage at Poulton Bridge, the construction being finished in two years including a bowstring swing bridge. A relatively small dock opened west of Poulton Bridge in 1931. Several Dock Board locomotives were engaged on building this dock, most of them from the Board's Engineer's Department (lettered M.D.E.) but a few Traffic Department engines were also seen. The work does not seem to have involved use of the Slopes Branch but the tip sidings alongside the curve from Bidston East to Bidston North were apparently extended to the site. Some spoil was spread around Bidston Moss but some, it is believed, was taken by rail to New Brighton for the promenade extension. The original dock was used for importing pit props, among other traffic, and huge piles of them built up between the quay and the railway sidings on the north side. The most likely destination for them was the North Wales coalfield, since the Manchester Ship Canal dominated the Lancashire market, so the Slopes Branch and the ex-Great Central line were probably the route followed by this traffic.

Finally, to end this section on a lighter note, widely remembered still are the elephants which, after a season in New Brighton, made their way in the traditional circus street parade to New Brighton station. They were bound for their winter quarters and were loose-coupled, trunk to tail, before stepping carefully into a waiting railway van. This regular traffic, in the 1940s and into the 1950s at least, must explain why there were elephants in a bogie van on the last passenger train from West Kirby to Hooton.

INDUSTRIAL SIDINGS AND LOCOMOTIVES

Hoylake Gas Works

Developments at Hoylake Gas Works during this period included the purchase of a Manning Wardle 0-4-0ST, Works No. 1136/91, second-hand from Electro Bleach of Middlewich at an unknown date, probably in the mid-1920s. It cannot have been a success because it was replaced by a new 4-wheeled Muir Hill tractor (Works No. 32/1927), of much lesser power but adequate for the work and remarkably durable.

The UDC built a vertical retort house (Woodall Duckham type) immediately after taking over but the old horizontal retorts were usable as late as 1935 and were still present at closure, though derelict. The new retort house was reached by extending the sidings across Moss Lane. In 1935, 8,929 tons of coal produced a much larger volume of gas for sale due to the more modern plant employed. The final tonnage before closure was about 11,000 per annum.

Wallasey Gas Works

As mentioned previously, coal continued to arrive at Wallasey Gas Works via the Wirral's Seacombe Branch throughout the LM&S era and the 1950s, right up until the works closed. For the whole of the LM&S period, the two Barclay 0-4-0STs, *W.G. Ellery* and *Eastwood*, new in 1897 and 1912 respectively, continued with their shunting duties around the gas and electricity works. Both locomotives were eventually sold to Cudworth & Johnson of Wrexham, *Eastwood* in 1948. Because C&J provided the local shunting contractors with most of their engines, both the ex-gas works Barclays were still to be seen around the district in subsequent years.

Ruston & Hornsby built diesel mechanical locos which became

Ex-Wallasey Gas Works Barclay 0-4-0ST *Eastwood* pictured on the MD&HB lines at Seacombe on 1st June 1950, when on hire from Cudworth & Johnson to haulage contractor W.J. Lee. Coincidentally, William Lee had provided haulage for wagons to the gas works prior to the gas company purchasing their first locomotive, *W.G. Ellery*, in 1897. *Eastwood* had left the gas works employ just two years before this photograph was taken. JOHN HORNE COLLECTION

very popular in the gas industry. Wallasey works had two of the small 44DS type, one of them new in 1943 and the other in 1947. They gave good service and both went to Wigan Gas Works in July 1962, after Wallasey closed. At Wigan, one locomotive yielded spares which kept the other in service until this gas works, in turn, closed in favour of supplies from more modern works elsewhere.

Wallasey Corporation Electricity Supply
Wallasey's electricity supply had begun on 1st February 1897, from an inland site in Seaview Road where the tram sheds were later built. A new works using steam turbines was opened next to Wallasey Gas Works in 1914; it had the advantages of railway access and of cooling water from the Great Float. Initially, the works apparently had its own siding connection direct to the Seacombe Branch but, after the war, this connection was removed and the works was served by a line running back from the gas works sidings. Gas works locomotives then delivered the coal.

In 1923, a 33kV link was made with Birkenhead and Wallasey supplied a rapidly increasing share of the town's load until 1st January 1934, when the CEB transferred the business to Liverpool. Wallasey's demand was more than halved; the works had burned about 50,000 tons of coal in 1933 but needed only 22,400 tons in 1935. The 'units sent out' briefly matched the 1933 peak in 1953 but the running hours (and therefore efficiency) were low, mostly at peak hours.

New Brighton Promenade, Edmund Nuttall, Sons & Co. Ltd
The 'New Promenade' at New Brighton was constructed in 1935-39 behind a massive concrete sea wall, a westward extension of the older sandstone block promenade walls which stretch from Seacombe to New Brighton. Not all residents or visitors looked favourably on this work, since it partly concealed the picturesque Red Noses and Yellow Noses, which were sandstone outcrops, and spoiled a fine sandy shore backed by large dunes. The contractor was Edmund Nuttall, Sons & Co. Ltd.

In a talk to the Liverpool Engineering Society, the Wallasey Borough Engineer reported that *'These narrow gauge lines were worked by at least six Ruston and Hornsby four-wheeled diesel locomotives.'* They were supplied new to this contract and were later moved to Bungay. There was also a substantial standard gauge layout, which brought in the necessary cement, aggregate and steel reinforcement although sand (once washed) was already plentiful. There was also a need for fill and some of it was said to have come from Bidston. The first Bidston Dock contract had already finished but perhaps the material had been stored on site.

The long-established 'Sand Siding' from New Brighton station was extended to serve the worksite. The gradients must have been fierce since the difference in levels is about thirty feet and it is no surprise that Nuttalls brought in four powerful six-coupled locomotives. They were among nine or ten near-identical Hunslet saddle-tanks with 14ins x 20ins cylinders, which had been bought new for building the King George the Fifth dry dock at Southampton, where they all worked from 1931 to 1935. This contract had been a joint effort by Nuttall and John Mowlem & Co. but the locomotives appear to have all been Nuttall's property, including the one named *Mowlem*. There may have been earlier engines on the New Brighton job but the four which moved there from Southampton were:

Nuttall, Hunslet works No. 1685/1931
Mowlem, Hunslet works No. 1686/1931*
Southern, Hunslet works No. 1688/1931
Cunarder, Hunslet works No. 1690/1931
* renamed *Wallasey*

Contractors had an engaging custom of naming their locomotives, often after places where they had worked. Most of the Southampton engines were so named but *Mowlem* was no longer appropriate so it was renamed *Wallasey*. Their work done, *Wallasey*, *Southern* and *Cunarder* were noted to be in store by July 1937. *Wallasey* left the New Brighton contract that year to help build the new Southern Railway branch to Chessington but *Southern* and *Cunarder* (and also

Wagons from all of the 'Big Four' railway companies are present in this early 1930s view of the sand siding near New Brighton, with the Irish Sea providing the background. MARTIN JENKINS COLLECTION

LEFT: Edmund Nuttall, Sons & Co's 0-6-0ST *Wallasey* at Wallasey Sand Siding on 7th July 1937, near the end of the engine's time on the New Brighton promenade contract. Note the chauldron-style contractor's wagons in the background, used for transporting the sand.

BELOW: Nuttall locomotives *Southern* and *Cunarder*, also photographed on 7th July 1937, were definitely 'in store'. They were to remain on site until 1939, whilst *Wallasey* departed soon after these pictures were taken, bound for Chessington. BOTH JOHN WARD COLLECTION, COURTESY JOHN HORNE

perhaps *Nuttall*) remained after the work was finished, until 1939. Then came a great demand for all kinds of contractor's plant to build ordnance factories and the like, and all four Hunslets served on such work. All of them continued to move around, lasting into the 1950s and 1960s. *Cunarder* survives to this day, although it has now been altered to a side-tank, and has run on the preserved line at Swanage.

The rump of the Sand Siding remained for many years, ending at a locked gate on the LM&S boundary and was partly electrified. Wind-blown sand had been a serious problem in the neighbourhood, not least to the Wirral Railway whose track would have been buried without constant attention. The planting of star grass failed to stabilise the sand dunes but the 'New Promenade' did at least solve that problem.

The Sand Siding was extended in connection with the New Brighton promenade contract in the mid-1930s. One of the contractor's locomotives can be seen but as all four were near identical, which one is not known. Note the steam shovel, digging out the sand and loading it into the wagons out of sight behind the locomotive. MARTIN JENKINS COLLECTION

A PORTION OF THE MERSEY DOCK ESTATE AT BIRKENHEAD.

An aerial view of Birkenhead Docks circa 1930. The goods coming through it passed mainly onto the GW, LM&S and L&NER (previously GW, L&NW, and GCR) but some traffic filtered down to the Wirral. Prior to the Grouping, the short connection over Wirral metals between the GCR's Bidston sidings and the docks had proved very useful for the company, at one time generating more income than all their other goods activities put together. Birkenhead North Goods and the locomotive depot can be seen in the right foreground, partially obscured by the word 'Birkenhead'. The line performs a shallow 'S' as it runs on past and along Beaufort Road, a short way down which was the boundary with the Mersey Docks & Harbour Board. At the other end of Beaufort Road can just be made out the great fan of sorting sidings. In the left foreground is Wallasey Pool or Poulton Bridge and in the middle distance beyond that can be seen Wallasey Gas Works, with the electricity works just visible in front. The course of the Seacombe Branch can just be made out curving round to the left, with the terminus being just off picture in the far distance. The Great Float West runs through the centre of the view, with Duke Street swing bridge (in the open position) visible centre left, whilst Vittoria Dock can be seen in the centre background. NEIL PARKHOUSE COLLECTION

New Brighton goods yard looking west circa 1939, with a typical selection of post-Grouping and private owner wagons. By the late 1930s, miscellaneous goods traffic was concentrated at Birkenhead and stations such as this handled only full load and coal traffic. The POs include a Gresford Colliery wagon, which one would expect to see here, and one for E. Foster Ltd of London and Emsworth, Hampshire, well out of its area. Pooling arrangements for wagons were brought into force in 1939, which meant wagons could be sent anywhere and would explain the presence of the Foster wagon here. GLYNN PARRY COLLECTION

PRIVATE OWNER WAGON OPERATORS IN THE LM&S ERA

Numerous coal merchants were in business in the area served by the Wirral system but few are known to have owned their own wagons. Cain Bros, coal merchants, operated from Duke Street, Birkenhead and Wallasey from the early 1930s. Prior to this, one Thomas A. Cain was listed as a coal merchant at 74 Keble Road, Bootle in 1894 (*Kelly's Directory*) but no link to Cain Bros has been found, nor any reference to Cain owning wagons. He does not appear in *Gore's Directory* for 1900. A photograph of 10-ton wagon No. 3 appears in *Private Owner Wagons, A First Collection* (Keith Turton, Lightmoor Press, 2003). This Gloucester RC&W photograph was taken in September 1933. The wagon was supplied second-hand at that time and painted with the owner's name within a large diamond or lozenge-shaped frame, possibly inspired by Lunt of Birmingham. Cains were not listed among coal merchants in the 1938 *Colliery Year Book*. However, they are said to have been trading from 471 Cleveland Street, Birkenhead (which is near Duke Street) and 6 Seaview Road, Wallasey.

In 1966, Clarke Bros & Co., were noted as still trading at 23 Rudd Street, Hoylake, Cheshire. In about 1935, the Gloucester RC&W Co. let one 10-ton wagon on hire to this firm. The agreement was renewed for a further five years on 11th May 1939, whilst they were listed as coal merchants in the 1938 *Colliery Year Book*, at the same address. R.J. Geill, coal merchant of Seacombe, owned at least one wagon, which is shown in a Hurst Nelson official photograph. However 10-ton wagon No. 2 is marked 'Load to South Reserve', so it may not have run on the Wirral when new. Meanwhile, Parr Bros of Station Yard, Hoylake, were listed as coal merchants in the 1926, 1933 and 1938 *Colliery Year Book*. Presumably, they were related (sons?) to the S. Parr whose office appears in the view of Hoylake yard on page 64. He is believed to have owned wagons, because his name appears on Railway Clearing House lists but whether or not Parr Bros also had their own wagons is not known.

A number of Wirral coal merchants are known to have leased wagons from the Gloucester Railway Carriage & Wagon Co. in the 1930s. Thomas Melone was at 12 Morley Road, Poulton, Wallasey. Gloucester re-let two 10-ton wagons to him for three years from 15th September 1938, although he was not listed among coal merchants in the 1938 *Colliery Year Book*. However, the New Brighton Coal Co. Ltd of 83 Brighton Street, Wallasey were listed and they had renewed an agreement for three 10-ton wagons for three years from 14th October 1937. W.N. Parkhouse (Coals) Ltd were based at 32 Birkenhead Road, Seacombe. The GRC&W Co. were recorded as having re-let two 10-ton wagons to Parkhouse for three years from 10th November 1938 but again he was not listed among coal merchants in the 1938 *Colliery Year Book*. Finally, Chas Pearce at 26 Magazine Lane, Wallasey, renewed his agreement for two 10-ton wagons for three years from 15th September 1938. He is also listed in the 1938 *Colliery Year Book*.

Hoylake & West Kirby Urban District Council had taken over both the gas and electricity works and their private sidings on the south side of Hoylake station. In 1938, the gas works carbonised 8,927 tons of coal; it ceased production in 1954. The Gas Department had wagons painted red with white lettering. A 7-plank wagon, with HOYLAKE on the top three, UDC GAS WORKS on the 5th and HOYLAKE in small lettering bottom right on the 7th plank was noted in May 1941, far from home and in use as a 'pooled' wagon. Hoylake Electricity Works operated from 1901 to about 1930-35 but whether it had its own wagons is not known.

Wallasey Corporation Gas Department owned three 12-ton mineral wagons, which were built by W.R. Davies Ltd of Wigan in August 1929 and numbered 43-45. They were seven-plank, had side and end doors only, and were registered by the LM&SR. The gas works was connected both to the Wirral Railway's Seacombe Branch and to the lines of the Mersey Docks & Harbour Board. Other wagons noted were numbered 2, 3, 81 and 127; they were painted red. The gas works locomotives also shunted the adjacent electricity works but whether the Electricity Department had their own wagons is not known.

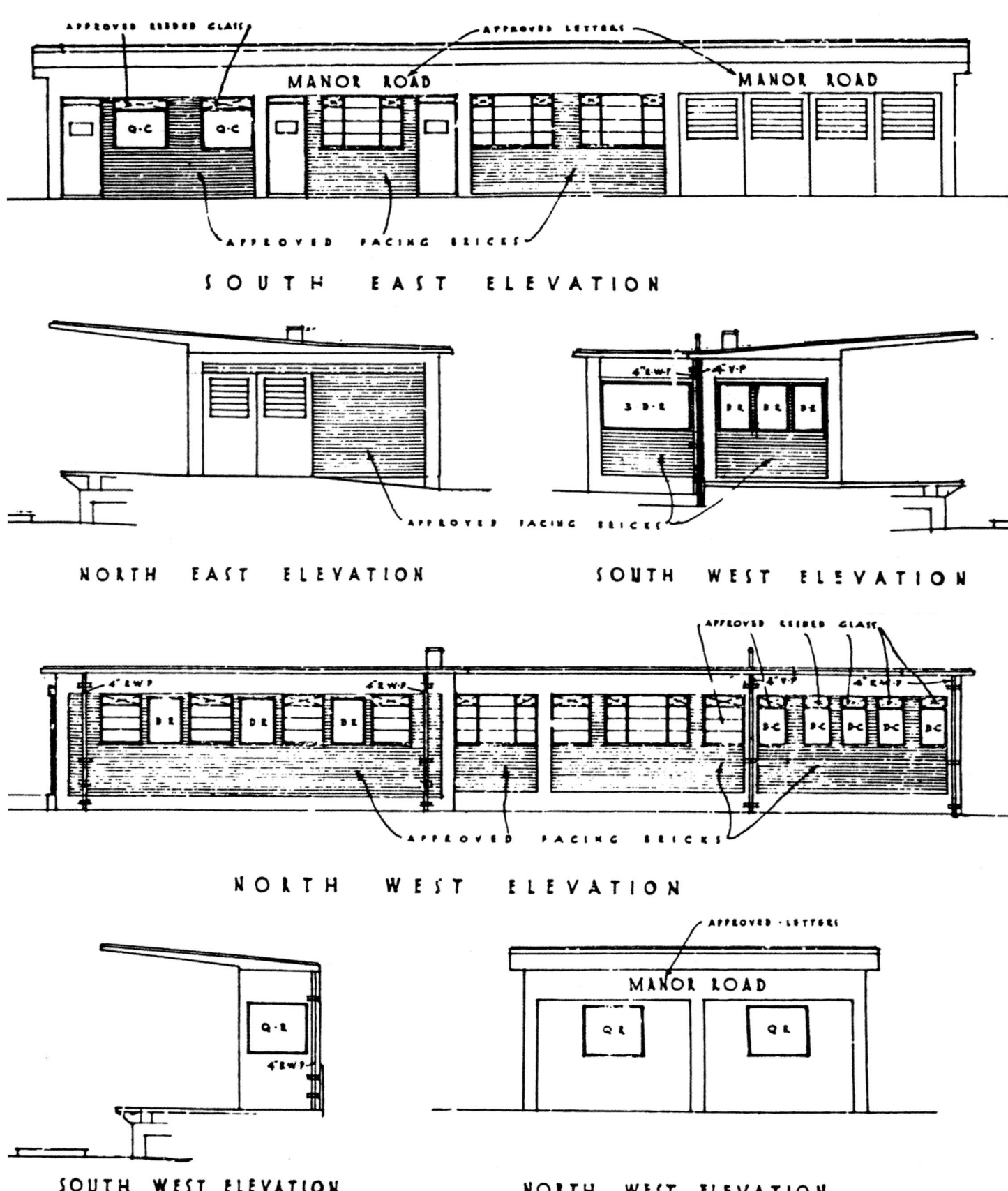

An official drawing of Manor Road, a new station which was opened on 15th May 1940, over two years after electrification. The design and construction methods were slightly different from the other rebuilt stations on the line, though the overall appearance is similar. Note the clear lines of the roof and the omission of the valances. (Not to scale)

An L&NE Seacombe-Wrexham train headed by an unidentified ex-GC Class 'C13' 4-4-2T locomotive approaches Bidston station on a misty day in the mid 1930s. The L&NE (ex-GC) sidings and the locomotive depot water tank are in the foreground. N.N. FORBES

THE SECOND WORLD WAR

The early months of the Second World War were relatively uneventful. The through coaches to and from London Euston were withdrawn from September 1939, never to be resumed. The blackout regulations required immediate attention to be given to restricting lighting both on trains and on stations. Metal shoe-guards, faced with rubber, were fitted between the positive shoes and the equaliser bars to obviate flashing over to earth, arising from intense sparking because of iced conductor rails experienced during the winter of 1939-40. A positive development was the opening, on 15th May 1940, of a new station named Manor Road, between Meols and Hoylake. This had been part of the 1938 electrification scheme but had been delayed by procedural difficulties. Train services were modified to take account of changes in demand, caused by the restriction of entertainment facilities and the reluctance of the public to travel during the hours of darkness. However, as the war machine expanded and new factories recruited labour, the demands on the service increased. Exhortations by the government to take holidays at home brought thousands of passengers on to the New Brighton and West Kirby trains at summer weekends.

During 1940-41, Merseyside was subjected to intensive aerial bombardment and the Wirral lines, being close to the Birkenhead docks, were very much in the firing line. However, despite the severity of the air raids, particularly those in December 1940, and March and May 1941, the line came off relatively lightly. The Mersey was less fortunate and, of course, incidents on that line interrupted the through service. However, Herculean efforts on the part of staff restored services in remarkably short times. A high explosive bomb which fell on Liverpool Central CLC station in the early hours penetrated the underground line, exploding between two six-car trains in the sidings. Both trains were extensively damaged, one car beyond repair, but the mess was cleared up in time for services to commence on time next morning. In the same week, a bomb penetrated the tunnel between Park and Hamilton Square, resulting in one side of the brick tunnel collapsing, blocking both roads. A shuttle service of buses ran for eight weeks whilst Beckwith Street was opened up to give access to the tunnel.

The worst incident occurred on the night of 12th/13th March 1941, when two land mines fell on the Duke Street overbridge, damaging one span, virtually demolishing Birkenhead Park station buildings and the Mersey Railway carriage shed which contained a six-car train, and leaving an enormous crater in the main line tracks. The staircase approaches to the platforms were also badly damaged. The debris was cleared in a very short time, with through services, not stopping at Park, being restored in five days. Meanwhile, a temporary booking office was built, the staircases were repaired and the station was reopened after eleven days. One wonders how long it would have taken in the early years of the 21st century. On the same night as this incident, the carriage shed on the Down side at Birkenhead North was destroyed resulting in the total loss of two Control Trailers and two Trailers. A bomb damaged the Down platform at Wallasey Village station, Harrison Drive bridge received a direct hit and another bomb fell on the Seacombe Branch near Liscard & Poulton station; the breakdown crane from Chester assisted in the clearance of the line and services were quickly restored. At no time was the under-river service stopped and reliability was far superior than that prevailing in the closing years of the 20th century.

New sidings connecting Birkenhead North with the south side of Bidston Dock were laid in 1941-42, probably by War Office labour to handle military traffic. A staff hut and telephone line to Cavendish Sidings (west of Duke Street) were also provided, the latter being

ABOVE & BELOW: Two views of the street level main building at Birkenhead Park station after being hit by high explosive German parachute mines on the night of 12-13th March 1941. Despite the devastation, trains were running through the platforms again in five days and temporary offices and stairways were built to enable the station itself to reopen after eleven days. Note the Dennis flatbed lorry in the foreground of the lower view, drafted in no doubt to assist in clear-up operations and also the badly damaged houses in the background. The station building was eventually demolished and replaced by a much smaller structure. BOTH T.G. TURNER COLLECTION

disconnected by War Office contractors in 1947. The strategic importance of the Wirral and Mersey lines to the war effort was recognised in high places and emergency plans were made to guard against the consequences of the loss of a substantial amount of rolling stock. The LM&S considered lending some Euston-Watford stock and asked London Transport if they could increase their peak hour Bakerloo Line workings to Watford to make good the shortage of stock which would have resulted but this idea was not pursued. However, London Transport had a number of compatible withdrawn 1906 Hammersmith & City and Metropolitan trains in store, pending disposal to a scrap dealer with whom the contract had already been signed. So eighteen H&C and six Metropolitan cars were overhauled, converted, repainted in LM&S colours and renumbered at London Transport's Acton works. They were then made up into four six-car trains and transferred to the Wirral between November 1941 and early 1942. Two were stored at Hoylake and two in the sidings west of Birkenhead North; however, they never saw public service although they made a few crew-training sorties. In 1945, after the war ended, they were reclaimed by the scrap merchant and taken to Chesterfield for breaking up.

This six-car Mersey Railway train has just passed under Harrison Drive bridge, between Wallasey and New Brighton stations, in February 1947. The end car is No. 13, a 1926 First class car which became M28417 after Nationalisation but the leading three-car set comprises 1903 Westinghouse-designed stock built by George Milnes & Co. at Hadley, Shropshire. This is the section of line which in earlier years was often buried in sand. The promenade and Liverpool Bay are to the left and one of the many golf courses served by the line is to the right, although here seemingly populated by picnickers. This view should be compared with that on page 73, taken close to here over forty years earlier. N.N. FORBES

Well known railway photographer H.C. Casserley paid a visit to Birkenhead just after WW2, on 19th October 1946, and took several pictures of the electric units at Park station. Here Motor Coach No. 28676 heads an arrival from West Kirby, with the Up starter indicating the imminent departure of another train. The piles of sleepers in the left background would seem to indicate that the siding was used by the pw department. H.C. CASSERLEY, COURTESY R.M. CASSERLEY

The Immediate Post-War Years

The Second World War ended in 1945 – in Europe in May and in the Far East in August. During the war years, both rail and road transport had been obliged to discourage non-essential traffic. During the blackout there was a reduced demand and late evening services were designed to cater only for the needs of essential workers. Sunday services were reduced. Local bus services finished running at 9.0-9.30pm, so the absence or sparsity of feeder services to the railway stations to some extent also affected demand.

During the war, summer Sundays had often seen packed trains carrying visitors to New Brighton and West Kirby. The end of the 'Is Your Journey Really Necessary' campaign eventually unleashed a huge pent-up demand of pleasure travellers. Hordes of day visitors descended on New Brighton and, to a lesser extent, Moreton, Hoylake and West Kirby, in the summer months. There were many summer excursions from inland towns, too. These trains used the CLC Manchester-Chester line and then the L&NE (ex-GC) line to Bidston. Because of the sharp curve at Bidston Junction and the limited running-round facilities at New Brighton, it was often necessary for the Birkenhead North-based LM&S tank engines to haul these trains between Bidston and New Brighton. Stabling of rolling stock during the day could also be problematical and on very busy days the stock had to be worked back to Bidston GC yard. Meanwhile, it took some time for the longer distance coach services to become fully operative, as there were restrictions on the radius within which excursions could be run while petroleum products remained on ration for some years after the war. This added further to the railway's popularity.

The railways could not immediately resume a full peacetime service. There were rolling stock shortages because of arrears of maintenance and manpower shortages. Many railwaymen serving in HM Forces, having seen more of the world outside railway employment, decided not to return to work on the railway, as there were many opportunities which paid better wages. The first task was to resume late evening services. The off-peak 20-minute frequency was adequate in most cases, so weekday services remained little changed. Higher demand during school holidays etc. could be satisfied by running six-car trains. The transition from wartime to peacetime conditions was therefore gradual and the loss of military and industrial traffic associated with wartime activities was counterbalanced by the revival of commercial activity in Liverpool city centre, as a start was made on rebuilding the badly damaged city infrastructure.

Nationalisation of the railways from 1st January 1948 had no noticeable effect on the Wirral. It has been said that it took three years before the powers that be in the London Midland Region realised that the Mersey Railway was now their responsibility and they started to integrate it with the Wirral Section!

LEFT: Motor Coach No. 29285, showing the LMS lettering and roundel. H.C. CASSERLEY, COURTESY R.M. CASSERLEY

A 6-car set waits to depart for West Kirby on 19th October 1946, with Motor Coach No. 29285 at the non-driving end. Note the LM&S target-style running in board on the platform. It is believed these were erected with the electrification works, replacing the earlier Wirral Railway nameboards. In the background, on the bridge, can be seen the rather austere replacement for the bomb damaged station building. H.C. CASSERLEY, COURTESY R.M. CASSERLEY

ABOVE: In marked contrast, the old matchboard-sided, clerestory-roofed Mersey Railway stock was also still in operation alongside the sleek new units. Here, Motor Coach No. 9 glides to a halt with a train from across the river.
BELOW: As passengers still mill around the carriages, the driver of Mersey Railway Motor Coach No. 32 waits for the 'off' signal from the guard before heading back to Liverpool. BOTH H.C. CASSERLEY, COURTESY R.M. CASSERLEY

A six-car train of Mersey Railway stock enters West Kirby station in November 1953. The end for these units was drawing near and some of their replacements can be seen in the carriage sidings in the background. To their left, the goods yard is still busy, mainly with coal traffic, as is the yard at the ex-GW/L&NW Joint line station to the left. Note the check rail on the sharp curve leading round to this station. N.N. FORBES

Another Mersey Railway train at speed at Carr Lane Crossing, between Meols and Moreton, heading towards Birkenhead in November 1953. The train is comprised of original Milnes cars of 1903. N.N. FORBES

CHAPTER 4

FROM BRITISH RAILWAYS TO MERSEYRAIL

The nationalisation of the railways on 1st January 1948 made little immediate difference to the Wirral. The Mersey became 'London Midland Region (Mersey Section)' but over two years were to elapse before the Mersey and Wirral electric lines were fully integrated and worked as one system, and even then the allocation of rolling stock remained unchanged. In 1950, malachite green began to replace maroon on the ex-LM&S stock and, initially one First class Mersey car was similarly treated, a gold line being added below the windows. Additionally, 'BRITISH RAILWAYS' transfers were applied at cantrail level to all stock in the same style as 'MERSEY RAILWAY' had been, officially described as 'Caslon Old Face modified' which was reminiscent of the style used on American railroads earlier in the century. From about 1952, the new livery was gradually extended to the Mersey stock. The latter were also renumbered in a series close to existing LM Region EMU stock, though the 'M' prefix was never applied to them; their old

RIGHT: This 6-car train of mixed Mersey Railway stock has just passed the site of Warren Halt as it approaches Harrison Drive bridge, between Wallasey and New Brighton, in June 1955. Note the signal in the opposite direction, on a much shorter post, is also 'off', for a New Brighton train. JOHN GAHAN, COURTESY TED LLOYD

BELOW: Another Mersey Railway 6-car unit is seen departing Wallasey Grove Road station in August 1953. Like other Wirral stations, the goods yard here seems mostly to have been used for coal traffic in later years. JOHN GAHAN, COURTESY TED LLOYD

Withdrawn ex-Mersey Railway, 1903 clerestory-roofed Milnes-built stock awaiting disposal alongside the carriage shed at Birkenhead North. GLYNN PARRY COLLECTION

Two views of the reconstructed island platform at Seacombe. ABOVE, the footplate crew of 'Jinty' 0-6-0 No. 67414 chat with the guard as they await departure time for the 2.31pm to Wrexham on 29th August 1954. The second picture, BELOW, is taken from the old disused wooden boarded No. 1 platform and again shows a Wrexham train, loaded to three coaches, waiting to leave. ABOVE: JOHN WARD COLLECTION, COURTESY JOHN HORNE; BELOW: MARTIN JENKINS COLLECTION

numbers were painted on the nearside buffer and retained on some interiors, for the benefit of the maintenance staff who knew the idiosyncrasies of every car off by heart.

As the 1950s advanced, the elderly Mersey trains became unreliable and it was decided to replace these with new stock similar to the LM&S 1938 units. Twenty-four three-car trains were ordered, plus two trailers and two control-trailers to replace those lost in the air raid in March 1941. In 1954-55, the signalling on the ex-Mersey lines was modernised and traction-bonding of the running rails and impedance-bonding at all double block joints was carried out. The fourth rail return was abolished in December 1955 so, for their last few months in service, the Mersey trains ran as three-rail on their own former territory. As there was no longer a need for twin train-stops, the open type electro-pneumatic train-stop units installed in the 1920s were replaced by modern all-enclosed units, on which the stop-arm emerged from the side of the box; all with single train-stops were on the six-foot side.

The replacement stock started to arrive in the summer of 1956 and the Mersey stock was gradually withdrawn, the first being M28432 (ex No. 39) in July and M28414/27 (ex No's 10 and 34) and their associated trailers in March 1957. They were at first stored in sidings all over the combined system, then their footboards were removed and they were taken via Hooton to Horwich to be broken up. The one exception was M28405 (ex No. 1) which went to Derby to be restored to its original open-ended condition, the intention being to exhibit it in the Liverpool museum. Unfortunately, it was totally destroyed in a fire in the paint shop. With the demise of this stock, the Birkenhead Central workshops were closed and all maintenance was

A former Mersey Railway train stands in a siding at Birkenhead North after withdrawal in the late 1950s. Note that all the steps have been removed and an Electrical Department Match Wagon (DM137824) has been attached to enable the unit to be coupled to a locomotive. The loop siding on which the train is standing ran on beneath the road bridge, parallel with the main line, and connected directly to the sidings at the electric car sheds. The bridge, which carried Wallasey Bridge Road over the line, also provided the viewpoint for the top photograph on the previous page. *J.B. McCann*

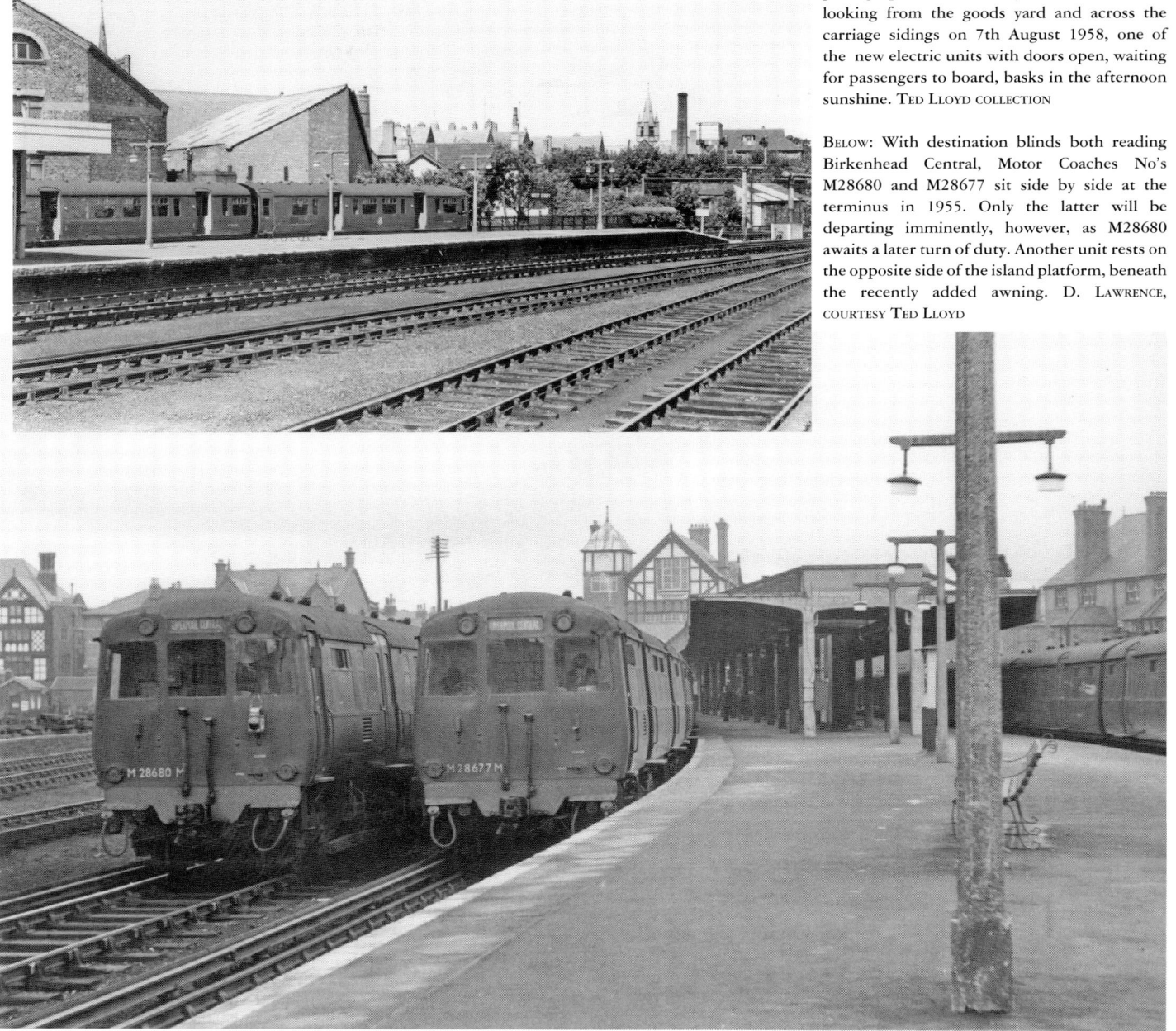

LEFT: The new order is illustrated in these two photographs of West Kirby. In this view, taken looking from the goods yard and across the carriage sidings on 7th August 1958, one of the new electric units with doors open, waiting for passengers to board, basks in the afternoon sunshine. TED LLOYD COLLECTION

BELOW: With destination blinds both reading Birkenhead Central, Motor Coaches No's M28680 and M28677 sit side by side at the terminus in 1955. Only the latter will be departing imminently, however, as M28680 awaits a later turn of duty. Another unit rests on the opposite side of the island platform, beneath the recently added awning. D. LAWRENCE, COURTESY TED LLOYD

thereafter carried out at Birkenhead North.

With favourable economic conditions in the port and city of Liverpool, the commuter traffic continued to expand and the combined electric services between the Wirral and Liverpool were among the most intensive in Britain. All peak hour and many Sunday trains had six cars, and high standards of punctuality and regularity were maintained.

There was some work done on improving the infrastructure, perhaps the most noticeable to the travelling public being the long overdue reconstruction of the island platform at Seacombe, with a proper stone surface and paved edges. Thereafter, platform 1 on the south side, which remained surfaced with sleepers, became disused. The station was also renamed, becoming plain Seacombe from 5th January 1953.

An internal committee was set up in October 1954, whose remit was *'to report on the conditions on the Mersey and Wirral lines and submit immediate short term recommendations and proposals for any longer term improvements thought desirable'*. This followed publication in the Liverpool *Evening Express* of an article headed 'Grandad's Railway is a Horror'. It claimed that nearly a million passengers a week were crowded into trains in worse conditions than would be allowed for cattle; criticised the appearance of stations; suggested that at peak times there was almost hand-to-hand fighting for lifts; condemned conditions generally and stated that British Railways was content to accept this state of affairs and do nothing except *'reap the harvest of gold that pours into the booking offices'*. The eight man committee, chaired by A.J.D. Thomas of the Chief Operating Superintendent's Department, got down to work promptly, presenting its report in March 1955. However, its recommendations were almost wholly confined to the ex-Mersey Railway lines, dealing with replacing lifts with escalators at James Street and Hamilton Square, and eliminating interchange problems at Rock Ferry. The sole recommendation for the Wirral lines was the replacement of the DC lighting supply at stations with a local AC supply.

Closure of the Seacombe Branch

The popularity of the ferry crossing at Seacombe declined in the later 1950s, as more and more passengers from the Wrexham service found it more convenient to transfer at Bidston to the electric service direct to Liverpool. The decision to close the Seacombe Branch met with little opposition, perhaps because it was proposed to provide an alternative service which, on the face of it, appeared to be superior. The steam-hauled passenger service on the Seacombe Branch was reduced to thirteen weekday and three Sunday trains to Wrexham, and was then withdrawn after final operation on Sunday, 3rd January 1960. It is of interest to note that, until the very last day, the notice board outside the station included New Brighton in the places served. By that time, a rail journey from Seacombe to New Brighton would have involved two changes – at Bidston and Birkenhead North.

In its place, from 4th January 1960, a diesel multiple unit service ran between New Brighton and both Wrexham and Chester (Northgate)

ABOVE: The new passenger entrance to the reconstructed platform at Seacombe on 1st August 1957, with an unidentified Ivatt 'Prairie' tank running round its train. The rebuilding did not include any overhead protection for passengers, however. J.P. WILLIAMS

RIGHT: Ivatt tank No. 41234 at the buffer stops at Seacombe, whilst in the process of running round its train on 7th August 1955. The proximity of the station to the ferry terminal is indicated by the looming presence of the 1933-built Seacombe ferry clock tower in the left background, which replaced the earlier hydraulic tower. JOHN WARD COLLECTION, COURTESY JOHN HORNE

The new platform arrangements at Seacombe left the original station building isolated on the disused wooden platform, as this view, taken on 1st August 1959 looking towards the buffer stops, shows. Note the uneven boarding on the old platform. The station was becoming even more run-down as it neared the end of its life, whilst the platform upgrading was completely spoilt by the lamps supported in battered oil drums. R. DYER, COURTESY TED LLOYD

LEFT: The last days of Seacombe in January 1960. This angle shows that a new fence had been erected to prevent access to the abandoned southern platform, whilst the ticket barrier was moved slightly nearer the train. J. McWATT

BELOW LEFT & RIGHT: The exterior of Seacombe station pictured circa 1955, left, and again in January 1960, shortly before closure. Notice that the advertisement for trains, large enough to catch the eye of passengers emerging from the ferry terminal some 250 yards away, includes New Brighton. The through service had closed forty-nine years earlier, in 1910, and two changes – at Bidston and Birkenhead North – would have been required to make the journey in 1960, by which time there was a six-minute bus service making the trip in twelve minutes. Note that apart from advertising the destinations, the board also served to hide the ramshackle collection of buildings that had formed the station. JOHN WARD COLLECTION, COURTESY JOHN HORNE

approximately alternately at combined hourly intervals; there were fourteen trains on weekdays and six on Sundays. However, on summer Sundays and Bank Holidays until August Bank Holiday 1966, excursions (and occasionally the timetabled service) headed by steam engines regularly operated from Wrexham to New Brighton. They were hauled by ex-GWR 0-6-0 pannier tanks or post-war Fairburn 2-6-4Ts, water being taken at Neston. Two rakes of non-corridor stock were kept at Wrexham especially for them. However, the new costing methods decreed that the level of traffic was unsatisfactory and the Chester service, by then DMU operated, was withdrawn on 9th September 1968, the conductor-guard system being adopted on the remaining New Brighton-Wrexham trains from 20th April 1969. From 4th January 1971, the weekday service ran to and from Birkenhead North instead of New Brighton, which was still served by the DMU's on Sundays. The Merseyside Passenger Transport Executive (MPTE), which had just become involved in railway affairs, provided some financial support and paid for the installation of a crossover at Birkenhead North to provide cross-platform interchange facilities. The Sunday service was diverted to Birkenhead North from 11th January 1976 but in 1978, MPTE withdrew financial support for the Wrexham service, except in respect of payment for acceptance, within the PTE area, of multi-journey, pensioners' and disabled persons' tickets. The service was then cut back to Bidston from 2nd October 1978. It is interesting to note that twelve new Derby-built DMU sets were allocated for this service in 1960, eight for operations and four for spares, a sad commentary on reliability standards.

In the later years of the Seacombe branch, BR experimented with Stanier and Fowler 2-6-2T and post-war Ivatt 2-6-2T locomotives,

ABOVE: Ex-L&NER 0-6-2T No. 69329 waits to depart with the 12.45pm to Wrexham service, sometime prior to October 1955. JOHN WARD COLLECTION, COURTESY JOHN HORNE

ABOVE RIGHT: Ivatt tank No. 41234 with the usual three coaches for Wrexham, on 7th August 1955. As well as the ferry clock tower, the towers of the Liver Building also feature in the right background. JOHN WARD COLLECTION, COURTESY JOHN HORNE

RIGHT: A Wrexham service departs a forlorn looking station on a murky February day in 1959. JIM PEDEN

BELOW RIGHT: On an altogether more cheerful summer's day at the beginning of July 1957, Ivatt 'Prairie' tank No. 41232 has just arrived bunker first with a train from Wrexham. JIM PEDEN

BELOW: Ex-L&NER 4-4-2T No. 67442 gently leaks steam from several points on 20th August 1955, as departure time nears for the 4.33pm service to Wrexham. JOHN WARD COLLECTION, COURTESY JOHN HORNE

ABOVE: Ex-L&NER engines continued to appear at Seacombe into the 1950s, until replaced on the Wrexham services by BR Standard types. Here, 4-4-2T No. 67412 (L&NE No. 5171) poses between the bridges on 10th August 1953, amidst the detritus of track renewals. The locomotive had only a few months left in service, being withdrawn in May 1954. H.C. CASSERLEY, COURTESY RICHARD CASSERLEY

RIGHT: Seacombe station on 1st August 1958. Note the signal box in the background. J.P. WILLIAMS

BELOW: The curved approach to Seacombe, seen here on 1st July 1957 from the lead compartment of No. 41232's train. The line passed beneath three overbridges before reaching the station. JIM PEDEN

in an effort to replace the elderly ex-GC Class 'C13/14' 4-4-2Ts but these were unpopular with drivers because of their inability to maintain a good head of steam on the steep incline from Shotton to Buckley Junction. Some of the Fowlers were the same ones which had been ousted from the Seacombe Branch when the Seacombe-West Kirby passenger service had been withdrawn in 1938. From 1957, the Class 'C13-14's had mostly been replaced by post-war Class '3MT' 82xxx 2-6-2T locomotives but an interesting side effect of integration at the Wrexham end of the line was the occasional appearance on the Seacombe Branch, hauling goods trains, of ex-GW Collett 0-6-2T engines. Some of these worked on to the dock lines via the Slopes Branch. The last passenger train from Seacombe was hauled by No. 41201, whilst the last into Seacombe at 10.20pm was headed by No. 82031, which then worked empty stock to Chester.

RIGHT: Bidston Dee Junction with a Wrexham-Seacombe train approaching Bidston station on a damp day in December 1959. The West Kirby line runs straight ahead, behind the locomotive. These trains, which were invariably tank engine hauled, seem generally to have been worked bunker first to Seacombe, although quite why this method of working prevailed is not clear. N.N. FORBES

RIGHT BELOW: A Seacombe bound train passes Seacombe Junction in May 1954. The train is comprised of at least six carriages, much longer than normally seen on the branch, so is likely to be a special working of some sort. There is a reporting code on the smokebox door of the locomotive but it is too indistinct to make out. Note that the coaches are all in British Railways red & cream ('blood & custard') livery, again not normally seen on Seacombe Branch workings, whilst the locomotive is heading 'smokebox first' to the terminus. The lines branching off to the left connected to the Bidston Dock ore sidings. MARTIN JENKINS COLLECTION

BELOW: Ivatt tank No. 41231 clears Bidston West Junction and approaches Bidston station on 22nd March 1957 with a Seacombe-Wrexham service. The prominence of the ore cranes at Bidston Dock, which could be seen from miles around, is mentioned in the text and they are clearly visible here in the right background. A 'J39' on Bidston shed can just be glimpsed on the extreme right of the picture. JOHN WARD COLLECTION, COURTESY JOHN HORNE

Top: Taken on 10th October 1953, the four photographs on this page follow a sequence. In this first picture, the 9.35am from Wrexham drifts into Seacombe station behind Robinson 4-4-2T No. 67412. This locomotive, built by the Great Central at Gorton in 1903 as No. 5171, had only a few months of service left, being withdrawn in May 1954.

Above Left: The service was well patronised still at this time, as can be seen by the sizeable throng of passengers making their way down the platform.

Above Right: No. 67412 has now run round its train prior to making the return journey to Wrexham. Some of the train crew chat as they wait for the few passengers to amble along the platform. Note, that in this more relaxed era, the disused platform was not out of bounds to railway enthusiasts, who will shortly also climb aboard the train!

Left: The morning light combined with the smoke and steam from the engine provide for an atmospheric glimpse of Liscard & Poulton station, viewed from the same train as it heads back to Wrexham. All H.C. Casserley, courtesy R.M. Casserley

Bidston station, positioned as it was in the middle of several junctions with frequent passing trains, was an obvious attraction for railway enthusiasts and was thus well photographed. Here, however, noted railway photographer Henry Casserley has captured the station in a quiet period, during a lull between services, on 19th September 1959. The lack of surrounding habitation was starkly evident in this direction. H.C. CASSERLEY, COURTESY R.M. CASSERLEY

A similar quiet moment at Birkenhead North station, in an undated view probably taken in the 1960s. Note the white sighting panel on the footbridge for the upper quadrant signal arm. The decorative cast iron spandrels supporting the island platform canopy are also worthy of note. TED LLOYD COLLECTION

ABOVE: Leasowe station on 26th May 1978, looking towards Birkenhead, with semaphore signalling still in place, along with the level crossing gates and the signal box controlling all of this. N.D. Mundy

RIGHT: Moreton station on the same day, this time looking towards West Kirby. Did the distinctive 1930s architecture provide inspiration for a well known model railway manufacturer based just across the River Mersey? N.D. Mundy

LEFT: Meols station, photographed some years earlier on 20th September 1959, looking towards Birkenhead. Here, station staff have enhanced the look of the Up platform with some attractive flower beds. All of these stations remain open and well patronised today. H.C. Casserley, courtesy R.M. Casserley

ABOVE: A nice study of the interior of Hoylake station, in between trains sometime in the mid 1950s. It is easy to understand why the new architecture of the LM&SR in the 1930s found immediate favour with passengers and, indeed, continues to do so today. The only significant losses to progress from this view are the signal box, crossing gates and semaphore signals. R.M. CASSERLEY COLLECTION

ABOVE: The exterior of West Kirby station, on 26th May 1978, with a BR 'double arrow' on the Merseyrail nameboard above the canopy. Again, this attractive collection of buildings, complete with the distinctive clock tower, continue to provide a welcoming prospect to passengers today. N.D. MUNDY

RIGHT: A useful study of the platform concourse beneath the glass roof at West Kirby in 1968, with period signs and 'railway clutter' in evidence. Parking here is no longer possible. TED LLOYD COLLECTION

New Brighton station on 7th June 1965 with ex-Great Western '57xx' Class pannier tank No. 4683 about to couple up to its train of five carriages. This was probably a scheduled New Brighton-Wrexham service about to be worked under conditions described in the *Supplement to the Working Time Table* as '*diesel made steam*', the normal DMU having been assigned to other duties. Fortunately, the water tower was still in place on the end of the platform to cover for such eventualities. The goods shed was closed by this date but the yard still seems to be in use for some coal traffic. This view makes an interesting comparison with that on page 46, taken over half a century earlier. COURTESY ONLINE TRANSPORT ARCHIVE

RIGHT: A steam 'Jubilee Special' headed by ex-LM&SR 2-6-2Ts No's 2236 and 2213, conveying girls of West Kirby County High School from West Kirby to Chester (Northgate) on 26th April 1963. The train loaded at the Joint station because it was too long for the Wirral station's platform. It is seen here just departing and about to join Wirral section metals. After a reversal at Bidston, the Special then followed the ex-GC tracks to Chester. GLYNN PARRY COLLECTION

ABOVE: A panoramic view from Seacombe Junction signal box, with BR Standard Class '3MT' No. 82021 passing on a Seacombe-Wrexham train. In the right background can be seen Bidston Dock ore sidings, with an unidentified Class '9F' ready to depart for John Summers' steel works at Shotwick. COURTESY ONLINE TRANSPORT ARCHIVE

LEFT: A distant view of shunting underway at West Kirby station in January 1952, as seen from the Joint station platform. Goods activities at Wirral line stations seem rarely to have been photographed. TED LLOYD COLLECTION

Goods Traffic – New Beginnings, Decline and Closure

The early years of British Railways on the Wirral were marked by the arrival of much new goods traffic. From the early 1950s, John Summers & Sons developed their Shotton site as an integrated steel works, with coke ovens and blast furnaces. A fleet of eight-wheeled hoppers were built to carry iron ore to the works from the new ore dock at Bidston, Birkenhead. Although only a short length of Wirral metals was traversed, the traffic was heavy and lasted nearly three decades. Further new traffic followed in 1953, with the opening of Cadbury's biscuit factory on the north side of the West Kirby line, adjacent to Moreton station. A private siding was laid with access by a trailing junction, with the Up line controlled by a ground frame west of Leasowe station and the firm acquired its own diesel shunter to work it. This traffic lasted until 1971.

Traffic to the north side of the docks had gradually faded away, landmarks being the closure of Birkenhead (Dock Road) L&NE (ex-GC) station on 1st August 1955 and the ex-CLC East & West Float depot on 23rd June 1959, the latter triggering the closure of Slopes Branch. Use of the Seacombe Branch for goods traffic as far as Oakdale Sidings continued until 5th December 1960, when the line beyond Liscard & Poulton station was abandoned. Latterly, coal to Wallasey

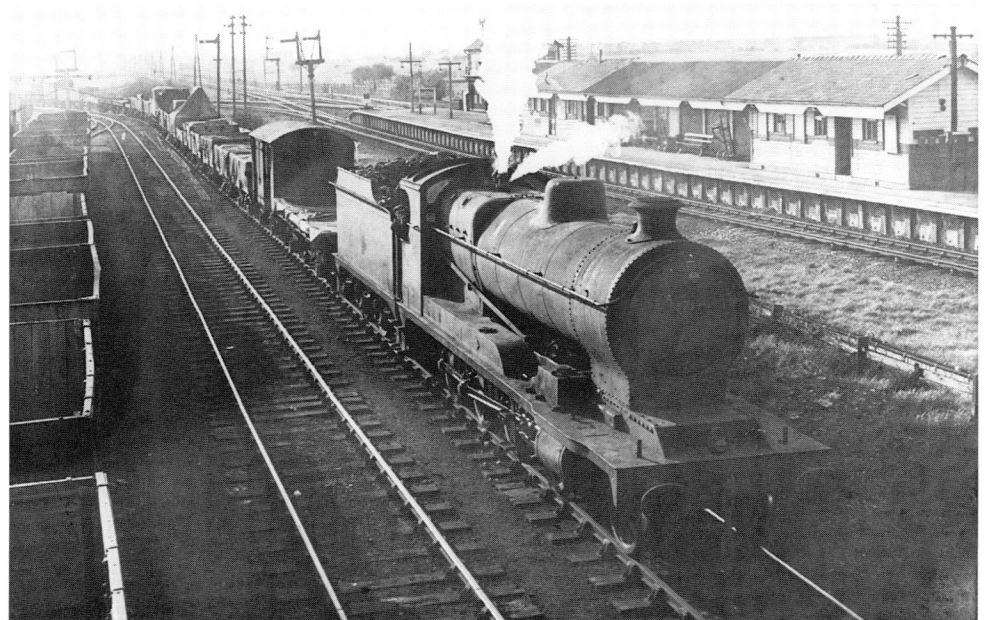

ABOVE: This low angle view of ex-L&NE 0-6-2T No. 69274, arriving at Bidston with a Seacombe-Wrexham train circa 1954, also shows the concrete platform wall supports, the wires and pulleys working the signal, and the footbridge, a favourite vantage point. JOHN WARD COLLECTION, COURTESY JOHN HORNE

LEFT: In steam days, there was always a variety of locomotive power to be seen at Bidston because of traffic arriving at the ex-GC sidings. Here, on 22nd March 1957, Robinson 2-8-0 No. 63717 is just arriving with a freight from Gorton. Most of the wagons will shortly transfer the short distance over Wirral metals to Birkenhead North. In the background, the piecemeal growth of the facilities at Bidston station are clear. JOHN WARD COLLECTION, COURTESY JOHN HORNE

gas and electricity works had comprised the only traffic. The last use of the rump of the line was for the storage of wagons and the branch closed completely on 17th June 1963. Sadly, the job which made the greatest impact on the Wirral lines was the Wallasey-Liverpool road tunnel and its approach road, which obliterated much of the Seacombe Branch. The tunnel opened in 1971 but on the section not used, several of the original bridges remain. Flats were erected on the site of Seacombe passenger station.

Goods workings to Hooton via West Kirby persisted until 1959 and probably until the Hooton-West Kirby line closed. A Guards' Journal, filled in by W. Jones of Hooton on Monday 20th November 1959, describes his working day, partly behind Class '9F' 2-10-0 No. 92045, with Driver Williams from 6C. This train was known to the staff as the 'Hooton Docker'. They left Hooton ten minutes late at 4.30am with twenty-nine 'Class 1' loose-coupled mineral wagons. Ten minutes were allowed at West Kirby for water but only five were taken, arriving at Moreton just five minutes down. Four loaded wagons were detached for Cadbury's and ten minutes spent shunting. Departure was again five minutes late and another fifteen were lost awaiting signals at Bidston East, so that arrival at Birkenhead North was twenty minutes late at 6.30am. The '9F' probably returned to Bidston to await iron ore duties. Guard Jones then made his own way back to Hooton and worked a long van train to Levers at Port Sunlight, leaving at 11.20am and arriving at 11.33 with sixty wagons on.

ABOVE: This aerial view of West Kirby dates from circa 1960 and clearly shows the Wirral station on the right, with its short clock tower and the canopy erected over the island platform in connection with the 1938 electrification. The Joint station, terminus of the Hooton branch, can be seen above left but most of the sidings which filled the ground between the two stations, particularly those on the Wirral side, are disused. Passengers transferring between the two lines had to walk along the road in the background. JOHN RYAN COLLECTION

RIGHT: 'Jinty' No. 47627 shunts the pick-up goods at Hoylake station on 20th May 1964. The picture is looking west with what was to be the last surviving Wirral signal box, the level crossing and the 1937 concrete footbridge much in evidence. The train is 'wrong line', so will be under the watchful eye of the signalman. RAY WALKINGTON

The new policies following the Beeching Plan led to the virtual elimination of goods traffic from the former Wirral lines. Facilities were withdrawn from West Kirby with the closure of the line to Hooton on 7th September 1962, from Moreton on 18th March 1963 and from Hoylake, New Brighton and Wallasey (Grove Road) on 30th October 1965. Goods traffic at the former Bidston GC yard ceased on 29th July 1968 and a steel works (which has since been demolished) was later built at the east end. From early 1965, domestic coal traffic was handled at a new Coal Concentration Depot operated by the Co-operative Society on the site of the sidings at Birkenhead North. The depot was run down in the early months of 1993 and the last coal train is believed to have arrived on 18th February. The last movement between Birkenhead North and Rock Ferry over the dock lines was by a Class '08' shunter on 10th May 1993 but the line is still more or less intact and is officially just mothballed. The curve from Bidston West to Bidston North Junction, used until 1978 by one Saturday New Brighton-West Kirby train, was officially closed on 28th November 1983, having been traversed by a Railway Correspondence & Travel Society tour two days earlier. A little used double track siding, suitable for use as a refuge by Wrexham-Bidston trains, eventually replaced it.

Bidston Dock and the Iron Ore Traffic

The firm of John Summers & Sons had established their iron and steel works on the banks of the River Dee at Shotton in 1896. Summers had traditionally used pig iron brought in from the Potteries. However, in 1952 the factory was expanded to a fully integrated iron and steel works using imports of iron ore, with its own coke ovens and blast furnaces, turning the ore into steel strip and plate. The previous year, agreement had been reached with the Mersey Docks & Harbour Board to install unloading facilities for imported iron ore on the north side of Bidston Dock. Bidston Dock was extended to 10.5 acres and connected directly to the Wirral line at Seacombe Junction, the first time the ex-Wirral system had direct connection to any dock, whilst the enlarged dock reached almost to the New Brighton Branch.

The ore was to be conveyed over the Bidston-Wrexham line to Shotwick, on the eastern bank of the Dee, where a new marshalling yard was built. New sidings, accessed by a double track junction at Seacombe Junction, were provided by agreement between BR and the Dock Board, who paid one sixth of the £38,000 cost; the former Wirral Railway was therefore traversed for a distance of just under half a mile to Dee Junction. In the other direction, the new line followed the curvature of the Seacombe Branch for a short distance. An initial tonnage of 750,000 per annum was predicted, rising to 1,250,000 tons. The layout included ten-road exchange sidings and a connecting line to Birkenhead North sidings, which was laid later. Shunting at Bidston Dock was carried out by Rea Ltd, who operated the unloading equipment, diesel shunters moving four loaded wagons at a time into the departure sidings. Considerable strengthening of bridges and upgrading of the permanent way was carried out on the Wrexham line as a train of loaded hopper wagons weighed almost 1,000 tons. There were quite severe gradients between Bidston and Neston, 1 in 75 near Woodchurch and in other parts mainly at 1 in 100 and 1 in 120. Steam trains were allowed forty-eight minutes for the 12½ mile journey and there was a speed limit of 35mph.

The first train left Bidston Dock on 18th September 1952 hauled by an ex-L&NE Class 'O4' 2-8-0 tender locomotive. These engines, to a Robinson design, had been introduced by the Great Central in 1911. They had small boilers, Belpaire fire-boxes, steam and vacuum

Ex-L&NER Class 'O1' 2-8-0 No. 63689 at Bidston shed circa 1955. This locomotive was new from Robert Stephenson & Co. in 1918, as part of a large batch of Class 'O4' 2-8-0s built for military use, becoming ROD No. 1617. It entered L&NER stock in 1924, being renumbered 6341, subsequently becoming No. 3689 in the 1946 L&NER renumbering. In 1945, the engine was rebuilt to Class 'O1', in which form it is seen here, awaiting its next turn of duty, perhaps on one of the heavy ore trains or a freight back to Gorton. Although looking a little work stained here, No. 63689's paintwork suggests a relatively recent overhaul and its long and useful career finally came to an end in 1965. JOHN WARD COLLECTION, COURTESY JOHN HORNE

The ex-Great Central shed at Bidston on 13th April 1957, with a typically diverse selection of locomotives on view. On the left is Class 'O4' 2-8-0 No. 63649 (ex-ROD No. 1608, ex-L&NE No. 6365), one of the type which worked the ore traffic when it began operating in 1952 but which had been superseded on these turns by the date of this photograph by the other two freight classes on view here. At the shed entrance is a Stanier '8F' 2-8-0, the next class brought in to haul the heavy ore trains, whilst to its right is an example of the final type associated with the traffic, Class '9F' 2-10-0 No. 92045. On the far right can be seen the unmistakable bunker end of an interloper, an ex-GWR pannier tank, which is probably visiting for coaling and watering, having arrived from Hooton via West Kirby. Pannier tanks were occasionally seen on Wrexham-New Brighton excursions in later years. TED LLOYD COLLECTION

brakes and water scoops, and were based at Bidston shed, where the allocation was considerably increased. The 'O4's handled this traffic alone for almost three years until 1955, when they were augmented by three Class '9F' 2-10-0 locomotives, No's 92045/6/7, which had a tractive effort of almost 40,000lbs and were eminently suitable for the gradual climb from Bidston to Neston. As the traffic increased, Stanier and ex-War Department Class '8' engines also appeared on this work. This mixture of motive power continued until 1961, when more '9F's were drafted into the area. These included No's 92165/6/7, the only '9F's with double chimneys and mechanical stokers, and No. 92079, the former banking engine on the Lickey incline. The wagons were loose coupled and these 1,000-ton trains relied on the braking power of the locomotive and brake van. Class '9F's were permitted to haul eleven hoppers, ('9F' Crosti's ten) and Class '8' locomotives only eight. Engines worked boiler first to Shotwick and tender first to Bidston.

The 8-wheeled hopper wagons built by Charles Roberts & Co. for this traffic were very similar to the successful limestone hoppers built in the 1930s by the same firm for ICI. Surprisingly, and unlike the further ICI hoppers then being delivered, the Summers batch were not fitted for continuous braking, although they did have the same Gloucester-type plate-back bogies. The name SUMMERS was painted on the upper, parallel-sided part of the hopper, where it fitted neatly into the spaces between the vertical stiffeners. With the Nationalisation of the steel industry, the British Steel Corporation repainted these hoppers in blue with their logos and the large letters B S C in white. They carried the prefix BSSH and the Tops code PHO. After British Steel ceased steelmaking at Shotton in 1983, many of these wagons were purchased for further use by ICI Northwich. Thirteen were refurbished with roller bearings and vacuum brakes before re-entering traffic as ICIM No's 19152-64.

The large cranes which were installed to unload the iron ore were visible for many miles and were forerunners of the container cranes now familiar at major ports. This was not a 'merry-go-round' operation; individual wagons or small groups were shunted under the loading hoppers by Rea's locomotives and assembled into trains. 'Bidston Dock Exchange Sidings' comprised five lines but BR trains were forbidden to enter sidings 2 and 3 'until the Guard has ascertained by telephone from the Person in charge of the Weighbridges, that the siding on to which the train is to proceed is clear.' There were weighbridges at the Dock end of 2 and 3 sidings, and arriving trains with empties were placed on 1, 3 or 5 sidings unless those were all occupied.

In 1954, there were eight paths on weekdays, with loaded trains passing Seacombe Junction at 12.55am (MX), 3.15am, 6.25am and 10.00am (SX), 2.00pm, 3.00pm (SX), 6.00pm (SO), 6.43pm (SX) and 8.59pm (SX). There were five loaded trains on Saturdays and none on Sundays. Departures from 'Bidston Dock North Side' were nominally five minutes earlier than the passing times at Seacombe Junction. Engines left Shotwick Sidings with an empty train forty-nine minutes after arrival with loaded ones. Forty-six minutes were allowed for passing Seacombe Junction, the same journey time as for the loaded trains, except that most of the Down workings added an extra ten minutes for taking water at Neston North. By the summer of 1958, the usual train was a 2-10-0 with either ten or eleven bogie hoppers. They would pick their way carefully across the electric lines, through Bidston station and Dee Junction before the regulator could be opened wide. The exhaust noise was impressive and could be heard for miles as the 1,000-ton trains climbed the hills. Some residents were disturbed to the extent of winning a reduction in their rates, hardly surprising when the first southbound train passed Seacombe Junction at 12.55am (Mondays excepted)! The Working Time Table allowed forty-six minutes for Up trains from passing Seacombe Junction to arriving at Shotwick Sidings, near the steelworks. Just one Up train, the third of the day, was allowed sixty-one minutes because there was a ten minute stop at Neston North for water.

A classic view of one of the John Summers' ore trains, seen departing Bidston Dock behind Class '9F' No. 92045 in July 1958. The train consists of eleven loaded hoppers and a brake van, the maximum load permitted, whilst No. 92045 was one of the first three '9F's assigned to Bidston shed specifically for this traffic. Photographed from the footbridge at Bidston station, the unloading cranes at the dock can be glimpsed through the smoke in the background. On the right, the ex-GC sidings for traffic bound for Birkenhead docks can also be seen. Note also the layout of Bidston West Junction, which was revised during the electrification work in the mid 1930s. JOHN WARD COLLECTION, COURTESY JOHN HORNE

RIGHT: Blizzard conditions at Bidston shed on 19th January 1958, with No. 92045 once more in residence and a second unidentified '9F' behind. On the left, a Robinson 2-8-0 sits with a rake of wagons on the coaling road. JOHN WARD COLLECTION, COURTESY JOHN HORNE

BELOW: In altogether more pleasant spring sunshine, No. 92046 stands alongside the water tank at Bidston shed. Taken on 22nd March 1957, Bidston West Junction and the ore dock cranes again feature in the background. JOHN WARD COLLECTION, COURTESY JOHN HORNE

The traffic was erratic as it depended on the arrival of ships. On some days there would be no trains but when three ships arrived together, as occasionally happened, 60,000 tons had to be conveyed and trains would run day and night. However, complaints from local residents about the deafening exhaust noises eventually resulted in the cancellation of night working.

Bidston shed closed on 11th February 1963, after which the ore traffic locomotives were shedded at Birkenhead (Mollington Street), which was reached over Dock Board lines. During this period, the allocation included the Franco-Crosti boilered '9F's (No's 92020-9), which differed from other members of the class by having double-barrelled boilers and no smoke deflectors. However, by the time they arrived at Birkenhead their Crosti pre-heaters had been sealed and they had been adapted for orthodox working. Although the number of Birkenhead-based '9F's had dwindled from more than fifty to twenty-four by the end of October 1967, the class continued to handle the ore traffic until the end of steam and the last steam-hauled train ran on 6th November 1967. It was 'driven' by Sir Richard Summers, Director in Charge at Shotton, a former Chairman of John Summers & Sons Ltd and a former Director of the LM&SR. The train

was hauled by Standard Class '9F' No. 92203, one of the last steam locomotives to be built for BR in 1959, which had been specially cleaned up and given white buffers and smokebox door ironwork. It was subsequently saved for preservation by the wildlife artist David Shepherd and named *Black Prince*. Meanwhile, the real crew of No. 92203 later joined Sir Richard for lunch, when they were presented with engraved ashtrays and cheques with which to entertain their fellow workers at Bidston shed.

Class '47' diesels then took over the ore traffic (No. D1956 was noted at Shotwick when the last steam train arrived), although pairs of Class '25's were also used occasionally. The Class '47's operated singly and sometimes had difficulty controlling these unfitted trains. Trains were run on average every two hours but on Sundays, with greater line capacity available, there were often hourly departures. Locomotives sometimes returned from Shotwick with just their brake vans, leaving empties to be returned in one train of a maximum of thirty-three wagons. This traffic continued until the crisis in the steel industry led to Shotton works being rationalised, the last ore being

ABOVE: A pilotman descends from the cab of Class '47' No. 47315 at Birkenhead North on 21st September 1985, whilst a Merseyrail train passes on the main line.

RIGHT: No. 47303 swings out of the dock sidings with a lengthy coal train on 25 January 1986. With the new M53 approach road viaduct in the background, this view makes an interesting comparison with that on page 197.

BELOW: No. 47315 is seen a little earlier in its journey on 21st September 1985, alongside Beaufort Road, Birkenhead. ALL TED LLOYD

ABOVE: A close up of Bidston Dock on 4th December 1983, showing one of the giant cranes used for unloading the ore. By this date, the ore traffic had finished and Rea's shunter *Labrador* is here seen shunting a rake of steel mineral wagons being loaded with scrap metal. *Labrador* was the sole Yorkshire Engine Co. locomotive (Works No. 2732/1959) operated by Rea's. JOHN WARD COLLECTION, COURTESY JOHN HORNE

RIGHT: *Wabana* was another of Rea's diesel shunters at Bidston Dock but quite different in appearance to *Labrador*, having been built in 1953 by Stephenson & Hawthorn, Works No. 7814 (Drewry Works No. 2500). JOHN WARD COLLECTION, COURTESY JOHN HORNE

smelted in March 1980. The last train from Bidston ran on 2nd April, feeding a stockpile of 150,000 tons to be conveyed by rail to Llanwern, South Wales, in thirteen 100 tonne rotary tipplers hauled by two Class '37' locomotives. After closure of the furnaces, the works was reduced to rerolling and coating strip made in Scotland but although the steel coils reached Shotton by rail the traffic did not involve the Wirral lines. The single line between the exchange sidings and Birkenhead North, which is believed never to have been used, is still *in situ* in a semi-derelict condition but the ore handling equipment has long been dismantled and Bidston Dock was filled in between 2001 and 2003.

The Shotton iron ore trains had been the heaviest flow of freight ever seen on the former Wirral system and it was fortunate for the electric services that the ore traffic shared their tracks only briefly. In fact, there were gaps in the iron ore shuttle service to coincide with the morning and evening rush hours. The locomotive work was strenuous because of the switchback character of the ex-Great Central line and because the 'modern' bogie hopper wagons, introduced by John Summers, had no continuous brakes, unlike the pre-war ICI limestone hopper wagons of which they were otherwise a copy.

Shunting at Bidston Dock: Rea Ltd and Rea Bulk Handling Ltd
Rea Ltd, who already operated the smaller ore wharf at Duke Street, Birkenhead, were chosen to work the new Bidston terminal. A Drewry/Vulcan diesel locomotive had been demonstrated in 1951 and now the extended Bidston terminal became the first part of the dock railways to be worked entirely by diesel engines, although (hired) steam locomotives deputised when the diesels were stopped.

Two views of one of Rea's shunters beneath one of the loading cranes at Bidston on 25th January 1986. The nameplates have been removed, so it is not possible to positively identify the locomotive. TED LLOYD

The terminal was actually 'opened' around Christmas 1953 by the 1918 Avonside 0-4-0ST *Brian*. This engine belonged to Cudworth & Johnson of Wrexham but spent the years 1950-1964 hired to William J. Lee, Shunting Contractor of Seacombe. These hired locomotives were numerous at Birkenhead and often spent odd weeks working for other contractors or industrialists. In this instance, Rea themselves could have hired *Brian* from C&J or perhaps they paid William Lee for the engine and crew, or just the engine.

The permanent shunting engines at Bidston were designed and supplied by the Drewry Car Company Ltd of London, who sub-contracted out their construction to several manufacturers. *Wabana* was an 0-4-0DM built by Robert Stephenson & Hawthorns, while *Narvik* was an 0-6-0DM built by Vulcan Foundry. Having decided to own rather than hire their locomotives, Rea kept the association with the Drewry Car Co. and had another six of their designs from various builders – *Pepel*, *W.H. Salthouse*, *Pegasus*, *Kathleen Nicholls*, *Dorothy Lightfoot* and *Teucer* – whilst a single 0-4-0DE, named *Labrador*, was also purchased from the Yorkshire Engine Company. The various shunting contractors did not invest in diesel engines and were put out of business by BR, who cut the rates after purchasing a surprising number of 0-6-0 diesels from Hudswell Clarke. However, these were soon redundant when both dock and rail traffic continued to decline. Rea's fleet survived longer, though its use became intermittent, thanks to the Bidston terminal.

After the abrupt end of the iron ore shuttle, a considerable tonnage remained in the stockpile on Bidston wharf. The weight was enormous but the wharf was designed to cope with it. This material was gradually recovered and sent to the Shelton steelworks at Etruria and elsewhere.

Bidston Dock and Imported Coal

Around the same time the steelworks closed, Britain began to import coal for electricity distribution. Reversing a century-old flow, the Central Electricity Generating Board chose Bidston Dock as a coal import terminal, where the existing transporter cranes, sidings and weighbridges were ideal for the job. Rea put their locomotive fleet in good order for this new work. When *Theseus* was overhauled between November 1980 and July 1981, she was finished in pale blue, the last to be so repainted. The locos *Narvik*, *Labrador*, *Pepel* and *Dorothy Lightfoot* were all employed at Bidston on this work by July 1981. The coal came from a stockpile at Rotterdam, having originated in South Africa, China, Columbia and Australia, but it was still half the price of British deep-mined coal. Most of it went in trains of thirty or thirty-two hopper wagons from Bidston to the generating station at Fiddler's Ferry, over the Dock Company's connecting line from Birkenhead North to Canning Street, then through Hooton and Warrington. However, the traffic ceased after 30th July 1981.

A certain amount of scrap metal was then put on rail at Bidston but only a few wagons at a time. *Labrador* remained at Bidston, its windows boarded up, and five more Rea locomotives stood idle at Duke Street. After four years, the coal traffic resumed; trains ran to and from Fiddler's Ferry between 8th July 1985 and 9th May 1986. Class '47' or '56' locomotives were used and there were three paths on weekdays, plus two on Saturdays and Sundays, although not all were used. At first, they left Bidston Dock at 12.20pm and 7.40pm daily. Sometimes the returning empties were left at Cavendish Siding and No. 03162 was used to trip them the last few miles to Bidston, where it was possible to see the family likeness between *Narvick* and the Class '03'. After 1986, the traffic was switched to Gladstone Dock, Bootle, where a new terminal was built.

The electricity industry was under political pressure to use British coal but the delivered price of imports was between £34 and £37 per tonne, a fraction of home-mined coal. When the CEGB's collier *Lord Hinton* arrived in Bidston Dock in October 1989, she had probably loaded in Rotterdam. Rea's locomotives again came out of hibernation but were now without their nameplates. Although the odd train ran to Fiddler's Ferry, most of this coal was taken to Rugeley or Ironbridge power stations. Haulage was by pairs of Class '20's with the occasional Brush Class '47'; their day started with an 04.40am departure from Crewe to collect the empties. At Bidston, these were exchanged for a loaded train made up by Rea's engines, the return departure from Bidston being late afternoon. Class '20' engines had seldom been seen on the Wirral before these events. They were already thirty years old but some were still working in 2007. The last departure was probably on 15th November 1989, when No's 20106 and 20140 were noted near Birkenhead North No. 2 box with thirty-four southbound hoppers at about 3.00pm. Today, regular trains of imported coal continue to operate to Fiddler's Ferry but now they run from Liverpool docks via the Bootle Branch and Edge Hill.

There was to be no more traffic from Bidston Dock. Seacombe Junction signal box had been retained solely for the Bidston Dock traffic and now stood disused, rather out of plumb as its foundations subsided, after the coal traffic ended. British Rail's engineers wanted to remove the box and the junction to save maintenance but other departments were loth to surrender the traffic potential of the dock connection. Both were satisfied by the laying of a long single track which joined the dock sidings to those at Birkenhead North, near to the carriage washer. This lay parallel to the electric line, inside the curve, and was declared ready for use on 6th November 1989. The old junction had already been disconnected. The remains of the signal box were removed, a task made easier in March 1988 when the locals set fire to it. However, the new connecting line was never used. Bidston Dock was filled in between 2001 and 2003, and Peel

Bidston Dee Junction signal box, seen here on 28th September 1968, replaced the original Wirral Railway structure, having been built by the LM&SR in 1938 as part of the electrification works. It also took over the role of Bidston West Junction, which allowed the closure of that box, something which the Wirral itself had mooted nearly three decades earlier. The frames for the three new LM&S-built boxes were supplied, appropriately, by the Railway Signal Co. Bidston Dee Junction box was closed on 20th November 1994, under Stage 2 of the Merseyrail IECC Scheme. JOHN WARD COLLECTION, COURTESY JOHN HORNE

Holdings, who control the Mersey Docks & Harbour Company, now have plans for housing and a shopping centre on the site.

Bidston Coal Concentration Depot

The coal yards at Wirral line stations were shut between 1962 and 1965. New Brighton, perhaps the busiest, closed on 30th October 1965, along with Wallasey Grove Road and Hoylake. Traffic had declined, due largely to the traditional open fire being replaced by central heating and gas fires. The remaining trade was transferred to a 'Coal Concentration Depot' at Birkenhead North, from which the merchants had to collect their loads. There was a degree of mechanisation, which offset the added road haulage, but the business continued to decline. The depot was close to the carriage washer at Birkenhead North and one might have expected clean but still wet carriages to gain a film of coal dust. Perhaps this was why the washer was seldom used.

The depot was not really in Bidston but on the site of the former steam locomotive workshops and shed at Birkenhead North. All the remaining engine shed buildings were cleared to make way for the depot, save only the water tank. The depot was managed (perhaps owned) by the Birkenhead Co-operative Society and was operating by the end of 1964, the first such depot in the north west of England. Three block trains per week fed the depot from North Staffordshire, plus about 300 tons by ordinary services from North Wales. A rail throughput of 85,000 tons of coal per annum was expected but whether this was ever achieved is not known. About 15,000 tons of locally produced-Phimax and coke were also dealt with each year, delivered to the depot by road.

From February 1989, coal was arriving in thrice-weekly trains from Washwood Heath; these came over the dock lines from Rock Ferry, usually hauled by a Class '37'. The depot was later worked by the Lancashire Fuel Company, who had a larger depot at Rathbone Road, Liverpool. In 1973, they transferred a small 0-4-0 diesel-electric locomotive from Liverpool to the Bidston depot. The engine was unusual in that it was built jointly by Brush Traction of

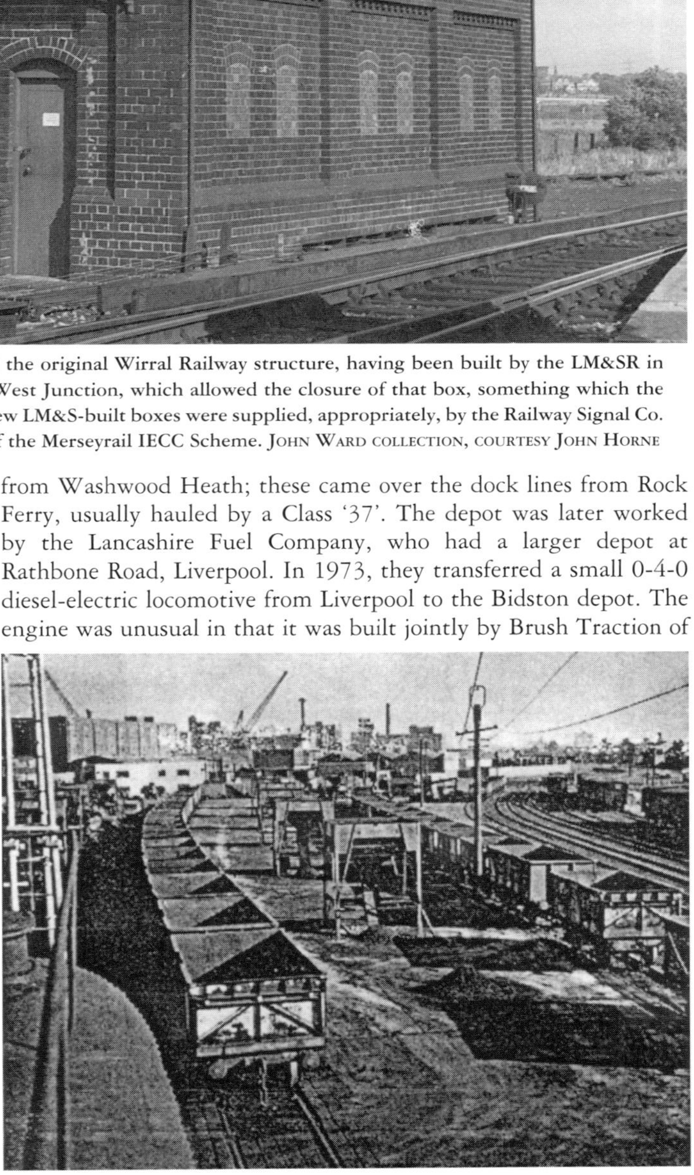

The Co-operative Society Coal Concentration Depot at Birkenhead North was the first in north west England, handling almost 2,000 tons of coal per week from Staffordshire and North Wales collieries. Here, unloaded wagons are seen on the left, with the goods lines on the right and Joseph Rank's flour mill in the background, left. JOHN HORNE COLLECTION

Mobile hoppers used for bagging solid fuel are loaded by grab cranes at the Coal Concentration Depot. JOHN HORNE COLLECTION

Loughborough and Beyer Peacock of Manchester. Both firms gave it a works number, these being 102 and 7859 respectively. However, it could be said that the Beyer Peacocks kept at Birkenhead North in times past were rather more elegant than this one. Five of these 200-230hp locomotives were built for stock and as demonstrators. They did not sell well, although one became BR No. D2999.

Through the 1980s, there was a train of coal hoppers most days, usually of twelve or fifteen, with the heaviest traffic in the spring when discounts were offered. By September 1991, coal was coming mostly from Newport, Gwent and was tripped to Birkenhead from Ellesmere Port. By this time, there were only two BR staff based at Duke Street for the whole dock system, a Head Shunter who also did the paperwork and an Under Shunter. With the end of the Bidston Dock coal traffic, the Coal Concentration Yard provided the last freight traffic on the former Wirral Railway and the only traffic on the MD&HCo's (the Dock Board had been privatised) connecting line from Birkenhead North to Canning Street North and the main network. BR Departmental stock was sometimes seen on this line, such as a pair of Plasser & Theurer tamping machines in 1988, although whether they had been working or were just taking a short-cut home is not known.

The depot was run down in the early months of 1993 and the last coal train is believed to have arrived on 18th February. The last movement between Birkenhead North and Rock Ferry over the dock lines was by a Class '08' shunter on 10th May 1993. The line is still more or less intact, although tarmac covers some level crossings and its owners regard it as 'mothballed'.

Cadbury-Schweppes Foods Ltd, Moreton

The factory was built in 1953-56 on the north side of the line, just east of Moreton station, with a trailing connection from the Up line and a ground frame. A new locomotive, an 0-4-0DM by Hudswell Clarke, works No. D1012/56, was delivered in a red-brown livery and lettered *Cadbury 17*. The traffic was mostly in vans. Initially there was a path for an early morning train which left Birkenhead North at 4.30am each Monday, Wednesday and Friday only. It arrived at Moreton ten minutes later, shunted until 5.20am and then scuttled back to North with the empties before it could get in the way of the first passenger trains. There is some evidence that deliveries were attempted during daylight hours but delays to the

'Jinty' tank No. 47622 passing Bidston station on 22nd March 1957 with a train of vans from the Cadbury-Schweppes factory at Moreton. The rear of the train has just cleared Bidston Dee Junction, with the box on the right. GLYNN PARRY COLLECTION

RIGHT: The Cadbury's van train, here headed by Class '8F' 2-8-0 No. 48436, is seen trundling through Leasowe station. Presumably, a more suitable engine was not available on this occasion. The cantilevering of the roof structure, adopted for most of the stations rebuilt for the electrification, is clearly revealed. COURTESY ONLINE TRANSPORT ARCHIVE

BELOW: A grubby unidentified 'Jinty' 0-6-0 eases a train of vans from Cadbury's factory over the Mersey Docks & Harbour Board's line alongside Beaufort Road, Birkenhead, in July 1966. A single line still exists here but is classed as 'mothballed'. The location is identical to that of the Class '47' and ore train on page 204. N.N. FORBES

electric trains were hard to avoid; their frequency was then every twenty minutes.

In July 1954, an addition to the WTT read *'It is now permitted to propel 10 wagons on the Down line from Bidston East Junction to Moreton'*. This unusual procedure involved the train being pushed out of Bidston GC yard onto the Wrexham line, drawn forward through Bidston station and then pushed through a crossover and away on the Down line (engine in rear) to the crossover just short of Moreton station. Here, the train was pulled onto the Up line before reversing once more and being pushed into Cadbury's siding. The alternative was to work the traffic round via Hooton and West Kirby, using only the Up line through Leasowe; this may have been the original method and, as already described, was used for mineral traffic to the works in 1959. However, after the closure of the Hooton-West Kirby line the more complex procedure certainly applied and Class '3F' 'Jinties', 'Crabs', Stanier 2-6-4Ts, Class '5' and Class '8F' locomotives successively performed it. Making so many turns on the screw reverser must have been tiring and eventually authority was given to propel up to ten vehicles 'wrong line' on the Up, all the way from Bidston to Cadbury's. This traffic survived the withdrawal of goods facilities from the Wirral line stations and was combined with trips to the last traditional coal yard in the district, at Upton station on the ex-GC line. After the closure of Bidston Sidings on 29th June 1968, this traffic was handled from Morpeth Dock, latterly by a diesel shunter; it ceased in 1971. Cadbury's locomotive was then placed on a plinth outside the factory. It was, however, rescued and moved first to the Llangollen Railway and then, more recently, to the Cadbury's Museum at Bournville.

This 4-wheeled, petrol-driven rail tractor, built by Muir Hill Engineering Ltd of Manchester in 1927, was used for shunting at Hoylake Gas Works and is pictured in the siding alongside the main line on 9th October 1954. The works had closed in June 1954 and it is known the tractor was subsequently taken to Birkenhead Gas Works in October, so it is likely this photograph was taken when it was being prepared to make that journey. JOHN HORNE COLLECTION

Wallasey Corporation Electricity Supply

Tonnages of coal to Wallasey power station were around 34,000 per annum in the 1950s. There was a scheme in the late 1950s to install an oil-fired boiler but whether this was carried out is uncertain. A number of peak-load stations were converted to oil firing at that time. Wallasey generating station is believed to have closed at about the same time as the gas works, the Seacombe Branch losing its two major freight customers, which hastened its closure.

Wallasey Gas Works

An 0-4-0 fireless locomotive built in Germany by Hohenzollern (Works No. 4311/1925) made a brief appearance at Wallasey Gas Works about 1949. It had inside cylinders, a rare feature for a fireless. There was a surplus of steam on the gas works but it came at a price and the charging point for the locomotive could equally have been within the electricity works, where both boiler pressure and capacity were higher. This engine belonged to Cudworth & Johnson, who sold it to the British Enka factory at Aintree near Liverpool. The 'Brenka' had another fireless, also German, and both worked into the 1960s.

The closure of Wallasey Gas Works effectively spelt the end for the Seacombe Branch.

Hoylake Gas Works

Hoylake Gas Works last made gas on 28th June 1954. The Muir Hill tractor which had been used for shunting the siding was then towed to Birkenhead (Hind Street) Gas Works, via Hooton, in the pick-up goods but the train went too fast and the tractor's transmission was damaged. The locomotive was subsequently scrapped at Birkenhead Gas Works, having been judged beyond economical repair.

Wallasey Gas Works owned a number of locomotives over the years, as well as their own fleet of wagons. In 1949, they acquired this fireless locomotive from Hohenzollern A.G. für Lokomotivbau of Düsseldorf. It was the only fireless locomotive working in Britain to have inside cylinders and looked rather toy-like. It was eventually sold to British Enka Ltd at Aintree, where this picture was taken in April 1957. The gas works received a small Ruston Hornsby diesel locomotive in 1943 and another in 1947. JOHN HORNE COLLECTION

A view of the bus/rail interchange at Leasowe, one of several developed by Merseyside Passenger Transport Authority, with a Class '503' EMU *en route* to West Kirby unloading passengers, whilst the waiting Metro-Scania bus is bound for Manor Drive, Upton. Note the end door of the train, necessitated when the Liverpool loop line, built on tube principles, was opened in 1977. This interchange still functions in 2009 and a car park has been added on the other side of the road. The picture was taken from the signal box, now closed, which controlled the level crossing gates. Barriers, operated remotely from Sandhills control centre, have now been substituted. Note the cars are already period pieces too. MERSEYSIDE PTE, COURTESY JOHN HORNE

Contrasting styles at Birkenhead North station on 14th March 1988. On the left is one of the ex-LM&SR Class '502s', with Motor Coach No. 28690 nearest, whilst one of the BR designed Class '508' units, No. 508 124 is on the right. Many would say that the lines of the former are the more elegant. GLYNN PARRY COLLECTION

MERSEYRAIL

Traffic on the Wirral lines continued to be buoyant throughout the 1960s but in the 1970s changes in shipping handling methods and the decline of a number of traditional industries led to massive job losses in Liverpool, over 30,000 being lost in the city centre alone. These events impacted on every walk of life on Merseyside and created unemployment levels well above the national average. Simultaneously, the effect of television on evening traffic and the slow erosion of all public transport traffic by private motor vehicles affected passenger levels on the suburban rail services. However, there was a belief in Liverpool that the region's network of railway lines, including the electrified Wirral and the ex-L&Y lines to Southport and Ormskirk, were a valuable asset capable of further development, to create a rapid transit system which would be free of

A Class '503' in green livery heads for New Brighton, with the Seacombe Junction signals prominent in the right foreground. With the complete cloure of the junction, these have since been removed, along with the rest of the semaphore signalling on the Wirral system. ONLINE TRANSPORT ARCHIVE

the Department of Transport, had commissioned the Merseyside Area Land Use and Transportation Study (MALTS), the report of which strongly recommended the development of the railways. Parliamentary powers were obtained to divert the Wirral lines to a new loop line beneath Liverpool city centre and to extend the Southport and Ormskirk lines from Exchange (which was to be closed) to Liverpool Central (Low Level). There were other ambitious plans which were only partly implemented and these included a burrowing junction at Hamilton Square, to increase the line capacity of the Wirral lines by eliminating conflicting movements, and the extension of electrification beyond Rock Ferry to Ellesmere Port and Chester. Many new stations were proposed only one of which, at Town Meadow Lane (sometimes called Arrowebrook), between Moreton and Meols, was on the Wirral lines. The necessary additional time was built into the train diagrams but as the population in the area never reached the required minimum level, the station was not built, though it remains a possibility if conditions change. Meanwhile, First class travel was abolished on the Wirral lines from 3rd May 1971.

The detailed development of the Merseyrail network is outside the scope of this book and has been dealt with comprehensively in the present author's *Merseyrail Electrics – The Inside Story* (NBC Books, 2001). In 1975, the 1938 and 1956 rolling stock was classified '503' by BR; by this time it was showing its age and becoming increasingly unreliable. The Wirral 1938 stock outlived the newer Southport/Ormskirk Class '502' stock because of the cleaning methods employed at Birkenhead North. They were 'dry cleaned' using a paste put on with rags at regular intervals by dedicated ex-Mersey men, whereas the '502's were washed and, by the time of withdrawal, the bodies were rotten.

The Wirral lines, with forty-three 3-car units, were operated on the basis of eighteen 6-car trains in service at peak periods, four units as traffic spares, two units under repair at Birkenhead North and one away on four-yearly overhaul at Horwich works. The last of the 1938 stock to be overhauled at Horwich was despatched in December 1982. Visits to Horwich were stepped up as the Class '503's had to be altered to run in the one-way Loop tunnel, end doors being fitted to allow emergency evacuation of passengers; the 'bus lines', the cables at conductor rail voltage which connected the three vehicles so that current could be taken from any shoe of a unit had to be eliminated. The latter involved a detailed review of

the congestion which was gradually clogging up road transport services.

Bus operations everywhere were in serious financial difficulties and the government enacted the Transport Act 1967 which established Passenger Transport Authorities and Executives to co-ordinate public transport services in the larger conurbations. These bodies were given powers to determine the level of local rail services and to finance them. The Merseyside PTA (the political body) and Executive (the operator) came into existence in 1969. In the meantime, the Merseyside local authorities, in conjunction with

ABOVE: Class '502' EMU No. M28394M inside the shed at Birkenhead North. This view is taken from a booklet produced by Liverpool fire brigade, as instruction for their crews in the event of one of the units catching fire inside a tunnel. COURTESY JOHN RYAN

BELOW: A commemorative plaque was placed on a Class '502' unit (No. 28690) to celebrate, somewhat belatedly on 14th March 1988, the award of the George Medal for bravery to a railway employee, Ivor T. Davies (right), who, by making safe an incendiary bomb during the 1939-45 war, prevented a disastrous explosion. The Mayor and Mayoress of Wirral were present for the ceremony. GLYNN PARRY

ABOVE: The preserved Class '502' set at Birkenhead North, showing the Ivor T. Davies commemorative plaque just beyond the first doors. After separation of the centre trailer from the driving units, the three have now been reunited at Coventry, though the trailer, in particular, has deteriorated in condition. Note that the leading car has been modified with a centre door for operation in the Liverpool Loop tunnel. GLYNN PARRY

LEFT: Class '508' EMU No. 508 103 has just departed Birkenhead North station bound for Liverpool and is seen passing under Ilchester Road bridge. T.B. MAUND COLLECTION

BELOW: A wintry scene photographed from the footbridge at Bidston on 7th March 1970, showing two three-car units heading towards Birkenhead. The viewpoint gives an excellent panorama of Bidston West Junction, with the double line to the left leading to New Brighton and the goods line to Bidston Dock, and the unloading machinery for the iron ore towering in the background. Part of the urban area of Wallasey is visible on the left and Joseph Rank's flour mills dominate the skyline on the right. Note, however, that Bidston locomotive shed and the ex-GC sidings on the right have all been removed. GLYNN PARRY COLLECTION

conductor rail gaps and their reduction wherever possible to less than 41 feet between the shoes of the motor vehicles; this was difficult to achieve at some level crossings.

Three 6-car sets were transferred to Liverpool to work the newly electrified Kirkby and Garston lines. The Liverpool city centre Loop line and the Hamilton Square burrowing junction were both opened on 9th May 1977. Whilst new Class '507' trains were used to replace Class '502' stock on the Liverpool lines, it was decided to transfer similar Class '508' stock from the Southern region to replace Class '503' trains. The first '508' sets (No's 508042-3) were delivered to Birkenhead North on 28th November 1981 but, after modification, were sent to Liverpool to provide extra rolling stock needed on the Northern Line. The first '508' set entered service on the Wirral on 8th June 1984 and, by 29th March 1985, when the last Class '503' train ran, there were thirty 3-car units in service, a reflection of the fall in traffic. Most of the '503's were scrapped at Cavendish Sidings on the dock lines or at Mollington Street shed, Birkenhead. With the closure of Hall Road works on the Liverpool-Southport line, stock for all the Merseyrail lines is maintained at Birkenhead North and there is free interchange of '507' and '508' units throughout the system. In 1994, all the remaining signal boxes on the Wirral lines were closed when the Merseyrail Central Control system, based at Sandhills, Liverpool, was extended.

THE WIRRAL LINES TODAY

The layout of Birkenhead Park station has, over the years, been much simplified and now consists of just two through roads either side of an island platform. The line westwards leading to what, since 1926, has been called Birkenhead North is unchanged, though there is just a loop there, put in at the expense of the Passenger Transport Executive, as a terminal for the Wrexham trains, though they no longer run east of Bidston. The sidings and goods depot have all gone, as have the Great Central sidings and the engine sheds. On the right, there stands the depot and workshops for all the EMUs on the Merseyrail network, with minimal siding accommodation. One line on the Down side follows the contours of our route and leads to the now abandoned branch into the Bidston Dock ore sidings, which were previously joined to the main line at Seacombe Junction. The Bidston triangle no longer exists, the north-western sector having been truncated to two little-used sidings suitable for accommodating a Wrexham train, though these are rarely used. Seacombe Junction no longer exists and the line thence to Wallasey Village on the Down side is more urbanised. The whole area is dominated by the approach roads to the M53 motorway.

At Wallasey (Grove Road) the goods shed and sidings have been abandoned and there is a commuters' car park. Similarly at New Brighton, the former goods station and coal yard have been cleared and warehouses have been built on the site. There is still room for stabling a train, however.

The Seacombe branch closed in January 1960 and few traces remain. The station site is covered by housing and the trackbed from a point close to Seacombe Junction has been used as the link road between the Wallasey-Liverpool road tunnel and the M53 motorway, the cutting having been widened as necessary. The Slopes Branch, too, has disappeared without trace. From 1952-67, the ore sidings at Bidston Dock were connected to the Wirral lines at Seacombe Junction but the junction was removed, a connection with Birkenhead North siding, probably never used, remaining *in situ*. Bidston North Junction is no more, the westbound curve having been truncated to two sidings as already mentioned. All the sidings at Bidston have gone, though Dee Junction remains. At Leasowe, the LM&SR installed a 10 foot standard signal box for the sole purpose of working the level crossing gates. These are now worked remotely from the Sandhills Control. The siding on the Up side west of Leasowe station, in use for a number of years as access to Cadbury's biscuit factory, has now been removed, as have both sidings at Moreton. Between Moreton and Meols a site has been set aside for a proposed Town Meadow station but it seems unlikely that this will be built in the foreseeable future. The new passenger station opened at Manor Road in 1940 is of the brick and concrete design chosen for all the stations rebuilt for the electrification.

At Hoylake, the electricity and gas works sidings have been abandoned, as has the goods depot and coal siding on the other side of the line. On reaching West Kirby, there are no traces remaining of the Joint Line to Hooton, closed in 1962, a new road and local government building now occupying the site. The goods depot at West Kirby has gone but some carriage sidings are still in use.

Manor Road station in 2009, showing how well the architecture blends in to the current scene. This station was opened in 1940. The '508' Class EMU, in the latest Merseyrail colours of grey and yellow, is seen arriving at the westbound platform, whilst the other two views show the eastbound or Up platform. ALL A.D. MAUND

The terminus at West Kirby, showing the new simplified track layout following closure and demolition of the signal box in the mid 1990s. C.E. HEYWOOD

Appendix 1
The Wirral Railway's Accident Record

The Wirral was a very safe railway. There had been one fatal accident in the period immediately before the Wirral was formed. This occurred on 8th February, 1888 when the 7.04pm Up passenger train collided with a Down special train about half a mile north of the station cabin and 80 yards inside the Hoylake Down distant signal. Injuries were suffered by five passengers on the Up train and six railway employees. The fireman of the Up train later died of his injuries.

The Up train comprised locomotive No. 7, one of the 1887-built 0-4-4 tanks, hauling seven coaches with a total weight of about 110 tons. The special consisted of new stock which had been assembled for inspection by the directors and was hauled by 2-4-0T engine No. 3; it weighed approximately 90 tons. The Locomotive Foreman, Mr Lathom, was riding on No. 3 with the driver and fireman.

The 6.45pm ordinary Down train from Birkenhead Park arrived while the Up train was still in the station. It was covered by a train ticket as the Train Staff was to follow with the special. The train ticket was handed by the fireman to a porter-signalman at Hoylake, who unsuccessfully tried to find the stationmaster before the Up train left. The latter, contrary to the regulations, was accustomed to sending the Up train off with a train ticket made out before the Down train, with the Train Staff, arrived. The signals were set for the Down special, carrying the Staff, to run into Hoylake. Both trains were running at slow speed, estimated at between 12 and 20mph, on level track, with good visibility, on a curve with a radius of 80 chains (one mile). The drivers and firemen of both trains should have seen each other if they had been keeping a proper lookout. The engine of the special and the first coach were derailed and the second coaches of both trains were badly wrecked. Both engines were extensively damaged and about 60 yards of track was torn up.

Colonel F.H. Rich, who conducted the Board of Trade Inquiry, said in his concluding remarks:

'... the result of a total disregard by the company and several of their officers and servants of regulations under which this railway has been worked. The railway has not been worked on the block system in connection with Train Staff, as was agreed by the Secretary in his letter to the Board of Trade dated 1 April 1878. If it had been the collision could not have occurred.'

After a lengthy inquest on the fireman of the Up train, the jury brought in verdicts of manslaughter against the stationmasters at Hoylake and Birkenhead Docks, the Hoylake porter-signalman and the driver of the Up train. They were bailed to appear at the County Court, charged with *'having feloniously killed and slain Thomas William Stretch, a fireman employed by the Seacombe, Hoylake & Deeside Railway'* and were committed to the Assizes at Chester where they appeared on 8-9th March 1888. The porter and the driver were acquitted but the two stationmasters were found guilty. The Hoylake man was sent to prison for six months without hard labour and the Birkenhead man was bound over in his own recognisance of £50. There was public sympathy for the latter and a special performance was held at a local theatre to raise funds towards his legal costs.

Over thirty years elapsed before another fatal accident, the only one to occur during the ownership of the Wirral Railway and within a few weeks of its absorption by the LM&SR. It was uncomplicated, being a straightforward case of signals being passed at danger. The accident happened on 6th December 1922 and involved the 4.00pm Up train hauled, coincidentally, by locomotive No. 7 and a Down train drawn by 4-4-4T No. 14. The former comprised a 4-wheeled Brake Third at each end and a set of 8-wheeled vehicles, whilst the Down train was made up of two 8-wheeled, one 6-wheeled and four 4-wheeled carriages. The Up train collided sidelong on a crossover road at Birkenhead Park station with the 4.18pm Down train, which was just departing. The vacuum brake was operative except on the middle wheels of the 6-wheeler. An invalid lady passenger, travelling in a wheel chair in one of the van compartments, was thrown from her chair and died from her injuries; eight other passengers sustained serious injuries and thirty-six suffered from shock. Although stock was extensively damaged, there was no derailment other than the raising of some wheels from the rails; the track suffered little damage.

At the subsequent inquiry for the Ministry of Transport, the Inspector, Lt. Col. Mount, held the driver of the Up train to blame for failing to see that the outer home signals at Birkenhead Park were set at danger. Despite the limited facilities available, No. 7 was repaired at Birkenhead Docks. This included straightening of the badly buckled mainframes and front end, and rehabilitation of the cylinder casting; a new cylinder block was fitted. It was most unfortunate that the Wirral's freedom from fatal accidents should have been spoiled so close to the end of the company's independent life.

No. 7's front end embedded in the end First class compartment of one of the 8-wheeled coaches of the 4.18pm Down train. The locomotives buckled mainframe is evident from this view. The driver of No. 7, aged 68 and with 40 years exemplary service on the Wirral, misread the outer home signal in failing light and then failed to see the inner home signal at the tunnel mouth due to its being obscured by the smoke of a departing train. Thus the Wirral missed an historic fatal accident free record by just 25 days!
KEN LONGBOTTOM COLLECTION, COURTESY TED LLOYD

Appendix 2
The Final Years of Mechanical Signalling on the Wirral
Merseyside Railway History Group

Despite the electrification works and extensive modernisation programme carried out by the LM&SR in the 1930s, mechanically operated boxes and semaphore signalling survived on the Wirral line until the 1990s. Several of the original Wirral Railway boxes were replaced during these works but a few survived until the final abolition of mechanical signalling on the Wirral, with the opening of Stage 2 of the Merseyrail Integrated Electrical Control Centre (IECC) scheme in 1994.

In the early years, the Wirral Railway was operated on the train staff and ticket system. The early photograph of Hoylake on page 12 indicates that primitive signals, by Stevens & Co. of Southwark, were supplied at the stations but these seem to have been posts with lamps and not semaphore arms. Exactly when the line was equipped with full mechanical signalling has not been ascertained but the 1888 accident report, when the trainstaff and ticket system was still in use, makes reference to numerous signals and to the station cabin at Hoylake. It is likely that these tiny cabins were sited on the various station platforms and operated by certain designated platform staff, such as that at Moreton.

The railway was resignalled on the Sykes lock & block system in the latter years of the 19th century, so most of the signal boxes and the signals, provided by the Railway Signal Co. Ltd, dated from then. In 1906, there were seventeen signal boxes in existence on the Wirral Railway: Birkenhead Dock No. 1, Seacombe Junction No. 1, Birkenhead Dock No. 2, Seacombe Junction No's 2 & 3, Bidston East Junction, Slopes Branch Junction, Bidston West Junction, Liscard & Poulton, Dee Junction, Seacombe Goods Yard, Meols, Seacombe & Egremont, Moreton, Wallasey, Hoylake, New Brighton and West Kirby. Of these, Liscard & Poulton was shortly to close or be reduced to ground frame status, with the station signals then being controlled from Slopes Branch Junction, whilst Seacombe Junction No's 2 & 3 box shut with the closure of the New Brighton Loop in 1914. The list also does not include Leasowe, which was never a block post, nor that at Birkenhead Park, which was a joint box with the Mersey Railway. The Wirral boxes were of all timber

construction and painted a mid green, with a darker shade used for the bargeboards and other details.

The rest remained untouched until the electrification programme of the 1930s, with new LM&SR boxes being provided at a number of locations, as replacements for the original cabins. Those replaced were: West Kirby, Moreton, Leasowe, Dee Junction (and renamed Bidston Dee Junction), Bidston East Junction and Seacombe Junction No. 1. Bidston West Junction was closed and replaced by an extended frame in the new Bidston Dee Junction box, whilst the larger new box at West Kirby allowed the closure of the Joint box at the ex-GW/L&NW line station adjacent. The two Birkenhead Dock boxes were renamed Birkenhead North in line with the renaming of the station. The only other box on the system, at Carr Lane Crossing, was, like Leasowe, not a block post but purely to control the crossing and associated signals. Apart from signal renewals and occasional replacement of other equipment such as new frames, these were the last major changes to the signalling on the Wirral until the late 1980s.

ABOVE: The end of semaphore signalling on the Wirral. A pile of scrap signals and other ancillary equipment awaits collection in the yard at Birkenhead North in early 1995. C.E. HEYWOOD

LEFT: One of the ex-LM&SR Class 503 EMUs in British Railways green livery arriving at Hoylake station with a train for Birkenhead Park in the 1950s. Although the station was completely rebuilt for the electrification of the line, the signalling survived untouched and is pure Wirral Railway, all supplied by the Railway Signalling Company of Fazakerley, Liverpool. As well as the timber-built box, the wooden crossing gates and lattice post signals are also worthy of note. TED LLOYD COLLECTION

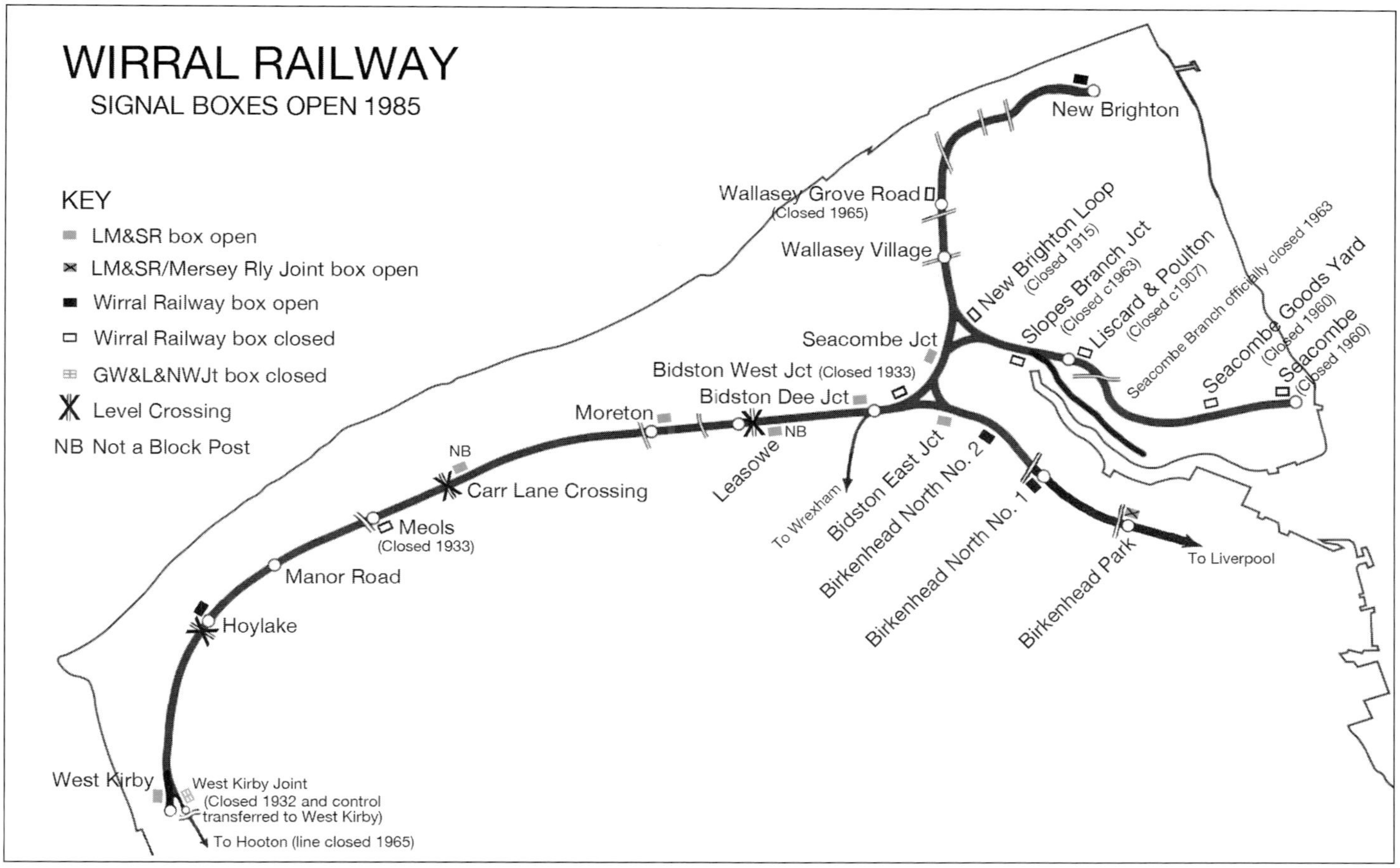

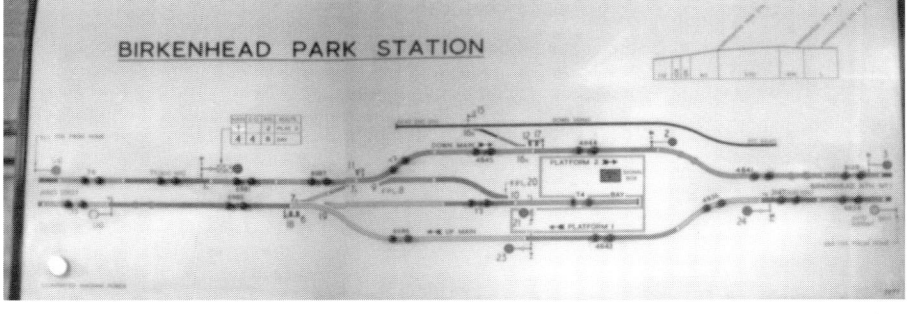

WIRRAL RAILWAY
SIGNAL BOXES OPEN 1985

KEY
- ▪ LM&SR box open
- ✱ LM&SR/Mersey Rly Joint box open
- ■ Wirral Railway box open
- ▫ Wirral Railway box closed
- ▨ GW&L&NWJt box closed
- ✖ Level Crossing
- NB Not a Block Post

Birkenhead Park station box was built by the LM&SR as part of the improvements carried out during the electrification of the line in the 1930s and replaced the earlier Wirral Railway box. The Mersey Railway remained an independent concern until Nationalisation, so the box, although built by the LM&S, was managed by a Joint Committee. These views, taken shortly before the box closed on 28th February 1988, by which time colour light signals had already replaced the semaphores, show the exterior, the lever frame and the control panel. The lever frame, a BR design which was spare from another job never carried out, was installed in 1972 when the bay platform seen on the control panel was added, whilst at the same time the working area inside the box was reduced by partitioning off one end. As built, the box had been equipped with a 60 lever frame. The additional peak hour services which had necessitated the new bay platform were not a success and were discontinued within a decade. The new platform was demolished in 1992 and services at Birkenhead Park today operate either side of a single island platform. Note the locking room floor was sunk into the platform, which meant the box appeared lower in height than its contemporaries on the Wirral. ALL K. SPENCER

ABOVE & RIGHT: Exterior and interior views of Birkenhead North No. 1 box, which was sited at the western end of the Up platform, hard up against Wallasey Bridge Road bridge. This original timber-built Railway Signal Co. structure was finally closed on 9th September 1994 and demolished over the following two days. The cut down levers in the (original) frame worked motorised points or electric colour lights. After closure of Birkenhead Park box, Track Circuit Block working was applied from Birkenhead North No. 1 to James Street box (Liverpool), with the colour light signals at Park also controlled from here. Modifications had also been carried out to the track and signalling when the New Brighton-Wrexham DMU service transferred to Birkenhead North in 1971. TED LLOYD; GLYNN PARRY

BELOW: Looking back towards Birkenhead from the depot washer roads, with Birkenhead North No. 2 box in the middle background, amidst an array of BR tubular post semaphore signals. The combined starting and distant signal on the main line was controlled from Bidston East Junction and Birkenhead North No. 1 boxes respectively. M. TUPPEN

ABOVE: Birkenhead North No. 2 box looking towards West Kirby, with Bidston East Junction box also visible in the left background, indicating how closely spaced the North No's 1 and 2 boxes and East Junction box were. The combined starter and distant signal applied to the Up & Down Goods Road on the right, whilst farther right still can be seen the recently installed Washer Road. Note that a number of the signals through here were colour lights by this stage. GLYNN PARRY

RIGHT: Birkenhead North No. 2 interior, showing the 25 lever BR frame transferred here from Halewood East around 1979. C.E. HEYWOOD

BELOW RIGHT: The indicator for the Down goods home signal was slotted with Bidston East Junction and is shown in the 'On' and 'Off' positions. M.P. ATHERTON

BELOW: The sad end for Birkenhead North No. 2 box, after an arson attack in November 1994, following closure on 15th September. C.E. HEYWOOD

RIGHT: A photograph of Bidston East Junction box under construction alongside the Wirral Railway cabin it replaced can be found on page 158. This view, taken from the access roads to Birkenhead North depot, shows the LM&SR design box near the end of its working life. Comprising a timber upper storey on a brick base, the box was much larger than the one it replaced, which suggests that it had control over a larger number of duties than the earlier cabin, presumably to do with the new traction depot on the site of the earlier carriage sheds. Closed on 9th September 1994, the box was demolished three days later. M. TUPPEN

LEFT & RIGHT: Two photographs looking in opposite directions out of the front of Bidston East Junction box. LEFT, an empty EMU comes off the depot. The Washer Road was a new section of line which was only brought in to use in January 1984 and controlled from Birkenhead North No. 2 box, visible in the background. In the second view, RIGHT, a train from West Kirby is seen crossing the junction, with the line to New Brighton curving off to the right. Behind the train, note the lower arm of the bracket signal, the outer distant for Birkenhead North is also 'off', which was apparently quite unusual. C.E. HEYWOOD

BELOW: Bidston East Junction signalling diagram, 1994. The frame had 45 levers, of which 10 were spare. The box connected to Birkenhead North No. 1 to the east and Bidston Dee Junction to the west, both quite near. However, Seacombe Junction box had closed by this date, so to the north the connection was with New Brighton box. Note the mixture of semaphore and colour light signals, particularly around the junction, and also the Up & Down Goods Road labelled as heading to the Docks, although the line was officially 'mothballed' by this date. CHRIS LITTLEWORTH, SIGNALLING RECORD SOCIETY

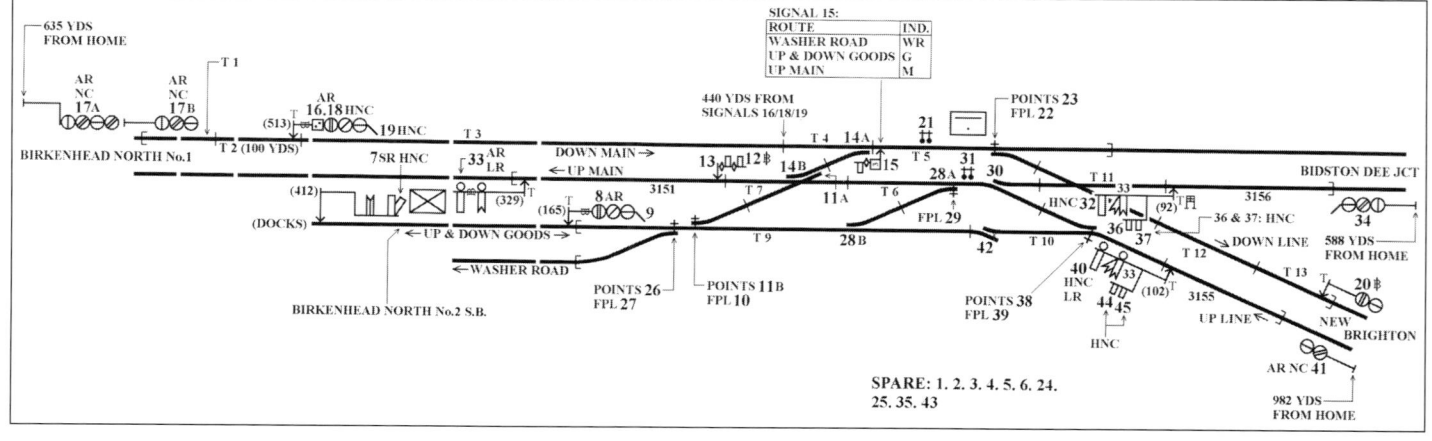

RIGHT: Bidston East Junction was another BR standard frame which arrived on the Wirral second-hand, coming from Exhibition Junction (Liverpool) in 1977. The interior was in immaculate condition, even down to plastic covered lever handles. C.E. HEYWOOD

BELOW: The Up starting signal being pulled off. The plastic lever handles made the traditional use of dusters by signalmen to protect their hands unnecessary. C.E. HEYWOOD

CENTRE RIGHT & RIGHT: Following final closure of the Seacombe Branch in 1963, Seacombe Junction box's last function was to control the ore traffic emanating from Bidston Dock. This was another LM&SR box, dating from 1933, built because the west to north side of the junction was realigned and the old Wirral Railway box was in the way. The 35 lever frame was most appropriately supplied by the Railway Signal Co. and was extended by another 10 levers in 1953 when the new double junction connecting to Bidston Dock was laid in. In 1969, colour light signals were installed for the New Brighton line and BR simplified the track layout in 1972, moving the junction back almost to its original position. The ore traffic finished in 1980 but trains of imported coal ran until 1986. The box closed on 13th March 1988, its end hastened by the lack of a water supply and by its poor structural condition; it had developed a pronounced sag as shown in the exterior view. Night duties here involved long periods of inactivity, as illustrated by the picture right! This box was another destroyed by arson, in 1989. COURTESY TED LLOYD; H.J. LEADBETTER

LEFT: After the closure of Seacombe Junction, New Brighton box fringed with Bidston East Junction. Due to a lack of space, the box was sited on the opposite side of Portland Street bridge to the station, which meant that the signalman did not have a view of the platforms or the goods yard. The box is seen here in largely original condition, complete with the distinctive bargeboards as fitted by the Railway Signal Co. It is believed that the lower floor windows, a standard RSC fitment, were boarded over at a later date and that the box was not supplied in this condition. G. NIGHTINGALE

ABOVE: A close up of the frame in New Brighton box, indicating its local origins. C.E. HEYWOOD

ABOVE: New Brighton box was the subject of two arson attacks in March 1989. The first did only minor damage but the second was more serious. Paraffin was removed from the ground and inner home signals, the locking room door was forced and the liquid poured all over the walls, before being set alight. The damage was extensive and the box was put out of action. This view shows the soot blacked interior of the upper floor.
ABOVE RIGHT: The immaculately restored interior.

RIGHT: The box was beautifully repaired, although the new plastic-framed, double-glazed windows looked a little out of place. BR also opened up the locking room floor windows, whilst the signalmen provided some extra 'TLC' in the form of hanging baskets and planters filled with flowering plants. Note the wheelbarrow placed in between the rodding coming out from the base of the box. All this effort, however, was sadly to be very short lived. New Brighton box was closed on 9th September 1994 and had been demolished by the December of that year. The building spent the last few years of its life in a white and dark blue paint scheme, as did the other surviving wooden boxes on the Wirral, although the white had aged to a creamy hue on most of the others. Note that access to the box was from both road and rail level. ALL M.P. ATHERTON

Bidston Dee Junction was another 1930s LM&SR structure, similar in design to several of the other boxes built then and much larger than the Wirral box it replaced, as it took over the duties of Bidston West Junction box which was closed and demolished. The presence of the stovepipe chimneys in the lower of the two exterior views indicate that it is slightly earlier than the upper picture. The colour light signal on the platform was installed in 1978 with the cutting back from Birkenhead North of the Wrexham service, thus allowing for bi-directional working so that trains could reverse out of the platform. The interior view, below left, shows the 65 lever frame installed by the LM&S and supplied, as were all of the frames in the new Wirral boxes built at this time, by the Railway Signal Co. Ltd. Note the letters 'LMS' cast into the ends of the frame with the maker's name (bottom right). Many of the lever description plates had been replaced or renewed with more modern examples over the years but the three shown in the photograph below were still original. Did any of these survive the imminent closure of the box on 17th September 1994 and its subsequent demolition on 20th November? M. TUPPEN; GLYNN PARRY; C.E. HEYWOOD; C.E. HEYWOOD; C. E. HEYWOOD

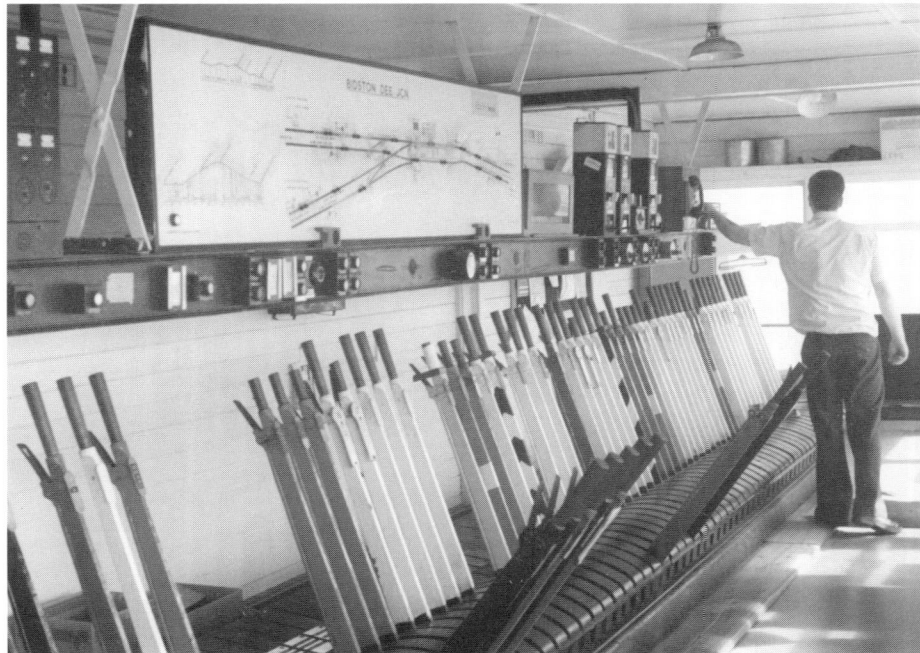

The smart little box at Leasowe was another provided by the LM&SR in the 1930s, when the station here was rebuilt. It replaced the original RSC cabin on the platform, as seen in the earlier pictures of the station. Leasowe was never a block post and the station did not have a goods yard or sidings, so the function of the box was solely to operate the level crossing and its associated signals. Beautifully maintained, the upper storey was painted in the white and dark blue colour scheme, whilst the base, like all of the other LM&SR Wirral boxes, was built of dark red engineering bricks. Note the steps winding round the back of the box. It is recorded that the gates were a source of constant nuisance to local motorists, because of the intensive train service, and were often under repair due to having been rammed!
M. TUPPEN; C.E. HEYWOOD

Leasowe box also closed in 1994 but seemingly some months earlier than the other remaining signal boxes. It too was demolished and the gates replaced by half barriers, although a keeper was still stationed in the adjacent relay room to operate them, until control was eventually passed to Sandhills, the crossing being monitored by CCTV. Here, a maroon & cream liveried Merseybus double-decker passes over the crossing during the transition period. The new protecting colour light signal on the left was 'live' but the old semaphore signal, complete with Bidston Dee Junction distant arm, had yet to be felled.

Moreton was a block post, so the cabin provided here by the LM&SR in 1932 was larger than the one at Leasowe, again replacing an original RSC box which was sited on the platform. The new cabin was actually a second-hand L&NWR box, which is thought to have come from Blaenau Ffestiniog. It was positioned on the Up side, opposite the connection to the goods yard, although this had long since been removed by the time of this photograph. The brick-built coal bunker for the box was also long out of use but had been left in place. The box was unusual in having three nameboards, an L&NWR pattern one on the front and LM&SR ones at each end. Note the distant arm on the signal was by this date 'fixed'; there is no controlling wire to it, nor balance weight on the post. M. TUPPEN

Moreton signal box closed after the last booked movements on 17th September 1994 and was demolished on 13th November. On this intensively worked passenger railway, there was little sentiment unfortunately in regard to these old structures. These two interior views record a little of the detail of what was lost when this box was shut. The top view shows the block switch, of L&NWR pattern, which allowed the box to be 'switched out'. In the event of this, the electrical switch next to it allowed for the telephones at the User Worked Gates (UWG) at Carr Lane Crossing to be switched to Hoylake box. The cast iron warning bell sounded an alert if the intermediate block stop signal was passed at danger. The picture of part of the Down line levers on the left shows the single lever which worked the home and distant Meols intermediate block signals. This was painted red at the top with a band of yellow below. BOTH C.E. HEYWOOD

A pre-fabricated concrete hut was provided at Carr Lane, complete with a Midland pattern lever frame to operate the signals protecting the crossing and repeater instruments to indicate the state of the line. It was not a block post and the crossing was converted to UWG operation from 5th December 1993. The main picture shows a West Kirby train passing the crossing, the protecting signal arms having been removed following conversion. BOTH C.E. HEYWOOD

Hoylake box was provided by the Railway Signal Co. in 1889, having been commissioned by the Seacombe, Hoylake & Deeside Railway, although until 1895 it was positioned at the other end of the station. It was moved so as to watch over the road crossing, when the line to West Kirby was doubled, at which time it is thought the original 13 lever frame was extended to 21. The box remained in largely original condition, apart from new windows probably installed to ease maintenance, right up to closure. This occurred on 17th September 1994, after which the intention by Wirral Borough Council was to preserve this gem of early railway signalling history. Regrettably, a lack of co-ordination between WBC and Railtrack saw the box demolished on 20th-21st September. The two interior views both show the gate wheel, which was apparently quite awkward, the signalman having to brace himself against the front of the box in order to turn it. In the lower picture, note the recently fitted guard over the mechanism, which had suddenly been deemed a hazard after a hundred years of use! M. TUPPEN; M.P. ATHERTON; M.P. ATHERTON

This tour of the last mechanical signal boxes on the Wirral Railway ends at the terminus at West Kirby. This LM&SR box was built in 1932 and was something of a hybrid, basically L&NWR in design but with Midland style windows. It was much larger than the timber-built RSC structure it replaced, as it also combined the duties of the ex-L&NWR & GWR box at the Joint station adjacent. This was an L&NWR design box, built in 1886, which is shown in the photograph bottom right and which was removed after closure in 1932. The new box, right, was thus also designated a joint box, between the LM&SR and the GWR. In the interior view, below right, note the large bank of white painted levers at the far end. These had become redundant following the closure of the old joint line branch to Hooton in 1962, whilst the goods yard at the terminus had also gone around the same time. Rationalisation of the passenger roads had seen the layout cut back to two lines either side of the island platform, with the two loops either side reduced to sidings, by the time of the closure of the box on 17th September 1994. It was demolished on 24-25th September. The picture below is of one of the last semaphores here, the Down inner home signal, which was equipped with a 'theatre' indicator below the 'calling on' arm to route trains into the relevant platform or siding. M.P. ATHERTON; C.E. HEYWOOD; JOHN RYAN COLLECTION; C.E. HEYWOOD

Appendix 3
Miscellany

LOCOMOTIVE HEADLIGHT CODES		
	Passenger (White light)	Goods (Green Light)
Seacombe-West Kirby	o x x	o x x
Seacombe-Park	o o x	NIL
Seacombe-New Brighton	o x o	o or o x o o x
Park-West Kirby	x x o	o x o
Park-New Brighton	x o x	x o x
New Brighton-West Kirby	x o o	x o o

LOAD FOR GOODS ENGINES 1906

Engine No.	New Brighton and Seacombe	West Kirby
1, 2, 5-11	380t	440t
3, 4	220t	290t
12, 13	440t	620t
14, 15	320t	500t

Estimated weight including weight of truck: Coal 15 tons; Bricks 16 tons; Sleepers 12 tons; Cement in bags 13 tons; Roadstone 15 tons.
[The low limit for No's 14 and 15 on the Seacombe & New Brighton branches is intriguing. It was only 64% of the load permitted to West Kirby, a lower ratio than for any of the other locomotives.]

CRANE POWER						
	1904		1938		1956	
	t	c	t	c	t	c
Hoylake	5	0	5	0	5	0
Liscard & Poulton	5	0	5	0	-	-
Moreton	5	0	-	-	-	-
New Brighton	5	0	1	5	1	5
Seacombe	5	0	5	0	-	-
Wallasey	5	0	-	-	-	-
West Kirby	5	0	5	0	5	0

TICKET PUNCH NUMBERS
As at August 1925
New Brighton   7W
Special Examiners S
Road side stations W
Bidston   966 No. impressed & semi-circular piece punched out
Birkenhead Park   967 No. impressed, P cut out
Seacombe   968 No. impressed & semi-circular piece punched out
West Kirby   969 No. impressed & semi-circular piece punched out

ELECTRICAL EQUIPMENT POWERED BY LIVERPOOL CORPORATION SUPPLY
As listed for application for traction current supply for Wirral Section 1936
GT HOWARD ST
1 x 15 hp capstan for hauling empty and loaded wagons for sugar traffic to and from Tate & Lyle's delivery conveyor.
2 x 60 hp wagon hoists used for lifting loaded wagons from the railway line on one level to the railway line on another.
SANDON DOCK
1 x 15 hp capstan for hauling empty and loaded wagons for general merchandise in the vicinity of the warehouse.
1 x 15 hp traverser used for transferring empty and loaded wagons from former L&Y section of the LMS to the former Midland section of the LMS.
1 x 5 hp traverser used for transferring empty and loaded wagons from one track to another for positioning against the quay.
GARSTON
2 x 30 hp capstans used for moving banana traffic to and from ships.
EDGE HILL
1 x 50 hp traverser used to move wagons laterally.
2 x 27 hp capstans used for hauling empty and loaded wagons from sidings into the warehouse and vice versa.
EDGE HILL LOCO
1 x 15 hp capstan for moving empty and loaded coal wagons.
STANLEY
3 x 15 hp capstans for hauling empty and loaded wagons for meat traffic between Dock Railway and Liverpool Corporation Abattoir.
BANK HALL LOCO
1 x 15 hp capstan for hauling empty and loaded coal wagons.
Capstans used for 30-50 ft movements.

ENGINE WHISTLES

Drivers Approaching	To or from	Whistle
Dee Junction	West Kirby line	1
	Dee & Birkenhead line	2
	Dee & Birkenhead main line and Goods sidings	3
	Goods sidings to Shunting Neck	1 long 2 short
	Goods sidings to Up main line	1 long 1 short
	Main line to Main line	4 short
	Main line to Platform sidings	1 short
Bidston West Junction	To Seacombe & Egremont	1
	To Birkenhead Park	2
	Main line to Main line	4 short
Seacombe Junction	Seacombe & Egremont and West Kirby	1
	Seacombe & Egremont and Birkenhead Park	2
	New Brighton and Birkenhead Park	3
	New Brighton and West Kirby	1 long 1 short
	Main line to Main line	4 short
Bidston East Junction	To West Kirby	2
	To New Brighton or Seacombe & Egremont	3
Birkenhead Docks No. 2	To Birkenhead Park	2
	Down Main to or from Down Goods line	1 long 1 short
	Up Main to and from Up Goods line and Engine Shed	1 long 2 short
	Down Main to and from Up Goods line and Engine Shed	1 long 3 short
	Main line to Main line	4 short

Appendix 4
The Locomotives of the Wirral Railway and its Predecessors

Name/No.	Date of Delivery	Wheel Arrangm't	Maker	Cylinders	Wheels	Notes	Disposal
ASHTON?	1866	2-2-2T?	Sharp?	Inside	?	Ramsbottom Ornamental chimney	Haydock Colliery
MAGNET?	1867?	0-6-0T?	Fox Walker	?	?	Possibly rebuilt	Unknown colliery
DIAMED	11.5.70	?	?	?	?	Bought from A. Young for £100	?
36 COMET	1875	2-2-2WT	LSWR	Inside 14½ins x 20ins	D 5ft 6ins L/T 3ft 6ins	Built Nine Elms 1852	Scrapped 7.1883
1 WEST KIRBY	1877	2-4-0T	Yorkshire Engine Co. No. 356	Outside 14ins x 20ins	D 5ft 0ins L 3ft 4ins	Withdrawn 6.1891	To Josiah Hardman Milton, Staffs 1892
2 BIRKENHEAD	1877	2-4-0T	Yorkshire Engine Co. No. 357	Outside 14ins x 20ins	D 5ft 0ins L 3ft 4ins	Withdrawn 6.1891	Talk o' th' Hill Colliery 1894
3	3.1879	2-4-0WT	Sharp & Sons 1850	?	?	Built for Monmouthshire Rly. Sold to Budd & Holt 10.1873. Resold 11.1873 to Neath & Brecon (No.14A)	Stationary Engine 1884
3	8.1885	2-4-0T	Beyer Peacock 2408	15ins x 20ins	L 3ft 6½ins D 5ft 0¼ins	Fitted with vacuum brakes and cylinders bored out to 16ins 12.1887. Withdrawn 2.1914	R. Smith for scrap
4	8.1885	2-4-0T	Beyer Peacock 2676	15ins x 20ins	L 3ft 6½ins D 5ft 0¼ins	Fitted with vacuum brakes 12.1887 Withdrawn 1.1913	R. Smith for scrap
5 (Wirral 2)	4.1887	0-4-4T	Beyer Peacock 2826	16ins x 24ins	D 5ft 2ins T 3ft 0ins	Reboilered by Vulcan and Davies & Metcalfe's brake ejector fitted 1909. LMS 6770	Broken up 11.1923
6	4.1887	0-4-4T	Beyer Peacock 2827	16ins x 24ins	D 5ft 2ins T 3ft 0ins	Reboilered by Beyer Peacock 1909 Withdrawn 6.1921	Ballast engine 1921-22

Wirral Railway No. 8 in one of the usual spots for photography, alongside the Birkenhead Docks water tower around 1910. The LM&S withdrew all seven of these Beyer Peacock built 0-4-4Ts shortly after Grouping. JOHN ALSOP COLLECTION

No.	Date	Type	Builder	Cylinders	Wheels	Notes	Disposal
7 (Wirral 5)	8.1887	0-4-4T	Beyer Peacock 2863	16ins x 24ins	D 5ft 2ins T 3ft 0ins	Reboilered by Vulcan and Davies & Metcalfe's brake ejector fitted 1909. LMS 6771	Broken up 11.1923
8	8.1887	0-4-4T	Beyer Peacock 2864	16ins x 24ins	D 5ft 2ins T 3ft 0ins	LMS 6772	Broken up 10.1923
9	7.1888	0-4-4T	Beyer Peacock 2975	16ins x 24ins	D 5ft 2ins T 3ft 0ins	Reboilered by Beyer Peacock 1909. LMS 6773	Broken up 4.1924
1	7.1892	4-4-2T	Beyer Peacock 3465	16ins x 24ins	L 3ft 0ins D 5ft 2ins T 3ft 9ins	Reboilered by Beyer Peacock 2.1914. LMS 6830	Withdrawn 2.1924
7	4.1894	0-4-4T	Beyer Peacock 3605	17ins x 24ins	D 5ft 2ins T 3ft 0ins	LMS 6774	Scrapped 1.1924
10	4.1894	0-4-4T	Beyer Peacock 3606	17ins x 24ins	D 5ft 2ins T 3ft 0ins	LMS 6775	Scrapped 4.1924
11	3.1896	4-4-4T	Beyer Peacock 3808	17ins x 24ins	L/T 3ft 0ins D 5ft 2ins	Screw reversing gear and Gresham & Craven combination ejectors. Cylinders enlarged to 18ins. Withdrawn 6.1919. Ballast engine	Broken up 2.1920
12	4.1900	0-6-4T	Beyer Peacock 4120	18ins x 26ins	D 5ft 3ins T 3ft 1in	Equipped as 11 above. LMS 6848	Withdrawn 2.1924
13	5?.1900	0-6-4T	Beyer Peacock 4121	18ins x 26ins	D 5ft 3ins T 3ft 1in	Equipped as 11 above. LMS 6849	Withdrawn 10.1923
14	6.1903	4-4-4T	Beyer Peacock 4493	17ins x 24ins	L/T 3ft 1in D 5ft 3ins	Equipped as 11 above. Belpaire firebox. LMS 6850	Withdrawn 7.1924
15	6.1903	4-4-4T	Beyer Peacock 4494	17ins x 24ins	L/T 3ft 1in D 5ft 3ins	Equipped as 11 above. Belpaire firebox. LMS 6851	Withdrawn 5.1924
3	2.1914	0-4-4T	Beyer Peacock 5742	18ins x 26ins	D 5ft 6ins T 3ft 1in	LMS 6776	Broken up 7.1928
4	2.1913	2-4-2T	LNW 2127	17ins x 20ins	D 4ft 8½ins LT 3ft 3ins	Built Crewe 1877. Webb side tank. Ex-LNW 2282. LMS 6758 (not carried)	Scrapped 4.1927
11	6.1919	2-4-2T	LNW 2523	17ins x 20ins	D 4ft 8½ins LT 3ft 3ins	Built Crewe 1882. Webb side tank. Ex-LNW 969. LMS 6759 (not carried)	Scrapped 4.1927
16	11.1919	2-4-2T	LNW 2725	17ins x 20ins	D 4ft 8½ins LT 3ft 3ins	Built Crewe 1884. Webb side tank. Ex-LNW 889. LMS 6760 (not carried)	Scrapped 4.1924
17	1.1921	2-4-2T	LNW 2637	17ins x 20ins	D 4ft 8½ins L/T 3ft 3ins	Built Crewe 1883. Webb side tank. Ex-LNW 284. LMS 6761	Scrapped 7.1928
6	6.1921	2-4-2T	L&Y 39	18ins x 26ins	D 5ft 8ins L/T 3ft 7¾ins	Built Horwich 1890. Ex-L&Y 1041. LMS 10638 not carried, then 6762. BR 46762	Withdrawn 2.1952

Key: Wheel Dimensions: L – Leading; D – Driving; T – Trailing

Wirral Railway No. 11, an ex-L&NWR side tank built in 1882. The engine arrived on the Wirral system in June 1919 and this photograph was taken at Birkenhead Docks shortly after. JOHN WARD COLLECTION, COURTESY JOHN HORNE

Appendix 5
The Electric Rolling Stock

CLASS 503
One unit has been preserved and is stored at SREA Coventry.
Motor cars built by Metropolitan Carriage & Wagon Co. Ltd; some trailer cars by Metro-Cammell and others by Birmingham Railway, Carriage & Wagon Co. Ltd. Electrical equipment by British Thomson-Houston Co. Ltd. 4 x 135hp BTH motors. End doors fitted during 1970s.

MOTOR OPEN BRAKE SECOND
Body dimensions 58ft 0ins x 8ft 8ins x 9ft 11ins: weight 36 tons: 58 seats
24 cars. M28371M-M28394.
19 cars. M28672M-M28690M

TRAILER OPEN COMPOSITE
Body dimensions 56ft 0ins x 8ft 8ins x 9ft 11ins: weight 20 tons: 40 1st cl./15 2nd cl. seats
19 cars. M29702M-M29720M
26 cars. M29821M-M29846M

DRIVING TRAILER OPEN SECOND
Body dimensions 58ft 0ins x 8ft 8ins x 8ft 11ins: weight 21 tons: 68 seats
26 cars. M29131M-M29156M
19 cars. M29271M-M29289M

1st class abolished 3rd May 1971.

1938 STOCK

MOTORS	TRAILERS	DRIVING TRAILERS
28672	29702	29271
28673	29703	29272
28674	29704	29273
28675	29705	29274
28676	29706	29275
28677	29707	29276
28678	29708*	29277*
28679	29709	29278
28680	29710	29279
28681	29711	29280
28682	29712	29281
28683	29713	29282
28684	29714	29283
28685	29715	29284
28686	29716	29285
28687	29717*	29286*
28688	29718	29287
28689	29719	29288
28690	29720	29289

* Vehicles destroyed in air raid on 12/13th March 1941.
Replaced on 2nd July 1956 by new vehicles 29831, 29155 & 29832, 29156.
Motor cars of these sets used as spares or for depot shunting 1941-56.

A train for Liverpool Central waits to depart West Kirby in April 1955, with ex LM&SR Motor Open Brake Second M28680M of the 1938 stock leading. These sets were later designated Class '503' by British Railways. On the right is some of the ex-Mersey Railway stock, shortly to be withdrawn with the arrival on the Wirral of the 1956-built units. By this date, they were probably only used on peak hour services. R.M. CASSERLEY

1956 STOCK

Motors	Trailers	Driving Trailers

Original formations which were changed soon after introduction.

Motors	Trailers	Driving Trailers
28371	29843	29140
28372	29841	29132
28373	29838	29131
28374	29845	29137
28375	29821	29138
28376	29822	29146
28377	29823	29139
28378	29844	29134
28379	29824	29145
28380	29825	29135
28381	29837	29142
28382	29826	29147
28383	29840	29150
28384	29828	29151
28385	29839	29152
28386	29842	29149
28387	29846	29153
28388	29829	29133
28389	29833	29136
28390	29830	29154
28391	29827	29148
28392	29834	29143
28393	29835	29144
28394	29836	29141

Original formations which were changed soon after introduction.

Motors	Trailers	Driving Trailers
28371	29838	29131
28373	29843	29140
28381	29827	29148
28387	29829	29136
28388	29846	29153
28389	29833	29133
28391	29837	29142

WARTIME EMERGENCY STOCK FROM LONDON TRANSPORT 1941-42

LMS No.	LT No.	Origin
Motor Cars		
E1	2233	Hammersmith & City
E2	2230	Hammersmith & City
E3	2200	Metropolitan
E4	2227	Hammersmith & City
E5	2239	Hammersmith & City
E6	2537	Metropolitan
E7	2207	Metropolitan
E8	2228	Hammersmith & City
Trailers		
E11	9228	Hammersmith & City
E12	9259	Hammersmith & City
E13	9224	Hammersmith & City
E14	9241	Hammersmith & City
E15	9231	Hammersmith & City
E16	9222	Hammersmith & City
E17	9255	Hammersmith & City
E18	9220	Hammersmith & City
Driving Trailers		
E21	6238	Hammersmith & City
E22	6203	Metropolitan
E23	6255	Hammersmith & City
E24	6241	Hammersmith & City
E25	6211	Metropolitan
E26	6582	Metropolitan
E27	6259	Hammersmith & City
E28	6254	Hammersmith & City

MERSEY RAILWAY STOCK WHICH WORKED OVER THE WIRRAL SECTION

Mersey No.	BR No.	Built By	Date New	Notes
1st Class Motor Cars				
1-12	M28405-16	Geo. Milnes	1903	
13	M28417	Cravens	1923	
14	M28418	Cravens	1925	
3rd Class Motor Cars				
26-37	M28419-30	Geo. Milnes	1903	No. 30 rebodied at Wolverton LMS in 1942 after air raid damage
38	M28431	Cravens	1923	
39	M28432	Cravens	1925	
1st Class Trailers				
51-62	M28787-98	Geo. Milnes	1903	No. 58 rebodied at Wolverton LMS in 1942 after air raid damage. No. 62 converted from composite trailer No. 119 in 1908.
63		Geo. Milnes	1903	Originally composite trailer No. 110. Converted to 1st class in 1908 and renumbered 63. Converted to 3rd class in 1937 and renumbered 75.
64	M28799	Cravens	1925	
3rd Class Trailers				
75-83	M29157-65	Geo. Milnes	1903	
84		Geo. Milnes	1903	Damaged beyond repair 1940. Replaced by new car No. 112, 1944.
85-92	M29166-73	Geo. Milnes	1903	
93-95	M29174-76	Geo. Milnes	1903	Converted from composite trailers No's 116-118, 1908.
96-99	M29177-80	Geo. Milnes	1903	
100-101	M29181-2	Cravens	1925	
102-111	M29183-92	Gloucester RC&W Co.	1936	
112	M29193	LMS Wolverton	1944	Replacement for No. 84 destroyed in air raid.

Appendix 6
The Wirral Railway in 1914
by Basil Mercer
(From *The Railway Magazine*, July 1914)

Although the London & North Western and Great Western Joint line from Chester to Birkenhead is quite an old-established institution, it is only in recent years, comparatively speaking, that the Wirral Peninsula has been given adequate railway communication with the surrounding districts. Now, of course, there are many lines in this region – the Chester & Birkenhead, with the branch from Hooton to West Kirby; the Great Central (formerly Liverpool & North Wales Railway) from Bidston to Connah's Quay, Chester and Wrexham; and the Mersey Railway, which owns the famous tunnel and leads to Rock Ferry on the one hand and Birkenhead Park on the other, connecting with the joint railways at the former place and with the subject of this article at the latter. The Wirral Railway fills up the gap left by the above-mentioned lines: it runs from Birkenhead Park station and from Seacombe (adjacent to the pier, used by the Mersey ferry steamers) to New Brighton and West Kirby. The line opens up a splendid suburban district, besides providing an all-rail route to New Brighton, beloved of pleasure-seekers.

Beauty spots in South Lancashire are not unlimited in number, and the more popular of them have during recent years become rather densely populated. Consequently, the business people of Liverpool cast their eyes 'across the water', as the saying goes, and the movement to the Wirral district has become so large a factor that 'the other side' is now sometimes referred to as 'The dormitory of Liverpool', owing to the number of people who reside on the Cheshire side of the Mersey and travel across or under the water daily to and from business. Until the Wirral Railway was opened access to Liverpool from West Kirby was over the joint railway companies' lines via Hooton, a somewhat indirect route. Nowadays, West Kirby is easily and quickly reached by the direct line of the Wirral Railway, either from Seacombe or by means of the Mersey Railway. This latter line, since its electrification, affords a quick and comfortable route to the other side of the river, its great advantage being independence of the weather. Fogs are sometimes so bad on the Mersey during the winter months that the ferry service is somewhat interfered with. However, notwithstanding climatic conditions, or perhaps because of the wonderfully smart working of the Mersey ferry steamers, the route to places in the Wirral via Seacombe Pier is very popular.

Places of interest on the Wirral Railway are numerous. The commercial interest, though not prominent (the Wirral is pre-eminently a passenger line), is seen at the Birkenhead end of the line, where there is communication with the lines of the Mersey Docks & Harbour Board.

Commencing a journey at Seacombe, we pass these junctions and the western end of the 'Great Float', upon which are situated the magnificent Birkenhead Docks. Passing through Liscard & Poulton, the wooded slopes of Bidston Hill appear, as also does the somewhat *maigre* [French: *Meagre, miserable, stingy*] Bidston station. On the summit of the hill is the Northern Observatory, and it is said that the telescope through which the Transit of Venus was first observed is preserved in the building. Leasowe Castle, sometimes called 'Mockbeggar Hall', next claims attention. It was built in 1593 by Ferdinando, Earl of Derby, and in the 16th century was a place of importance; a race course was laid out near by upon which the first 'Derby' took place. Indeed, the Wallasey Stakes are still in the bill at Epsom. To-day the buildings are in the hands of the Trustees of the Railwaymen's Convalescent Homes, a most excellent and well-managed institution, also maintaining the older 'Home' at Herne Bay in Kent. The antiquary may find in the vicinity a submarine forest, and, which is of more consequence to the majority, the beach is excellent for bathing; this last, indeed, is common to most places on the Wirral Railway.

We next come to Moreton and Meols, growing townlets on a coast which is famous for its '*winds that blow from the south*', or rather, south-west, which winds are predominant for ten out of the twelve months. The railway now takes a south-westerly direction, and brings us to Hoylake. Here the Deeside shores may be said to begin, and here may be witnessed the wonderful Turneresque sunsets for which the locality is famous. Hoylake may also be called the mother home of the '*royal and ancient game of golf*', and within its demesne are situated the links of the Royal Liverpool Golf Club. Nor are archaeological interests wanting. Accessible at low water is the Island of Hilbre, mentioned in Domesday Book and site of a monastery founded in one of his better moments by King John. In the 16th and 17th centuries Hoylake was an important port, the bulk of the trade between England and Ireland being carried on there. It was the point of William the Third's departure for the Emerald Isle in 1690.

The attractions of Edwardian New Brighton; the tower and boating lake, circa 1908. NEIL PARKHOUSE COLLECTION

West Kirby, which is the *ultima thule* [Latin: *Most distant destination*] of the Wirral Railway, is round the corner, and overlooks the extensive Sands of Dee, where Mary in the old song went '*to call the cattle home.*' Owing to its situation and to the ozone from the aforesaid sands, West Kirby is one of the most beneficial spots in England for anyone needing the open air cure. It is a cheerful little town with plenty going on, while the view from the hills behind the town is a treat for the jaded town-dweller, embracing as it does the Bay of Liverpool and the Dee Estuary, while the mountains of North Wales form a striking background.

The other section of the Wirral Railway is shorter but equally important. Leaving the West Kirby line before we come to Bidston station, the train heads northwards and enters the district of Wallasey, which is served by two stations. This '*ancient village*' of the old chronicles has a splendid shore on the open Irish Sea, and is a favourite residential place. Turning in an easterly direction and running along the picturesque littoral, New Brighton is reached. This place, which is known all over

LEFT: Children build sandcastles whilst donkey carts wait on the left to give rides along the beach at West Kirby circa 1910. NEIL PARKHOUSE COLLECTION

BELOW: Victoria Road, New Brighton, bustling with trippers and visitors around 1908. A couple of electric tramcars wait at the tram terminus and the pier looms large in the background. NEIL PARKHOUSE COLLECTION

the world as a pleasure resort, and is a favourite suburb of the Liverpolitans, almost rivals Blackpool in its lavish provision of entertainments, while not the least of its charms is the ever-varying panorama of the sea-borne traffic of Liverpool. From the Mersey frontage we may see such famous leviathans as the *Mauretania* and *Aquitania*, to mention only two among many, while the *Ben-my-Chree*, of the Isle of Man Steam Packet Company, and the Liverpool & North Wales steamer, the famous *La Marguerite*, are also features of interest. And yet the place is not at all spoilt in spite of the millions of trippers who visit it; fine houses with well-kept gardens grace the promenade, while the resident has choice of either sea or river view.

The history of the Wirral Railway goes back to 1863, when the Hoylake Railway Company was incorporated, with powers to make railways from Birkenhead and Poulton to Hoylake. In 1865 further extensions were authorised, to New Brighton and Parkgate, but the full powers were not then exercised. Changes took place a few years later, in 1872, when the Hoylake & Birkenhead Rail & Tramways Company was founded to acquire the lines of the Hoylake Company. In the following year, 1873, powers were obtained to make an extension to West Kirby, and to make a short line at the Birkenhead end connecting the Dock lines of the Mersey Dock & Harbour Board.

In 1881, powers were obtained to change the name of the Company to the Seacombe, Hoylake & Deeside Railway Company, and to make an extension to Seacombe. The latter powers were not, however, exercised until some years later, the extension to Seacombe being opened in 1895. The terminus, since re-named Seacombe & Egremont, is situated close to the ferry to Liverpool. A further extension from Wallasey to New Brighton was opened in 1888.

The Wirral Railway Company was incorporated in 1883, and by the Acts of 1884, 1885 and 1888 was authorised to construct railways in the county of Chester connecting with the Great Central near Connah's Quay; the existing Seacombe, Hoylake & Deeside Railways, and the Mersey Railway.

The partially completed line from Bidston to Connah's Quay was, by the Act of 1889, transferred to the joint ownership of the Great Central and Wirral, Mersey and Connah's Quay Railways. The connection with the Mersey Tunnel Railway at Birkenhead Park station was opened in 1888. In 1891 the various undertakings were amalgamated under the name of the Wirral Railway Company.

As mentioned before, there are two routes from Liverpool to the Wirral stations. The Seacombe ferry steamer from the landing stage at Liverpool connects with the West Kirby service, the journey, including the change from boat to train, taking only 33 minutes. Seacombe station is also the place of departure for Great Central trains to Chester and Wrexham. The other route, via the Mersey Railway and Birkenhead Park, serves both sections of the Wirral Railway, the electric trains of the former conveying the passenger through the great tunnel, now happily free from mephitic vapours. By this route West Kirby is 28 minutes from Liverpool, the journey to New Brighton taking 21 minutes.

The Wirral Railway derives the bulk of its revenue from passengers, the amount received from goods being only a fifth of that from passenger traffic, albeit there are important goods connections at Birkenhead Docks. With, however, a short mileage, fourteen miles in all, and that mainly to rising residential places, it is not surprising that this should be the case.

Coming to the equipment of the line, we find a high standard of maintenance. All of the mileage is double track and laid with bull-head rails 30 ft long, weighing 85 lbs to the yard. The stations, as may be seen from the illustrations, are neat and adequate, with the exception of Bidston, the dominant colour being a pleasing shade of green. New Brighton, Hoylake and West Kirby are particularly good, especially the last mentioned.

As might be expected from the nature of the country, the uphill work demanded of the engines is not of a serious character. There are, however, a few banks, Liscard being the summit on the Seacombe line, with rises at 1 in 100 and 1 in 150 from that place and 1 in 100 and 1 in 125 on the other side. The approach to New Brighton is a two-mile rise mainly at 1 in 100,

terminating with 1 in 88. The West Kirby line is gently undulating and calls for no special effort, except on Bank Holidays, when the train loads provide problems for the engines to solve on all the routes.

The locomotive stud consists of fifteen tank engines, there being six different types. Although there are no tender locomotives, some very interesting examples of construction may be seen. For the goods traffic powerful 0-6-4 engines are employed, with 5ft 3in driving wheels and 18in by 26in cylinders; they weigh 62 tons. There is a little 2-4-0 and one of the 4-4-2 type. The Wirral possesses three engines of the interesting and uncommon 4-4-4 wheel arrangement; these are fine machines with a large reserve of power, while their extensive bunker and tank capacity enables them to work long turns when required. These have driving wheels 5ft 2in diameter, 17in by 24in cylinders, and a weight of $59\tfrac{3}{4}$ tons. The most numerous class of engine on the line is the popular 0-4-4 tank, over half the stock being of this type. A considerably enlarged edition has just been added in the shape of No. 3. This smart engine is a great favourite both with her designer and driver, and the class will probably be added to in the near future. No. 3 has 5ft 6in driving wheels, cylinders 18in by 26in, and weighs in working order $54\tfrac{1}{2}$ tons; she is the only engine on the line with a Belpaire firebox, and carries 2,000 gallons of water and 3 tons of coal. One engine remains to be mentioned, No. 4, formerly the property of the London & North Western Railway. As this machine, of the familiar double-ender type with 4ft 6in driving wheels, is so well-known, mention will suffice without description. But it is an interesting change of ownership. All the Wirral locomotives, with the exception of No. 4, have been built by Messrs Beyer, Peacock & Co., of Manchester.

Turning to the carriage department, we find that the Wirral has taken the lead in one very useful improvement of stock – the mounting of two old coach bodies on a long underframe carried on bogies. It will be remembered that the London, Brighton & South Coast Railway has done a great deal of this kind of work with very beneficial results to the comfort of the passenger. It is, of course, obvious that there are many cases where the body of a four or six-wheel coach differs in no respect from the body of a bogie vehicle belonging to the same company. Of course, in the case of a small line like the Wirral heavy mechanical construction is not undertaken. The under-frames for these re-builds came from the Consett Iron Company, and the bogies from Messrs Pickering. The body work, or what might be called the cabinet-maker's work, is done by the Wirral Company's own men at Hoylake, as also is the painting. The underpart of the coach and the metal work is dealt with at the shops adjacent to Birkenhead Docks station, and the coach is completed at Hoylake. There are several varieties of eight-wheel coaches on the line, from 54ft to 59ft in length and varying a little in their internal arrangements. There are eight-bodied firsts, coaches with four firsts and four thirds, others with five firsts and four thirds, and some excellent brake thirds having five or seven compartments. There is also a very fine bogie brake composite with two first saloon compartments, one third saloon, one third-class compartment and a brake. The firsts are most artistically decorated, and the whole coach reflects great credit on the Brush Electrical Company, who are the makers. All the above-mentioned stock rides perfectly and compares favourably in this respect with any in England.

The remainder of the passenger stock is composed of four and six-wheel coaches of the usual type, but with fittings corresponding to the bogie stock, and all in thoroughly good condition. The bulk of the stock has been purchased from the Midland and Mersey Railways, and serves its purpose very well after renovation. Incandescent gas is the illuminant, and the coaches are painted a rich shade of chocolate. The goods rolling stock is of the ordinary type, and is adequate to the needs of the traffic. The engines are painted black and somewhat resemble in finish the locomotives built at Crewe Works.

As we have seen before, the Wirral has important connections with its neighbours. Passenger traffic is exchanged with the Great Western and London & North Western Joint Railway at West Kirby, where there is also a physical connection which is useful for goods traffic. With the Great Central's Wrexham & Chester line the Wirral has close connection, the trains of the former company using the latter's line from Bidston to Seacombe. Trains run in connection with this service and provide Liverpool with an alternate rail access to North Wales. But it is with the Mersey Tunnel Railway that the Wirral has most intimate relations. By means of close connections at Birkenhead Park, the Wallasey and West Kirby districts are brought very close to Liverpool. There is a change of train at Park station, but as there is no change of platform the inconvenience is but slight.

This last point brings to our notice the fact that the Wirral has powers to electrify its line. The matter is one for financial experts, but from '*information received*' it would not be a great surprise to the railway world if this took place within the next decade. When this electrification becomes an established fact it will be possible to have through trains from the Wirral country right into Liverpool over the Mersey Railway. The idea is well within the region of practical politics, for the district is developing by leaps and bounds, and facilities in the shape of increased train services will be demanded to such an extent that electrification will be the only solution of the traffic problem.

An account of the Wirral Railway would be incomplete without mention of the able and energetic Traffic Manager, Mr J.H. Burns. What Mr Burns has done for the line is better expressed by reviewing the vast improvements which have taken place under his regime. With Mr Burns' name we may couple those of Mr T.B. Hunter, the Locomotive Superintendent, and Mr E.S. Wilcox, the Engineer. We may safely say that the fortunes of the Wirral Railway are in good hands under these three gentlemen, aided as they are by an energetic and courteous staff.

Grange Road, West Kirby, in the early years of the 20th century, when it was still safe to walk in the road! The Wirral Railway's station, with its distinctive castellated clock tower, is on the left. NEIL PARKHOUSE COLLECTION

Index

Accidents, 15, 31, 101, 217
Air Raids, 62, 156, 177
Anglo-American Oil Co's siding, 54
Ashton locomotive, 10, 12, 14, 15

Barker, E.G., 81, 84
Bateman, John Frederick, 8
Beyer, Peacock & Co., 19, 28, 29, 81, 86, 87
Bidston (GC) shed, sidings and yard, 42, 49, 203
Bidston Dock sidings, 7, 191, 197, 200, 206
Bidston station, 10, 11, 18, 38, 42, 43, 48, 150, 164, 193, 198, 208,
Bidston-Wrexham line, 31, 32, 34, 38, 43, 72, 187, 189,
Birkenhead Central station, 18, 21, 22, 23,
Birkenhead Dock Road goods (GC) station, 42, 135, 198,
Birkenhead Docks & West Cheshire Junction Railway, 7, 8, 16,
Birkenhead Docks/North goods station, 10, 13, 21, 24, 42, 49, 56, 106, 132, 142, 146-9, 171, 184, 207
Birkenhead Docks/North passenger station, 10, 11, 14, 21, 22, 24, 27, 49, 105, 193, 211-3, 220
Birkenhead Improvement Commissioners, 10, 14, 17,
Birkenhead locomotive, 15, 16, 29
Birkenhead (Mollington St.) engine shed, 203
Birkenhead Park station, 24, 27-9, 38, 102-4, 135, 155, 168, 177-8, 180
Birkenhead Tramways Co., 19, 21
Birkenhead Woodside ferry/station, 8, 14, 16-18, 43, 72, 156, 180-1
Birkenhead, Chester & North Wales Railway, 18
Birkenhead, Lancashire & Cheshire Junction Railway, 7

Board of Trade Inspections, 10, 28, 57, 59
Bradshaw's Guide/Manual, 76
Brassey & Co., Thomas, 11, 19

Brunlees, James, 8, 24
Burke Wood, M, 33
Burns, J.H., 79, 81, 94, 100

Canada Works, 11
Carr Lane Crossing, 73, 182, 227-8
Carr, S.J., 81
Carriage & Paint Shop, 33
Cavendish sidings, 50, 51
Cheshire Lines Committee, 32, 42, 48, 68
Chester & Holyhead Railway, 38
Coal Concentration depot, 207
Comet locomotive, 12, 14-16, 29
Contract tickets, 44, 68, 81, 100
Crane Power, 231

Darby, J.H., 24
Davies, John, 33
Davies, Thomas Wilberforce, 34-6, 57, 59
Dean, J.H., 24, 35, 57
Dee & Mersey Junction Railway, 8
Diamed locomotive, 13, 14

Egerton, Sir Robert, 24, 33, 100
Electric Current Supply, 76, 231
Electrification, 74, 150, 152, 154, 156-9, 161, 166, 186,
English McKenna Process Co.'s siding, 48, 54, 55, 57, 62,
Evans, Thomas, 10
Everitt, J., 8, 10
Excursion traffic, 44, 80

Fairburn, C.E., 153, 189
Fares, 14, 18, 28, 39, 43, 76, 79, 80, 100
Fearon, F.G.W., 14
Fox, Adam, 10, 11, 14
Fox, Charles/Douglas, 24, 28, 33

Gladstone MP, W.E., 23, 34
Goods traffic, 22, 38, 47, 55, 56, 132, 169
Gorsey Lane, 34, 62, 78
Goulding, James, 18
Grand Junction Railway, 13
Great Central Railway, 38, 42, 44, 56, 68, 72, 73, 93, 94, 105, 131, 201
Great Drain – see River Birket
Great Float, 7
Great Western Railway, 7, 8, 15, 31, 32, 35, 48, 54, 55, 59, 63, 131, 134, 189
Green Lane station, 22, 152

Hamilton Square station, 22, 186
Haswell, W.D., 21, 33
Hobson, G.A., 33, 34
Hoylake & Birkenhead Rail & Tramway Co., 10, 14
Hoylake & West Kirby UDC, 100, 166, 175
Hoylake station, 12, 27, 48, 54, 64, 124, 125, 131, 138, 154, 159, 161, 162, 195, 199, 218, 229
Hunter, T.B., 81, 106, 148

Iron Ore traffic, 64, 198, 200-5

Jackson, Thomas H, 24, 33, 76, 81, 100-1
James Street station, 22, 186

Kirtley, F., 18

Lancashire & Yorkshire Railway, 13, 132
Leasowe station, 36, 37, 45, 74, 119, 120, 159, 194, 198, 209, 211, 226
Leigh, Cortez, 152, 153
Liscard & Poulton station, 34, 38, 47, 78, 116-8, 170, 177, 192,
Littledale, Harold, 8, 21, 23
Liverpool Central Low Level station, 38
Loads for Goods engines, 231
Locomotive Headlight Codes, 231

One of twelve lowbridge Leyland Titan TD1 buses introduced by Crosville in 1928-29 seen in use on the West Kirby-Liscard service, near the goods yard entrance to West Kirby station around 1930. This and the service to Birkenhead Park station were highly competitive with the Wirral Railway. Later deliveries had enclosed rear ends and these open-staircase models were rebuilt as such in 1936. MIKE DAY COLLECTION

Locomotives, 29, 30, 82-94, 132, 136, 143, 144, 146
London & North Eastern Railway, 131, 154, 170
London & North Western Railway, 7, 8, 13, 19, 31, 32, 48, 54
London through carriages, 133, 134, 177
London, Midland & Scottish Railway, 6, 55, 59, 63, 131, 134,

Magnet locomotive, 13, 14, 15,
Manchester, Sheffield & Lincolnshire Railway, 8, 19, 21, 22, 32,
Manor Road station, 176, 215
Meakin, George, 24, 35, 57
McHenry, James, 10
Medley, J.E., 15, 16, 18
Meols station, 10, 123, 141, 153, 159, 163, 194
Mersey Docks & Harbour Board/Co., 7, 13, 18, 19, 35, 38, 42, 48, 55, 59, 171, 201
Mersey Railway, 18, 21, 22, 27-9, 32, 43, 74, 76, 79, 152, 168, 179, 181-5
Merseyrail, 211, 212, 215
Merseyside PTA/PTE, 211
Moreton Brick & Tile Co.'s siding, 65, 119, 121
Moreton station, 10, 121, 122, 139, 153, 164, 169, 194, 227
Mostyn, Lord, 8

Nationalisation, 180, 183
Neath & Brecon Railway, 11, 15, 16, 18, 32
Neston, 8, 22, 189, 201
New Brighton station, 8, 19, 21, 24, 26-8, 46, 65, 67, 100, 115, 140, 159, 161, 196
North Wales & Liverpool Railway Committee, 38
North, Frederic, 21, 24, 33

Oakdale Sidings – See Seacombe & Egremont goods
Omnibus services (horse), 10 11 14
Overend & Gurney, 11

Padeswell Hall, MP, A.C. S., 14
Parkgate, 8, 19, 80, 133
Passenger rolling stock, 28, 66, 94-9, 131, 136, 166-8, 178, 214
Peto, Betts, Brassey & Jackson, 100
Piercy, Benjamin, 7
Poole, Braithwaite, 7, 10, 11
Prenton branch railway, 21, 22
Private Owners' Wagons, 46, 47, 63-5, 107, 175
Private sidings, 48, 54, 57-63, 171, 172, 175, 215

Railway & Canal Commissioners, 43
Railway Signal Co. Ltd, 52, 59, 70
Railways (Agreement) Act, 1935, 166
River Birket, 7, 8, 24, 42, 50, 85, 105, 159
Robertson, (Sir) Henry Beyer, 21, 100
Robertson, Henry, 19, 21, 23, 24, 28, 29

Sand siding, 54, 115, 172, 173
Seacombe & Egremont goods station, 48, 52, 53, 57, 59, 61, 78, 116
Seacombe & Egremont passenger station, 35-9, 48, 69, 72, 79, 116, 134, 135, 140, 151, 155, 159, 184, 187-190, 192
Seacombe branch, 33, 34, 37, 43, 97, 161, 198
Seacombe Dodger, 76, 78, 99
Seacombe Junction, 24, 49, 110, 111, 117, 119, 191, 197, 201, 206
Season Tickets – see Contract Tickets
Sharp & Sons/Sharp, Stewart & Co., 11, 13
Shaw, Joshua, 152, 154
Signalling, 30, 31, 45, 53, 71, 73, 85, 103, 154, 158, 199, 207, 212, 218, 221-5, 227, 229, 230
Slopes Branch, 39, 40, 79, 117, 171, 198
Smith, Richard, 35, 38
Stamp, Sir Josiah (Lord), 152, 166
Stanley of Alderley, Lord, 8
Starbuck, George, 16, 17
Stephenson, Robert, 33

Tickets, 11, 44, 78, 80, 129, 152
Ticket Punch Numbers, 231
Tomkinson, James, 24, 33
Townson, W.W., 17
Train, George Francis, 17, 19
Tramways, 14, 16-9, 21, 27, 28, 78
Transport Act 1967, 212

Vacuum Oil Co's siding, 54
Vulcan Foundry, 14, 30
Vyner, Robert/ R.C. de Grey, 7, 8, 11, 14, 16, 21, 23, 24, 27, 32

Walker, James, 14
Wallasey (Grove Road) station, 27, 47, 112, 113, 115
Wallasey ferries, 43, 44, 72, 187
Wallasey Local Board/UDC/borough, 10, 34-6, 38, 42, 59, 62, 151, 172, 175, 210
Wallasey Village station, 77, 78, 159, 177
Warren station, 28, 41, 56, 79, 111, 114, 115, 140
Wartime services, 177
Welsh Railways Union Act, 32
West Kirby (Joint) station, 31, 37, 68, 75, 126-8, 165, 182, 199
West Kirby (Wirral) station, 18, 28, 31, 36, 75, 126, 127, 151, 153, 159, 165, 182, 186, 195, 197, 199, 216, 230
West Kirby locomotive, 15, 16
Wilcox, J.S., 81
Wirral Railways Co. Ltd, 23, 24, 33
Wirral Railways Committee, 38
Working Time Tables, 25, 42, 67, 135
Wrexham, Mold & Connah's Quay Railway, 7, 8, 19, 21, 32, 34, 38, 93

Yorkshire Engine Co. Ltd, 15, 82
Young, Alexander, 11, 13

Class '9F' No. 92045 with a train of empty Summers' ore hoppers at Bidston West Junction circa 1960. Bidston observatory can just be made out on the wooded top of Bidston Hill in the centre background. IAN BOUMPHREY